Ethics and War

What are the ethical principles underpinning the idea of a just war, and how should they be adapted to changing social and military circumstances? In this book, Steven P. Lee presents the basic principles of just war theory, showing how they evolved historically and how they are applied today in global relations. He examines the role of state sovereignty and individual human rights in the moral foundations of just war theory, and discusses a wide range of topics including humanitarian intervention, preventive war, the moral status of civilians and enemy combatants, civil war, and terrorism. He shows how just war theory relates to both pacifism and realism. Finally, he considers the future of war and the prospects for its obsolescence. His clear and wide-ranging discussion, richly illustrated with examples, will be invaluable for students and other readers interested in the ethical challenges posed by the changing nature of war.

STEVEN P. LEE is Donald R. Harter Professor in Humanities at Hobart and William Smith Colleges in Geneva, New York. He is the author of *Morality, Prudence, and Nuclear Weapons* (Cambridge, 1993) and *What Is the Argument? Critical Thinking in the Real World* (2002), the editor of *Intervention, Terrorism, and Torture: Contemporary Challenges to Just War Theory* (2007) and the co-editor of *Ethics and Weapons of Mass Destruction* (Cambridge, 2004).

Cambridge Applied Ethics

Titles published in this series:

Ethics and War

An Introduction

STEVEN P. LEE

Hobart and William Smith Colleges

CAMBRIDGE
UNIVERSITY PRESS

CAMBRIDGE UNIVERSITY PRESS
Cambridge, New York, Melbourne, Madrid, Cape Town,
Singapore, São Paulo, Delhi, Tokyo, Mexico City

Cambridge University Press
The Edinburgh Building, Cambridge CB2 8RU, UK

Published in the United States of America by Cambridge University Press, New York

www.cambridge.org
Information on this title: www.cambridge.org/9780521898836

First published 2012

Printed in the United Kingdom at the University Press, Cambridge

A catalogue record for this publication is available from the British Library

Library of Congress Cataloguing in Publication data
Lee, Steven (Steven P.)
  Ethics and war : an introduction / Steven P. Lee.
    p.   cm. – (Cambridge applied ethics)
  Includes bibliographical references and index.
  ISBN 978-0-521-89883-6 – ISBN 978-0-521-72757-0 (pbk.)
  1. Just war doctrine.   2. War–Moral and ethical aspects.   I. Title.
  B105.W3L44 2012
  172′.42–dc23   2011038187

ISBN 978-0-521-89883-6 Hardback
ISBN 978-0-521-72757-0 Paperback

In memory of my parents,
Bob and Marguerite Lee

This conference should be, by the help of God, a happy presage for the century which is about to open. It would converge in one powerful focus the efforts of all States which are sincerely seeking to make the great idea of universal peace triumph over the elements of trouble and discord. It would, at the same time, confirm their agreement by the solemn establishment of the principles of justice and right, upon which repose the security of States and the welfare of peoples.

Czar Nicholas II on the opening of the Hague Peace Conference of 1899

Contents

Figures and tables

Figures

Tables

Preface

War is a horror, a scourge of humanity. There is no other way to describe it. It is, along with pestilence, famine, and death, one of the Four Horsemen of the Apocalypse, and war is a significant contributor to the other three. Much of the human-caused suffering our species has endured over time has been the result of war. Yet there is an ethics of war. The *just war tradition* is an intellectual effort, spanning two millennia in the West, to come to moral terms with war. It is an attempt to balance the horror of war against the poor arrangements of the world that leave participation in organized inter-group violence as sometimes the only instrument available to rectify major injustices. This need makes war barely tolerable, while the horror demands its constraint. The ethics of war lies in that balance.

Just war theory is a systematic account of the ethics of war constructed from the materials of the just war tradition. This volume examines just war theory and its basis in the tradition. In addition to offering an account of the elements of the tradition, I argue for the thesis that the tradition is able to provide a moral analysis of contemporary war, despite the radical changes that war has undergone. I do this by developing a version of just war theory that takes these changes into account. In other words, I test the adequacy of the tradition by presenting a theory coming out of that tradition that (I argue) offers a satisfactory moral analysis of the nature of war as we find it in the twenty-first century.

The just war tradition has developed, in part, as a practical effort to limit the horror of war. This is both a strength and a weakness of the tradition. Its practical orientation is a strength to the extent that the tradition has had an impact on military practice, lessening the human suffering of war. The tradition has, arguably, been able to impose some restraint on the application of state power in its most naked and violent form. To succeed in this, the tradition exemplifies the characteristic I call tolerable divergence, meaning that the theories' prescriptions do not fall so far outside the practically acceptable that they are treated by decision makers as irrelevant. This strength in the tradition has a corresponding weakness. The tradition has had to compromise with the political and military reality of war. In contrast, an account of the morality of war founded in a more free-floating moral theory, such as a Kantian formalism or a Millian utilitarianism, would not be compromised in this way. The just war tradition is a compromise with the moral ideal. But a morality of war grounded in the moral ideal would have less of an impact on the practice of war.

The just war theory I present differs from other such theories in two respects. First, at the level of justice in going to war (*jus ad bellum*), other just war theories tend to be collectivist in that they give special moral weight to states and to state sovereignty. In contrast, my approach, while it recognizes that war is conflict between social groups, shifts the locus of primary moral value from collectives to individuals, founding *jus ad bellum* in individual human rights. Second, at the level of justice in the conduct of war (*jus in bello*), the tables turn. Traditionally, *jus in bello* has been regarded as based in the rights of individuals, combatants and civilians, because the actors at this level are individual combatants, and some surprising implications of this individualistic approach have been raised by recent commentators. In contrast, I introduce a collectivist element into our moral understanding of *jus in bello*, collectivist in the sense that the moral liability to attack in war may be based more on who you are than what you have done.

Because this volume concerns the just war tradition, it does not offer an extended discussion of the alternative tradition of *realism*, which develops a normative account of war primarily in terms of what is in the national interests of states. There are, however, important relations between the two traditions, and some of these are discussed.

It is appropriate here to express my debt to Michael Walzer's *Just and Unjust Wars*, the most significant work on the ethics of war in the past half century. Walzer's arguments and responses to them animate a large portion of this text.

By way of acknowledgment, I begin by thanking my many students in courses on the morality of war over the years, who have stimulated my thought and helped me to get clearer on a number of the issues discussed in this book. Some have valiantly made their way through earlier versions of some of these chapters. Thanks are also due to my home institution, Hobart and William Smith Colleges, which has provided me with an opportunity to teach in this area and granted me leaves important in the gestation of this work. Hobart and William Smith is a superb institution in the liberal arts tradition, providing an atmosphere conducive to research as well as teaching.

I would like to thank my editor, Hilary Gaskin, for giving me the opportunity to write this book and encouraging my efforts in that direction. Also, thanks are due to the anonymous reviewers for the Press, who helped make this a better book.

I have been working on these topics for over a decade, and during that time I had three fellowships that were very helpful. In 2003–2004, I held a Resident Fellowship at the Center for the Study of Professional Military Ethics at the United States Naval Academy. While in Annapolis, I had the freedom to pursue my work and the opportunity to observe the care the military academies take in instructing future combatants in the morality of war. Special thanks to Albert Pierce, Director of the Center, and to Colonel Michael Campbell. In 2007, I held a Research Fellowship at the Centre for Ethics, Philosophy, and Public Affairs at the University of St Andrews. I owe special thanks to John Haldane, the director of the Centre, and to Nicholas Rengger. In 2008, I was the H. L. A. Hart Visiting Fellow, at the Centre for Ethics and the Philosophy of Law in University College, Oxford. There I had the opportunity to work with Henry Shue and four of his graduate students, Seth Lazer, Janina Dill, Per Ilsaas, and Zahler Bryan in the "war workshop," a weekly seminar, in which I had the chance to try out some early and rough portions of this text.

Several friends read and commented on portions of the manuscript, including Stephen Nathanson, Frederik Kaufman, Henry Shue, Karen Frost-Arnold, Scott Brophy, Derek Linton, and Eric Barnes. To them I owe many thanks for their help in allowing me to avoid some of the mistakes the manuscript surely contained.

Finally, the greatest thanks to Cherry Rahn, my life partner, for all the help and support she has given me through the writing process.

1   Understanding war in moral terms

> In the exercise of arms, many great wrongs, extortions, and grievous deeds are committed, as well as rapine, killings, forced executions, and arson.
>
> Christine de Pizan[1]

> Even war is a good exchange for a miserable peace.
>
> Tacitus[2]

War is monumentally destructive, deeply tragic, and, to many, morally incomprehensible. War involves death on an awful scale. In the war between Vietnam and the United States (1960–1975), an estimated 2.3 million people died. In warfare in the Democratic Republic of the Congo between 1998 and 2007, an estimated 5.4 million people died. In World War II (1939–1945) an estimated 70 million people died. In the many wars that occurred in the period from the end of World War II until 2000, an estimated 41 million people died.[3] It is claimed that in the 3,500 years of recorded history, there have been only 270 years of peace, and that the United States has enjoyed only 20 years of peace since its founding.[4] In

---

[1] Christine de Pizan, *The Book of Deeds of Arms and of Chivalry*, ed. Charity Cannon Willard (University Park, PA: Penn State University Press, 1999), p. 14. Used by permission of Penn State University Press.

[2] Cornelius Tacitus, *The Annals*, from *The Complete Works of Tacitus*, trans. Alfred Church and William Brodribb (New York: Modern Library, 1942).

[3] The Congo Wars estimate is from Benjamin Coghlan *et al.*, "Mortality in the Democratic Republic of Congo: An On-Going Crisis," report of the International Rescue Committee, www.theirc.org/sites/default/files/resource-file/2006-7_congoMortalitySurvey.pdf, accessed July 12, 2010. The other estimates are from Milton Leitenberg, *Deaths in Wars and Conflicts in the 20th Century*, 3rd edn. (Ithaca, NY: Cornell University Peace Studies Program, Occasional Paper #29, 2006).

[4] L. Montross, *War through the Ages*, 3rd edn. (1960), pp. 83–86, 313. Cited in James E. Bond, *The Rules of Riot* (Princeton University Press, 1974), p. 7.

war, people suffer and die in appalling numbers and in appalling ways. It says something important and terrible about humans that we are capable of engaging in such destructive activities. In the face of such devastation, what sense does it make to talk about the ethics of war? Isn't the very phrase an oxymoron? War seems to be a moral outrage, not to be tolerated. Yet people do talk about war in moral terms. They distinguish between the morally acceptable and the morally unacceptable in wars and ways of fighting. There are deep relations between war and morality, despite any initial appearance to the contrary, and it is these relations we will explore in this book. Despite the moral horror that war can be, it is sometimes the morally preferable choice.

1.1 Rwanda, 1994

From April to June of 1994, 500,000 to 1 million citizens of the Central African state of Rwanda were slaughtered by their compatriots. The victims were primarily members of the Tutsi ethnic group, and the murderers members of the Hutu ethnic group. The Hutu perpetrators set out to destroy the Tutsis. It was a clear case of *genocide*, the worse such case since the Holocaust of World War II. Genocide is a systematic effort to destroy "a national, ethnical, racial or religious group, as such."[5] In a genocide, a large number of people, men and women, young and old, are killed for no reason other than that they belong to the group into which they were born. Genocide is perhaps the worst moral act humans can commit, and attempts to stop it from happening are, correspondingly, morally imperative.

But stopping it would have required the use of military force; it would have meant going to war with Rwanda, with the Hutu government in power that was controlling the genocide. That war, had it occurred, would have been a *humanitarian intervention*. There is good reason to think that it could have been successful. Control of the genocide was centralized in the Rwanda government, and it was a low-tech affair, most of the killings done with machetes. At the time of the genocide, there was a UN peace-keeping operation of about 2,500 troops on the ground in Rwanda, led

---

[5] The 1948 UN Convention on Genocide, reprinted in William Schabas, *Genocide in International Law: the Crime of Crimes* (Cambridge University Press, 2000), p. 565.

by Canadian Lieutenant-General Roméo Dallaire. As the genocide began, Dallaire urged his superiors at the UN to increase the size of his force and give it a mandate to stop the killing. Instead, the international community looked the other way and the Security Council of the UN reduced his force to 270. Dallaire argued that a force of only 2,500 troops, in addition to the 2,500 he already had, deployed by mid April, could have "saved hundreds of thousands of lives."[6] The expectations, then, were that many lives could have been saved with only a relatively small number of casualties from the military action. This sort of example makes the case that going to war, despite its moral costs, can sometimes be the morally correct thing to do.

1.2 Morality, self-interest, and national interest

Whatever the reason for going to war, it is important to impose *limits* on war. As bad as any war is, it could always be worse, and the limitations that the parties at war often recognize when they restrict when and how they fight keep war from being worse. All cultures through history, it seems, have recognized that there should be limits on war. War has always been understood as a *normative* activity, an activity bound by rules, however often the rules are recognized in the breach. The international relations theorist Hedley Bull noted that war "is an inherently normative phenomenon … unimaginable apart from rules by which human beings recognize what behavior is appropriate to it and define their attitude toward it."[7] The rules that limit war distinguish war from mere savagery or barbarity, however savage and barbaric war may seem. The ethics of war is a study of the moral reasons for limiting war. Almost any limits may be morally valuable, since they would lessen the overall destruction, but certain kinds of limits are of special moral interest, and it is these limits we will investigate.

We begin this account of the ethics of war with a brief discussion of ethics or morality in general. (I will use the terms "morality" and "ethics"

---

[6] Gregory Stanton, "Could the Rwandan Genocide Have Been Prevented?" *Journal of Genocide Research* 6, no. 2 (2004), pp. 211–228, at pp. 221, 222. For an account of how the world looked the other way, see Samantha Power, *A Problem from Hell: America and the Age of Genocide* (New York: Basic Books, 2002), chapter 10.

[7] Hedley Bull, "Recapturing the Just War for Political Theory," *World Politics* 31, no. 4 (July, 1979), pp. 588–599, at p. 595.

interchangeably.[8]) All of us view the human world through the lens of morality. We see the actions of others (and of ourselves) in moral terms, and we judge those actions and their agents accordingly. Morality is a universal human phenomenon. It is an application of *moral values* to human actions. For a person's actions to be morally acceptable, they must respect those values. One important moral value is *justice* or *fairness*. We act justly, for example, when we take no more than our fair share of some benefit (such as a ration of food), and unjustly when we take more than our fair share. We may *want* more than our fair share, but in order to act morally we set aside that want and take only our share in order to be fair to others. If we do act unjustly by taking more than our fair share, we usually recognize that we are doing something wrong, and often try to keep such actions secret. Moral issues arise when persons interact. Morality concerns rules for how people should treat each other. In acting morally, we take account of the *interests* of others. For example, when we take only our fair share, we take account of the interests of others who deserve their fair share.

There are other values besides moral values. There are, for example, *prudential values*, which concern only a person's own interests, not the interests of others. When people act prudentially, they act in terms of what they believe to be their *self-interest*, in terms of what they want for themselves. There is nothing wrong with acting prudentially, when this does not conflict with acting morally. Most self-interested actions are not selfish actions. But moral and prudential values often do conflict, as when morality requires us to take only our fair share, and we want or need more. Morality places limits on a person's pursuit of self-interest. This conflict between morality and self-interest is a reason that it is sometimes difficult to do what is right. (Another reason is that it is not always clear what is right.)

States also have interests, and, like persons, states often act on those interests. (I generally use the term "state" to refer to the political units often also called nations or countries.) More precisely, the leaders of a state often act in what they believe to be their state's interests. The self-interest

---

[8] These terms are sometimes distinguished. See, for example, Terry Nardin, "Ethical Traditions in International Affairs," in Terry Nardin and David Mapel (eds.), *Traditions of International Ethics* (Cambridge University Press, 1992), pp. 1–22, at pp. 2–6.

of a state is its *national interest*. As persons have a strong prudential interest in their individual security, states have a strong prudential interest in their *national security*. As persons may have a prudential interest in taking more than their fair share, states may have a prudential interest in expanding their power at the expense of other states, taking what justly belongs to other states. They might see such expansion as a matter of national security. As a person's pursuit of individual self-interest may conflict with morality, so may a state's pursuit of its national interest. In both cases, these conflicts are sometimes pursued through force and violence. The morality of war is about the use of force to settle such conflicts. States sometimes pursue their national interests through the use of force against other states, and, when they do, we have war. Often, when states pursue their national interest through war, their actions are morally wrong. Our concern in this book is moral limitations on the pursuit of national interest through military force.

Morality may be represented by *rules*. "Take only your fair share" is one. Another is "keep your promises," and, of course, "do not kill (or murder)." The rules embody moral values. To justify a moral rule is to show that it better embodies moral values, that it is closer to the moral truth, than other possible rules. People may disagree about what the correct moral rules are and about what to do when moral rules conflict, as they sometimes do. How are such disagreements resolved? People justify claims about moral rules and how conflicts among them should be resolved through *arguments*, that is, by giving *reasons* for the moral claims they make. When we disagree about moral issues, as we often do, the response should be (and often is) for each side to present reasons for the moral claims it is making. This presentation of arguments is the *critical* aspect of morality. Some arguments are strong and others are weak. The moral claims that have the strongest arguments behind them are the ones we should accept. In the morality of war, as in other areas of morality, there are many disagreements and consequently many reasons and arguments that arise when we debate the issues. In this book, we consider these reasons and arguments.

But the prior question is: can morality be applied to war? Let us put the question this way: is it possible to distinguish morally acceptable wars and ways of fighting from morally unacceptable wars and ways of fighting? There are three views that deny this is possible.

[margin handwritten note:] WE CAN GIVE REASONS TO JUSTIFY MORAL RULES. ARGUMENTS CAN BE WEAK OR STRONG. WE CAN BE PERSUADED TO CHANGE OUR MINDS.

(1) *Value relativism*: according to this view, there are no objective or universal moral values on which our moral beliefs can be based or through which we can judge human behavior, including behavior in war.

(2) *Realism*: realism is the view that morality does not apply to the relations among states, including states at war, nor to individuals engaged in those wars, even though it may apply to individual actions within a society.

(3) *Pacifism*: according to pacifism war is not morally acceptable in any form, however limited it is. Moral values rule out war.

These three views question in different ways the claim that morality applies to war.

1.3 War and peace, just war and just peace

Before we consider these views, it will be helpful to define war, as well as its opposite, peace. The term *war* is used in a variety of ways, some uses being more central than others. But we need to settle on a definition to be used in our discussions.[9] At first glance, it seems that war could be defined as *armed conflict between states*. This definition would show why the Olympics are not a war; though they are a conflict (or competition) among states and individual athletes, they are not armed conflict. This definition also shows why a shoot-out among gangsters is not a war, because, though it is an armed conflict, it is not between states. Conflicts are the stuff of human life, but fortunately most are not armed. A conflict is armed when it involves physical violence and the use of lethal weapons. The effort to avoid war is largely an effort to keep conflicts from becoming armed, to settle them peaceably.

But some revisions of the definition are required. For one thing, a war is different from a skirmish. An isolated case of two soldiers exchanging a few shots across a border is not a war (though it may lead to one). War is armed conflict on a large scale. To take account of this, we may refine the definition: war is *large-scale armed conflict between states*. But this definition is too restrictive. In addition to wars between states, there are wars

---

[9] On the definition of "war," see Yoram Dinstein, *War – Aggression and Self-Defense*, 4th edn. (Cambridge University Press, 2005), pp. 3–15.

within states. In civil war, the groups in armed conflict are from the same state. This suggests the following revision: war is *a large-scale armed conflict between states or other large organized groups*. The *belligerents*, the organizations at war, may be less than states, but they must be of sufficient size and must fight as an organized group. War is not armed conflict between individuals who are isolated or in small social groups, but between large social groups. A situation of violent lawlessness involves armed conflict, but it is not war, because those fighting are generally not fighting as representatives of large groups.

That the social groups in war must be *organized* is important. War is conducted through military hierarchies in which those fighting (the individual *combatants*) have assigned roles, some giving orders and others obeying them. There is a small group at the top, the leaders, civilian or military, who direct the entire group and seek to control what it is doing. The members of this leadership group can, through their individual decisions, initiate war or end it, because they can effectively order their combatants to begin or to stop fighting. A military hierarchy establishes discipline and accountability on the part of the combatants. War may seem to its participants and victims like random violence, but it is not. For all its devastation, war is a socially organized affair, and so it is a normative activity, conducted through rules (some of which are moral) that control and limit the actions of those involved.

This definition of war (large-scale armed conflict between states or other large organized groups) obviously differs from some ways that the term "war" is used. For example, it differs from the way it was used by the seventeenth-century English political theorist Thomas Hobbes, who, in his great work *Leviathan*, famously claims that, in the absence of government, there would be "such a war as is of every man against every man."[10] He seems to mean that without government, violence would be frequently used by individuals in pursuit of their own ends without organizational control. Such free, unorganized violence is not war in our sense.

Some other uses of the term *war* include: the cold war, the war on drugs, gang wars, the war on poverty, culture wars, and the war on disease or hunger. These are not wars in our sense (though gang war may come close). These secondary, metaphorical uses of the term are fine, so

[10] Thomas Hobbes, *Leviathan* (Indianapolis, IN: Hackett Publishing, 1994), p. 76.

long as we recognize that they are metaphorical. They may mistakenly lead us to believe that we should use a military approach to the problem they label. We do not fight the war on poverty or cancer the way we fight a military conflict, nor perhaps should we fight the war on drugs in this way. One example of this problem is the "war on terrorism." After the September 11, 2001 attack on the World Trade Towers in New York, the US administration declared a "war on terrorism," and proceeded to fight this "war" in a largely military way. Critics of the administration's policies argued that the United States was misled by the term "war on terrorism" into believing that a military approach was the most effective way to deal with the problem. To take another example, the war on crime may not best be fought by military forces in the streets of our cities.

In addition, it is important to note that war is a *purposive activity*. States choose to go to war; they go to war with goals in mind. When states go to war, it is often because their leaders believe the goals they have for their states, usually connected with settling conflicts with other states, cannot be achieved by non-military means. States usually prefer to pursue such goals with non-military means, if they can. The goals that leaders seek in war are broadly *political goals*. War is the pursuit of political goals by military means, an insight of the nineteenth-century Prussian philosopher of war Carl von Clausewitz, who observed that war is "a true political instrument, a continuation of political intercourse, carried on with other means."[11] But, despite its purposive nature, war is no ordinary political instrument. Its exceeding moral costs set it apart from politics as usual.

There is another important definitional point. *War* may refer to the overall military conflict between the belligerents, that is, to the military actions by all sides in the conflict taken together, as in "World War II." But *war* also refers to the military struggle of each side in an armed conflict considered by itself. A war in the former sense is composed of at least two wars in the latter sense. "World War II" refers to two different wars: (1) the war of the Allied Powers (the United States, Britain, the Soviet Union) against the Axis Powers (Germany, Italy, Japan) and (2) the war of the Axis Powers against the Allied Powers. I will use *war* in the second sense, because the moral rules of war may yield different judgments when

---

[11] Carl von Clausewitz, *On War*, ed. and trans. Michael Howard and Peter Paret (Princeton University Press, 1989), p. 87.

applied to the different sides. War is the military struggle of one side in an armed conflict. For the purposes of moral assessment, Inis Claude notes, "it is essential to divide wars into their component parts, giving separate consideration to the war of A against B and to the war of B against A, the two half-wars that together constitute the A-B war."[12] Often, one side is fighting a morally acceptable war, and its opponent is not. Most people would say, for example, that from 1939 to 1945, the Allied Powers fought a morally acceptable war of defense against the morally unacceptable war of aggression by the Axis Powers. It is rare or impossible for each side to fight a morally acceptable war.

Combining the last two points, our revised definition is:

Definition: war is the use of force for political purposes by one side in a large-scale armed conflict where both (or all) sides are states or other large organized groups.[13]

Given this definition of war, what is *peace*? One way to define peace is simply as the absence of war: peace is a state in which there is no large-scale armed conflict between states or other large organized groups. (Of course, at any one time, some parts of the world may be at peace, while others are not.) But this is not quite satisfactory. In the absence of war, a society may have overall what we could call a negative or a positive social order. A negative social order includes an abundance of unnecessary human suffering due to political factors, as in the case of a repressive government that exploits those over whom it rules and does not respect their rights. On the other hand, a positive social order lacks such large-scale suffering, as when people are allowed to flourish under a government that respects and protects its citizens' rights. A positive social order is just, and a negative social order is unjust. An absence of armed conflict, then, may represent either a *just peace* or an *unjust peace*.

The difference between just and unjust peace indicates how war may be morally justified. First, consider an insight of the late-period Roman

---

[12] Inis L. Claude, Jr., "Just War: Doctrines and Institutions," *Political Science Quarterly* 95, no. 1 (Spring 1980), pp. 83–96, at p. 84.

[13] The force involved in war is often violent. When the term "military force" is used, it must be kept in mind that the force is mainly violence, though the term is appropriate because in war the military often does its work through the threat to inflict violence, as when combatants are forced to surrender.

philosopher Augustine that the "end of war is peace."[14] The end to which Augustine refers is not the time at which a war is over, for if it were, the claim that the end of war is peace would simply be a repetition of the claim that peace is the absence of war. Rather, in Augustine's claim, "end" refers to the purpose for which a war is fought. A war is fought in order to achieve peace. But the claim that peace is the end of war does not make much sense if peace is merely the absence of war, because one can always have peace, of a sort, simply by choosing not to fight and accepting the demands of an aggressor. Rather, states often fight wars to avoid one kind of peace (domination) and to achieve another kind (independence). If state M goes to war to dominate state N, M fights for an unjust peace, a peace in which it dominates N. But N goes to war to defend itself against the imposition of that unjust peace and to restore a just peace in which it retains its independence. If N declines to fight and accepts M's domination, it would have peace, but an unjust peace.

A war that is morally justified or acceptable is a *just war*, while a war that is not is an *unjust war*. There is a close connection between the ideas of just peace and just war, as well as between unjust peace and unjust war. Because N is fighting for a just peace, its war may be a just war, and because M is fighting for an unjust peace, its war is an unjust war. The ancient Roman orator Cicero asserts: "Wars, then, ought to be undertaken for this purpose, that we may live in peace, without injustice."[15] A war should be fought, he suggests, if it is meant to avoid injustice, that is, if it is fought to achieve a just peace. A just peace may be something morally worth fighting for.

But thinkers are divided on this, even against themselves. In addition to the above comment, Cicero is also reputed to have said that an unjust peace is better than a just war. The two remarks are inconsistent. If a war ought to be fought to achieve a just peace, then a just war may be morally better than an unjust peace. The pursuit of a just peace could make war morally justified. Benjamin Franklin seems to be similarly conflicted. On the one hand, he claimed: "There never was a good war or a bad peace."[16]

[14] Augustine, *City of God*, book XIX, chapter 12, in Reichberg *et al.* (eds.), *The Ethics of War: Classic and Contemporary Readings* (Oxford: Blackwell Publishing, 2006), p. 79.

[15] Cicero, *On Duties*, in Reichberg *et al.* (eds.), *Ethics of War*, p. 52.

[16] Benjamin Franklin, Letter to Josh Quincy, September 11, 1783, quoted in Jay M. Shafritz, *Words on War* (New York: Prentice Hall, 1990), p. 463.

But on the other hand he gave strong support to the American Revolution, fought to avoid the unjust peace of continued British domination of the Colonies. This sort of conflict brings us back to a consideration of value relativism, realism, and pacifism, which deny that morality can distinguish good from bad wars.

1.4 Value relativism

The fact that morality is a universal human phenomenon does not imply that there are universal moral values. Value relativism is the view that there are no common moral or ethical standards that apply to all persons or all societies, no universal moral standards to which a person can successfully appeal in thinking about or arguing about a moral issue. There are two main types of value relativism, *individual relativism*, which asserts that moral values are relative to the individual, and *cultural relativism*, according to which moral values are relative to a social group. Individual relativism is a form of moral subjectivism, which is the view that moral beliefs are merely subjective, that there is nothing objective, nothing independent of an individual's beliefs to which they correspond or refer. Individual relativists often hold the view that moral opinions are simply *preferences*, individual likes or dislikes, and there are no independent standards to which to appeal in seeking to resolve differences in moral beliefs. Moral values would be non-relative only if there were such a standard.

Cultural relativism, on the other hand, allows moral standards independent of the individual, namely, the moral standards of that individual's culture. These standards are not universal, because they differ among social groups. But because the standards are independent, an individual's moral views may be in conflict with those of her social group, and in that sense mistaken. According to the individual relativist, a person has no independent basis for criticizing the moral views of another. According to the cultural relativist, a person may have a basis for criticizing the moral views of a member of her culture, a basis provided by the value standards of the culture to which both belong. There may be no independent basis, however, on which members of different cultures can criticize each other's moral beliefs. Because there may be no moral standards applying to conflicts across cultures, in the case of the morality of war, cultural relativism can come to the same as individual relativism when armed conflict is international and occurs between groups with different cultures.

Debates about value relativism are complicated, and there are versions of these doctrines that are more sophisticated and harder to argue against than the simple ones I have sketched. Nevertheless, there are good reasons to think that individual value relativism is mistaken and that cultural value relativism, even if it were true, would not undermine the possibility of a uniform morality of war. I will sketch three arguments on this issue. The first concludes that individuals consistently act as if value relativism is false, even while they believe it is true. The second questions a key way in which people tend to look at the world that gives relativism much of its misleading plausibility. The third argument shows that even if value relativism were true, it would not undermine the morality of war.

The first argument is that moral views cannot be mere preferences because we treat them differently. Everyone has likes and dislikes, preferences, in food, music, and so forth. Preferences are not something we argue about. Take preference in ice cream flavors. If we happened upon two adults arguing about what the best flavor of ice cream is, we would find it quite strange and would think they must be spoofing. A person cannot be right or wrong in her preferences, and that is why it makes no sense to argue about them. Preferences are merely subjective. But we argue about moral matters all of the time without thinking it strange to do so. We give reasons for or against moral beliefs and the morality of actions. To argue about something, however, assumes that there is an independent standard according to which the conflicting claims can be judged. Not only do we argue as if there were independent values, but we generally act that way as well. In choosing how to act, we consider the moral implications of what we are doing and usually take them very seriously. When we choose not to follow our moral beliefs, we recognize that we have done something wrong. If values were relative, it would not make sense for us to treat morality as seriously as we do.

All of this reflects the *critical* aspect of morality. Moral beliefs arise initially through a person's upbringing, and because upbringings differ, it is not surprising that moral beliefs also differ. But we are free to change our moral beliefs (or affirm the ones we have) as a result of personal reflection and critical thought. When people argue about moral claims, sometimes minds are changed. Critical assessment of our own moral beliefs may

WE DON'T HAVE SERIOUS ARGUMENTS ABOUT WHICH FLAVOR OF ICE CREAM IS THE BEST

lead us to recognize that they should be modified or abandoned in favor of others. So, even though different people hold different beliefs about the morality of war, this does not indicate that there are no independent standards for judging which of these beliefs are true and which are not.

Though this argument presents a strong case against individual relativism, however, it does not necessarily undermine cultural relativism. In the case of cultural relativism, there is an independent standard of morality within a culture, and if the moral beliefs of members of a culture are at odds, there is a basis for determining which beliefs are more correct. Moral argument between members of a culture becomes meaningful as debate over what the moral values of that culture in fact are.

The second argument, on the other hand, applies against both individual and cultural relativism. The plausibility of value relativism, in either form, comes from a way of looking at the world that draws a sharp contrast between *facts* and *values*. Facts are definite things out there in the world, hard, sharp, often easy to determine, and the same for all. As Aristotle remarks, fire burns the same in Athens as in Persia. But values are not like that at all, say defenders of value relativism. We often can determine whether a factual claim is true simply by opening our eyes, but our senses cannot tell us whether moral claims are true. Also, there is often universal agreement about factual claims, while notoriously little agreement about many value claims. Consider the apparent intractability of the abortion debate; it seems there will never be a generally accepted resolution.

But such a sharp contrast between facts and values does not hold up to close scrutiny. Many facts are not easily determined and cannot be directly apprehended by the senses, for example facts about events that happened in the distant past. But facts about the present can also be difficult to determine. Consider the question: what is the temperature at the center of the sun? This is clearly a factual question, yet it is about a fact that will never be apprehensible by direct or indirect (instrument-assisted) observation. No instrument could be placed at the center of the sun to provide us with temperature readings. In this respect, the question is similar to: when is a war morally justified? Consider the claim that the temperature at the center of the sun is about 15 million degrees centigrade. This claim is true or false, but there is no way through observation to tell which. The same may be true of the claim that a war is justified when it is in self-defense against aggression. Another similarity between these two claims is that the way in which we determine whether they are true or false is by an appeal to a *theory*, astrophysical theory in one case and moral theory in the other. *Just war theory* is a moral theory.

According to the third argument there may be a meaningful morality of war even if value relativism were true. There is, as a matter of fact, considerable agreement across cultures on some basic moral ideas, agreement sufficient to underwrite a morality of war whose values are independent of particular individuals and cultures. To think about this, consider two ideas from the American philosopher John Rawls. Even though different cultures may have different *comprehensive doctrines* regarding moral values, often connected with the dominant religion in that culture, there is an *overlapping consensus* among these doctrines on some moral basics.[17] These universally accepted moral basics are a sufficient foundation for just war theory because the scope of *justice* in the just war theory is a limited one. Consider holy wars, like the religious wars that plagued Europe in the seventeenth century or the current struggles of some religious extremists. Holy wars are fought in the name of morality, and they are sometimes sanctioned by the full sense of the morality of the comprehensive doctrine of the religions in question, which may include the idea that other faiths be suppressed. But a holy war is not a just war, as understood in just war theory. In just war theory, justice is a minimal moral notion, largely limited to the idea that individuals and states should be free of outside interference. Just war theory, as it has come to be understood in the modern age, is consistent with the idea of religious tolerance, refusing to justify war on religious grounds. The existence of international law, which is recognized, if not always adhered to, by virtually all states and which follows closely the principles of just war theory, is evidence that there is a sufficient overlapping consensus among cultures to support the universality of the moral values in just war theory. International law is discussed below.

1.5 Realism

Realism is a tradition in the study of international relations (including war) that claims that morality does not apply to the actions of states. It is a tradition generally in opposition to the main tradition focusing on the

---

[17] John Rawls, *The Law of Peoples* (Cambridge, MA: Harvard University Press, 1999).

ethics of war, the *just war tradition*, which is the tradition out of which just war theory comes. The value relativist would agree with the realist that morality does not apply to the actions of states, but for different reasons. The relativist believes there are no independent moral standards, while the realist believes that though there may be such standards, they simply do not apply to international relations. Moral standards may apply within societies, but not between societies. There is something about international relations that precludes the application of moral standards. This is indicated, in the case of war, by another saying of Cicero's: "In times of war, the laws fall silent."[18]

Thus, realism denies what the just war tradition assumes, that morality can be applied to the behavior of states at war. Realism may be traced back to the ancient Greek historian Thucydides, who presents a realist understanding of war in his commentary on the Peloponnesian War between Athens and Sparta.[19] According to the realist, states act on their national interest to the exclusion of morality. Realism entails "the primacy of self-interest over moral principle."[20] Realism does not deny that there are moral standards, but regards them as inapplicable to international relations. As international relations theorist Hans Morgenthau notes, the international sphere is autonomous from the moral realm. "The realist defense of the autonomy of the political sphere against its subversion by other modes of thought does not imply disregard for the existence and importance of these other modes of thought."[21] Realism is sometimes identified with the claim that *might makes right*, but it is more accurate to say that for the realist, there are no standards of moral right applicable in the international sphere.

Why does realism regard morality as inapplicable in international relations? What is special about such relations? The answer involves an appeal to several key ideas in terms of which realists see the world: international anarchy, human nature, national interest, power, necessity, and the basis of morality. Though there are different forms of realism, these features

---

[18] Cicero, *On Duties*, in Reichberg *et al.* (eds.), *Ethics of War*, p. 51.

[19] Thucydides, *The Peloponnesian War* (Oxford University Press, 2009).

[20] Steven Forde, "Classical Realism," in Nardin and Mapel (eds.), *Traditions of International Ethics*, pp. 62–84, at p. 62.

[21] Hans Morgenthau and Kenneth Thompson, *Politics among Nations*, 6th edn. (New York: Knopf, 1985), p. 16.

are generally characteristic of them. According to realists, states exist in a condition of *international anarchy*, by which they mean that there is no hierarchical authority that can sanction the behavior of states in their relations, no effective international government. This feature is joined with the view that certain motivations characterize *human nature*, such as aggressiveness and self-interest. When these two features are coupled, the result is that the key concern of states is to protect themselves from depredations by their neighbors. Their primary *national interest* becomes survival, a goal that can be secured only by their *power* to keep other states at bay; national interest is "defined in terms of power."[22] Power is largely a function of military capability, which can defeat or deter attacks by other states and secure the state's national interest in other ways. International behavior is characterized as a realm of *necessity*, in the sense that survival, which is what is at stake under the condition of anarchy, supersedes moral considerations. Realism represents "the subordination of morality to political necessity."[23]

The idea that national interest supersedes moral considerations is an implication of a particular view about the *basis of morality* held by realists. This view is represented by one of the classic realists, Thomas Hobbes. Hobbes argued that in a *state of nature*, where people are without a government and so lack a public agency to make and enforce law, no one would be secure from attack by others.[24] The result would be constant threat and interpersonal conflict, in which life would be "nasty, brutish, and short." The solution to this chaos is to establish a government through a *social contract* among the members of a group to create a central coercive authority, a sovereign, which would, through the making and enforcing of laws, provide individuals with the physical security lacking in the state of nature. In Hobbes' view, the basis of morality is physical security; morality can apply only when individuals have it. An effective coercive authority is necessary for the applicability of morality. In the absence of physical security, morality can gain no footing because moral behavior would then make a person more vulnerable to attack, and self-preservation is all-important.

---

[22] *Ibid.*, p. 5.
[23] Jack Donnelly, "Twentieth-Century Realism," in Nardin and Mapel (eds.), *Traditions of International Ethics*, pp. 85–111, at p. 96.
[24] Hobbes, *Leviathan*, pp. 74–78.

Morality cannot apply unless acting morally can be expected to be in a person's long-term self-interest, as it would not be in a state of nature. A reasonable expectation of reciprocity, where my restraint in not attacking others will be met by a similar restraint by them, must hold for morality to be binding, and such an expectation is possible only under a coercive power that can enforce the rules.

If we apply Hobbes' argument to the international realm by putting states in place of individuals, we get the realist vision of international relations. (This idea of drawing conclusions about states by comparing them with individuals is referred to as a *domestic analogy*.) States, unlike individuals within states, are in a Hobbesian state of nature, with no central authority to guarantee reciprocity of moral behavior. There is no world government to make and enforce laws, so there is among states a war of all against all. (Hobbes explains that in a state of nature, though war need not be constant, it is a constant threat, ready to break out at any moment.) Consequently, as in a state of nature among individuals, morality is not applicable between states and so there is no morality of war.

HOBBESIAN ANARCHY

Hobbes identifies three sources of conflict in a state of nature, what he calls *causes of quarrel*, namely, competition, diffidence, and glory. *Competition* causes quarrel due to scarcity and human acquisitiveness. *Glory* causes quarrel due to the human tendency to seek to outdo others. *Diffidence* is a mistrust of others, and it causes quarrel because what we fear about others in a state of nature is that they will attack us. Diffidence may compel individuals to initiate attacks on others to avoid expected attacks on them by those others. Diffidence has a reflexive, self-reinforcing character, in that even if we do not fear others on the grounds of their competitiveness or glory-seeking, we may expect they may choose to attack us out of their own diffidence, their fear of our future attack. Diffidence can lead states to initiate war on defensive grounds, that is, to go to war not out of competition or for glory, but in defense against an expected attack. Defensive wars are usually reactive, but diffidence can lead to anticipatory wars initiated on defensive grounds. Such wars are referred to as preventive wars or preemptive wars, and we discuss these in Chapter 3. The role of diffidence highlights the function of international anarchy in the realist world-view (the *structural* aspect of the theory), while competitiveness and glory-seeking highlight the function of the human-nature aspect in the realist world-view. The form of realism called *classical realism* emphasizes

SOURCES OF CONFLICT

STRUCTURE AND HUMAN NATURE

the human-nature aspect of the theory, while a more recent version of realism, *neorealism*, emphasizes the structural aspect.[25]

There are different ways of understanding the theoretical role of realism. One way, sometimes referred to as *descriptive realism* (also as explanatory or analytical realism), is to understand the theory as primarily providing a description of how states in fact act in their relations with other states. This is an implication of the first part of Hobbes' argument applied to international relations: in a state of nature, individuals, concerned with self-preservation, would not act in a moral way. The claim that states in fact behave as if they had no moral obligations toward each other is an *empirical* claim. It is not by itself a *normative* claim about how states *should* behave. But the empirical claim leads naturally to a normative claim, which understands the theory as prescriptive. *Prescriptive realism* includes the claim that states should not treat their relations with other states in moral terms. Because other states do not act morally in their international relations, no state should do so. This form of realism relies on Hobbes' claim that no state has moral obligations toward other states in a situation where acting morally can leave a state more vulnerable to attack. Prescriptive realism implies that states ought to act only in their national interest, and it is based on the claim of descriptive realism that states act only in that way.

Another, very different, way of understanding realism may be referred to as *moralized realism*. One form of moralized realism concludes that leaders have a *moral* obligation to act in their nation's interest because of their role as leaders and that this obligation weighs more heavily than other obligations they may have. Leaders must act according to national interest not because morality does not apply to their actions, but because morality requires that they do so. The most important and overriding moral duty of national leaders is to serve the interests of the states they lead. This is a *role obligation* they take on in assuming a leadership position. In their international actions, including the wars they fight, they should act morally by pursuing the national interest. One reason sometimes given for this position is that, while individuals are free to sacrifice their interests

---

[25] W. Julian Korab-Karpowicz, "Political Realism in International Relations," *Stanford Encyclopedia of Philosophy* (Fall 2010), http://plato.stanford.edu/entries/realism/, accessed December 29, 2010.

for moral ends, leaders are not free to do this for the citizens of the states they lead.

A second form of moralized realism concludes, like prescriptive realism, that states should act in their relations with other states out of national interest, not for explicitly moral reasons. (Basing foreign policy on explicitly moral reasons rather than national interest is sometimes referred to as *moralism*.) But moralized realists advocate this position, ironically, out of moral concern. States should not act for explicitly moral reasons because, when they do, they are likely to make matters morally worse. The consequences will be morally better if states go to war only from nation interest. For instance, some moralized realists who were critics of the 2003 US invasion of Iraq opposed the war because the stated purposes of the war were, in large part, explicitly moral, specifically, to combat the evil of terrorism and to depose an oppressive tyrant. (Another stated purpose was a matter of national interest, to disarm Iraq of weapons of mass destruction, though these turned out not to exist.) These critics would contend that their concerns were borne out, as the war was a moral disaster for both Iraq and the United States. Going to war only for reasons of national interest, as realists recommend, has better moral outcomes. The realists' opposition to the Iraq War shows, by the way, that realists are often cautious opponents rather than militant advocates of war.

Something close to this second form of moralized realism is discussed by American philosopher Charles Beitz under the label *heuristic realism*. This is "a cautionary view about the role that normative considerations should be allowed to play in practical reasoning about international affairs." Heuristic realism "warns of the predictable kinds of errors that can occur when moral considerations are applied naively or in the wrong way."[26] Beitz, following the American diplomat and theorist George Kennan, suggests some reasons for such a warning. First, action taken for explicitly moral reasons may be initiated without the consequences or their unpredictability being adequately taken into account. Second, such action may be undertaken without due consideration for whether the state has the ability and the will for the necessary follow-through (for example, the need for "nation building" after the military victory). Third, such action

---

[26] Charles Beitz, *Political Theory and International Relations*, new edn. (Princeton University Press, 1999), pp. 186–187.

may be taken not in a carefully reasoned way, but because of a popular moral clamor for something to be done.[27]

A fuller discussion of realism would reveal it to be a more subtle and sophisticated position than here represented, and a more difficult position to argue against than might at first appear. But consider briefly some criticisms. First, descriptive realism is simply false. In fact, states often act internationally as morality requires, even when this is against their national interests. The descriptive realist might respond that such behavior only *appears* to be against their interests, arguing that leaders recognize that it is often in a state's interest to have a reputation for acting morally. States (as well as individuals) can behave morally from different motives, and sometimes those motives are prudential rather than moral, as when action is undertaken only for the sake of a good reputation. But the fact that one can behave morally for different reasons is not relevant here. Descriptive realism, at least insofar as it supports prescriptive realism, is a doctrine about how states act, not what their motivations are. On the Hobbesian argument, states are justified in ignoring moral rules only if other states cannot be expected to act in accord with those rules. If states often do act in accord with moral rules, whatever their motives, prescriptive realism loses its support. Thus, this criticism of descriptive realism is also a criticism of prescriptive realism. Other criticisms of descriptive and prescriptive realism focus on challenges to the domestic analogy it involves, arguing that states under international anarchy are not relevantly similar to individuals under a Hobbesian state of nature.[28]

There are also arguments against the versions of moralized realism discussed earlier. The first version, that leaders have a *moral* obligation to act in their state's interest due to their role as leaders, misunderstands the nature of moral obligation. Granted that leaders do have such an obligation, it does not follow that it is always overriding. When there are moral reasons both for and against an action (as when there is a conflict of moral duties), determining the morally correct thing to do involves weighing the opposing reasons against each other, determining which reason in those circumstances has greater force. One cannot guarantee in advance, as this version of moralized realism assumes, that a leader's obligation to pursue the national interest will always be the strongest. To appeal to another

---

[27] *Ibid.*, p. 190.   [28] *Ibid.*, pp. 36–50.

domestic analogy, a mother has a very strong moral duty to feed her young children, but also a moral duty not to steal food from other hungry children. When these two moral reasons conflict, the duty not to steal food would often outweigh the duty to feed one's own. Likewise, it may be in the national interest of a hungry nation to invade another hungry nation to obtain its food stocks, but the leader's duty to pursue the national interest may in this case be weaker than the moral duty not to deprive another state of what it needs.

The second form of moralized realism is based on the assumption that when states act on explicitly moral reasons rather than on their national interest, they will make matters morally worse. But this assumption, while often true, may sometimes be false. As Beitz argues, heuristic realism does not show that leaders should never make foreign policy decisions for reasons that are explicitly moral rather than directly in the national interest, but rather that states should be cautious when doing so, given the ways that such actions can backfire or be counterproductive.[29] When all the facts are carefully considered, it may turn out that acting on the explicitly moral reason will lead to the best moral outcome.

Heuristic realism, though it is not realism in the standard sense, represents a grain of truth in the realistic approach to international relations and war. It offers some salutary practical advice for how leaders should reason about foreign policy decisions. This is indicated by its being *heuristic*. Because leaders are prone to miscalculate when they seek to imbue their foreign policy with moral principle, they should consider very carefully what they are doing, and, indeed, treat national interest as the default approach, so to speak, in their decision making. Counsels of realism may provide, Beitz suggests, a set of mid-level maxims or rules of thumb for leaders' practical decision making in foreign policy.[30]

There is another grain of truth in realism. In war, a great deal may be at stake, sometimes the lives of millions and the fate of nations. If morality were to pose a major obstacle to a state's pursuit of core national interests, it would likely be ignored. This idea may be referred to as the *principle of tolerable divergence*. If morality is to have an impact on behavior, the divergence between what morality requires and what prudence demands must be tolerable. If international morality were to require extreme sacrifice of

EXCELLENT POINTS

---

[29] *Ibid.*, p. 21.   [30] *Ibid.*, p. 190.

[margin note: THE JUST WAR TRADITION AIMS TO BE PRACTICAL]

national interest, it would be ignored and so rendered irrelevant. The just war tradition exhibits tolerable divergence; it has developed so as to be a practical guide to wartime decision makers. It does not require saint-like behavior, as anti-war pacifism might. The just war tradition, as discussed in Chapter 2, has developed in the moral space between realism and pacifism. The realist vision of international relations has had a continuous impact on the just war tradition throughout its development. So the contemporary realist's claim that the just war tradition should be disregarded ignores the fact that realism has, so to speak, already had its input. The demands of prudence have already been spoken for in the tradition.

1.6 Pacifism

Now we turn our attention to pacifism. Pacifism as it applies to war does not allow for a distinction between just and unjust wars because it rules out all wars. The pacifist denies that a war can be just even when it is fought to bring about a just peace. The pacifist would embrace the claims of Cicero and Franklin that an unjust peace is better than a just war (because no war is just). Pacifism, in general, is opposed to the use of force or violence against other persons, and it may take different forms, as represented in Figure 1.1.

Some people regard pacifism as an individual option, a "lifestyle choice," as a principle that should be held only by those who think that it is right for them. This may be referred to as *particularistic* pacifism. For the particularistic pacifist, pacifism is an individual preference, and it does not and should not apply to those who do not prefer it. In fact, particularistic pacifism is consistent with moral relativism and is not, strictly speaking, a moral view at all. As a moral view, pacifism, like any moral view, is *universalistic*. A moral rule is universal because it applies to everyone in the kind of situation in which the rule is relevant. If pacifism is a correct moral view, it is a view to which everyone should adhere, whether they recognize it or not.[31]

Universalistic pacifism may be *complete* or *partial*, complete when it applies in all situations, partial when it applies only in some. (Partial

---

[31] On the different forms of pacifism, see Douglas Lackey, *The Ethics of War and Peace* (Englewood Cliffs, NJ: Prentice-Hall, 1989), pp. 6–7.

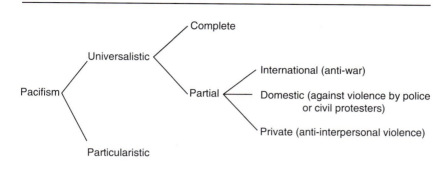

Figure 1.1   Forms of pacifism

pacifism is universalistic because it applies to everyone in the kinds of situation in which it is relevant.) *Complete pacifism* is the view that it is never morally justified to use violence against other persons. For the complete pacifist, not only is war morally wrong, but so is violence in civil or interpersonal contexts, such as individual self-defense. In contrast, *partial pacifism* is the view that violence is morally unacceptable only in certain kinds of situations. Three forms of partial pacifism are *international pacifism*, *domestic pacifism*, and *private pacifism*. The international pacifist is an anti-war pacifist, but may find some forms of domestic or private violence acceptable. The domestic pacifist is opposed to violence in civil contexts such as political action and policing, but not necessarily to violence in war. Mahatma Gandhi and Martin Luther King, Jr. were known for their domestic pacifism, as least as concerns violence in political protests, though they may have been complete pacifists. The private pacifist is opposed to the use of violence in private contexts. Our interest is in international or anti-war pacifism.

Universalistic pacifism, whether complete or partial, may be either conditional or unconditional.[32] *Unconditional pacifism* is the view that there are no exceptions to the anti-violence rule, that when moral rules conflict, the anti-violence rule always takes precedence. *Conditional pacifism*, on the other hand, is the view that, while the anti-violence rule applies to everyone, it may sometimes be overridden by other moral rules that apply in the

---

[32] The strongest form of pacifism is unconditional complete pacifism.

same situation. For example, a rule against private violence in self-defense would be conditional if it could be overridden in cases where violence is necessary to save not oneself, but other innocent people. Conditional anti-war pacifism would allow exceptions to the rule that war is not permitted. This is a position advanced by American philosopher Larry May, under the label of contingent pacifism. "Contingent pacifism is opposed to war not on absolute grounds but on contingent grounds, namely, that war as we have known it has not been, and seemingly cannot be, waged in a way that is morally acceptable."[33]

What is the argument for pacifism, whether complete or partial? Speaking generally, there are two broad moral theories that may be appealed to when seeking to justify a moral position, *deontological theory* and *consequentialist theory* (*utilitarianism* is one well-known form of consequentialist theory). A deontological theory grounds morality in certain basic duties or obligations that moral agents have, often duties or obligations requiring respect for human rights. An action is right or wrong depending on whether it is required, prohibited, or permitted by those duties. ("Deontology" is from the ancient Greek, meaning roughly "logic of duty.") In contrast, a consequentialist theory grounds morality in the examination of the moral value and disvalue of an action's consequences. The moral value is the benefit to all persons affected by the action, while the moral disvalue is the harm to them. Some consequentialist theories (such as utilitarianism) take the benefit to be pleasure or happiness and the harm to be pain or unhappiness. For a consequentialist, whether an action is morally acceptable depends on the overall expected value of the action (its value minus its disvalue) as this compares with the overall expected value of alternative actions.

A rough deontological argument for anti-war pacifism would be this: all persons have a basic moral duty not to kill others, and war involves such killing, so war is morally prohibited. A rough consequentialist argument for anti-war pacifism would be this: in the light of the tremendous destruction it brings about, the consequences of going to war are always worse, in terms of overall expected value, than the consequences of not going to war.

[33] Larry May, *Aggression and Crimes against Peace* (Cambridge University Press, 2008), pp. 25–26.

But do these arguments support conditional or unconditional anti-war pacifism? From the deontological perspective, a common feature of our moral lives is that we often face a conflict of moral duties, a situation in which we have two or more moral duties that cannot all be satisfied because they require incompatible actions. For example, a duty to aid someone in distress may be in conflict with a duty to keep a promise. When this sort of conflict occurs, we must compare the two duties to determine which is weightier, which one overrides the other, given the circumstances. There is sometimes a conflict between (1) a duty not to kill others and (2) a duty not to allow innocent people to be killed by others. These two duties would conflict when the only way to fulfill duty (2) is to kill the prospective killer, thereby violating duty (1). This kind of conflict of duties arises in the context of war, and when it does, it may at least sometimes be that duty (2) would override duty (1), in which case military violence would be acceptable. This suggests that a deontological perspective supports conditional rather than unconditional anti-war pacifism.

The consequentialist argument for anti-war pacifism is based on what may be called the *principle of uncertain expectations*. When a state is considering going to war, it expects certain outcomes, and it makes its decision based on those expectations. If leaders are considering war from a consequentialist perspective, they will want to know whether the expected outcomes of going to war will be better than those of not going to war. But there is much uncertainty in war, with luck and chance playing a central role in the outcome. The philosopher Richard Norman observes: "A major war involves social upheaval on a huge scale, eluding effective human control, and its outcome is almost bound to be unpredictable."[34] To take account of this uncertainty, when considering the expected outcomes of our actions, we factor in not only the overall value of the outcome, but also the likelihood or probability of its occurrence. In doing this, we *discount* the overall value of an outcome by its likelihood, producing what is known as an *expected value*. For example, if an outcome is thought to have a 50 percent probability, its value will be counted at one-half in the consequentialist calculations. Expectations for outcomes are *reasonable* when the probability estimates used in arriving at the expected value are based on reliable evidence and careful calculations. Consequentialist calculations,

[34] Richard Norman, *Ethics, Killing, and War* (Cambridge University Press, 1995) p. 210.

then, should be based on *reasonable expectations*. This is especially important in the moral assessment of war, given that its consequences are so uncertain.

The principle of uncertain expectations relies on an important feature of war, namely, that we can generally be more certain of harmful consequences than of beneficial ones. First, the harms are usually more immediate, occurring in the shorter term, while the benefits would occur later in time. Given that short-term predictions are generally more accurate than long-term predictions, the benefits should be more heavily discounted than the harms. Second, serious harms will occur no matter who wins, while the hoped-for benefits will occur only if the side doing the calculations wins. But every war has a loser. This too implies that the benefits must be more heavily discounted.

> *Principle of uncertain expectations*: in war, the foreseen harms are significantly more likely to occur than the foreseen benefits, so, in terms of reasonable expectations, the benefits must be discounted more heavily than the harms in the consequentialist calculations, making it more difficult for the expected value of the war to turn out positive.

This principle supports the consequentialist case for anti-war pacifism, but in a qualified way. It cautions against expecting war to produce a positive outcome, but it allows the expectation of a positive outcome, if the stakes are high. Thus, the principle supports conditional rather than unconditional anti-war pacifism.

Consider briefly three other consequentialist arguments for anti-war pacifism. First, pacifists argue that violence begets violence, so that military violence creates a situation in which future violence is more likely, and so tends to be counterproductive. For example, the side that loses will want to take revenge, and other parties, observing the benefits achieved by the winner, will take the lesson that violence can be an effective way to get results. But the tendency of violence to beget violence is only a tendency; it does not show that going to war will always have worse consequences than avoiding it. Second, pacifists argue that there is an alternative to violence that can achieve the defensive purposes for which violence is often used, namely, *civilian defense*.[35] Under civilian defense, aggressors, rather

[35] See Gene Sharp, *The Politics of Nonviolent Action*, 3 vols. (Boston: Porter Sargent, 1973).

than being met with violence, would face a massive campaign of civilian non-cooperation. The assumption is that aggressors need the cooperation of the population of a conquered state to achieve the benefits that led them to undertake the invasion. Absent that cooperation, aggressors will eventually recognize the futility of their occupation and depart. The possibility of civilian defense shows that pacifism is not the same as passivism; pacifism calls not for acquiescence in aggression, but for militant, though nonviolent, resistance to it. But civilian defense is a controversial idea, and the claim that it would work depends on various empirical assumptions that may not hold in all cases. One is that an aggressor will always seek to exploit the population of the occupied state economically rather than to destroy it or drive it away to make extra room for its own population.[36]

The third argument focuses on the huge loss of life characteristic of recent wars, as indicated by the sobering numbers cited at the beginning of the chapter. Moreover, the ratio of civilian to combatant deaths in war has been increasing in the past hundred years. By one estimate, the ratio of civilian to combatant deaths, which was about one to eight at the beginning of the twentieth century, had flipped by the end of the century, shifting to a ratio of eight to one.[37] The death of civilians in war is especially problematic from a moral perspective. The increasing numbers of war dead, with the increasing proportion of them civilians, may be an inevitable feature of contemporary wars in our age of insurgencies, ethnic rivalries, terrorism, and the spread of sophisticated and destructive weapons technology, and it supports the view that contemporary war cannot be morally justified from a consequentialist perspective.[38] But this argument, like the other two, supports conditional rather than unconditional antiwar pacifism because it is consistent with exceptional situations in which reasonable expectations about outcomes would morally favor war.

So, both deontological and consequentialist arguments for anti-war pacifism support its conditional form rather than its unconditional form. Even if most wars would not be morally justified, some could be. Following

[handwritten margin note: IS CONDITIONAL PACIFISM REALLY A FORM OF PACIFISM? ISN'T PACIFISM UNCONDITIONAL ALMOST BY DEFINITION?]

---

[36] As was Hitler's intention regarding areas in Eastern Europe Germany occupied in World War II. For a similar criticism of civilian defense, see Michael Walzer, *Just and Unjust Wars* (New York: Basic Books, 1977), pp. 329–335.

[37] Mary Kaldor, *New and Old Wars*, 2nd edn. (Stanford University Press, 2006), p. 9.

[38] This argument is developed by Robert Holmes, *On War and Morality* (Princeton University Press, 1989).

these arguments, then, what the pacifist should do is to investigate the (perhaps unusual) conditions under which war would be morally justified. But this is precisely what just war theory is about. Just war theory seeks to determine the conditions under which war is morally acceptable. In that sense, conditional anti-war pacifism is not inconsistent with just war theory. Both theories seek to discover the conditions under which war may be justified. As May notes, "contingent pacifism is consistent with some forms of Just War theory."[39] The question for both theories is how just wars should be distinguished from unjust wars.[40]

An interesting consequentialist argument against anti-war pacifism is put forth by the British philosopher Elizabeth Anscombe. She argues that the advocacy of pacifism can lead to greater bloodshed in war because it can undermine belief in moral constraints within war.[41] Just war theory considers not only moral constraints on going to war, but also moral constraints on how a war is fought. Anscombe is concerned with the latter. Because the pacifist claims that wars should not be fought at all, those influenced by pacifism will tend to believe that there are no moral limits *within* war (as opposed to the moral prohibition of war itself). If those people find themselves in war, the lesson they may draw from pacifism is that if a war is being fought, there are no constraints on how it is fought. As a result, they may fight without constraint, causing greater destruction. Specifically, Anscombe argues that the major moral constraint within war is the rule not to attack civilians, so that if one is fighting a war without recognizing this as a constraint, civilians will be freely attacked.

[handwritten margin note: HOW MANY PACIFISTS ACTUALLY REASON THIS WAY?]

1.7 Just war theory

Realism and (unconditional anti-war) pacifism agree that there is no moral distinction to be made between just and unjust wars; none is prohibited or all are prohibited. The problems we have seen with these two positions

---

[39] May, *Aggression and Crimes against Peace*, p. 33.

[40] For one proposal on reconciling just war theory and anti-war pacifism, see James Sterba, *Social and Political Philosophy: Contemporary Perspectives* (New York: Routledge, 2001), pp. 18–22.

[41] Elizabeth Anscombe, "War and Murder," in E. Anscombe (ed.), *Ethics, Religion, and Politics* (Oxford: Blackwell, 1981), pp. 51–61, specifically, pp. 55–58.

suggest that an ethics of war should focus on a position that would recognize such a distinction. Just war theory is such a position.[42] Just war theory seeks to determine the conditions for distinguishing just from unjust wars. Just war theory gives content to the idea of an ethics of war, and so it allows an engagement with ethics by those wielding political and military power. In one respect, the basis of both realism and pacifism is the notion that war is pure barbarism and savagery, and there is no way to regard it as anything else. To this, the realist responds that we must accept it and not attempt to restrict it with fine moral concepts, while the pacifist responds that we must reject it completely. Both the realist and the pacifist let leaders off the moral hook. Realism does this directly, but pacifism does this indirectly. In practice, the pacifist allows leaders to ignore morality regarding matters of war because it permits them to say: "It's a dangerous world out there, and if morality tells me that I cannot use military force at all to protect my state, then I must ignore morality."

IN PRACTICE?

But the idea that war is mere savagery is close to the way Hobbes used the term in his claim that without government there would be a "war as is of every man against every man." We rejected the idea that violence among isolated individuals is an instance of war. Because war is conducted by a large organization, it is inevitably conducted in a limited way. War is designed to serve the organization's ends, and it cannot do so unless it is limited. The organization, usually a government and its military, exercises control over the violence in order to achieve its goals. War is a human institution, and as such it is inherently normative, an activity bounded by rules. War is not a natural catastrophe such as an earthquake, but a human creation. But these limits are not necessarily moral limits. Morality adds its own restraints to the use of violence in war, partly in an effort to make war less destructive. These restraints are what just war theory studies. When these restraints are respected, war may be viewed as morally acceptable.

The central question of ethical thinking about war, as the just war theorist James Turner Johnson notes, is: "How can the use of force serve just ends?"[43] The same question can be asked of a government's use of force

---

[42] Other moral theories may recognize such a distinction as well, but they are not forms of just war theory because they are not connected with the just war tradition.

[43] James Turner Johnson, "The Broken Tradition," *National Interest* (Fall 1996).

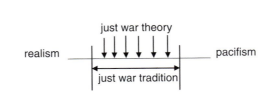

Figure 1.2   Just war between realism and pacifism

within society. To answer this, political philosophers sometimes pose another question: what is the difference between the taxman and the gunman? The taxman's use of force is thought sometimes at least to be just, while the gunman's is not. But both use force or the threat of force to take your money against your will, so how can one of the activities be moral and the other not? Isn't the phrase "the ethics of taking someone's money by force," like the phrase "the ethics of war," an oxymoron? The answer is that there are moral limitations on the taxman's extractive activities, and those activities may be morally acceptable when those limitations are respected. The moral limitations have to do, in large part, with the legal and moral legitimacy of the government for which the taxman works.

One way to view the relationship between realism, pacifism, and just war theory is that just war theory occupies a middle position between the extremes of realism and pacifism. Johnson notes, "in the ongoing argument between foreign policy realists and idealists [pacifists], the just-war tradition of moral reasoning about the use of force has played a crucial mediating role."[44] We could imagine the positions on the spectrum in Figure 1.2.

Realism claims that no wars are unjust, while pacifism claims that all wars are unjust. The just war tradition is between them because it claims that some wars are just and some not. Realists criticize the just war tradition for interfering with states' ability to fight, and pacifists criticize it for seeking to legitimize what cannot be legitimated.[45] As the figure indicates, the just war tradition is an interval on this line, rather than

[44] Ibid.
[45] C. A. J. Coady, *Morality and Political Violence* (Cambridge University Press, 2008), p. 11.

a point. The tradition encompasses different versions of just war theory, represented in Figure 1.2 by vertical arrows. In this way of delineating the differences among versions of just war theory, they differ in that some are closer to realism, so include weaker moral constraints and are more permissive regarding the use of force, while others are closer to pacifism, so include stronger moral constraints and are more restrictive regarding the use of force.

There are two main dimensions of moral questions in just war theory. First, there are questions about when it is justified to go to war, which wars are just and which are unjust. We have primarily been discussing questions at this level. This dimension of just war theory is known by the Latin phrase *jus ad bellum*, justice *of* war. Second, there are questions about how force can be used in wars, how war should be fought. This dimension of just war theory is known as *jus in bello*, justice *in* war. *Jus ad bellum* is (in part) about what *ends* justify going to war, while *jus in bello* is about what *means* may be used in pursuit of those ends. (Although these terms represent ideas seen throughout the history of the just war tradition, they did not actually come into common use until the 1930s.[46]) *Jus ad bellum* will be discussed in Chapters 3 and 4 and *jus in bello* in Chapters 5 and 6.

Just war theory is the result of a long intellectual tradition in the West, extending back thousands of years to the writings of philosophers in ancient Greece and Rome. This intellectual history is referred to as the *just war tradition*. Just war theory is an attempt to provide the best account of the ethics of war. It draws freely on the just war tradition as a source, but the two are not the same. The just war tradition is composed of a series of interrelated ideas and arguments by various authors offered over a long period of time, and it contains many conflicting and inconsistent elements. In contrast, a just war theory is an attempt to create a consistent and unified account of the ethics of war. The theory is selective in the ideas it borrows from the tradition, and it seeks to develop those ideas in a comprehensive way.

[handwritten margin note: JUSTICE OF WAR]

[handwritten margin note: JUSTICE IN WAR]

[46] Robert Kolb, "Origins of the Twin Terms *Jus ad Bellum/Jus in Bello*," *International Review of the Red Cross*, no. 320, pp. 553–562, www.icrc.org/web/eng/siteeng0.nsf/htmlall/57J NUU?OpenDocument&View=defaultBody&style=custo_print, accessed September 2, 2010.

The next chapter offers a brief history of the ideas and arguments of the just war tradition.

1.8 Just war theory and international law

There exists in our time an extensive and elaborate international law of war, known as International Humanitarian Law (IHL). The content of IHL borrows many of its elements from the just war tradition, and it overlaps considerably with just war theory, though they are not identical. Just war theory and IHL relate to each other much as do morality and domestic law (law within a society). Much of domestic law is a codification of basic moral rules. For example, the moral rule against murder is codified in a law against murder. Of course, some law is contrary to morality, and efforts to reform existing law are often attempts to bring it more into accord with morality, for example when women were given the right to vote. The energy behind the campaign for female suffrage was in large part due to the moral principle then being recognized in society that it is unjust to deny women equal rights of citizenship. In addition, much of the support that domestic law enjoys among citizens is due to their belief that what the law requires corresponds roughly with what morality requires. If the law were to depart too far from moral values, the law would come to be seen as illegitimate and would be less effective at controlling behavior.

Much the same could be said about the relation between IHL and just war theory. The IHL is largely the institutionalization of just war theory, and efforts to reform IHL are largely driven by the desire to bring it more fully into accord with just war theory. International law is different from domestic law in certain respects. For example, international law has no effective system of sanctions or punishments for states that are violators, and international law has no single or commanding source, a role played in domestic law by a legislature. These differences have led some to deny that international law is really law.[47] But international law operates in many ways like its domestic counterpart. For example, despite lacking a formal legislature, international law has clear sources of law, on the basis of which international courts are able to pass judgments on cases that come before them. The sources of IHL include international agreements,

---

[47] See H. L. A. Hart, *The Concept of Law* (Oxford University Press, 1961), chapter 10.

customary principles and rules, decisions of international courts, and the writings of legal specialists.[48]

The institutionalization of just war theory through IHL has made moral obligations in war enforceable, as the institutionalization of morality in domestic law makes it enforceable. The creation of law is, in this respect, a great boon for morality. In addition, the institutionalization of just war theory, as mentioned in our discussion of value relativism, has ensured its practical universalization. The global reach of international law, as shown for example by the near universal membership of states in the UN, means that just war theory is no longer exclusive to the European intellectual tradition, but has global reach. The global acceptance of just war theory is further guaranteed by our earlier observation that the justice that the theory seeks to instantiate is a minimal notion of justice common to the variety of comprehensive doctrines existing in the world.

* * *

One of the greatest challenges to just war theory is to provide an account that is relevant and applicable to the great variety of armed conflicts through history. In terms of scope, armed conflicts have ranged from those with near global involvement, such as World Wars I and II, to the 1963 Sand War, a border dispute between Morocco and Algeria. In terms of lethality, the range extends from the nineteen armed conflicts of the twentieth century with over a million fatalities each to the United States invasion of Grenada (1983), with ninety-seven killed. In temporal terms, the range extends from conflicts like the Six Day War between Israel and the Arab states (1967), to the Hundred Years War (1336–1453), between the English and the French over control of territory in modern-day France. The extent of civilian casualties ranges from the minimal civilian destruction of the Falkland/Malvinas War between Argentina and Britain, with three civilian deaths,[49] to the Congo Civil Wars at the turn of this century, which involved over 5 million civilian deaths.

---

[48] Adam Roberts and Richard Guelff, *Documents on the Laws of War*, 3rd edn. (Oxford University Press, 2000), p. 4.

[49] The three civilians, killed by accidental British shelling, were Mrs. Susan Whitley, Mrs. Doreen Bonner, and Mrs. Mary Goodwin. www.ppu.org.uk/falklands/falklands3. html accessed June 8, 2009.

Perhaps the most theoretically problematic difference is that between inter-state armed conflict, where the opponents are different states, and intra-state armed conflicts, where the opponents are from the same state. Inter-state armed conflicts have been our dominant model of war, but in recent decades, the majority of armed conflicts have been civil wars, and civil wars have had an especially high number of civilians dying, as the Congo Civil Wars show. The focus of discussion in the next few chapters will be mainly on inter-state armed conflicts, but in Chapter 7 we will explore civil wars and the extent to which an account of war based on the inter-state model can be applied to wars in an intra-state context.

2 The just war tradition: a brief history

It is not for man to make wasteful use of his fellow-man.

Seneca[1]

In the Western intellectual tradition, systematic thinking about the ethics of war goes back to ancient Greece. The body of thinking that developed in that tradition over the centuries is referred to as the just war tradition. Efforts to organize the insights of the just war tradition into a single coherent understanding of the ethics of war are instances of just war theory. To introduce our discussion of just war theory in the remainder of this book, this chapter offers a brief history of the just war tradition, of the ideas that developed in this tradition. The characteristic feature of both the just war tradition and just war theory is an effort to *limit* war, both in its frequency and in the savagery with which it is fought.

2.1 Vitoria and the Spanish war against Native Americans

Following the European discovery of America by Columbus, various states in Europe waged war against and exploited the native populations of the New World.[2] Consider the Spanish aggression in Latin America. In 1493, the year after his initial voyage, Columbus, sailing again for Spain, returned to the Caribbean and began a conquest of the Taino people of that region. In 1519–1521, the Spanish, under Hernán Cortés, conquered

---

[1] Lucius Seneca, *Moral Epistles*, trans. Richard Gummere, Loeb Classical Library (Cambridge, MA: Harvard University Press, 1925), Epistle 88.

[2] In addition, these populations suffered "demographic collapse" as a large portion of their number died due to the diseases carried by the Europeans to which the natives had no immunity.

the Aztec civilization in present-day Mexico. In 1532–1533, the Spanish, under Francisco Pizzaro, conquered the Inca civilization in present-day Peru. These wars of conquest were fought primarily for the precious metals to be had. Many of the surviving natives were put under systems of forced labor. An empire was established, which "in extent and population, and cultural diversity … exceeded even [that of] ancient Roman, previously the standard of imperial power."[3]

What was the European reaction to the morality of these wars? The Spanish crown declared in 1500, in the midst of the conquest of the Taino, that the natives were "free and not subject to servitude," but this declaration "kept a loophole open for Spanish colonizers to legally enslave any Indians taken in so-called 'just-wars' – which colonists characterised as any violence they conducted against resisting Natives." The Spanish conquerors did adhere to the Spanish law of conquest by reading to the natives a script, referred to as the *requerimiento*, ordering the Indians immediately to accept Spanish rule and convert to Christianity or face punishment. If the natives refused, the resulting violence against them was regarded by the Spanish as a just war. The *requerimiento* included the sentence: "The resultant deaths and damages shall be your fault, and not the monarch's or mine or the soldiers." When the script was read, "Attending witnesses and a notary usually certified in writing that the *requerimiento* had been read and ignored by the usually uncomprehending Indians, thus justifying the death and destruction that so often followed."[4]

In 1513, King Ferdinand "called a commission of theologians and civil and canon [religious] lawyers to discuss the matter," resulting in the first colonial legislation, the Law of Burgos.[5] Prior to this, natives were under a system of compulsory labor referred to as *repartimiento*. The Law replaced the *repartimiento* by the *encomienda*, a more paternalistic approach to exploitation. Under the old system, the natives were forced to travel sometimes great distances from their villages to the sites of their compelled labor. The Law declared that instead the natives should "be brought to dwell near the villages and communities of the Spaniards who inhabit

---

[3] Michael McDonnell, "The 'Conquest' of the Americas: The Aztecs," www.anzasa.arts.usyd.edu.au/ahas/conquest_overview.html, accessed August 3, 2008.

[4] *Ibid.*

[5] Anthony Pagden and Jeremy Lawrance (eds.), *Vitoria: Political Writings* (Cambridge University Press, 1991), editors' introduction, p. xxiii.

that Island, so that they may be treated and taught and looked after as is right."[6] The Law apparently had little effect in changing the behavior of the Spanish masters, and the natives themselves probably saw little difference. More to the point, paternalistic exploitation is no more justified than is non-paternalistic exploitation. A recent statement by the descendants of the Taino people sums up the situation.

> Our ancestors faced genocide and enslavement, under the "repartimiento" and "encomienda" system of Spanish Colonial Rule. The objective of these systems was to Christianize our Peoples and protect us from our own "infidel state". According to the Crown only by forcibly denying us our freedom and appropriating our labor could our civilization and assimilation be successful.[7]

The clearest contemporaneous European intellectual reaction against the moral acceptability of the Spanish conquests came from one of the main figures in the just war tradition, the Spanish theologian Francisco de Vitoria (c. 1485–1546). Vitoria, a distinguished professor at the University of Salamanca, gave a lecture in 1539, "On the American Indians," discussing the Spanish conquest from the perspective of just war thinking.[8] The first substantive question he addresses is whether the natives had "true dominion" over the lands they inhabited. While the natives were not Christians and their behavior was barbarous from a European perspective, Vitoria argued, this did not show that they lacked dominion over their lands. He concluded that "the barbarians undoubtedly possessed as true dominion, both public and private, as any Christian."[9]

This claim establishes the presumption that it was wrong for the Spanish to dispossess the natives of their land, and Vitoria then critically addresses a series of alleged justifications for dispossession, proposed reasons to set the presumption aside. In response to one such reason, that the natives refused voluntarily to accept Christianity, Vitoria argues that this is not

[6] "The Laws of Burgos," http://faculty.smu.edu/bakewell/BAKEWELL/texts.burgoslaws.html, accessed August 3. 2008.

[7] United Confederation of Taino People, "Sacred Sites and the Environment from an Indigenous Perspective," www.yachaywasi-ngo.org/TainoSpeech.pdf, accessed August 6, 2008.

[8] Francisco Vitoria, "On the American Indians," in Pagden and Lawrance (eds.), *Vitoria*, pp. 231–292.

[9] *Ibid.*, pp. 239–251, quotation p. 250.

a matter about which people may be coerced. Not only is such coercion morally unacceptable, but also it is incoherent because true religious faith must be voluntarily chosen. "Belief is a matter of will, but fear considerably diminishes the freedom of will." Another reason offered was that natives are sinners, to which Vitoria responds, given the natives' dominion over their lands, the Europeans had no right to punish them for their sins.[10] He also argues that the establishment of empire is not a just cause for war.[11]

Vitoria's arguments show that just war thinking can pose a serious challenge to the way in which great powers conduct military affairs. But the apparent failure of these efforts to substantially change Spanish military policies in the New World must be acknowledged.

2.2 The origins of the just war tradition: early developments

The most significant figure in the early development of the just war tradition was Augustine (CE 354–430). Augustine, a convert to Christianity and a bishop of the early Church, took ideas about the ethics of war that had earlier developed in Greece and Rome and combined these with features of Christian doctrine to produce a synthesis of historical importance. We will first examine some of the earlier thinking from which Augustine drew.

One of the intellectual giants of the ancient world was the Greek philosopher Plato (427–347 BCE). Though Plato grew up at a time of great upheaval caused by the prolonged and disastrous Peloponnesian War (431–404 BCE) between the Greek city-states of Athens (his homeland) and Sparta, he does not devote much attention to war in his writings. One discussion of it occurs in his dialogue *Republic*, in which he describes an ideal, completely just political community (or city-state). In Plato's dialogues, the main speaker is his teacher Socrates, who was put to death by Athens for his public philosophizing. At one point in *Republic*, Plato has Socrates say that the Greeks should fight "like people who know one day that they will be reconciled." With this attitude, "they won't ravage Greece or burn her

---

[10] *Ibid.*, pp. 265–275, quotation p. 272.

[11] Despite this criticism, Vitoria notes that there may be a legitimate basis for war by Spain against the natives, if the natives interfere with the preaching of the Christian religion. *Ibid.*, pp. 284–286.

houses, nor will they agree that in any of her cities all the inhabitants –
men, women, and children – are their enemies."[12] While Plato regards
these limits as applying only when Greeks fight fellow Greeks, not when
they fight barbarians, the kind of limitations he advocates (do not attack
civilians and their property) and the reason he offers for them (because
we will need to reconcile with our opponents once the war is over) will
become important aspects of later just war thinking.

Aristotle, another intellectual giant of the ancient world and a student
of Plato, endorsed his teacher's claim that war should be waged with reconciliation in mind: "peace, as has often been repeated, is the end of war."[13]
Elsewhere, Aristotle distinguished two kinds of justice. "Of political justice part is natural, part legal, – natural, that which everywhere has the
same force and does not exist by people's thinking this or that; legal, that
which is originally indifferent, but when laid down is not indifferent."[14]
Legal justice (also called *conventional justice*) varies from society to society,
while *natural justice* is universal. Rules of legal justice, for example, which
side of the road to drive on, exist by convention. Absent such rules, the
side of the road one uses is a matter of indifference, but not in societies
with such a rule. In contrast, natural justice "everywhere has the same
force." The rules of natural justice or morality apply to all societies.

This distinction between natural and conventional justice is important
for several reasons. First, it is vital in showing that some justice (natural
justice) is universal, even though some justice (conventional justice) is the
result of agreement and may vary from culture to culture. When two societies are at war, there are moral rules binding both of them, however
different their views of conventional justice. Second, among the rules set
forth in just war theory, some are in the category of natural justice and
some in the category of conventional justice, and the difference between
them is important to note. Third, the idea of natural justice (later called
natural law) is crucial in later efforts to shift just war theory from a religious to a secular foundation.

---

[12] Plato, *Republic* (Indianapolis, IN: Hackett Publishing, 2004), p. 371a.

[13] Aristotle, *Politics* (Cambridge University Press, 1988), p. 1134a15. Regarding the
equivocation of this claim discussed in the first chapter, Aristotle clearly meant that
the *purpose* of waging war is achieving a good peace.

[14] Aristotle, *Nicomachean Ethics*, (Indianapolis, IN: Hackett Publishing, 1998), p. 1134b.

The sources of the just war tradition are also found in the ancient Roman legal institutions established to govern war, for example in *jus fetiale*. The *fetiales* was a group of religious leaders whose approval was necessary before Rome could go to war. Approval followed a prescribed procedure: Roman officials took a grievance of alleged offences by another state to the *fetiales*, which oversaw the sending of ambassadors to the offending state demanding reparations. If the offending state refused, the *fetiales* could give its permission for Rome to go to war, determining that the war could be legally waged. This requirement is, in part, a *procedural* limitation on war, in the sense that legally there could be no war unless the procedures of the *jus fetiale* were satisfied. A contemporary example of a procedural limitation on war is the provision in Article 1, Section 8 of the United States Constitution that "Congress shall have the power … to declare war," though in recent decades, this limitation has been effectively ignored by the Executive Branch. Of course, procedural limitations are meant to embody also *substantive* limitations, because they require an independent judgment about the substance of the case for going to war. For example, the *fetiales* would judge whether the alleged grievance was sufficient to justify war.[15] If the law worked as it was supposed to, Rome could not engage in unprovoked aggression, but could go to war only in response to a wrong or an offense committed against it. This idea of justified war as a response to a wrong would prove central to the developing just war tradition.

The Roman orator Marcus Tullius Cicero (106–43 BCE) had a strong influence on Augustine. In his work *On Duties*, he observes: "There are two types of conflict: the one proceeds by debate, and the other by force. Since the former is the proper concern of a man, but the latter of beasts, one should only resort to the latter if one may not employ the former."[16] Peaceful resolution of disputes, involving persuasion, debate, and negotiation, are proper for humans; war-making is for beasts. War may be fought only if peaceful means of resolving the underlying conflict are not available or effective. Cicero, like Aristotle, takes the view that the proper end

---

[15] Dinstein, *War – Aggression and Self-Defense,* 4th edn. (Cambridge University Press, 2005), pp. 63–64, and by Alex Bellamy, *Just Wars* (Cambridge: Polity Press, 2006), p. 19. Bellamy argues that the *fetiales* did not have a great practical impact, often the fate of rules that seek to limit war.

[16] Cicero, *On Duties* (Cambridge University Press, 1991), pp. 14–15.

of war is a just peace. For Cicero, limitations on the use of force flow from this fact.

Cicero regards natural justice as a dictate of nature "established not only in nature, that is in the law of nations, but also in the laws of individual peoples [that] one is not allowed to harm another for the sake of one's own advantage."[17] Thus, no state should use force to take advantage of another.

> Now surely it is absurd to say, as some do, that they would not deprive a parent or brother of anything for their own advantage, but that there is another rationale for the rest of the citizens. Such men decree that no justice and no fellowship exist among citizens for the sake of common benefit, an opinion that breaks up all fellowship in the city. There are others again who say that account should be taken of other citizens, but deny it in the case of foreigners; such men tear apart the common fellowship of the human race.[18]

We owe foreigners the same respect we owe compatriots and our own family, not to take from them wrongfully for our own advantage. This would rule out aggressive war, in which the aggressor seeks to take from another nation for the aggressor's own advantage. Such aggression would "tear apart the common fellowship of the human race." This is a statement of *cosmopolitanism*, the view that all humans are, in a moral sense, part of a single community.

But elsewhere Cicero suggests that it is possible to fight a just war for the sake of empire.[19] This initially appears puzzling because a war for empire seems to be a clear case of harming another for the sake of one's own advantage. The international relations theorist Alex Bellamy proposes a way to resolve this puzzle, suggesting that "by bringing more lands into the [Roman] empire … greater peace and happiness could be brought to humanity [so that] there is no contradiction between fighting for the glory of Rome and fighting to preserve the peace."[20] On this view, the route to realizing the cosmopolitan ideal is through the unity and the civilizing benefits of the global empire of Rome, and global unity is achieved not through humanity choosing to unite, but through humanity being forcibly united by Roman wars of conquest.

---

[17] *Ibid.*, p. 108.   [18] *Ibid.*, p. 110.   [19] *Ibid.*, pp. 16–17.
[20] Bellamy, *Just Wars*, pp. 19–20.

2.3 The origins of the just war tradition: Augustine

During Augustine's life, Rome, perceived as the guarantor of civilization, adopted Christianity as its official state religion. At the same time,
Rome was coming increasingly under assault by barbarian forces at its
borders. The historical conjunction of these two, the political triumph
of Christianity and the increasing vulnerability of Rome, created a special intellectual problem for Augustine as a Christian. Could he reconcile
Church doctrine, often understood as pacifist, with the political responsibility the Church had acquired by becoming the official state religion, to
see after the security of Rome (and so of civilization)? In addressing this
problem, Augustine laid the foundations of the just war tradition.

Augustine, like Aristotle and Cicero, claims that the end of war is peace:
"The desired end of war is peace, for everyone seeks peace, even by waging
war, but no one seeks war by waging peace." But, as we saw, peace can be
just or unjust. There is a difference between "the peace of the iniquitous"
and "the peace of the just," and war may be permissible to achieve the
latter.[21] To understand how Augustine reconciled Christian doctrine and
war, we need to understand what he thought morally wrong with war. The
answer is surprising. What is "to be blamed" in war is not "that those who
will die someday are killed," but rather the motivations of those who fight:
"the desire for harming, the cruelty of revenge … the lust for dominating,
and similar thing – these are what are justly blamed in war."[22] Acting out
of these negative motivations is harmful to the soul, and the soul is more
important than the body, both because the soul continues after the death
of the body and because, unlike our ability to exercise control over how we
act, we cannot always exercise control over whether we die.

Augustine uses this focus on negative motivations to reconcile Christian
doctrine with waging war. The strongest Christian argument for pacifism
is based on the so-called *precepts of patience*, the New Testament teachings
not to return evil for evil, such as Jesus' admonition to turn the other
cheek. According to Augustine the precepts of patience concern not out-
ward behavior, but inward motivation. The precepts "must always be

---

[21] Augustine, *The City of God*, in Reichberg *et al.* (eds.), *The Ethics of War: Classic and
Contemporary Readings* (Oxford: Blackwell Publishing, 2006), p. 79.

[22] Augustine, *Against Faustus the Manichean*, in Reichberg *et al.* (eds.), *Ethics of War*, p. 73.

observed with respect to one's interior disposition, and a spirit of benevolence must always permeate the will so as to avoid returning evil for
evil."[23] What is important morally is not whether one strikes another, but
how one strikes another, whether or not it is out of feelings of revenge,
anger, or hurt. It may be acceptable to strike another in "a spirit of benevolence," as a parent might strike a child.

But there is another step in the argument. For Augustine, killing in
individual self-defense is morally questionable because killing to defend
one's body shows a "lust" for continued earthly existence, one of the negative motivations he proscribes. This objection, however, does not apply to
killing in defense of others because such killing can be undertaken in a
detached or benevolent way. In a defensive war, combatants defend others
(their compatriots). "In killing an enemy, the soldier acts as an agent of the
law. That is why he can easily fulfill his duty without lust."[24] In killing an
enemy, a combatant may be motivated by the duty to follow orders, or by
benevolence or charity in regard to the ones whose lives are threatened by
the enemy. All of these are positive, permissible motivations.[25] This shows,
contrary to pacifism, that war is *morally possible*, not necessarily morally
wrong. But under what conditions is war just? Though Augustine gives no
succinct list, three criteria can be gleaned from his writing.

The first is that a just war must be fought out of positive rather than
negative motivations. The second is that a war must be defensive, for only
then can it be an act of benevolence or charity. Augustine, however, understands defensive war quite broadly: "As a rule just wars are defined as
those which avenge injuries."[26] ("Injuries" here is sometimes translated
as "wrongs.") But this formulation is problematic for Augustine. The language of *avenging* seems to lose the connection with defending others, for
one avenges an injury only after it has been inflicted and the damage done.
Moreover, *avenging* an injury seems to require that one acts out of *vengeance*, which is one of the negative motivations. But he offers a different
formulation that avoids these problems. In a just war, he asserts, "soldiers

[handwritten marginal note: NEAT TRICK: KILLING WITH-OUT SINFUL MOTIVATION.]

---

[23] Augustine, *Letter 138, to Marcellinus*, in Reichberg et al. (eds.), *Ethics of War*, p. 73.

[24] Augustine, *On Free Choice of the Will*, in Reichberg et al. (eds.), *Ethics of War*, p. 75.

[25] Augustine here seems to ignore or downplay the fact that combatants may also be
killing enemies in defense of their own lives.

[26] Augustine, *Questions on the Heptateuch*, in Reichberg et al. (eds.), *Ethics of War*, p. 82.

serve peace and the common well-being."[27] The peace they seek must be a just peace, which serves the common well-being, not an iniquitous peace, which does not. When the common well-being of a community is under threat from a military attack, the combatants countering that threat are serving the common well-being of their community. Augustine's third criterion requires that a war be fought under an effective authority, that "the authority and deliberation for undertaking war be under the control of a leader."[28] This criterion, as we saw, is necessary to distinguish war from random violence, and it also makes it possible for combatants to act on the positive motivation to obey authority, rather than one of the negative motivations.

Introducing the contrast between combatants and their leaders opens an account of the ethics of war to greater moral complexity. Augustine notes: "Perhaps the iniquity of giving the orders will make the king guilty while the rank of a servant in the civil order will show the soldier to be innocent."[29] The combatants in an unjust war may not be morally responsible for the injustice of the war, if they do not themselves fight out of the negative motivations that presumably determine the actions of their leaders. Instead the combatants can act out of the motivation to follow orders, even if the orders are unjust. This argument suggests the difference between *jus ad bellum*, morality of waging war, and *jus in bello*, morality in the conduct of war, though Augustine does not develop this distinction. In fact, just war thinkers prior to the modern era have little to say about *jus in bello*.

Finally, Augustine introduces the idea of *necessity*, or *military necessity*, and considers the role it plays in the morality of war. Just wars are wars fought out of necessity, he asserts. In a sense, we do not choose to fight just wars, because fighting them is forced upon us by the opponent choosing to wage unjust war against us. While just wars are wars of necessity, unjust wars are wars of choice. Augustine observes: "The will should be concerned with peace and necessity with war, so that God might liberate us from necessity and preserve us in peace … Let necessity slay the warring foe, not your will."[30] This idea of necessity plays a complex role in

---

[27] Augustine, *Against Faustus*, in Reichberg *et al.* (eds.), *Ethics of War*, p. 81.
[28] *Ibid.*   [29] *Ibid.*, p. 82.
[30] Augustine, *Letter 189, to Boniface*, in Reichberg *et al.* (eds.), *Ethics of War*, p. 79.

later just war thinking, often being used as an alleged excuse or justification for those who fight. An appeal to necessity allows states to claim that they are not responsible for the harm their wars do because they did not choose to fight, but are instead forced (by necessity) to fight.

Let me sum up some the key ideas and distinctions from the last two sections. (1) The purpose of war should be to achieve a just peace, and a war is just only then fought for this purpose. (2) There is a distinction between natural justice, which is universal and applies to all, and conventional justice, which may vary. (3) Limitations on war may be *formal* (procedural) or *substantive*. Formal limitations are largely matters of conventional justice, whereas substantive limitations may be matters of natural justice. (4) There is, in a moral sense, a human community, composed of all persons. In addition to the *polis* (city), there is a *cosmopolis*. Both Cicero and Augustine bring us from the particular to the universal, Cicero through the idea of multiculturalism under law, and Augustine through the idea of universal religion. (5) The criteria for a just war include: first, that it is fought out of positive rather than negative motivation; second, that it is meant to avenge an injury or serve the common well-being; and third, that it is conducted under authority.

2.4 The medieval synthesis

The Catholic Church in the Middle Ages undertook practical efforts, beginning around the turn of the millennium, to limit various aspects of warfare through the movements called "The Peace of God" (beginning around 990) and "The Truce of God" (beginning around 1050).[31] These movements sought to limit the damage of warfare by prohibiting the military from assaulting clergy, women, travelers, shepherds, and agricultural workers and by setting aside times that warfare was to be in abeyance, such as Sundays. Also put off limits were farm animals and olive trees, and certain kinds of weapons were prohibited, such as incendiaries (those designed to cause fire).[32] These were attempts to establish conventions that would limit war, not eliminate it. The restrictions were

---

[31] For a discussion of these movements, see James Turner Johnson, *Just War Tradition and the Restraint of War* (Princeton University Press, 1981), pp. 124–131.
[32] Reichberg *et al.*, *Ethics of War*, pp. 93–97.

justified primarily on pragmatic grounds, rather than on arguments from natural justice, and were non-universal, applying only to wars among Christians.

The religious exclusivity of these limitations on war is consistent with a roughly contemporaneous development, the Crusades. The Crusades, lasting roughly from 1095 to 1274, were a series of wars fought by Christians against Muslims to retake sites in the Holy Land. These were holy wars, fought for moral reasons, but they were not just wars, in our sense. As discussed in the last chapter, the sense of justice in just war theory is a minimal one, one that could be accepted by members of different social groups holding a variety of comprehensive moral doctrines. This minimal sense of justice includes a notion of mutual toleration of differences of religion, since otherwise it could not be accepted by different religions. The just war tradition would come more fully around to this view as it detached itself from its religious roots. Later medieval thinkers adopted a perspective that was increasingly secular.

Another strand in the development of just war thinking in the Middle Ages was the idea of *chivalry*, a code of conduct adopted by members of the aristocratic class of knights beginning in the thirteenth century.[33] Much of the fighting during this period was done by knights, partly because outfitting combatants with the required horses and armor was expensive. Knights developed rules of behavior, a professional code, to distinguish themselves from other classes. The code represented a number of different ideals and virtues, such as honor, courage, service, protection of the weak, and avoidance of the vices of falsehood, greed, and idleness. Like other behavioral codes, however, it was often ignored in practice. But the aspect of the code requiring that knights fight only other knights gave rise to what later came to be called the principle of discrimination, the most important rule of *jus in bello*.

The major just war thinker of the Middle Ages is the theologian Thomas Aquinas (*c.* 1225–1274), who created the medieval synthesis referred to in the title of this section. Though he wrote relatively little on war, his discussion succinctly drew together the threads of just war thinking that had come before him, especially in the work of Augustine. Aquinas' work represented the high point of *scholasticism*, an approach to intellectual inquiry

[33] On chivalry and its relation to just war theory, see Bellamy, *Just Wars*, pp. 40–44.

that sought to understand the world through reason in a way compatible with Christian teachings.

Like Augustine, Aquinas argues that it is not always sinful to wage war. He outlines three criteria a war must satisfy to be just, parallel to Augustine's three criteria discussed earlier. The first is that a just war must be fought with "the authority of the sovereign by whose command the war is to be waged." A *sovereign* is the ruler of a state, a leader without an earthly political superior. In support of this *legitimate authority* criterion, Aquinas offers two arguments. First, a just war cannot be fought by private individuals, or by lesser public officials, because they have no need to take up arms. Because they have an earthly superior, they have a way to appeal nonviolently for the rectification of injustices they have suffered. But, without an earthly superior, sovereigns have no one to whom they can appeal regarding injustices they or their states have suffered at the hands of other states. They are themselves responsible for rectifying the injustice, and sometimes violence may be required. Second, sovereigns are the ones with the moral obligation to use force to protect their subjects from harm, whether the source of that harm is internal or external to the state. "As it is lawful for them to have recourse to the sword in defending that common weal against internal disturbances, when they punish evil-doers … so too it is their business to have recourse to the sword of war in defending the common weal against external enemies."[34]

Sovereigns, when protecting their subjects against internal harm, should act through law, but how can they do so when protecting them from external harm, given that the international arena lacks law under which the sovereign can act? According to Aquinas, there is no need for human law to play this role; instead sovereigns can wage war under natural law. Natural law is the law of God as revealed to humans through reason, while human law (conventional law or positive law) is law that is enacted in particular states.[35] Aquinas' idea of natural law is related to the idea of natural justice in Aristotle and Cicero. It is universal morality. From the natural law, "we can discern what is good and evil," and, coming from

NATURAL LAW

---

[34] Aquinas, *Summa Theologica*, trans. Fathers of the English Dominican Province, vol. 9 (London: Burns, Oates & Washbourne, 1916), p. 501.
[35] *Ibid.*, vol. 8, pp. 9–21.

God, natural law "is the same for all."[36] Human law should be informed by natural law, and when it is not, it is unjust law.

Natural law distinguishes just war from unjust war. Because humans understand natural law through reason, an account like Aquinas' can be presented without any direct reference to the tenets of Christianity or any other religion. Morality in general, from which we determine the morality of war, is the same for everyone and can be rationally determined by anyone. This is substantially a *secular perspective* on the morality of war, and it is a significant shift from a religious perspective which dominated previously in the just war tradition. Aquinas observes that "the theologian considers a sin principally as an offense against God, whereas the moral philosopher considers it as being contrary to reason."[37] Soldier-scholar Paul Christopher notes: "Augustine holds that revelation is always the foundational source of moral truth; Aquinas contends that humans can discover moral truths through reason."[38] One indication of Aquinas' appeal to reason is that he provides *arguments* for his claims, not simply relying on religious authority, and it is argument by which reason operates. Though Aquinas pushed the just war tradition in a secular direction, he was not himself a secularist. For him, natural law is from God, and he thought it necessary that reason provide the same conclusions as revelation.

Aquinas' second criterion is that a war must have a *just cause*. For him, "those who are attacked, should be attacked because they deserve it on account of some fault."[39] A state has a just cause for war when its opponent is at fault for wrongful actions. Recall that one of Augustine's formulations of the just cause criterion is that wars can be fought only to "avenge injuries [or wrongs]." Augustine and Aquinas share the view that a war is just only when the opponent has done something that makes it morally liable to attack, which is the case when it is at fault for some wrong or injury. This makes it morally permissible for the victim state to avenge that injury or wrong through war. Augustine and Aquinas thus share a *punitive* model of just cause, under which a just war is fought as punishment for

---

[36] *Ibid.*, pp. 12, 48.

[37] Aquinas, *Summa Theologica*, quoted in Paul Christopher (ed.), *The Ethics of War and Peace*, 2nd edn. (Upper Saddle River, NJ: Prentice-Hall, 1999), pp. 50–51.

[38] Christopher, *Ethics of War and Peace*, pp. 70–71.

[39] Aquinas, *Summa Theologica*, vol. 9, pp. 501–502.

wrongdoing. The political theorist Colm McKeogh finds this surprising. Aquinas had, he notes, effected a revolution in political theory by adopting the view that the purpose of rulers is the promotion of the common good, in contrast with Augustine's view that their purpose is to suppress sin. This suggests to McKeogh that Aquinas might also have moved away from Augustine's punitive model of just cause, but he did not do so.[40] The issue of whether or not just cause is punitive is a recurrent theme in the just war tradition.

The third criterion is that "it is necessary that the belligerents should have a rightful intention, so that they intend the advancement of good or the avoidance of evil." The *rightful intention* criterion can be traced back to Augustine's focus on avoiding negative motivations. "It may happen that the war is declared by the legitimate authority and for a just cause, and yet be rendered unlawful through a wicked intention."[41] Aquinas is trying to rule out wars where the just cause is simply a pretext, where the attacker goes to war for other, morally unacceptable reasons, and rationalizes the war by pointing to the just cause. This would occur, for example, when a strong state, wishing to exploit a weak state, goads the weak state into attacking it, thus providing it with a just-cause excuse for going to war against the weak state. Note, however, that Aquinas has shifted the nature of this criterion from Augustine's version of it. Augustine spoke of *motivations*, like lust or vengeance, whereas Aquinas speaks instead of *intentions*, like the intention to avoid evil.

[handwritten margin note: A JUST WAR CANNOT BE BASED ON A PRETEXT]

In addition to these three criteria, Aquinas hints at another that will be developed by future just war theorists. In his discussion of *strife* (the use of force among private individuals) he asserts that it is not a sin when it is a matter of individual self-defense. But individual self-defense must be conducted with "due moderation."[42] The point seems to be that the force used in individual self-defense should be appropriate to the attack to which it is a response, for example, by not exceeding what is necessary to ward off the attack. Just war theorists would later apply this idea to war, where it would become known as the criterion of *due care*. Indeed, the analogy (referred to as the *domestic analogy*) between individual self-defense and

---

[40] Colm McKeogh, "Civilian Immunity in War: From Augustine to Vattel," in I. Primoratz (ed.), *Civilian Immunity in War* (Oxford University Press, 2007), pp. 62–83, at p. 69.
[41] Aquinas, *Summa Theologica*, vol. 9, p. 502.   [42] *Ibid.*, p. 511.

national self-defense would later become an important part of arguments justifying war.

In contrast with Augustine, Aquinas sees nothing wrong with acting to save one's life because self-preservation is a natural instinct. In discussing individual self-defense, Aquinas introduces another distinction important in the just war tradition.

> Nothing hinders a single act from having two effects, only one of which is intended, while the other is beside the intention. Now moral acts get their character in accordance what is intended, but not from what is beside the intention, since the latter is incidental.

The intended effects of an action are of greater moral importance than the unintended effects.

> Accordingly, the act of self-defense may have a double effect: the saving of one's life, on the one hand, and the slaying of the attacker, on the other. Since saving one's life is what is intended, such an act is not therefore illicit, seeing that it is natural to everything to keep itself in existence as far as possible.[43]

Killing in self-defense has a *double effect*; one is the saving of one's own life and the other is the death of the attacker. In acting in self-defense, one may intend to save one's life, but not to kill the attacker, even though one knows the attacker will die. In such a case, the act is not necessarily morally wrong (illicit), despite the death of the attacker, because that effect is not intended.[44] But unintended effects have a weaker form of moral relevance. The act, "though proceeding from a good intention," may be morally wrong if the unintended effect is "out of proportion to the [intended] end."[45] Here we see the idea of *proportionality*: if the act as a whole is to be morally acceptable, the good of the intended end must be proportional to the harm of the actions foreseeable, though unintended effects. This became known as the *doctrine of double effect*, and we will see it applied by later just war thinkers to the question of what conduct in war is just (*jus in bello*).

---

[43] Aquinas, *Summa Theologica*, in Reichberg *et al.* (eds.), *Ethics of War*, p. 190.
[44] Note that we do not generally refer to a killing in self-defense as murder.
[45] Aquinas, *Summa Theologica*, in Reichberg *et al.* (eds.), *Ethics of War*, p. 190.

2.5 The state system and the secularization of the tradition

As the Middle Ages passed into the modern era, the just war tradition went through rapid development, partly in response to the revolutionary social changes of that time. In this section, we consider the just war tradition in the sixteenth and the first half of the seventeenth centuries. One important social change was the declining influence of the Roman Church. This decline was fostered by the Protestant Reformation, which opened the way for religious war within Europe, and by the increasing power of sovereign states. This represented a fundamental shift in how Europe was organized politically. The universalism represented by the Roman Empire and emphasized by Cicero was kept alive in the Middle Ages by the universalism of the Church, also with its center in Rome. But with political power flowing from the Church to the states, this form of universalism seemed increasingly implausible. This led to a basic realignment in just war thinking. The universalism of just war theory no longer had a political instantiation.

We begin this section by taking a broader look at Vitoria's views, then examining the work of his main successor, Grotius, who, in appreciation of the growing political power of the states, abandoned the scholasticism that Vitoria inherited from Aquinas and moved just war thinking in a new, more practical direction.

Vitoria, like Augustine and Aquinas, began by criticizing pacifism.[46] He also largely followed his predecessors in his account of just cause, asserting that the only just cause is "when harm has [wrongfully] been inflicted." In support of this, he argued that a ruler cannot have greater authority over foreigners than he has over his own people, and a ruler may use force against his own people only if they have done something deserving of punishment. Hence, a ruler cannot harm foreigners unless they have done something deserving of punishment (such as wrongful infliction of harm).[47] Moreover, as a wrong done by a subject must be of sufficient

---

[46] Vitoria, "On the Law of War," in Pagden and Lawrance (eds.), *Vitoria*, pp. 293–327, at pp. 297–298.

[47] *Ibid.*, pp. 303–304. This mode of argument, comparing what is permissible domestically with what is permissible internationally, is frequently used by Vitoria. It is a version of the domestic analogy.

gravity to justify severe punishment, a harm wrongfully inflicted by one state against another must be of sufficient gravity to justify war.[48] In his discussion of just cause, however, he goes on to make clearer than earlier theorists had what sorts of reasons for war are *not* just causes including the spreading of religion, the creation of empire, or the advantage of the rulers rather than the common good.[49] His rejection of empire as a just cause for war is, of course, part of his criticism of the Spanish attacks on the natives of the New World.

Justified wars, for Vitoria, fall into two classes: *defensive* wars and *offensive* wars. An offensive war is not, as one might think, a war of aggression, which he condemns. Offensive war is "war in which vengeance for an injury is sought" while defensive war is "war in which property is defended or reclaimed."[50] An offensive war is punitive. A single war may fall into both classes, as the purpose of a war might be both to recover land invaded by an attacker and punish the attacker (seeking vengeance) for taking the land. We could refer to defensive war as a matter of *rectification* and offensive war a matter of *punishment*. Vitoria follows Augustine and Aquinas in seeing war as having a punitive function, though he includes a rectificatory function as well.[51]

Vitoria claims that an armed conflict cannot be just on both sides (or, more precisely, that two opponents cannot at the same time be each fighting a just war against the other).[52] His argument for this takes the form of a *reductio ad absurdum*.[53] If both sides were just, then neither would be entitled to fight the other because it is not justified to attack those fighting a just war; but this is absurd because a just war is a war in which attacking the opponent is justified; so, it must be false that both sides can be just.[54] But Vitoria recognizes that, though both sides cannot be fighting a

---

[48] *Ibid*, p. 304.   [49] *Ibid*, pp. 302–303.

[50] *Ibid*, pp. 297–298. This is a difference between individual and national self-defense: individuals are not entitled to exercise vengeance for the wrongdoing (p. 300).

[51] These two ideas of war, however, may seem incompatible when we later consider the *in bello* rule against attacking civilians. See McKeogh, "Civilian Immunity," p. 72.

[52] But it may be that both sides in an armed conflict are fighting an unjust war.

[53] *Reductio ad absurdum* is a form of argument in which a position is affirmed by showing that the contradictory position leads to an absurd conclusion.

[54] Vitoria, "On the Law of War," p. 313. Vitoria uses this conclusion to support his claim that the expansion of empire is not a just cause; if it were, both sides in such a war would be just, those fighting for expansion and those resisting it. *Ibid.*, p. 303.

just war, both sides may *believe* they are fighting a just war. It is easy for a state to misjudge the justice of its own cause. Determining which side is just in an armed conflict is often inherently difficult, and, in addition, it is hard to be objective about one's own case. Some of those who wage an unjust war do so in good faith, believing their war is just. But, clearly, a war is not just simply because those fighting it believe it to be; true justice is an objective characteristic.[55] The possibility of mistaken belief about the justice of one's war leads Vitoria to recommend that a decision to go to war should be made very carefully, to ensure as much objectivity in the moral assessment as possible. This connects with our earlier discussion of the Roman *fetiales* and the idea of procedural justice. A good political or legal procedure for the moral assessment of war increases the likelihood of a correct determination of its substantive justice.

The fact that states may falsely believe their war to be just has important implications. One concerns moral responsibility. Normally, when a state is fighting an unjust war, it is morally responsible or culpable for that action; because it is doing something wrongful, it is morally to blame. But, according to Vitoria, states fighting unjust wars may sometimes be excused from moral responsibility. When a state falsely believes it is fighting a just war, that ignorance *may* be an excuse. For example, a killing might be excused when the perpetrator falsely believes it to be in self-defense, as when the victim is only an actor brandishing a toy gun; the killing is wrongful, but the killer is not to blame. But not all such ignorance is an excuse. To develop this point, Vitoria distinguishes between *vincible ignorance* and *invincible ignorance*.[56] Ignorance is invincible when the agent, given her circumstances, could not have known the truth. In contrast, ignorance is vincible when the agent should have known the truth, but was prevented from knowing the truth by his own passion. He may, for example, have been blinded by his nationalism or his patriotism into believing that his side was fighting a just war, when there was evidence to the contrary available to him. According to Vitoria, "invincible error is an excuse in every case," but not so vincible ignorance.

Another implication of this follows from Vitoria's distinction between true justice and *ostensible justice*. Ostensible justice is not true, objective justice, but the subjective belief in such. While an armed conflict cannot

[handwritten margin note: GREAT PURPOSE: VINCIBLE IGNORANCE]

---

[55] *Ibid.*, pp. 306–307.   [56] Vitoria, "On the American Indians," pp. 267–269.

be truly just on both sides, it can be ostensibly just on both sides, in which case it has, in the phrase of contemporary just war theorist James Turner Johnson, *simultaneous ostensible justice*.[57] Combining this point with the previous one gives this idea: when an armed conflict has simultaneous ostensible justice and the ignorance of those on the unjust side is invincible, then that side is not morally responsible for the wrong it does, and neither side can be blamed for fighting.

This idea initiates an important shift in thinking about *jus ad bellum*. An armed conflict cannot be just on both sides, and if we assume that one side is fighting an *ad bellum* just war, the distribution of justification, we might say, between the belligerents is *morally asymmetric*, in that one side is justified in waging war and the other is not. (Sometimes both sides are *ad bellum* unjust, in which case the relation between them is morally symmetric.[58] But in the discussion that follows, we leave such cases aside.) Vitoria continues to regard armed conflict as morally asymmetric in this sense, but his introduction of the ideas of ostensible justice and invincible ignorance provides a way of seeing it differently. When an armed conflict has simultaneous ostensible justice and the ignorance of the side falsely believing itself to be just is invincible, there is a sense in which the conflict is morally symmetric, in that neither side is to blame for its war. The symmetry lies in the realm of responsibility, not in the realm of true justice. In such a case, a just belligerent should regard its opponent as warring against it out of ignorance rather than malevolence.[59] Of course, only some wars are morally symmetric in this sense, since not all states fighting unjust wars are invincibly ignorant of the injustice.

But this idea of moral symmetry led to a gradual shift in just war thinking from an almost exclusive concern with *jus ad bellum*, to an increasing concern with *jus in bello*. Vitoria is on the cusp of this shift. James Turner Johnson puts it this way: "The belligerents should be chastened by this realization that both sides might seem equally to be in the right, and so

---

[57] This phrase is introduced by James Turner Johnson, *Ideology, Reason, and the Limitation of War* (Princeton University Press, 1975), p. 20.

[58] It is a matter of dispute how frequently armed conflicts are unjust on both sides. Some of the discussion in the next chapter bears on this issue.

[59] Nicholas Rengger, "The Jus in Bello in Historical and Philosophical Perspective," in Larry May (ed.), *War: Essays in Political Philosophy* (New York: Cambridge University Press, 2008), pp. 30–46, at p. 45.

they should be especially scrupulous in observing the *jus in bello*, the rules of war. The doctrine of simultaneous ostensible justice was thus intended to affect the *conduct* of war, not the *resort* to war."[60] Earlier theorists had given little attention to *jus in bello*, and one reason for this may be that they viewed *jus ad bellum* as largely determining the justice of how a war is fought. Because a war that is *ad bellum* unjust should not be fought, there is no just way to fight it.[61] A war that is *ad bellum* unjust is also *in bello* unjust.[62] One cannot fight an unjust war justly. Once we know that a war is *ad bellum* unjust, we know that it is also *in bello* unjust.[63] This may be called the *dependence view*, in that *in bello* judgments are dependent on *ad bellum* judgments. It implies that the moral asymmetry in *jus ad bellum* carries over to a moral asymmetry in *jus in bello*. But, if there is instead a sense in which *jus ad bellum* is morally symmetric, then in that sense *jus in bello* may be seen as morally symmetric as well. This dynamic plays itself out in the next two sections of our discussion.

The most important successor to Vitoria is the seventeenth-century jurist Hugo Grotius (1583–1645). Grotius, like Aquinas, developed a comprehensive view of the ethics of war by working the insights of his predecessors into a coherent theory. He is perhaps best known for the idea of *international society*, which is, as international relations theorist Hedley Bull asserts, "the notion that states and rulers of states are bound by rules and form a society or community with one another." This idea, Bull says, is "one of the classic paradigms in our understanding of "inter-state relations" and "right conduct therein."[64] It stands against the realist vision

---

[60] Johnson, *Ideology, Reason*, p. 20.

[61] Robert Kolb, "Origins of the Twin Terms *Jus ad Bellum/Jus in Bello*," *International Review of the Red Cross*, no. 320, pp. 553–562, www.icrc.org/web/eng/siteeng0.nsf/htmlall/57J NUU?OpenDocument&View=defaultBody&style=custo_print, accessed September 2, 2010.

[62] The phrases "*ad bellum* unjust" and "*in bello* unjust" are shorthand for "unjust from a *jus ad bellum* (or *jus in bello*) perspective," and similarly for wars that are just in these two ways.

[63] It does not follow that those fighting a just war are necessarily fighting it justly because there are moral restrictions on their conduct despite the justice of their cause. It follows only that there are some ways those fighting a just war can fight justly; there are no ways in which those fighting an unjust war can fight justly.

[64] Hedley Bull, "The Importance of Grotius in the Study of International Relations," in Hedley Bull *et al.* (eds.), *Hugo Grotius and International Relations* (Oxford University Press, 1992), pp. 65–93, at p. 71.

of Thomas Hobbes, according to which there is no society in the international realm. We saw a version of the idea of international society earlier in the idea of natural law, a law governing not only relations within states, but also international relations. Grotius is often claimed to be the father of international law, which plays an important role later in the just war tradition.

Grotius takes realism as the main opponent of just war theory, in contrast with earlier, less secular theorists, for whom pacifism was the main opponent.[65] He argues that realism, the view that "for a king or state with sovereign power, nothing which is in their interest is unjust," is false because a characteristic human trait is a "desire for society, that is, for community, with those who belong to his species – though not a community of any kind, but one at peace." It is such sociability that is the basis of international society, as well as domestic society, and this would be the case even if "there is no God."[66] Human sociality is at the basis of natural law, and it leads humans to create positive (that is, human-made) law for the promotion of community at all levels. Natural law forms the model of what positive law should be. The law of international society is the "law of nations" (*jus gentium*), and it covers relations in war. Grotius asserts: "I am in no doubt that there is some common law among nations which *applies to war and its conduct*,"[67] that is, a law which applies to both *jus ad bellum* and *jus in bello*.[68]

Grotius follows closely his predecessors in the general stipulation of just cause for war. "There is no other *reasonable* Cause of making War, but an Injury received."[69] He expands this category to include four specific kinds of just causes or ways of responding to injuries received: defense of self or property, recovery of property wrongly taken, exaction of outstanding debts, and the punishment of wrongdoing.[70] Regarding punishment,

---

[65] Reichberg, "Jus ad Bellum," in May (ed.), *War*, pp. 11–29, at p. 14.

[66] Hugo Grotius, *The Rights of War and Peace*, ed. Richard Tuck (Indianapolis, IN: Liberty Fund, 2005), Prolegomena, pp. 1745, 1747, 1748. Grotius is quick to add that the claim that there is no God cannot be supposed "without the greatest wickedness."

[67] *Ibid.*, p. 1753, emphasis added.

[68] Grotius did not use the terms *jus ad bellum* and *jus in bello*, as they were not introduced until the twentieth century. See Kolb, "Origin of the Twin Terms."

[69] Grotius, *Rights of War and Peace*, p. 393.

[70] This formulation of the four just causes is taken from introductory material in Reichberg *et al.* (eds.), *Ethics of War*, p. 400.

he asserts: "In a private war [such as individual self-defense] we have only a Regard to our own Defence, but the supreme Powers have not only a Right of Self-Defence, but of revenging and punishing Injuries."[71] The power of punishment is based on the moral asymmetry between the belligerents we discussed earlier. But, as we saw with Vitoria, there is also in Grotius movement away from this asymmetric view. Consider how he addresses "that much controverted Question … Whether War can be just and lawful on both sides." He responds: "As it regards the Action itself, War cannot be just on both Sides … But it may happen that neither of the parties in War acts unjustly. For no Man acts unjustly, but he who is conscious that what he does is unjust."[72] This follows Vitoria's view that the unjust may be excused from blame due to a sincere belief that what they do is just.

But this raises some questions. First, Grotius asserts that any *sincere* ignorance will excuse, while Vitoria asserts that ignorance has to be *invincible* to excuse. Sometimes Vitoria seems to understand invincibility in the same way that Grotius understands sincerity, but sometimes he understands it in a stronger sense, in the sense that invincible ignorance excludes ignorance due to *negligence*. Negligent ignorance is ignorance for which one is responsible ("she should have known"), and such ignorance is sincere but not invincible, in the stronger sense. Second, Vitoria had spoken of those who are invincibly ignorant of the wrongfulness of their war as being *excused*, whereas Grotius claims in the previous quotation that those ignorant of their military wrongfulness (invincibly or not) do not act unjustly, which suggests that they are *justified* in what they do, not merely excused.[73] This suggests, despite Grotius' initial disclaimer, that a war can, in some sense, be just on both sides. The idea that a war can be just on both sides is also implied by Grotius' idea of "public war," a war between two sovereign states. Speaking of public war, he observes: "War is often said to be just, not from the Cause whence it arises … but from some peculiar Effects of Right." The idea seems to be that a prerogative of sovereignty (the "Right" referred to in this quotation) is the waging of war. Sovereign states wage war at their own discretion, which means, in effect, that both sides are just, or at least not unjust. The moral asymmetry of

---

[71] Grotius, *Rights of War and Peace*, p. 416.   [72] *Ibid.*, p. 1130.

[73] *Excuse* is different from *justification*. A justified action is not wrongful, while an excused action is wrongful but the agent is not morally responsible.

war in the traditional just war view seems here to be replaced by a moral symmetry – an armed conflict may be just on both sides. This leads to a decline in theoretical importance of *jus ad bellum*, and, as suggested earlier, a rise in interest in *jus in bello*.[74]

2.6 The fall of *jus ad bellum*

Grotius died three years before the Peace of Westphalia, a pair of treaties by which the powers in Europe sought to end the Thirty Years War, a devastating religious war pitting Catholics against Protestants. The Treaties of Westphalia helped bring into being the modern international system of sovereign states, which is with us still. The historical development of state sovereignty had a profound effect on the just war tradition, for the powers of sovereignty came to be understood to include the discretion to wage war. If the waging of war is morally discretionary, then the moral difference represented by the distinction between just and unjust wars seems to disappear, as no war is unjust. To take a domestic example, a person may have the discretionary right to ignore a stranger's plea for help, in which case, though ignoring the plea may be morally wrong, the person does not act unjustly in doing so.[75] The idea is that a state, as sovereign, may similarly have a right to wage war, even when doing so is morally wrong, in which case the state does not act unjustly in waging war. Under this way of thinking, because *jus ad bellum* is concerned with the justice of war, moral symmetry replaces moral asymmetry at the *ad bellum* level. One of the effects of this is to bring just war thinking closer to realism. Indeed, this way of thinking led to the development of ideas such as *raison d'état* (a state may fight a war for its own reasons) and *competence de guerre* (the state has the legal right to wage war), which are realist doctrines asserting the discretionary right of states to wage war. But the moral philosophers did not, in general, see *ad bellum* symmetry in terms quite this strong.

The idea of moral symmetry between belligerents is evident in a comparison offered by the Italian jurist Alberico Gentili (1552–1608), who lived a generation before Grotius. Gentili compares warring with dueling:

---

[74] See Bellamy, *Just Wars*, p. 61.

[75] On this view, injustice and moral wrongness are separate characteristics; all unjust acts are wrongful, but not all wrongful acts are unjust.

"*bellum*, 'war', derives its name from the fact that there is a contest for victory between two equal parties, and for that reason it was at first called *duellum*, 'a contest of two'."[76] Gentili's reference to "equal parties" suggests moral symmetry, an equality in the exercise of their sovereign rights. The view was endorsed by the early eighteenth-century philosopher Christian von Wolff (1679–1754). Wolff, while admitting that "by natural law, a war cannot be just on both sides," claimed that "by the voluntary law of nations the war must be considered as just on either side … as regards the effects of the war."[77] One of the effects Wolff apparently had in mind concerns *jus in bello*, how states should conduct themselves in war.

The eighteenth-century theorist who perhaps best represents this new approach is the Swiss diplomat Emer de Vattel (1714–1767). Vattel agrees with Gentili and Wolff that a war may be considered just on both sides.

> Since Nations are free, independent, and equal, – and since each possesses the right of judging, according to the dictates of her conscience, what conduct she is to pursue in order to fulfil her duties, – the effect of the whole is, to produce, at least externally and in the eyes of mankind, a perfect equality of rights between nations … without regard to the intrinsic justice of their conduct, of which others have no right to form a definitive judgment.[78]

[handwritten margin note: THE EQUAL RIGHT TO WAGE WAR]

Here, again, we have the contrast between true ("intrinsic") justice and ostensible justice, justice "in the eyes of mankind." Vattel's understanding of ostensible justice is more developed than Vitoria's, however. Beyond Vitoria's idea that both sides may sincerely believe themselves to be just, Vattel claims that, given the nature of war in the real world, we must operate with a different sense of justice than "true" justice. Vattel sometimes referred to this alternative notion of justice as one supplied by the "voluntary law of nations."[79] We may refer to it as *operative justice*; it is the

---

[76] Alberico Gentili, *On the Law of War*, in Reichberg *et al.* (eds.), *Ethics of War*, pp. 372–373. This comparison between a war and a duel is another domestic analogy. Clausewitz uses the comparison as well: "War is nothing but a duel on a larger scale." *On War*, ed. and trans. Michael Howard and Peter Paret (Princeton University Press, 1989), p. 75.

[77] Christian von Wolff, *The Law of Nations Treated according to a Scientific Method*, in Reichberg *et al.* (eds.), *Ethics of War*, p. 474.

[78] Emer de Vattel, *The Law of Nations* (Indianapolis, IN: Liberty Fund, 2008), pp. 75–76.

[79] *Ibid.*, p. 590.

sense of justice with which we should operate in the actual moral assessment of war.

One sort of reason to prefer operative justice, in practice, to intrinsic justice, is *epistemological*, relating to what humans are able to *know*, especially in the context in which such knowledge is available for moral judgment and action. Gentili, for example, supports his version of this distinction by claiming that intrinsic justice is beyond our ken. Because of the "weakness of our human nature ... we see everything dimly, and are not cognizant of that purest and truest form of justice, which cannot conceive of both parties to a dispute being in the right." Because of this weakness, all we can do is to "aim at justice as it appears from man's standpoint," and, "if each side aims at justice, neither can be called unjust."[80] Another sort of reason is *metaphysical* in that it refers to the ultimate moral nature of states. By the very nature of sovereignty, states have the moral discretion to act by their own lights, and nothing they choose to do can be judged to be morally wrong. This reason may be less commonly offered because it suggests that there is no intrinsic justice at all. Finally, a third sort of reason is *pragmatic*, based on claims that acting according to operative justice rather than intrinsic justice produces morally better results overall.[81] Vattel claims that applying the rules of true or intrinsic justice would lead to war becoming "more cruel, more disastrous in its effects, and more difficult of termination," so that adopting the perspective of operative justice "is in the interest of the safety and welfare of the great society of the human race." War may be less destructive, if the rules of justice followed in war are those of operative justice rather than intrinsic justice.[82] Moreover, there can be no "other rule of conduct to be observed between nations, since they acknowledge no superior judge" to determine which of them has true or intrinsic justice on its side.[83]

Vattel introduces the expressions "war in due form" and "regular war" to refer to war as assessed in terms of operative justice, where war "is to be accounted just on both sides."[84] This is related to Grotius' idea of public

---

[80] Gentili, *Law of War*, p. 374.

[81] This is a form of consequentialist moral justification, discussed in Chapter 1.

[82] This is similar to the view of moralized realism, discussed in Chapter 1.

[83] Vattel, *Law of Nations*, p. 591.

[84] *Ibid.* See also Gregory Reichberg, "Just War and Regular War: Competing Paradigms," in David Rodin and Henry Shue (eds.), *Just and Unjust Warriors: The Moral and Legal Status of Soldiers* (Oxford University Press, 2008), pp. 193–213.

war. As Gregory Reichberg puts it, a regular war is "a contest between juridically equal belligerents [which] owing to their sovereign status … were deemed to possess a similar capacity to wage war, regardless of the cause that prompted the conflict."[85] He is speaking of moral or legal capacity. The states are moral equals, as a result of which each has the moral discretion to wage war. The idea, notes Michael Walzer, is that "war-making was the natural prerogative of sovereign states, not subject to legal or moral judgment."[86]

Reichberg refers to the just war tradition prior to the eighteenth century as based on the *just war paradigm*, and the tradition as it developed in eighteenth century, by Vattel in particular, as based on the *regular war paradigm*.[87] The just war paradigm regards *jus ad bellum* as morally asymmetric, only (or at most) one side being just, while the regular war paradigm regards *jus ad bellum* as morally symmetric, both sides being just. The just war paradigm implies "unilateral rights of war," a right to initiate war lying only with one side. In contrast, the regular war paradigm implies "bilateral rights of war," either side having a right to initiate war.

In the case of a war in due form, Vattel notes, "the lawfulness of its effects … do not, externally and between mankind, depend on the justice of the cause, but on the legality of the means in themselves."[88] This reference to *means* is a reference to *jus in bello*. Under the regular war paradigm, a state at war is judged in terms of *jus in bello* rather than *jus ad bellum*, because both sides have the discretion to wage war. Alex Bellamy remarks: "A just war was one waged by sovereigns and conducted in a just fashion."[89] Adherence to the rules of *jus in bello* alone determine whether a war is just, and these rules are the same for both sides. "Whatever is permitted to the one in virtue of the state of war, is also permitted to the other."[90] Under the regular war paradigm, the moral symmetry of *jus ad bellum* allows a moral symmetry of *jus in bello*, in the sense that the *in bello* rules apply equally to both sides. Under the just war paradigm, the combatants on the unjust side are not allowed to fight at all; under the regular war paradigm, the *in bello* rules apply to the combatants of both sides. This would later come to be called the *moral equality of combatants*.

MORAL EQUALITY OF COMBATANTS

---

[85] Reichberg, "Jus ad Bellum," p. 16.   [86] Walzer, *Just and Unjust Wars*, p. 63.
[87] Reichberg, "Just War and Regular War," pp. 193–194.
[88] Vattel, *Law of Nations*, p. 591.   [89] Bellamy, *Just Wars*, p. 62.
[90] Vattel, *Law of Nations*, p. 591.

2.7 The rise of *jus in bello* and the re-emergence of *jus ad bellum*

The regular war paradigm, Inis Claude notes, "stood essentially unchallenged in the eighteenth and nineteenth centuries," and the focus was on the symmetric rules of *jus in bello*.[91] This led to viewing belligerents as if they were "prize fighters rather than cops and robbers."[92] There is a moral symmetry between prize fighters; they are in a duel, and the rules of the fight apply equally to both fighters. The rules in a fight tend to be rules that reduce the harm from the contest, such as no hitting below the belt. War can be thought of as a fair fight, fairness being understood as adherence to the rules applying equally to both fighters. In contrast, the traditional just war paradigm thought of the relation between belligerents as like that between cops and robbers, or aggressors and defenders, where one side was in the right and the rules of conduct did not apply to both parties.

The development of *jus in bello* in this period was characterized by efforts on the part of the international community to set out rules for the conduct of war in international law. This was, in part, a moral effort to limit the damage that war causes. The body of IHL, as the law of war is called, consists largely in a series of treaties, often referred to as conventions, negotiated among states. This series began with the 1856 Paris Declaration on maritime war and included the 1864 Geneva Convention on the wounded and sick, several conventions coming out of the 1899 and 1907 Hague Peace Conferences, the 1919 Treaty of Versailles, which prohibited certain means of conducting warfare (as well as ending World War I), and the 1925 Geneva Protocol on gas and bacteriological warfare. After World War II, there were the 1949 Geneva Conventions (followed by the 1977 Geneva Protocols), the 1997 Ottawa Convention on anti-personnel mines, and the 1998 Rome Statute of the International Criminal Court.[93] All of these conventions are based on what Adam Roberts calls

---

[91] Inis L. Claude, Jr., "Just War: Doctrines and Institutions," *Political Science Quarterly* 95, no. 1 (Spring 1980), pp. 83–96, p. 89.

[92] *Ibid.*, pp. 91–92.

[93] Adam Roberts and Richard Guelff, *Documents on the Laws of War*, 3rd edn. (Oxford University Press, 2000), pp. 5–6.

the "principle of equal application," the idea that rules of conduct in war apply equally to both sides.[94]

The effort to create IHL was also spurred by great changes in warfare that occurred during this period, making war much more destructive.[95] Some of these changes were technological, such as the introduction of more effective firearms and more destructive explosives, and improvements in transportation and communications, allowing for large armies to be easily moved about and for better coordination in battle. Closer to our own time, there is the development of aircraft and missile technology, allowing attacks on the opponent's homeland over the heads of its armies on the battlefield, and the invention of nuclear weapons, increasing by several orders of magnitude the destructive capability in state hands. In our own time, we have the potential of technologies such as military robotics, cyber warfare, and genetically engineered biological weapons. Some of the changes were social, economic, and political, such as the extension of the franchise and the growth of nationalist and patriotic sentiment and politics, larger armies due to increased populations, better medical care, and universal male conscription, the economic resources to field large armies for extended times, and the growth in the effectiveness of government propaganda. Note that some of these changes seriously undermine the effectiveness, or perhaps even the relevance, of the key *in bello* rule that civilians are not to be attacked, and wars in the twentieth century involved increasing numbers of civilian deaths.

One of the social changes was an alteration in the class structure of the military. In the age of chivalry, combatants had been members of a small professional class, the knights, with their own professional code of honor in fighting. But the French Revolution changed this, introducing into military forces large numbers of peasants and later working-class men, who were not raised to fight, as the knights had been, and so lacked an inherent code of conduct to apply to their military activity. This led to discipline problems, including problems of military leaders in getting the men under them to behave according to a consistent set or rules. As a

---

[94] Adam Roberts, "The Principle of Equal Application of the Laws of War," in Rodin and Shue (eds.), *Just and Unjust Warriors*, pp. 226–254.

[95] For a discussion of some of the social and technological changes relevant to war, see Johnson, *Just War Tradition*, chapter 6.

result there were institutional efforts to ensure that ordinary combatants would act accordingly to the rules of IHL, including the issuing of formal military codes of conduct to fighting forces. One of the first of these was promulgated to Union forces during the American Civil War, "Instructions for the Government of Armies of the United States in the Field, General Orders No. 100," authored by Francis Lieber.[96] Descendants of this code are contained in the Field Manuals of the military services of the United States. They are closely related to *rules of engagement* now issued to forces in combat.

Despite IHL, wars became ever more destructive, and attention began to return to *jus ad bellum*. In the efforts to effectively limit war, *in bello* measures by themselves, however helpful, were proving inadequate. This became especially evident in the twentieth century, with the awful destruction of the two World Wars. If warfare was to be effectively controlled, efforts had to be made not simply to limit how it is conducted, but also to limit its frequency. This led to the re-emergence of *jus ad bellum*, specifically, as a subject of interest for international law. As Inis Claude observes, "The leaders of the international system set out, after World War I, to create the necessary international structures and procedures to give effect to a revived and revised just war idea [*jus ad bellum*]." Claude refers to the re-emergence of *jus ad bellum* as "neo-just war doctrine."[97] The result was "legal restrictions on the sovereign right to wage war," as with the Covenant of the League of Nations in 1919, the Kellogg–Briand Pact in 1928, and the prohibition of aggression in the UN Charter (1945).[98] According to the UN Charter, war is permitted only if it is in self-defense or is approved by the UN Security Council as an appropriate response to a threat to international peace and security. These agreements represent "a throwback to the *jus ad bellum* as conceived within the just war paradigm."[99] This return of *jus ad bellum* in the UN Charter is referred to as the *post-war settlement*. It represents a third paradigm, the *national defense paradigm*, so called because only national defense is a justification for war.

The new *ad bellum* paradigm was different from the old just war paradigm, and, to mark this difference, the post-war settlement is sometimes referred to (especially by its critics) as *jus contra bellum*, the idea that justice

THE UN CHARTER

---

[96] See Reichberg *et al.* (eds.), *Ethics of War*, pp. 565–573.

[97] Claude, "Just War: Doctrines and Institutions," p. 92.

[98] Reichberg, "Just War and Regular War," p. 209.   [99] *Ibid.*, p. 194.

requires the avoidance of war. The difference between the new paradigm and the old lies in what counts as just cause. Under the old, more permissive *jus ad bellum*, a just cause was "a wrong inflicted," and this could justify, for example, a war to retrieve stolen property, to exact payment of a debt, or, most significantly, to punish the offending state for its wrongdoing. But under the national defense paradigm, the notion of just cause is more narrowly conceived, allowing war only on grounds of defense (of self or others under attack) or to restore international peace and security (under Security Council approval). The punitive justification for war is eliminated. The philosopher Joseph Boyle notes: "One of the major developments of just war thinking in the twentieth century is the rejection of the legitimacy of this punitive conception of just cause, and the limitation of just cause to defense."[100]

One implication of the idea of *jus contra bellum*, Claude claims, is that it reduces justice to peacefulness, elevating peace over justice. "Peace is too important to be disrupted by those who are tempted to fight for values other than peace," so that the "preservation of peace took precedence over the promotion of justice."[101] This may be part of the reason that there have been efforts, after 1945, to reassert the old form of *jus ad bellum*, allowing fighting for values other than peacefulness. This most recent part of the story we save for a later chapter.

[handwritten margin note: PEACE HAS PRIORITY OVER JUSTICE]

2.8 Conclusion

Concluding this brief survey of the just war tradition, I raise two issues that will help to guide some of the discussion in later chapters.

The first issue is an apparent historical anomaly. Under the just war paradigm, through the seventeenth century, *jus ad bellum* was understood as morally asymmetric between the belligerents, in the way we have discussed, which led, at least implicitly, to *jus in bello* also being understood as asymmetric. In contrast, under the regular war paradigm, in the eighteenth and nineteenth centuries, *jus ad bellum* was taken as morally symmetric, as a result of which *jus in bello* was also then taken as symmetric. A pattern here is that *jus in bello* seems to follow the lead of *jus ad bellum*, so to speak; when

---

[100] Joseph Boyle, "Just War Doctrine and the Military Response to Terrorism," *Journal of Political Philosophy* 11, no. 2 (2003), pp. 153–170, at p. 161.

[101] Claude, "Just War: Doctrines and Institutions," p. 94.

Table 2.1. *Paradigms in just war theory*

	Jus ad bellum: moral relations of states	Moral character of that relation	*Jus in bello:* moral relation of combatants	Moral character of that relation
Just war paradigm	1. One state punishes the other for a wrong received	2. Asymmetric – unequal	3. Just combatants helping to punish unjust combatants	4. Asymmetric – unequal
Real war paradigm	5. Both states pursue their national interests (*raison d'état*)	6. Symmetric – equal	7. Combatants fighting each other to promote their national interests	8. Symmetric – equal
National defense paradigm	9. One state defends self against the other	10. Asymmetric – unequal	11. Combatants fighting to defend themselves against enemy combatants	12. Symmetric – equal

the latter is symmetric, so is the former, and when the latter is asymmetric, so is the former. But the current theoretical state of affairs is different. The return to *jus ad bellum* in the national defense paradigm is a return to moral asymmetry at that level, but *jus in bello* has continued to be regarded as symmetric, contrary to the earlier pattern. Roberts notes that the return of *jus ad bellum* has not led "to a weakening of the principle of equal application of the *jus in bello*."[102] This raises the question of why the current period is different in this regard, and whether this difference can persist, given the underlying moral logic of the theory. These relations are portrayed in Table 2.1. Cells (2) and (4) are the same, and (6) and (8) are the same, but (10) and (12) are different. Can (11) and (12) remain as they are?

[102] Roberts, "The Principle of Equal Application," p. 235.

The second issue concerns the relation between the law of war and the morality of war. The rise of IHL is seen by some as making the ethics of war irrelevant. Yoram Dinstein asserts: "It is totally irrelevant today whether or not a war is just. The sole question is: is war legal, in accordance with the Charter?"[103] But it is a mistake to think that the admirable and partly successful efforts to limit war through international law have made a study of the ethics of war unnecessary. On the contrary, consider the role of ethics in relation to law in the case of a domestic social order within a state. The importance of law within a state does not detract from the relevance and importance of ethics. Ethics has two crucial, related functions in relation to domestic law. First, ethics provides a position from which law can be endorsed or criticized. Ethics serves as one of the main factors in legal reform, such as the role of appeals to justice in the effort to change segregation laws in the American Civil Rights Movement. Second, ethical theory helps to provide a coherent account of existing domestic laws, so that we can better understand the law as a whole. Ethics can also serve these functions in regard to international law, specifically the law of war, endorsing or criticizing existing conventions regarding war and determining how they fit together into a coherent body of rules.

ETHICS
AND
LAW

[103] Yoram Dinstein, "Comments on War," *Harvard Journal of Law & Public Policy* 27, no. 3 (Summer 2004), pp. 877–892, at p. 880.

3   When is it just to go to war?

The life of states is like that of men. Men have the right to kill in the case of natural defense; states have the right to wage war for their own preservation.

Montesquieu[1]

War is constituted by a relation between things, and not between persons ... a relation, not between man and man, but between State and State, and individuals are enemies only accidentally, not as men, nor even as citizens, but as soldiers

Jean-Jacques Rousseau[2]

Great is the guilt of an unnecessary war.

John Adams[3]

This chapter and the next are devoted to *jus ad bellum*, the justice of war. *Jus ad bellum* is the morality of going to war, the morality of the decisions taken by leaders that initiate war. As the last chapter revealed, the conception of *jus ad bellum* in the just war tradition has changed over time. In this chapter we consider *jus ad bellum* in general, and under the national defense paradigm, in particular. This paradigm is the conception of *jus ad bellum* brought into being at the end of World War II by the post-war settlement, codified in the charter of the UN. The national defense paradigm

---

[1] Charles de Montesquieu, *The Spirit of the Laws*, in Reichberg *et al.* (eds.), *Ethics of War: Classic and Contemporary Readings* (Oxford: Blackwell Publishing, 2006), p. 477.

[2] Jean-Jacques Rousseau, *The Social Contract*, from *The Social Contract and Discourses*, trans. G. D. H. Cole (London: Dent, 1923), p. 12.

[3] John Adams, second president of the United States, wrote these words to his wife Abigail while he was under pressure, which he resisted, to declare war against France. Cited in Henry E. Mattox, "Like Father; Like Son," *American Diplomacy* (June 2004), www.unc.edu/depts/diplomat/archives_roll/2004_04–06/ed_father/ed_father.html, accessed May 26, 2010.

differs most significantly from the earlier just war paradigm in its rejection of war as *punitive*. Under the just war paradigm, a just cause for war was "a wrong received," making a just war a form of punishment for this wrong. Beginning in the eighteenth century, under the regular war paradigm, a sovereign ruler had the moral and legal discretion or right to go to war, so that, in effect, any cause was a just cause. A state could go to war "for a good reason, a bad reason or no reason at all."[4] When *jus ad bellum* staged a comeback in the twentieth century under the national defense paradigm, a just cause for war was limited largely to self-defense, without the punitive element. The national defense paradigm shares with the just war paradigm the moral asymmetry that justice cannot be on both sides in an armed conflict.

The main moral argument for the national defense paradigm is indicated by the opening quotation from the philosopher Montesquieu (1689–1755), who sets out the principal analogy, the *domestic analogy*, in terms of which the paradigm is both understood and morally justified. The domestic analogy is an analogy between states and individuals, and the analogical argument based on it is that because states are like individuals and individuals have a moral right to use force to protect themselves against attack, states do as well. The analogy is called *domestic* because it compares the international arena which states inhabit to the domestic arena inhabited by individuals within a state.[5] Political philosopher Michael Walzer relies prominently on the analogy in his account of *jus ad bellum*. The analogy involves, he notes, a comparison "of personal liberty and political independence."[6] As an attack by an individual interferes with the victim's personal liberty, aggression by a state interferes with the victim state's political independence. In both cases, attacks are prohibited and, if they occur, force in self-defense is morally justified.

The national defense paradigm shares most of its moral content with the current international legal regime of IHL. But claims that war is *morally* justified under this paradigm rely largely on the argument from the domestic analogy. In this chapter we explore *jus ad bellum* under the

---

[4] H. W. Briggs, quoted in Yoram Dinstein, *War – Aggression and Self-Defense*, 4th edn. (Cambridge University Press, 2005), p. 75.

[5] "Domestic" is used here to mean "within a state," not "within a family."

[6] Michael Walzer, *Just and Unjust Wars* (New York: Basic Books, 1977), p. 58. He discusses the domestic analogy at a number of places in this book.

national defense paradigm, and in the next chapter we consider criticisms of this paradigm and propose a new paradigm. The criticisms will focus on whether the argument from the domestic analogy is sound.

3.1 *Jus ad bellum* and the Gulf War

In the just war tradition, a war is just when it satisfies a set of criteria or conditions. As discussed in the last chapter, Aquinas, following Augustine, indicates three such criteria: just cause, legitimate authority, and rightful intention. Below is a standard list of *ad bellum* criteria drawn from the tradition, six in all, beginning with Aquinas' three. Following this is a discussion of how they apply in a particular case, the First Gulf War (1990–1991), fought under the auspices of the UN by the United States and others against Iraq, in response to Iraq's invasion of Kuwait.

For a war to be just, it must

(1) have a *just cause*;
(2) be declared by a *legitimate authority*;
(3) be fought with a *rightful intention*;
(4) show *proportionality* in the balance between the good and harm it does;
(5) be a *last resort*; and
(6) have a *reasonable chance of success*.

An important question in *jus ad bellum* is whether a war must satisfy all of these criteria to be considered just, or some of them only. Is each of these criteria a necessary condition for a just war? This question is addressed later in the chapter.

On August 2, 1990, Iraq invaded its neighbor Kuwait and occupied the country in short order. Tensions between Iraq and Kuwait had been building and were due, in part, to Iraq's dire economic straits following the devastating Iran–Iraq War (1980–1988). There were allegations that Kuwait was stealing oil from Iraq by pumping from a field that straddled their common border and that Kuwait was selling more oil internationally than it was allowed to do under agreements among oil producers, depressing the price of oil and harming Iraq's economy. Four days after the invasion, the UN Security Council imposed an economic embargo, prohibiting almost all trade with Iraq. Shortly thereafter, combat forces from several nations began to assemble in the deserts of Saudi Arabia, at its request, to protect it from further aggression by Iraq ("Operation Desert Shield"). On November 29, the Security Council authorized member states to "use all necessary means" (a diplomatic euphemism for armed force) to drive Iraq from Kuwait, if Iraq did not withdraw by January 15. On January 9, the US Secretary of State met with representatives of the government of Iraq, but no deal was reached. On January 12, the US Senate passed a resolution authorizing the President to use force, if necessary, to remove Iraq from Kuwait.

Some thirty states signed on to a Coalition against Iraq. An air war on Iraq began on January 17, and continued for over five weeks (involving 100,000 sorties). The land war ("Operation Desert Storm"), beginning February 24, met with swift success. Two days later, Iraq announced that it was withdrawing from Kuwait, and two days after that, the Coalition declared a ceasefire. Some on the Coalition side had opposed an early ceasefire, arguing that the forces should instead continue to the Iraqi capital Baghdad and depose the Iraqi leader, Saddam Hussein. Iraq suffered up to 35,000 combat deaths in the war, while the Coalition suffered only 240. Iraq had laid ruin to the infrastructure of Kuwait, kidnapped some Kuwaiti citizens, and set fire to many of its oil wells, creating an environmental disaster. The Coalition had destroyed a great deal of the infrastructure of Iraq.

In an effort to enforce the provisions of the ceasefire, the economic sanctions were to be kept in force until Iraq had met all of the terms. The enforcement regime included international inspections to guarantee that Iraq had destroyed and had not reconstructed its weapons of mass destruction (nuclear, biological, and chemical weapons). Iraq balked at some of the conditions, and the sanctions remained in place, in one form or another, for the next twelve years (until the Iraq War of 2003).[7] The number of Iraqi civilians killed during the war is estimated at up to 3,000. But many civilians, especially children, died later, as a result of two factors: (1) the destruction and disablement of many "dual-use" infrastructure targets,[8] such as electrical generating plants and water-pumping and

---

[7] Information from *MSN Encarta Encyclopedia*, http://encarta.msn.com/text_761551555__0/Persian_Gulf_War.html, accessed July 25, 2008.

[8] "Dual use targets" are features of a state's infrastructure that support both the military and the civilian population. One of the main *in bello* rules is that civilian targets should not be attacked.

sewage treatment systems, by the Coalition air attacks; and (2) the continuing impact of the economic sanctions on childhood malnutrition and illness.[9] One study estimates that in the period from the war until 2000, 350,000 Iraqi children under five died from these effects.[10]

How did the war against Iraq fare in terms of *jus ad bellum*? (1) Just cause, as understood under the national defense paradigm, was clearly satisfied. Kuwait was invaded and had a just cause to go to war in self-defense, as did any other states that chose to aid it in fighting the aggression. Although Kuwait may have harmed Iraq in the ways alleged (pumping Iraqi oil, depressing the price of oil), these provocations were not sufficient to justify Iraq's going to war. They did not give Iraq a just cause. (2) The legitimate authority criterion was also clearly satisfied. The use of armed forces by the Coalition was approved by the UN Security Council, and the role of the United States was approved by the United States Senate. (3) Rightful intention is more difficult to assess, partly because the meaning of the criterion is not clear. A state has a rightful intention in war when its main purpose in the war is consonant with its just cause. This seems to have been the case in the Gulf War because the Coalition did not take the war beyond achievement of the defensive objective, indicating that that was its intention.

(4) Proportionality is also difficult to assess, due to uncertainty not simply about the meaning of the criterion, but about what consequences should have been reasonably expected. To put it roughly, a war fails to satisfy the proportionality criterion when the harm it brings about is disproportionate to the good it achieves, in terms of reasonable expectations at the time the war started. The principal good of the war was the liberation of Kuwait and the reinforcement of the international rule against aggression. The reasonably expected harms were many, as in most wars. What about the many Iraqi children who subsequently died due to the Coalition's destruction of basic infrastructure? Could their deaths have been reasonably expected? Should concern about them be considered instead under

---

[9] Human Rights Watch, "Introduction and Summary," *Needless Deaths in the Gulf War*, www.hrw.org/legacy/reports/1991/gulfwar/, accessed June 18, 2009.

[10] A study by Richard Garfield of Columbia University, cited in David Cortright, "A Harder Look at Iraq Sanctions," *The Nation*, December 3, 2001. Saddam Hussein contributed to this toll by disproportionally allocating the smaller economic resources Iraq had under the sanctions to military and regime purposes.

jus in bello, as a matter of how the war was fought? There are many such questions and few clear answers.

It seems likely that the war satisfied (6), reasonable chance of success, given the Coalition's preponderance in military power, though some critics expressed concern that the Coalition forces would become bogged down in fighting the Iraqis.[11] But (5), last resort, is a source of some controversy. Critics argued that the war was not a last resort because the economic sanctions had not been given enough time to work. Proponents argued that the war was a last resort because Iraq had been given enough time to respond to the sanctions and the United States had gone the extra mile by negotiating with Iraq in early January. We now take a more detailed look at the criteria.

3.2 Just cause

A *cause* is a *reason* someone has for acting, as in the phrase "a cause worth fighting for." A cause in this sense can be just or unjust, depending on whether it is a reason that justifies the action. Another meaning of cause is *explanation*, as when historians claim that a cause of World War I was the assassination of Archduke Franz Ferdinand. But an explanation cannot be just or unjust. A just cause is a *justifying reason*, that is, a reason for an action, such as going to war, that morally justifies (or helps to justify) it. A state goes to war for a reason or reasons, which may be just or unjust.

Under the national defense paradigm the only just cause is self-defense. This is made clear in two provisions of the UN Charter, part of the basis for the post-war settlement:

> All Members shall refrain in their international relations from the threat or use of force against the territorial integrity or political independence of any state (Article 4, Section 2)
> Nothing in the present Charter shall impair the inherent right of individual or collective self-defense … (Article 51)

Jus ad bellum, under the national defense paradigm, follows international law in this regard. Aggression is outlawed, but defensive response to

---

[11] This is part of the reason that the first President Bush chose not to turn the Gulf War into a war of conquest of Iraq, a concern arguably justified by the fate of his son's war against Iraq twelve years later.

aggression is permitted. (There is a much-noted apparent inconsistency between these two provisions of the Charter, since the second allows defensive wars, while the first seems to rule out all wars, including defensive ones.) In Article 51, *collective* as well as individual defense is permitted. A state is allowed to militarily assist another state that is engaged in self-defense against aggression. As Michael Walzer puts it, aggression justifies not only a war of self-defense by the victim, but also "a war of law enforcement by ... any other member of international society."[12] This is the just cause pursued by the United States in the Gulf War – joining with Kuwait in a justified war of self-defense. (I will use the term "self-defense" to include cases in which a state goes to war to help defend another state that is a victim of aggression.)

The terms *self-defense* and *aggression* are, in a moral context, defined in contrast to each other. Self-defense is a response to aggression, and self-defense is morally justified and aggression is not. But how is the line between them to be drawn? The line is often drawn in terms of the "priority principle,"[13] according to which the aggressor is the state first to use force, and the defender is the state responding with a second use of force. For the priority principle, the morally relevant question is: who struck the first blow? But there are complications in defining aggression and defense in this straightforward way if our interest is in the moral relevance of the distinction. Some of these problems will come up later.

Two additional problems in drawing the line between self-defense and aggression are the sufficiency problem and the time-lag problem. The sufficiency problem concerns the level of military assault that justifies a defensive war. Not every military action is sufficiently serious to be a just cause for war. In the last chapter, we saw Vitoria's claim to this effect. For example, if one state fires a few shots across its border with another state, this is a use of military force, but it would not, in most circumstances, justify war in response. It is too trivial. But if a small military provocation is insufficient to justify war, perhaps it could justify a lesser military response. In IHL there is a recognized distinction between war and

---

[12] Walzer, *Just and Unjust Wars*, p. 62 (emphasis omitted). Walzer's use of "international society" recalls Grotius' introduction of that phrase.

[13] Myres McDougal and Florentino Feliciano, *The International Law of War: Transnational Coercion and World Public Order* (New Haven Press, 1994), p. 168.

"measures short of war" as defensive responses. Two such measures are "on-the-spot reactions," which occur when, for example, military patrols or ships at sea return fire after being fired upon, and "defensive armed reprisals," which occur when one state makes a small-scale military strike in response to its opponent's earlier small-scale attack. The former occur at the time of the provocation, while the latter occur at a time and place of the state's choosing.[14] Military responses are not all or nothing; there are lesser forms than war corresponding to lesser acts of aggression. *Jus ad bellum* could include an account of small-scale military *strikes* as "measures short of war."

The time-lag problem arises from a difference between two kinds of military self-defense: (1) a defense that seeks to thwart a military aggression in process, before it succeeds, as in Britain's efforts to avoid a Nazi invasion during World War II; and (2) a defense that seeks to "roll back" a military aggression that has (temporarily) succeeded, as in the Gulf War, where the defensive war was to retake an already occupied state. A war has a just cause in both kinds of cases. Consider the analogy with a purse snatching, where the victim has a just cause not only to try to hang on to the purse, but also to run after the thief and retrieve the purse after it has been taken. The time-lag problem is the question whether in (2) the length of time between the aggression and attempted roll-back has any bearing on the justifiability of the defensive efforts.

Consider the Falklands/Malvinas War between Britain and Argentina in 1982. The Falkland Islands (called the Malvinas by the Argentines) are off the coast of Argentina, but had for over 150 years been under the sovereignty of Britain as a British Overseas Territory. The islands were seized by Argentina in April, 1982. Britain succeeded in retaking the islands by June of that year, but the islands were under the control of Argentina for the couple of months it took the British to sail an expeditionary force to the South Atlantic to reclaim them. It seems clear that Britain's claim to have a just cause for retaking the islands, whatever its overall merits, was not invalidated by this delay. But would Britain's efforts to retake the islands been justified had it waited years? Argentina, after all, tried to justify its attack by pointing out that it had controlled the islands centuries earlier. It claimed to be retaking what had once belonged to it.

[14] Dinstein, *War*, pp. 219–231.

The time-lag problem raises a number of interesting and important issues. It seems that if a territory has been under the control of a state for a significant period of time, another state that earlier controlled the territory cannot justify retaking it by force, though this also depends on the wishes of the local population. For example, Michael Walzer has proposed as a moral principle governing such situations, "the land follows the people," meaning that the will of the inhabitants should be the determining factor when control over a territory is disputed.[15] Generally, however, just war theory stands opposed to *irredentism*, the effort by a state to justify the forceful taking of a territory it claims to have controlled in the distant past. If Mexico invaded the United States to retake territory in the Southwest it lost to the United States in the nineteenth century, it would not have a just cause, and its action would be treated as aggression, not delayed self-defense, if there is such a thing. It is worth noting that this feature of just cause helps to give just war theory a strong bias in favor of the status quo.

Just cause under the national defense paradigm shares one important feature with just cause under the just war paradigm, where a just cause is "a wrong received." Under the national defense paradigm, a state under attack surely has received a wrong at the hands of the aggressor. The wrong is that the victim's right to be free from attack has been violated.[16] The victim has not simply been harmed. There is a difference between a *wrong* and a *harm*. While a wrong is a species of harm, it is a special kind of harm; not all harms are also wrongs. Consider two actions of state S that harm state T: first, S increases its import tariffs, seriously damaging T's economy; second, S invades T, seizing some of T's resources. In both cases, S has seriously harmed T, and the harm to T may even be greater in the first case than in the second. Yet, in general, only in second case would T have been wronged by S. S had a moral obligation not to invade T, due to T's right not to be attacked, but S (absent a special treaty) had no moral obligation not to alter its tariff policy. T had a right not to be subject to armed attack, and S had a duty to respect that right. There are no such rights and duties in the first case.

---

[15] Walzer, *Just and Unjust Wars*, p. 55.

[16] Still, under the national defense paradigm the wrong received does not justify punitive war, as it does under the just war paradigm. A defensive war is not retributive punishment, but simply an effort to avoid or restore a loss.

This talk of wrongs, obligations, duties, and rights shows that just cause is understood in deontological terms. We mentioned the contrast between *deontological* and *consequentialist* moral considerations briefly in the discussion of pacifism in Chapter 1. Under a deontological approach, the focus of the moral assessment of an action is on the moral duties a person has, usually connected with respect for the moral rights of those to whom the duties are owed. In contrast, under a consequentialist approach the focus of moral assessment is on the full range of consequences an action has, including all the harms it brings about. From a deontological perspective, only those harms that are also wrongs are of moral concern. (Under a different version of consequentialism, *rule consequentialism*, what is assessed in terms of consequences are not individual actions but rules of action.)

The view that a just cause is a wrong received is one of the reasons for the view that an armed conflict cannot be just on both sides. A wrong goes only in one direction. In an armed conflict, each side harms the other, but each side does not wrong the other. The state that has a just cause has been wronged by its opponent, and the harm that that state does to its opponent in a just war of self-defense is not itself a wrong. The distinction between wrongs and mere harms is the source of the moral asymmetry between defender and aggressor. Inis Claude points out that "the injustice of one side typically provides the basis for the justice of the other; just war consists in opposing certain varieties of unjust behavior."[17] Of course, it may be (in cases of simultaneous ostensible justice) that both sides *believe* they are fighting a just war, each believing it is the side that has been wronged. But both sides cannot be correct in this view. Both sides can, however, be mistaken. Each side may be fighting an unjust war, as when, for example, each is fighting the other on the territory of a third state it is trying to conquer. Representing these various points, here is a formulation of the just cause criterion:

> Just cause (national defense paradigm): a war (or a measure short of war) engaged in by state S (or by another state coming to its aid) against state T must be a defensive response to a wrong of military aggression committed by T against S (so long as any time lag between aggression and defense is not too great).

[17] Inis L. Claude, "Just War: Doctrines and Institutions," *Political Science Quarterly* 95, no. 1 (Spring 1980), p. 87.

We need now to return to the question raised earlier: what counts as aggression and, correspondingly, what counts as defense? To do this, we look at a special case of just cause.

3.3 Just cause and anticipatory defense

A war has a just cause only if it is a defensive response to aggression. But hidden within this formulation is another problem, a different sort of time-lag problem. Must the aggression have begun before the defensive war is initiated? Can *anticipatory defense* be justified? The idea of anticipatory defense is a challenge to the priority principle, mentioned earlier, which defines aggression as striking the first blow. Can a first blow be defensive rather than aggressive? Theorists from the just war tradition take different views on this. Gentili says that it can: "No one ought to wait to be struck, unless he is a fool. One ought to provide not only against an offence which is being committed, but also against one which may possibly be committed."[18] But Grotius disagrees, arguing that it is not right "to take up Arms to reduce the growing Power of a Prince or State, which if too much augmented, may possibly injure us." He continues: "to pretend to have a Right to injure another, merely from a Possibility that he may injure me, is repugnant to all the Justice in the World: For such is the condition of present Life, that we can never be in perfect Security."[19] Anticipatory defense may be part of a quixotic effort to achieve perfect security, which can never be ours.

Anticipatory defense may be divided into two cases. First is the case where the anticipated attack is *imminent*. As an example, consider a hypothetical attack by the United States on the Japanese fleet near Hawaii in 1941, as it was about to launch its aircraft for the attack on Pearl Harbor.[20] The second case is where the anticipatory blow is struck some significant length of time before the anticipated aggression. As another example, consider the United States' invasion of Iraq in 2003 where the just cause was claimed to be an anticipated future aggression by Iraq with weapons of

[18] Alberico Gentili, *On the Law of War*, excerpts in Reichberg *et al.* (eds.), *Ethics of War*, p. 376.

[19] Hugo Grotius, *The Rights of War and Peace*, ed. Richard Tuck (Indianapolis, IN: Liberty Fund, 2005), p. 417.

[20] Dinstein, *War*, pp. 190–191.

mass destruction. The first case is referred to as a *preemptive war*, and the second case as a *preventive war*.[21] Can anticipatory defense ever be justified, and, if so, does the temporal difference between preemptive and preventive war make a moral difference?

Both preemptive war and preventive war involve a first strike, and so each violates the priority principle. If a first strike can be defensive, then the side responding with a second strike must be the aggressor, since otherwise the resulting armed conflict would be just on both sides. Many think that the temporal difference between the two cases allows a preemptive war, but not a preventive war, to be morally justified. Imminence is the key point. When an anticipated attack is believed to be imminent, there will generally be a much higher level of reasonable certainty that it will occur. Consider an analogy with an Old West gunfight. It is high noon on the streets of Dodge as Doc faces Slim. Doc could shoot Slim as Slim retrieves his gun belt from his saddle bags, in anticipation that Slim is going to try to shoot him. In that case, Doc's shooting Slim would be an analogue of preventive war. But Doc cannot at that point be certain that Slim will try to shoot him. Consistent with gunfighter morality, Doc waits to shoot until Slim stands ready with his hand moving toward his six-shooter, for then Slim's intention to shoot Doc is certain. In that case, Doc's shooting first would be an analogue of preemptive war. A gunfighter is not morally obligated to wait until he has been shot to shoot back.

Preventive wars, Michael Walzer notes, have traditionally been justified on "balance of power" considerations.[22] When a state sees the military power of its opponent growing, and its own in relative decline, it may be fearful of the opponent's future aggression and be tempted to launch a preventive war now to restore the balance of power between the two as a way of avoiding the aggression it anticipates will come when the opponent has increased its strength. Better to nip things in the bud. But the fear in this case is based on very uncertain expectations. The arms build-ups that generate such fear are, by their nature, opaque in intention; a build-up may be meant for either offensive or defensive purposes, to wage future aggression or simply to improve one's deterrence posture. Also contributing to the uncertainty is the fact that even if the opponent's current

International order would break down if states were permitted to start wars because of what they feared might happen in the distant future.

---

[21] I draw from a discussion of this issue in Walzer, *Just and Unjust Wars*, pp. 74–85.

[22] *Ibid.*, pp. 76–80.

intentions are to engage in aggression in the future, much can happen in the meantime to ensure that aggression will not happen.

The German theorist Samuel Pufendorf (1632–1694) notes: "Fear alone does not suffice as a just cause for war, unless it is established with moral and evident certitude that there is an intent to injure us."[23] Regarding anticipatory defense, Emer de Vattel urges a state "not to attack [its opponent] upon vague and uncertain suspicions, lest she should incur the imputation of becoming herself an unjust aggressor."[24] Preventive war should be understood not as defense at all, but aggression, even if the motivation is fear rather than desire for gain. Walzer endorses Pufendorf's point about the inadequacy of mere fear, fear not backed by a high degree of reasonable expectation regarding the anticipated aggression. To justify war, the fear must be a "just fear," one based on a sufficient threat.[25] Imminence is not by itself of inherent importance; rather it is a condition without which the level of reasonable expectation needed for a sufficient threat is not possible.

One moral objection to preventive war is that if it were permitted, war would become much more frequent. This is due to the dynamic of fear on which preventive wars are predicated. If states expect that their opponents might engage in preventive wars, their fear of being attacked would be that much greater, making them more likely to initiate preventive war, which, of course, would increase the likelihood that their opponents would initiate preventive war, in a vicious cycle of reciprocal fear. Those who wage preventive war believe themselves to be in the right, because they see themselves as acting defensively.[26] But the priority principle applies to them, and they are the aggressors. Another way to put the objection to preventive war is that it has no just cause. Vitoria observes: "It is quite unacceptable that a person should be killed for a sin he has

[margin handwritten note: THE CYCLE OF RECIPROCAL FEAR.]

---

[23] Samuel Pufendorf, *On the Law of Nature and Nations*, in Larry May, Eric Rovie, and Steve Viner (eds.), *The Morality of War: Classical and Contemporary Readings* (Upper Saddle River, NJ: Prentice-Hall, 2006), p. 92.

[24] Emer de Vattel, *The Law of Nations*, ed. Bella Kapossy and Richard Whatmore (Indianapolis, IN: Liberty Fund, 2008), p. 289.

[25] Walzer, *Just and Unjust Wars*, pp. 81, 84.

[26] This could contribute to the prevalence of simultaneous ostensible justice, discussed in the last chapter, as those fighting a preventive war believe themselves to be in the right, as do their opponents.

yet to commit."[27] A just cause requires a "wrong received," and prior to actual aggression, no wrong has been received. These arguments support the view that preventive war cannot be morally justified.

But, given the need for a "wrong received," it seems that this objection extends to preemptive wars as well. In a strict sense, however, it is misleading to refer to a preemptive war as anticipatory. It may be argued that the level of certainty or "sufficient threat" needed to justify a preemptive war can only be achieved when the attack has actually begun, in the sense that it has been set in motion, as when the gunslinger has begun reaching for his gun, even if the first blow has yet to land. The point is that a military attack is a complex event covering a period of time, and part of that event occurs before it bears fruit in the first blow. If the United States military had engaged the Japanese fleet off Hawaii before the Japanese aircraft were launched on December 7, 1941, this would be a justified preemptive war on the grounds that the attack, which involved the fleet's sailing to Hawaii, was already underway. Once a state has begun an attack, it has committed a wrong against its intended victim, even before the inevitable blow lands. Viewed in this way, preemptive war has a just cause. Israeli theorist Yoram Dinstein refers to "interceptive self-defense," the idea being that the state defends itself by intercepting an attack already in progress.[28] The suggestion is that preemptive war should be understood as a form in interceptive self-defense. Of course, if the attack is identified as a series of events beginning before the blow lands, the difficult question remains of when this series of events begins.

The problem of preemption is a serious one because waiting for the blow to land can put a state at a great military disadvantage, as the gunslinger would be if he waited to shoot until his opponent's bullet struck. In a confrontation, preemption may seem to be a matter of *military necessity*. In general, when a state has a just cause, its military response, whether anticipatory or not, is often said to be a matter of military necessity. Augustine argued that just wars are matters of necessity, and this idea is reflected in the remark of President John Adams at the beginning of this chapter,

---

[27] Francisco Vitoria, "On the Law of War," in Anthony Pagden and Jeremy Lawrance (eds.), *Vitoria: Political Writings* (Cambridge University Press, 1991), pp. 293–327, at p. 316. While Vitoria makes this comment in a discussion of *jus in bello*, the point may be applied to *jus ad bellum* as well.

[28] Dinstein, *War*, pp. 190–192.

where he implies the negative, that a war lacking military necessity is unjust. If aggression occurs, the victim state is *forced* to respond, sometimes for its very survival. This is especially the case with some preemptive wars where the victim, like the gunslinger, may not survive awaiting the blow. Augustine's view has given rise to the distinction between wars of necessity and wars of choice: just wars are of necessity; unjust wars are matters of choice. But in referring to wars with a just cause as necessary, it is important to appreciate a point of Michael Walzer's that war can be necessary only in the sense of being *indispensible* (to staving off aggression, for example), not in the sense of being *inevitable*.[29] Even a just war is a moral choice, and viewing a just war as inevitable, as Augustine seems to do, is a renunciation of moral responsibility for human agency. (Military necessity also plays a role in *jus in bello*, as discussed in Chapter 6.)

Just cause is perhaps the most important of the *ad bellum* criteria. But it is one of six, and establishes, at best, only a *prima facie* case for a war's being just. The other criteria still need to be consulted.

3.4 Legitimate authority and rightful intention

The second of Aquinas' three criteria, legitimate authority, is different from the other criteria in that it places a condition not on the characteristics of a war, but rather on how it is initiated. It is different in another sense as well. The criterion is at least partly incorporated within the definition of war. Recall that war involves armed conflict between states or other large organizations. Large organizations have authority structures which make decisions for the organization, such as whether it goes to war. So, it might be claimed the legitimate authority criterion is satisfied "by definition." Legitimate authority is about procedure in the initiation of war, while the other criteria concern matters of moral substance, about which the definition should be neutral. The question is whether the requirement that the authority be *legitimate* makes the criterion more than procedural.

Legitimacy may be understood as either legal or moral. Legal legitimacy may mean simply authority that is exercised in accord with the rules (or laws) of an organization. If so, the criterion is likely to be satisfied by any

---

[29] Walzer, *Just and Unjust Wars*, chapter 1.

war, understood as a conflict between large organizations. But if legitimacy is understood as implying some moral content, then the criterion goes beyond what is implied by the definition of war. The idea of legitimacy would have moral content, for example, if it required that a just war be initiated by an authority who rules in a morally acceptable way, such as by respecting the rights of the citizens.

Aquinas seems to require that this criterion have moral content when he speaks of the sovereign who declares war as one who pursues the care of the community, which is to say that he rules justly. But if we recall Aquinas' argument for this criterion, it is not clear that the sovereign who is entitled to declare war must meet such a moral standard. The reason that war can be declared by a sovereign is that he has, unlike his subjects, no one to whom to appeal should the state be treated unjustly by another state, leaving resort to war as the only alternative. But a sovereign lacks such a higher court of appeal whether or not he is a just ruler. As an example of an unjust ruler having the authority to declare war, consider Joseph Stalin, ruler of the Soviet Union during World War II. He was a paradigmatic murderous tyrant, but to claim that, as a result, he was not a legitimate authority would imply that the war he declared against the 1941 Nazi invasion did not satisfy that criterion, so was not a just war. This seems clearly false. This *reductio ad absurdum* argument supports the claim that legitimate authority does not have a moral content.

> Legitimate authority: a war must be initiated by some person or group with legal authority within a large organization, whether or not that person or group also has moral legitimacy as a ruler.

This implies that almost all war (as we have defined war) would satisfy the legitimate authority criterion, given that the *de facto* rulers of organizations capable of using force act under the rules (official or unofficial) of that organization in initiating war. (There could be, however, cases where the rules are contested or a ruler usurps the power to initiate war by going outside the recognized rules.) In any case, the moral status of a war is borne by the other criteria.

The third of Aquinas' criteria, rightful intention, requires that a war be fought with a morally acceptable intention. This requires that a war be fought for a just cause. A rightful intention is an intention to correct the wrong that is a just cause, in the case of the national defense paradigm, an act of aggression. The point of the criterion is to ensure that a state does not use the fact that a war has a just cause as a pretext to fight the war for another purpose, especially a nefarious purpose such as conquest or exploitation.

PRETEXTS ARE NOT ALLOWED

The ancestor of this criterion is Augustine's requirement that war not be fought with an unacceptable motivation, such as hatred or revenge. This suggests that the criterion could be one of "rightful motivation" instead of rightful intention.[30] But there are reasons to reject this. A motive is an underlying predisposition to act in a certain way (greed is an example), which may be indulged or resisted, while an intention is a purpose adopted for a particular action (as an intention to steal candy from that baby). It seems that our obligations concern our intentions rather than our motives. An individual's obligation not to lie, for example, requires that he act without the intention to deceive, whatever his motives may be in doing so. Another reason to avoid a criterion cast in terms of motives is that motives are usually mixed in human action. It may not be possible for an individual, let alone a state, to act with a pure, single motive. (This issue arises in the case of humanitarian intervention, discussed in the next chapter.) A person can reasonably be required to have a specific intention when acting, such as not to deceive, but not to have a specific motive. Intentions are under our control in a way that motives are not.

There are additional problems in understanding this criterion. First, it is not clear what it means for a state to have an intention, since it has no mind, and the mind is normally thought to be where intentions reside. Second, it is not clear how we can know, even for a person, what her intentions are, given that they are creatures of her mind, to which others do not have access. The solution to both of these problems is to recognize that we attribute intentions on the basis of behavior, in terms of what the actor actually does, whether the actor is an individual or a state. So, requiring that a state have an intention to correct the wrong that is its just cause means requiring that it behave in a certain way, specifically, that it do no more in the war than what would be consistent with that goal. The state's actions should not go beyond those necessary to achieve that intention.

---

[30] See the introduction to Terry Nardin and Melissa Williams (eds.), *Humanitarian Intervention*, Nomos 47 (New York University Press, 2006), pp. 9–10. For the reasons given, I think this suggestion should be rejected.

If they do, its intentions are different.[31] As Joseph Boyle expresses it, the "concrete goal" established by the just cause "strictly controls the actions for its sake."[32]

THE GOAL
CONTROLS
THE ACTIONS

A state may have additional intentions beyond the rightful intention, other purposes it seeks to achieve, for intentions can be multiple, as when one seeks to kill two birds with one stone. But additional intentions should be "lesser included" intentions, meaning that they should be achievable through the use of no more than the amount of military force necessary to achieve the rightful intention. Other allowable intentions, and the actions needed to secure them, should be "nested within" the intention, and the actions to secure it, that reflect the just cause. Having several intentions, Michael Walzer observes, is "morally troubling in wartime only if they make for the expansion or prolongation of the fighting beyond its justifiable limits or if they distort the conduct of the war."[33]

> Rightful intention: a war must be initiated with an intention to correct for a wrong that is a just cause (this is the rightful intention), and any other intentions must be achievable with no more than the amount of military force required to achieve the rightful intention.

3.5 Proportionality

Vitoria expresses the proportionality criterion as "the obligation to see that greater evils do not arise out of the war than the war would avert."[34] There is a sense in which proportionality is about the lesser of evils. The basic idea is that the moral cost of a war must not be out of proportion (or disproportionate or excessive) in relation to the moral cost the war would avoid. The idea seems simple, but it is not. The first question is the standard of moral cost. Should proportionality be measured in terms of wrongs or in terms of mere harms? As we saw earlier, when we compared

---

[31] Unless the behavior is due to the agent's mistaken belief about the means necessary to that end. I owe this point to Fredrik Kaufman.

[32] Joseph Boyle, "Just War Doctrine and the Military Response to Terrorism," *Journal of Political Philosophy* 11, no. 2 (2003), pp. 153–170, at p. 164.

[33] Walzer, *Just and Unjust Wars*, 2nd edn. (New York: Basic Books, 1992), p. xix.

[34] Vitoria, "On the Law of War," p. 315. Vitoria is speaking of *in bello* proportionality, but the point also applies for *ad bellum* proportionality.

the harm from a state's tariff policy with the harm from its seizure of territory, not all harms count as wrongs, and this is true even among the harms that war causes. As we shall see, there is good reason to consider proportionality in terms of wrongs rather than mere harms.

In terms of proportionality calculations, the evil that arises out of a war may be called the *created evil*, while the evil a war is meant to avert may be called the *resisted evil*. Proportionality is tied to just cause because the main resisted evil is the wrong that provides a just cause, such as an act of aggression, so that proportionality (at the *ad bellum* level) can be satisfied only if there is a just cause. But the reverse does not hold – just cause can be satisfied without proportionality being satisfied. The criterion is about balancing ends (averting the resisted evil) and means (the evils created by the war). Even when there is a just cause, the created evil may be out of proportion to the resisted evil. The point of proportionality, like the other criteria, is to make *jus ad bellum* more restrictive than just cause alone does; proportionality limits what a state can do in the name of a just cause.

Following Vitoria's formula, we must understand precisely what sorts of evils, understood as wrongs, are to be balanced against each other and how the balancing is to be done.[35] There are three factors to be deter-mined: (1) the resisted evils; (2) the created evils; and (3) a comparison of the two in terms of some metric.[36] The third requires a calculation com-paring the first and the second, balancing or weighing them against each other, determining where the greater evil lies.[37] In terms of the national defense paradigm, the idea behind (1) seems straightforward. When a state has a just cause for war, a wrong has been committed against it, and this wrong is an evil that a defensive war can resist and attempt to avert, either through stopping it from happening (as Britain stopped a Nazi invasion in 1940) or reversing it (as the Coalition did in pushing Iraq out of Kuwait in 1991). The resisted evil is a wrong, specifically, a failure to fulfill an obli-gation. Under the national defense paradigm, states have obligations not

---

[35] I have had great help in my understanding of proportionality through discussions with Henry Shue, though I do not think he would fully endorse my position.

[36] Thomas Hurka, "Proportionality in the Morality of War," *Philosophy & Public Affairs* 33, no. 1 (2005), pp. 34–66, at p. 38.

[37] The choice here is between prospective evils committed by different agents, not the more familiar sort of case where the prospective evils are due to actions of a single agent.

to attack other states, so the resisted evil is a wrong against a state, an act of aggression.

Moving to (2), it seems that the created evil, unlike the resisted evil, is a wrong, or set of wrongs, against individuals, rather than against a state. The created evil cannot be against a state because so long as a state is fighting a just war against its opponent it is not committing a wrong against that opponent. To say that a war is just is to say that it is not wrong to fight it, that no wrong is committed against the opposing state. If the proportionality calculation is to apply at all, the wrong committed by a state at war is against individuals, rather than against a state.[38] We may understand the wrongs against individuals in war as violations of *individual rights*. So, the created evil in war consists of individual rights violations.

But perhaps the created evil should include all harms instead of only the harms that are wrongs. In war a great deal of harm is done; many die or are maimed and considerable valuable property is destroyed. This is what makes war so terrible. This has led many to think that proportionality should be calculated in terms of all such harms, not simply in terms of wrongs. Not all the harms are wrongs. For example, when a state fighting a just war kills enemy combatants, these deaths are harms, but they may not be wrongs, precisely because the war is just. If we were to consider the created evil in terms of all the harms the war causes rather than the subset of these that are also wrongs, proportionality might be represented partly in consequentialist terms.[39] But a consequentialist understanding of the created evil will not work. The argument for this can be presented in terms of the domestic analogy. If a case of individual self-defense is justified, it presumably will have satisfied the domestic equivalents of the *ad bellum* criteria, including proportionality. If Jones is attacked by a pair of assassins, she is justified in killing both of them, if necessary to save her own life, and the same if the number of assassins is three, four, or more. So, no matter how great the harm she creates in saving her life, her actions are justified, so she would not have failed to satisfy the domestic equivalent of the proportionality criterion. The reason is that though Jones has

---

[38] My thinking here was assisted by Douglas Lackey's discussion of proportionality in *Ethics of War and Peace* (Englewood Cliffs, NJ: Prentice-Hall, 1989), pp. 40–41.

[39] It could be wholly consequentialist only if the *resisted* evil were also understood in consequentialist terms, that is, in terms of all harms the war was meant to avoid.

harmed the assassins in killing them, she has not wronged them, so their deaths do not count in calculating proportionality.

While many of the harms a state inflicts on individuals in fighting a just war are not wrongs, some are, and it is the latter that are relevant to the proportionality calculations. The wrongs may be referred to as *unjust harms*. The just harms, the harms that are not wrongs, are harms to those individuals who are *morally liable* to be harmed. A person has *moral liability* to be harmed if, due to her role or the choices she has made, she would not be wronged were she to be harmed. In our discussion of *jus in bello* in Chapters 5 and 6, we will consider in greater detail who is and who is not liable to be harmed in war. For now, speaking generally, we can say that combatants are liable to be harmed and civilians are not. If civilians are harmed, killed, injured, or deprived of important property, they have been wronged.[40] So, speaking roughly at this point, we can say that the created evil in war, the set of wrongs done to individuals, are harms done to civilians. The civilians harmed have had their rights violated.

A basic fact about war, which is behind the relevance of the proportionality criterion, is that in practice a state cannot wage war, even with a just cause, without committing wrongs, that is, without harming those who are not liable to be harmed. In practical terms, *the created evil cannot be zero*. Likely many civilians will be seriously harmed and killed by a state waging a war, whether or not the war has a just cause. This is a point emphasized by the anti-war pacifist: if unjust harm cannot be avoided, war is wrong, whether or not it has a just cause. We will return to this point shortly.

Before considering (3), we need to discuss some further points about how wrongs to individuals should be treated in proportionality calculations. First, a wrong should count in terms of the reasonable expectation that it will occur. An expectation is reasonable, recall, when it is carefully calculated in accord with the best information available at the time. Note that this will, in part, involve predictions by the leaders about their own future choices, as well as the future choices of the members of their military. The second point is that the mental state (in law, *mens rea*) of the person causing the harm is relevant to determining whether it is a wrong.

WHO IS LIABLE TO BE HARMED ?

---

[40] In Chapters 5 and 6, we consider an alternative view that combatants fighting in a just war are wronged when they are attacked.

The imposition of a harm is a wrong only if the harm was or should have been foreseen by the person imposing it. The harm may be a wrong not only if is deliberately intended, but also if it is merely foreseen or should have been foreseen. This recalls the distinction in the doctrine of double effect between harms that are intended and harms that are merely foreseen. The created evil is the total of the unjust harms leaders can reasonably expect to result from their war.

The third point concerns whether a state must include in its proportionality assessment wrongs committed by its opponent. When a state M launches a defensive war, its opponent N will respond with (further) military force, and this will involve its committing wrongs against individuals that would not have occurred without M's having gone to war. The question is whether these wrongs must be taken into account when M calculates proportionality. The answer seems to be no. In the domestic case, if some action of A results in B's committing a wrong, B's wrong is not, in general, also A's wrong, unless B is acting under A's authority. Otherwise A and B are responsible for their own wrongs. So wartime wrongs suffered by individuals in M committed by N do not count in M's proportionality calculations.

The final point concerns wrongs that are imposed after the war is over. Many people will be unjustly harmed after the war through delayed effects of actions taken by the other side during the war. For example, wartime damage to the opponent's civilian infrastructure may continue to impose harm on its citizens after hostilities have ceased, such as deaths due to damage of waste treatment plants or the radiation deaths of the former residents of Hiroshima that occurred long after World War II. Because they result from the war, these wrongs should be counted in proportionality assessments.

So, the created evil consists of the unjust harms, the wrongs to individuals not liable to be harmed (primarily civilians), that a state either intends to commit or foresees (or should foresee) that it will commit in a prospective war. The calculation of the created evil must be based on a reasonable expectation of the results of actions the state is likely to commit in the war, and include the unjust harms resulting from the war that occur after the war is over. Given the increasing ratio of civilian to combatant deaths through the series of wars of the past century, the created evil of a future prospective war, other things being equal, might be reasonably expected to be great. When it is great enough, the war will fail the proportionality criterion.

Consider now (3). How are the resisted evil and the created evil to be compared to determine whether the war satisfies *ad bellum* proportionality? But first, is such a comparison even possible, since it is not clear whether it is ever morally justified to commit a wrong, even for the sake of averting a wrong? If doing wrong is not allowed, even for the sake of averting other wrongs, then war becomes morally impossible. This *rights-absolutist approach*, as we may call it, supports the position of the anti-war pacifist.[41] A rights absolutist holds that it is never permissible to violate rights (that is, commit wrongs), even to avoid the occurrence of rights violations by others. The alternative idea, the *trade-off approach*, is that one can commit wrongs in order to avoid greater wrongs; in other words, one can violate rights in order to avoid a greater violation of rights. The goal of this approach is to minimize the overall number (and seriousness) of rights violations, even when this requires violating some rights. But to advocates of the absolutist approach, this makes no sense because one cannot justify violating rights for the sake of good consequences, even if those consequences include reducing the number of rights violations overall. Suggesting otherwise is akin to the view that two wrongs make a right.

It seems that the debate between just war theory and pacifism hangs on the question whether a rights-absolutist approach or a trade-off approach is correct, given that war cannot, in practice, be fought without wrongs being committed. We will return to this question again in the next chapter, when we consider a different *ad bellum* paradigm, but there is a way we can address the question in the context of the national defense paradigm. According to this paradigm, the resisted evil is a wrong to a state, and we have argued that the created evil consists of wrongs to individuals. Now it is plausible to claim that wrongs committed against states are worse evils, in general, than wrongs committed against individuals. Wrongs against states are of greater moral *significance*. In light of this, the trade-off approach seems more reasonable than the absolutist approach,

[handwritten margin note: WHY IS THIS PLAUSIBLE?]

---

[41] The rights absolutist assumes, problematically, that it is always possible to avoid committing wrongs, that a person's obligations to others never conflict, and that she cannot have an obligation to avoid someone's rights being violated by a third party. I question these assumptions in the next chapter.

for, in the context of war, a trade-off approach allows us through committing wrongs of lesser significance (wrongs to individuals) to avoid wrongs of greater significance (wrongs to states). This seems morally reasonable.

This idea of *significance* of wrongs suggests a scale of comparison that answers the question how the resisted evils are to be compared with the created evils. The question is whether the significance of the resisted evil is greater than the significance of the created evil. If the resisted evils are of greater significance, proportionality is satisfied, and if not, it is not. Note that the significance of the resisted evil in the case of aggression is not undifferentiated and can range from that involved in the seizure of a small bit of territory to that involved in complete conquest. The significance of the created evil is the total of the unjust individual harms the war would cause. Each is discounted by the reasonable expectations of the likelihoods that they would occur.

> Proportionality criterion (national defense paradigm): a war must be such that the reasonably expected created evil does not exceed in significance the reasonably expected resisted evil.[42]

This is, of course, a vague criterion, given the conceptual and empirical difficulties of calculating reasonable expectations of the resisted and the created evils, and given that there is an element of incommensurability in the comparison of wrongs against states (the resisted evil) and wrongs against individuals (the created evil). We will find a way to address the incommensurability in the next chapter, but the conceptual and empirical difficulties of the calculation seem inherent in the enterprise.

Because we are assuming, as the national defense paradigm suggests, that a wrong against a state is a much more serious matter than wrongs against individuals, most wars of self-defense will turn out to satisfy this criterion, but not all. Some resisted evils (such as the seizure of a small portion of territory) are of less significance than others (such as complete conquest), and in any case, a sufficient number of wrongs against individuals could tip the balance against the resisted evil. Consider an example of a war that would have failed proportionality. In 1968, the Soviet Union invaded Czechoslovakia to oust a liberal government that had sought to

---

[42] I formulate the criterion in terms of *expectations* under the assumption that their main purpose is *prospective*, to guide the actions of leaders and those advising them, rather than retrospective, to judge such actions.

distance itself from Soviet control. (Previously, Czechoslovakia had been a satellite state of the Soviet Union.) There were calls for the United States to intervene to protect the Czech government, and such a war would have had a just cause. But if the United States had gone to war, the war might have escalated into a nuclear war with the Soviet Union, the result of which would have been the deaths of millions of Soviet civilians. Given the reasonable expectations of vast civilian deaths, proportionality would not have been satisfied.

Note the relation between the created evil and the averting of the resisted evil. The resisted evil is averted only if the state adopts means of fighting that win the war. Alternative means of fighting are available to a state, given its resources and the response of its opponent, and the choices among the alternatives will affect the magnitude of the created evil. Some of these alternative means would be more likely to win the war than others. For example, a state may believe that it has to fight a war viciously to have a good chance of winning, but the more viciously it fights, the greater the created evil (given the increased risk to civilians), and as the significance of the created evil increases, the likelihood that proportionality would be satisfied decreases. There is a moral trade-off between the means of fighting adopted and the likelihood that the resisted evil will be averted. All of this is taken account of by measuring the evils in terms of reasonable expectations.

But the proportionality criterion is not in practice a very useful rule. Not only is it vague, but also, because it is vague, it is easily manipulated to produce the desired results and it is subject to self-deceptive assessments. One of the main sources of self-deception is the judgment states make that they will win their wars. Usually, both sides in an armed conflict believe that they will win, otherwise they would not engage in war. But they cannot both be right. The importance of the criterion, however, is that it allows the interests of individuals who may be wronged in a war to be considered. When we consider criticisms of the national defense paradigm in the next chapter, we will see good reason to bring more fully into the picture the interests of individuals wronged in war.

When a state, in applying the proportionality criterion, seeks to determine, based on reasonable expectations, the significance of the evil it would create and the likelihood of its averting the resisted evil, it must, as mentioned, make predictions of its own future behavior, or, more precisely, the leaders must predict how they will conduct the war and how their military will behave in fighting it. Making predictions about one's own future behavior may seem strange, but it is something that we do all the time, based on our understanding of our own character and past actions, to which is added some resolve about how we plan to behave in the future. But if this sense of resolve is unmodified by an understanding of our own character and past actions, it is little more than wishful thinking. The leaders need an understanding of the character of their own leadership and of their military forces, given the way they have fought in the past.

3.6 Last resort and reasonable chance of success

The last resort criterion is meant to ensure that, prior to initiating war, a state has considered available peaceful means of avoiding the resisted evil and attempted those among them that have a significant prospect of success. The point is that there are sometimes resorts other than war that could resolve a conflict that is heading toward war. If the other resorts were successful, the resisted evil could be averted without bloodshed. This criterion is simply an application of the general moral rule, called the *least harm principle*. Because war is so destructive, doing the least harm requires that one ascertain whether there are alternative, less destructive resorts that could avert the resisted evil. Any such alternatives should be tried first, making war the last resort. Charles Guthrie and Michael Quinlan note that the "last" in "last resort" means "least to be preferred."[43] Assuming that it is the most harmful means, war is always the least to be preferred means of achieving results in international relations. But war might not be the option least to be preferred, if another resort would actually cause more harm. Some would see this as the case with economic sanctions imposed on Iraq in the 1990s, arguing that the sanctions caused more deaths among civilians than a war to overthrow the regime would have.[44] This possibility, though it may be rare, should be taken into account in the last resort criterion.

[43] Charles Guthrie and Michael Quinlan, *The Just War Tradition: Ethics in Modern Warfare* (London: Bloomsbury, 2007), p. 33.

[44] This point is discussed by Simon Caney, *Justice beyond Borders* (Oxford University Press, 2005), p. 249. Even if this were the case with Iraq, however, this is unlikely to have justified the war option, for the war might well have failed other *ad bellum* criteria.

Sometimes there is no question that war is a last resort, that nothing else could achieve the results, as is usually the case when an invasion is under way, and it is clear that nothing but force could stop the invaders. This would also have been the case had there been a humanitarian intervention in Rwanda. But note that this may not be the case for a successful or accomplished invasion, where there may be time to attempt to force the invaders to withdraw by non-military means before force is used for this purpose. In the case of the 1991 Gulf War, where Iraq invaded neighboring Kuwait, Iraq quickly succeeded in occupying Kuwait before an outside military defense of Kuwait could be mounted, which allowed time for the application of economic sanctions in an effort (unsuccessful) to force Iraqi withdrawal before resort to force.

The last resort criterion is, in part, a call to give *diplomacy* a serious chance at resolving disputes that could lead to war. Diplomacy can often avert the resisted evil and stop war before it starts, as some have argued could have been the case with the Korean War, the Falklands War, and the Gulf War. The reference to diplomacy, however, shows that other resorts that should be tried before war may not achieve the whole of what the war would be fought to achieve, but something less. Diplomacy, after all, is an art of compromise, and so it may not avert all of the resisted evil. But the virtue of diplomacy is that while it may yield results less than war might have achieved, war would not necessarily have yielded those results, given that one side will lose and war comes with a great price tag in terms of blood and treasure. In war, at most one side achieves its goals, and both sides may lose in an overall sense. But with diplomacy, both sides can win, not everything they might want, but more than they might have achieved, when matters are viewed in terms of reasonable expectations. War is largely a zero-sum or negative-sum activity, while diplomacy is usually a positive-sum activity, with a win–win outcome.

The practice of diplomacy or conflict resolution involved in the application of the last resort criterion is an intellectual discipline and includes a set of skills that can be learned by training and advanced through intellectual study. Given the contribution these skills can make to advancing the state's interests without the costs of war, they receive only a pittance of support from states compared to the vast resources poured into military establishments. Part of satisfying this criterion should be to provide generous background support for such study and training, as well as for the international organizations, governmental or non-governmental, that play the often necessary role of outside mediation.[45] Greater support for the study of conflict resolution and for international mediation organizations would create a much richer background set of alternatives to war. Part of satisfying last resort is the long-range task of providing support for these background options. This point will be discussed again in the last chapter.

Last resort is an important moral requirement, but it has its critics. First, say the critics, it is not clear that the criterion can ever be satisfied. Given that there are always peaceful means yet to be tried, however unlikely of success, the criterion puts off war into the indefinite future. The Achilles of war can never overtake the tortoise of peaceful last resorts. Critics claim that the criterion is a backdoor route to pacifism. The criticism, as Michael Walzer suggests, is that the criterion "would make war morally impossible ... For we can never reach lastness, or we can never know that we have reached it."[46] Second, delaying a war to attempt peaceful means can make the war, if it must later be resorted to, more costly and less likely to succeed. He who hesitates may be lost, or may lose. Guthrie and Quinlan observe that "in conflict settings, time is often by no means neutral."[47] *Jus ad bellum* should be sensitive to the fact that war is sometimes necessary and that the dynamic nature of the events leading up to war makes timing crucial in the expected outcomes. But last resort, according to the critics, does not allow this. An example of this criticism is that the criterion can lead to appeasement of aggressors, as was shown by the period prior to World War II in Europe, whetting their appetites and making the eventual war more costly.

Some have sought to avoid such criticisms by stipulating that only *reasonable* peaceful resorts must be attempted prior to war. Reasonableness, in this context, would include two considerations: first, a temporal dimension, in recognition that delayed wars can be more costly, and, second, recognition of the likelihood of success of the other resorts. Employing

[handwritten marginal note: DIPLOMACY WORKS BEST WHEN IT'S BACKED UP BY THE THREAT OF FORCE]

---

[45] An example of this is the 1995 settlement of a border dispute between Peru and Ecuador, brokered by peace activist Johan Galtung. The states accepted Galtung's idea that they settle the dispute by turning the land into a bi-national park. See www.worldlingo.com/ma/enwiki/en/Johan_Galtung#cite_note-14, accessed May 28, 2010.

[46] Walzer, *Just and Unjust Wars*, 2nd edn., p. xiv.

[47] Guthrie and Quinlan, *Just War Tradition*, p. 33.

a peaceful, next-to-last resort takes time, so, if the resort fails, the war is delayed. Consider that a war may be fought at T1 or, at greater cost, later at T2, where the decision must be made at T1 whether to fight the war then or attempt a peaceful resort, which may or may not succeed. What we want to know is roughly whether it is worth the wait to fight the war, given the likelihood that the peaceful resort will succeed. If the benefit of avoiding the war, discounted by reasonable expectations of the likelihood that peaceful resort will succeed, is less than the increased cost of the war at T2, then the peaceful resort is not a reasonable last resort, and the last resort criterion should not require that it be attempted. So we have:

> Criterion of last resort: a war must be such that there is no peaceful resort that would be morally less costly than war and might avert the resisted evil (or something close to it) and that would satisfy the following condition: the value of what the peaceful resort could achieve, discounted by reasonable expectations of the likelihood that it would achieve that value, is greater than the cost, if any, of delaying the war until it has become clear that the peaceful resort has failed.

The criterion of reasonable chance of success is meant to exclude a war that is a hopeless cause, or close to it. Under this criterion, a state is prohibited from fighting a war, even with a just cause, if it does not stand a reasonable chance of winning. The point is that, given war's destructiveness, it should not be undertaken if the likelihood of success is low.[48] So understood, the criterion is partly reflected in the proportionality criterion, but it may be helpful to have it listed separately. Prudence would recommend this criterion, of course, but it is included in *jus ad bellum* to show that it is a moral requirement as well. Hugo Grotius says of the ruler, "Indeed it is not only Prudence, or Affection for his Subjects, that requires him to forbear engaging in a dangerous War, but very often Justice itself."[49]

But an important caveat in this criterion must be recognized. Note that in the case of individual self-defense against attempted murder, a high likelihood of failure does not stand in the way of the moral permissibility of fighting an attacker. Can we reason from a domestic analogy that something similar applies to war? We can, but only if the survival of the

---

[48] Guthrie and Quinlan point out that success does not necessarily require victory in a war as traditionally understood. *Ibid.*, p. 32.
[49] Grotius, *Rights of War and Peace*, p. 1145.

population is at stake. A state or group is morally entitled to fight for the very survival of its citizens, even if failure is very likely. For example, the violent efforts of the Jews in the Warsaw Ghetto to resist their being slaughtered by the Nazis in the spring of 1943 was surely justified, despite its being a lost cause.[50]

> The criterion of reasonable chance of success: a war must be such that the odds of success are not minimal, unless the war is for the very survival of the members of the state or group making the fight.

Like other *ad bellum* criteria this criterion is vague, and it is hard to see how it could be made more precise.

It is interesting that some would reject this criterion because they think that any war satisfying the other *ad bellum* criteria (especially just cause) is *obligatory*. Consider Vattel's claim: "Self-defence against unjust violence is not only the right, but the duty of a nation, and one of her most sacred duties."[51] Michael Walzer is tempted by Vattel's position, and like him is not too happy with the criterion of reasonable chance of success. He claims that a failure to fight against aggression is appeasement, and that appeasement is morally suspect, even when a war against aggression is unlikely to succeed. "When it comes to resisting aggression [just war theory] is at least permissive, sometimes imperative." Elsewhere, Walzer asserts that even when defensive war "seems imprudent, even hopeless ... We not only justify resistance, we call it heroic."[52] The reason, in Walzer's view, is that the international rules against aggression will be upheld only if their violations are countered with force, and there is no international police force to do the job. Against this idea stand the obligations leaders have not to lead their people to useless slaughter.

This completes our discussion of the six *ad bellum* criteria.

3.7 Does *jus ad bellum* depend on *jus in bello*?

In understanding *jus ad bellum* it is important to consider whether it is related to *jus in bello*. In discussing the rise of the regular war paradigm in

---

[50] Israel Gutman, *Resistance: The Warsaw Ghetto Uprising* (Washington, DC: United States Holocaust Museum, 1994). My thanks to Stephen Nathanson on this point.

[51] Vattel, *Law of Nations*, p. 487.

[52] Walzer, *Just and Unjust Wars*, 2nd edn., pp. xvi, 67.

Chapter 2, we mentioned the *dependence view*, the view that *in bello* judgments are dependent on *ad bellum* judgments. The relationship may apply in the other direction as well. So there are two separate claims: (1) *ad bellum* judgments depend on *in bello* judgments; and (2) *in bello* judgments depend on *ad bellum* judgments.

There are different ways in which one may be dependent on the other, but the sort of dependence we are concerned with involves the idea of a *necessary condition*. If P is a necessary condition for Q, Q cannot be true unless P is also true. For example, being female (P) is a necessary condition for being a mother (Q) – Q is true only when P is true. (But it does not work in reverse – being a mother is not a necessary condition for being female.) On this understanding, (1) is the claim that the truth of some *in bello* judgment is a necessary condition for the truth of an *ad bellum* judgment and (2) is the claim that the truth of some *ad bellum* judgment is a necessary condition for the truth of an *in bello* judgment. To represent necessary conditions, we may use hypothetical statements, which have the form "if A, then B" or "A, only if B" meaning that B is a necessary condition for A. We may formulate two *dependence theses*:

(DT1) A war is *ad bellum* just, only if it is *in bello* just; and

(DT2) A war is *in bello* just, only if it is *ad bellum* just.

We may refer to (DT1) as the *ad bellum* dependence thesis and (DT2) as the *in bello* dependence thesis.

Corresponding to each of these is an *independence thesis*, one denying the truth of (DT1) and another denying the truth of (DT2). Michael Walzer regards these independence theses as true. He claims that *jus ad bellum* and *jus in bello* are "logically independent," and that "it is perfectly possible for a just war to be fought unjustly and for an unjust war to be fought in strict accordance with the rules."[53] One way to express this difference between independence and dependence is to say that, according to the independence theses, *jus ad bellum* and *jus in bello* are related only *externally*, while according to the dependence theses, they are related *internally*.[54] In this section we consider the *ad bellum* dependence thesis, saving a discussion of the *in bello* dependence thesis for Chapter 6.

[53] *Ibid.*, p. 21. The latter claim, however, seems to be consistent with a weaker dependence relationship.

[54] Robert Holmes, On *War and Morality* (Princeton University Press, 1989), p. 176.

(DT1) is supported by British philosopher David Rodin, who asserts that "fighting in accordance with the *jus in bello* is one of the necessary conditions classically identified for war to be *ad bellum* just."[55] It is also supported by just war theorist William O'Brien, who asserts that "the *jus in bello* requirements ... have to be included in the comprehensive judgment as to a war's permissibility."[56] This way of putting it suggests that the truth of (DT1) could be represented by the addition of a seventh *ad bellum* criterion, a *dependence criterion*, according to which a condition for the *ad bellum* justice of a war is its *in bello* justice.[57]

> *Ad bellum* dependence criterion: a war must be fought in accord with *jus in bello*.

But there is a problem with this formulation. Larry May calls our attention to the fact that "we cannot determine whether [*jus in bello*] has been met in advance of fighting the war," because of our poor predictive abilities, and this leads him to suggest that the dependence criterion should require only that it "be likely that the conduct of the war will be proper."[58] But this is a familiar problem. In the case of other criteria, as we have discussed, one must judge in terms of reasonable expectations or likelihoods. This suggests the following formulation of the criterion, corresponding to a weaker version of (DT1):

> *Ad bellum* dependence criterion (revision 1): a war must be such that it is reasonably expected that it will be fought in accord with *jus in bello*.

Applying this criterion requires predictions of one's own future actions, but this is the case with the proportionality criterion as well. In addition, this formulation of the criterion allows it to be action guiding, which the original formulation does not.

---

[55] David Rodin, "The Ethics of Asymmetric War," in Richard Sorabji and David Rodin (eds.), *The Ethics of War: Shared Problems in Different Traditions* (Farnham, UK: Ashgate Publishing, 2006), pp. 153–168, at p. 160.

[56] William O'Brien, *The Conduct of Just and Limited War* (New York: Praeger, 1981), p. 35.

[57] The *ad bellum* dependence thesis might be represented in the criteria in other ways, such as by revising the rightful intention criterion to include an intention to fight a war justly.

[58] Larry May, *Aggression and Crimes against Peace* (Cambridge University Press, 2008), pp. 35, 113.

In defense of some form of an *ad bellum* dependence criterion, Larry May says: "Why should we think that a war that *cannot* or *is unlikely to* be waged with just tactics should ever be considered a just war from the outset?"[59] But there is an important difference between the claim that a war "cannot" and the claim that is "is unlikely to" be fought justly. The revised criterion corresponds roughly to the "is unlikely to" option. In regard to the "cannot" option, May offers this observation: "Think of a war that could be successfully waged only by annihilating the enemy State's cities ... It is questionable that such a war is just given the horrific consequences."[60]

Despite Walzer's explicit rejection of the dependence theses, he does argue implicitly for a "cannot" version of the dependence criterion. He gives some examples where the *ad bellum* independence thesis does not hold. One is the Vietnam War (1965–1973), in which, he argues, the only way that the United States could have won was with a war fought against civilians, making the war, if fought for victory, inevitably *in bello* unjust. (That is, if it were fought justly, it could not have been won.) The war could not be won justly. Here, he says, *jus ad bellum* and *jus in bello* "come together." Because the war could not be fought justly, it was *ad bellum* unjust.[61] Another example would be nuclear war. This implies that a weaker version of (DT1) is true, and it suggests a weaker version of the dependence criterion:

VIETNAM WAR

> *Ad bellum* dependence criterion (revision 2): a war must be such that it is reasonably expected that it *could be* won in accord with *jus in bello*.

Revision 1 may be referred to as the *justly fought* criterion, and revision 2 as the *justly winnable* criterion.

There are some arguments against the justly fought criterion. First, most *in bello* violations are committed by individual combatants, and some of these violations are effectively beyond the control of the leadership. The leadership can reduce *in bello* violations significantly by proper training and discipline of its combatants and by promulgating the proper rules of engagement, and, to the extent it fails in this regard, many of the violations would be its responsibility. But placing all of the responsibility for *in bello* violations on the leadership flies in the face of the moral division of labor between leaders (to whom *jus ad bellum* applies) and combatants

---

[59] *Ibid.*, p. 113, emphasis added.   [60] *Ibid.*, p. 114.
[61] Walzer, *Just and Unjust Wars*, pp. 195–196.

(to whom *jus in bello* mainly applies). Joseph Boyle remarks that "surely the inevitable but essentially private sins of soldiers – unless sanctioned or overlooked – do not necessarily flaw an otherwise justified war."[62] It seems implausible, given the inevitability of some *in bello* violations beyond the control of the leadership, that any such violations, by themselves, could make a war *ad bellum* unjust.

The problem lies partly in the one–many relation that exists between the actions to which *jus ad bellum* and *jus in bello* apply. For a given war, *jus ad bellum* applies to a single action, the initiation of war (or, at least, a small number of actions involving a small number of people in leadership positions), while *jus in bello* applies to a large number of actions involving a large number of combatants. It is a practical impossibility, and so not a reasonable expectation, that all of the latter actions would turn out to be just. The straightforward solution to this objection is to require only that a substantial portion of the actions in the war be just or that there are no or few egregious injustices in the conduct of the war. The criterion would then be:

> *Ad bellum* dependence criterion (revision 3): a war must be such that it is reasonably expected that it will be fought in *substantial* accord with *jus in bello*.

Of course, a difficulty this version poses is setting the threshold for substantial accord.

But there is another objection to the justly fought criterion represented by revision 3. Some military forces, due to their culture and training, are simply incapable of fighting with substantial *in bello* justice. One example might be the Russian army in its battle with rebels in the break-away province of Chechnya (beginning in 1994).[63] Of course, a state has an obligation to shape its military forces so that they will generally respect *jus in bello*, but this cannot be done overnight. If a state with a military that is unable to fight justly is invaded, it would not be able to fight a war that satisfied the dependence criterion, so that the *ad bellum* justice of its war would be under a cloud. This is an implausible implication. Again think of the Soviet Union in World War II when it was invaded by Nazi Germany. The sorry moral condition that the Soviet forces were probably in at the time

---

[62] Boyle, "Just War Doctrine," p. 161.
[63] Thanks to Per Ilsaas for this point and the example.

should not stand in the way of the claim that the Soviet Union was fighting a just defensive war. To take another example, consider a state that does not possess the technology it would need (but which it could have had, if it had devoted greater resources to military research in the past) to win a war without killing large numbers of civilians. Can it be denied the right to fight a defensive war? Note that this is also an objection to the justly winnable form of the *ad bellum* dependence criterion, given that the "could be won" in the formulation should be understood as "could be won with the military the state then has at hand." There is, then, some reason, though not conclusive reason, to regard the *ad bellum* dependence thesis, in any of its forms, as false.

3.8 *Jus ad bellum*: overall justice

Consider now the overall assessment of justice at the *ad bellum* level. When is a war just *on the whole*? How does satisfaction of the six (or seven) criteria relate to this overall judgment? There two related issues here. First, a question raised earlier: must a war satisfy all the *ad bellum* criteria to be just? Second, how permissive or restrictive of war overall should *jus ad bellum* be understood to be?

Must all the *ad bellum* criteria be met for a war to be just? Is the satisfaction of each of them a necessary condition for an overall judgment of justice, or is satisfying a subset of them sufficient for a just war? William O'Brien thinks they all are needed: "There are strong reasons for asserting that all of the conditions must be met. Such a requirement is consonant with the presumption against war and the positing of the just-war conditions as necessary to overcoming this presumption."[64] It seems reasonable, given the moral horror of war, to view just war theory as representing a *presumption against war*, and this supports the view that all the criteria must be satisfied, as O'Brien asserts. But it seems likely that there are few wars that satisfy all of the *ad bellum* criteria, so that few would be overall just. This is at odds with the wide-spread view that in most armed conflicts, one of the sides is just.

When we view a war as *ad bellum* just, we think primarily in terms of just cause. This seems to be the view of Michael Walzer, as just cause is

---

[64] O'Brien, *Just and Limited War*, p. 35.

the only one of the criteria to which he gives much attention, perhaps to the point of treating its satisfaction as sufficient for a war to be just. He says little about the other criteria, and he sometimes explicitly downplays their role. For example, he says that he does not discuss proportionality or last resort at length "because they [do] not seem to me … to help much in making the crucial moral distinctions."[65]

Overall *ad bellum* justice seems to be thought of in two ways, which we could label *full justice* and *prima facie justice*. A war would be fully just if it satisfies all of the criteria, but it could be *prima facie* just if it satisfies some (particular ones) of them. The judgment of *prima facie* justice would be subject to rebuttal and revision based on a consideration of the remaining criteria. Just cause clearly must be satisfied for *prima facie* justice. Just cause plays a special role among the criteria. For example, it is the criterion that shows that both sides in an armed conflict cannot be fighting a just war, so that if one side satisfies just cause, the other side's war cannot be just. In addition, some of the other criteria (such as proportionality and rightful intention) cannot be satisfied unless just cause is satisfied. If we did not have the idea of *prima facie* justice pegged to the just cause criterion, then the following argument might be conceivable. Imagine that powerful state M engages in aggression against weak state N, but that N's war is not fully just because, although just cause would be satisfied, some other criterion, such as proportionality, is not. M might then try to argue that its war is just because N's war is unjust. A focus on *prima facie* justice, as distinct from full justice, would blunt any such argument.

Now, consider the second question: how restrictive or permissive is *jus ad bellum*? In Chapter 1, we saw that the just war tradition occupies an interval between realism and pacifism, with different versions of just war theory occupying different points in that interval. Some versions of just war theory are less restrictive and closer to realism, while others are more restrictive and closer to pacifism. The possibility for this range of views is facilitated, in part, by the vagueness of the *ad bellum* criteria, which opens the theory up to different interpretations. The *permissivists*, as they may be called, favor a view of just war theory closer to realism; they are more likely to see war as an acceptable means of conducting international

---

[65] Walzer, *Just and Unjust Wars*, pp. xiii.

politics. In contrast, the *restrictivists* tend toward pacifism, endorsing the view that just war theory includes a presumption against war.

Permissivists argue that restrictivists do not take adequate account of political and military realities. First, they argue that a restrictive *jus ad bellum* is too simple, too black and white, to apply to wars in the real world, where the moral complexity and ambiguity are great. Second, they argue that a restrictive *jus ad bellum* does not allow political leaders sufficient latitude in using force to pursue justice and to protect their national interests. The first argument is especially critical of the role played by just cause in restrictivist theories, while the second is especially critical of the role played by the other criteria.

The first argument is similar to arguments that led historically to the regular war paradigm, discussed in the last chapter. The criterion of just cause may be clear in theory, but not in practice. First, the party that started an armed conflict cannot be easily determined often due to lack of sufficient information. Second, even with sufficient information, there are no dispassionate observers to arbitrate inevitable conflicts over the matter among the self-interested parties. Third, the answer as to who started the conflict is not always straightforwardly factual. For example, who was the aggressor in the American Civil War? The South fired the first shots, but they did so in response to the presence of the Union's military facility at Fort Sumter in South Carolina, from their perspective a clear aggression onto its territory. Fourth, even if we were confident about who started an armed conflict, it is not always clear that that party should bear complete moral responsibility for the conflict, as the just cause criterion seems to assume. The real world is simply less clear and straightforward than the theory. Adam Roberts observes: "Situations in which a clear and widely accepted distinction can be drawn between the just and unjust users of force are rare."[66]

While these points could be used to support the regular war paradigm, permissivists do not go that far. They see a continuing role for just cause, but understand it often to be unclear in its moral implications. They may, for example, understand just cause in terms of the idea of *comparative justice*,

---

[66] Roberts, "The Principle of Equal Application of the Laws of War," in David Rodin and Henry Shue (eds.), *Just and Unjust Warriors: The Moral and Legal Status of Soldiers* (Oxford University Press, 2008), pp. 226–254, at p. 248.

according to which armed conflicts generally have some justice and some injustice on each side. Each side has legitimate grievances against the other. There are "factors in the behavior of both sides that constitute contributory wrongs in the political situation that seems to require war as its solution," C. A. J. Coady notes.[67] The idea, as Gregory Reichberg puts it, is "that the rights and wrongs leading to war [are] distributed on both sides in such fashion that neither could claim an exclusive prerogative to use force."[68] In terms of just cause, neither side is completely in the right or completely in the wrong. Reflecting this view, theorists may ask, "which side is the *more* legitimate under the *jus ad bellum*," or say that we should go to war "only if we truly judge that there is substantially *more right* on our side than on his."[69] Permissivists take the idea of comparative justice as supporting their view because it makes war easier to justify in practice. Under comparative justice, judgments about which side has the just cause become more contestable, and neither side can be labeled as completely in the wrong.

The second argument against the restrictivists is based on the claim that a restrictive understanding of *jus ad bellum* does not allow leaders the political room they need to maneuver in order to pursue justice, to practice their statecraft, and to fulfill their obligations to protect their citizens. This argument, unlike the first, holds that more attention should be given to just cause and less to the other criteria. In this vein, James Turner Johnson argues against the "presumption against war" view of the restrictivists. Instead, he argues, just war theory should be understood to include a "presumption against injustice." He argues that the main concern in the just war tradition has been injustice, and force "provided the means to deal with it," while the concept "that force itself is a major problem originated only comparatively recently."[70] The presumption-against-war perspective puts "lesser, prudential considerations within *jus ad bellum* above major ones."[71] He observes that in contemporary discussions of just war theory,

---

[67] C. A. J. Coady, *Morality and Political Violence* (Cambridge University Press, 2008), p. 90.

[68] Gregorg Reichberg, "Just War and Regular War," in Gregorg Reichberg, Henrik Syse, and Endre Begby (eds.), *The Ethics of War: Classic and Contemporary Readings* (Oxford: Blackwell Publishing, 2006), p. 202.

[69] Roberts, "Equal Application," p. 248, emphasis added; Guthrie and Quinlan, *Just War Tradition*, p. 19, emphasis added.

[70] James Turner Johnson, "Just Cause Revisited," in Elliot Abrams (ed.), *Close Calls* (Washington, DC: Ethics and Public Policy Center, 1998), pp. 3–38, at pp. 27, 22.

[71] Johnson, "The Broken Tradition," *National Interest* (Fall 1996), p. 33.

the argument "has shifted away from the classic emphasis on the requirements of just cause, right authority, and right intention to the prudential
considerations of overall proportionality, last resort, and reasonable hope
of success."[72] The latter should be given less emphasis, leaving them more
to the judgment of leaders.

But these arguments against the restrictivists are not in the end con-
vincing. Against the first line of argument, note that the idea of comparative justice can cut both ways; it can be used by restrictivists as well
as permissivists. Restrictivists argue that a recognition that neither side
is completely in the right should cause states to behave with greater
moral caution, to acknowledge that their right to go to war is not as
strong as the standard idea of just cause might make them think. The
real world of war is so morally complicated that we cannot assign to
one side or the other in an armed conflict the full measure of justice.
The US Catholic Bishops observe: "The category of comparative justice is
designed to emphasize the presumption against war which stands at the
beginning of just-war teaching." As a result of the relativity of comparative justice: "Every party to a conflict should acknowledge the limits of
its 'just cause.'"[73]

The second argument against the restrictivists has some affin-
ities with the notion of tolerable divergence, mentioned in Chapter 1.
Tolerable divergence is the idea that, if it is to be practically relevant,
morality must not demand such sacrifice that it is likely to be generally
ignored. The second argument, in effect, is that because a restrictivist
presumption against war would hobble leaders in their ability to pursue
the legitimate interests of their states, it would fail the test of tolerable
divergence. But the case needs to be made that a restrictivist understanding is *in practice* intolerable and such as to make *jus ad bellum* irrelevant to
political leaders. While leaders tend to complain about any restrictions
put upon their freedom of action, it would have to be shown that war
could not be effectively conducted under a restrictivist understanding of
jus ad bellum.

---

[72] Johnson, "Just Cause Revisited," pp. 22–23, and "Broken Tradition," p. 34. The three
other criteria are not "prudential" in our sense, but moral.

[73] National Conference of Catholic Bishops, *The Challenge of Peace: God's Promise and our
Response* (United States Catholic Conference, 1983), paragraph 93. The bishops list
comparative justice as a separate criterion, in addition to just cause.

There are different ways to read the idea of a presumption against war. As a practical matter, it is about where the burden of proof lies in moral arguments for and against war. But more than this, the presumption against war seems to be a matter of how and which *ad bellum* criteria are emphasized. A presumption against injustice, which Johnson recommends, would focus on just cause and treat some of the other criteria as less important. A presumption against war would focus on these other criteria, especially last resort. For the idea of last resort, that war should be initiated only when there is no other choice, more than any other of the criteria, instantiates a presumption against war.

But the presumption against war has a more specific meaning, very much in line with the national defense paradigm and the post-war settlement. The spirit of the presumption is captured in the one of the labels given the post-war settlement by its critics: *jus contra bellum*, justice against war. Gregory Reichberg provides a helpful list of the features of presumption against war understood in this way: (1) a limitation of war to defensive war; (2) an emphasis on the reconciliation of states over the punishment of injustice; (3) a skepticism about the ability of leaders to make objective judgments of justice; (4) an emphasis on comparative justice; (5) a recognition that violence has an "inherent propensity," even when used for a just cause, "to exceed the measure of moral virtue."[74]

Points (3) and (5) on this list are salutary reminders of inherent features of all war that morally demand that we emphasize its avoidance, and they support a restrictivist understanding of *jus ad bellum*, which is characteristic of the national defense paradigm. But, as we saw in Chapter 2, there seems to have been a move away from the national defense paradigm in recent decades. Inis Claude argues that this is a return to the just war paradigm, which places greater importance on achieving justice through war than to maintaining peace. James Turner Johnson would agree that this is direction we ought to be taking. As Claude puts it:

> The world no longer seriously purports to accept the view that peace is unconditionally a higher value than justice. We have returned to the

[74] Gregory Reichberg, "Is there a Presumption against War in Aquinas's Ethics?" in Henrik Syse and Gregory M. Reichberg (eds.), *Ethics, Nationalism, and Just War: Medieval and Contemporary Perspectives* (Washington, DC: Catholic University Press, 2007), pp. 72–98, at p. 96.

medieval view that it is permissible and perhaps even desirable – and, conceivably, even mandatory – to fight to promote justice, broadly conceived. Evil ought to be overturned, and the good ought to be achieved by force if necessary.[75]

If we are indeed shifting away from the national defense paradigm to a view that gives greater importance to the use of violence to achieve justice, this suggests we are also shifting away from a restrictivist view of *jus ad bellum* and toward a more permissivist view. One contemporary manifestation of the shift away from the national defense paradigm is the growing acknowledgment of *humanitarian intervention* as a just form of warfare. We examine humanitarian intervention in the next chapter, where we should keep in mind the question of whether, as Claude and Johnson would suggest, this shift represents a move toward the permissivists' view. Indeed, the challenge posed by Claude for restrictivists, who appreciate the force of Reichberg's five features, but who recognize the legitimacy of humanitarian intervention, is to show that an allowance for humanitarian intervention does not lead to permissivism.

---

[75] Claude, "Just War," p. 94.

4   Sovereignty and human rights

> War … is so horrible, that nothing but mere Necessity, or true
> Charity, can make it lawful.
>
> Hugo Grotius[1]

> The law of nations may be deduced, first, from the general
> principles of right and justice applied to the concerns of individuals,
> and thence to the relations and duties of nations.
>
> Justice Story[2]

In the last chapter, we discussed *jus ad bellum* under the national defense paradigm, according to which only defensive war is justified. Given the priority principle, which is part of this idea of just cause, the first use of force is never justified.[3] This understanding of just cause is different from that during much of the history of the just war tradition. In particular, the just war paradigm, which characterized the tradition through the seventeenth century, did not accept the priority principle, and aggression was not the only wrong that could justify war. In this chapter, we continue our discussion of *jus ad bellum* by examining whether there is a need to revise our account of just cause in ways more consonant with the just war paradigm.

   In recent decades, a number of wars have been justified on humanitarian grounds. A *humanitarian intervention* is a war launched to rescue persons in another state suffering under a grave humanitarian crisis, such as genocide, mass enslavement, starvation, or ethnic cleansing, usually at the hands of their own government. Among the recent interventions

---

[1] Hugo Grotius, *The Rights of War and Peace*, trans. Jean Barbayrac (London: W. Innys, 1738), p. 507.

[2] Supreme Court Justice Story, *United States* v. *Le Jeune Eugenie*, 26 Federal Cases 832 (1822), pp. 846–848.

[3] Recall that preemptive war may fit this formula if the attack that is preempted is understood as already in progress.

widely viewed as justified on humanitarian grounds are India's invasion of East Pakistan (1971), which established the state of Bangladesh, the Vietnamese invasion of Cambodia (1978), which ended the genocidal Khmer Rouge regime, the Tanzanian invasion of Uganda (1979), which overthrew the murderous regime of Ida Amin, the Somalia intervention by the United States and others (1992), which made possible the delivery of needed humanitarian relief, the United States invasion of Haiti (1994) to reestablish a democratically elected president, and the Kosovo War (1999), an attack on Serbia by the United States and several European states, seeking to end the ethnic cleansing by Serbia of ethnic Albanians in Kosovo.

While humanitarian intervention has been controversial, both as a general concept and in its particular instances, it is commonly accepted that such a use of force is justified on some occasions. Yet this flies in the face of the national defense paradigm. It is a violation of the priority principle. To defenders of the national defense paradigm, it is simply aggression; a strict understanding of the paradigm leaves no room for a first use of force that is not aggression. Humanitarian intervention violates the sovereignty of the state that is attacked, which has committed no wrong against another state. It creates an exception to the national defense paradigm, which I will call the *humanitarian intervention exception*. I shall assume that this exception is morally acceptable and that humanitarian intervention is sometimes justified. There are critics of the humanitarian intervention exception, but much of the criticism is pragmatic or consequentialist rather than based on an in-principle defense of absolute sovereignty.[4] In this chapter, I take up the question of how *jus ad bellum* should be understood in order to accommodate the humanitarian intervention exception. To begin the discussion, consider the Kosovo War.

4.1 The Kosovo War

Following the dissolution of the Soviet Union and the achievement of independence by its former client states in Eastern Europe around 1990, one of

YUGOSLAVIA WAS NOT A SOVIET CLIENT STATE!.

---

[4] For some criticisms, see Adam Roberts, "The Road to Hell: A Critique of Humanitarian Intervention," *Harvard International Review* 16, no. 1 (Fall 1993), pp. 10–13, and Jennifer Welsh, "Taking Consequences Seriously: Objections to Humanitarian Intervention," in Jennifer Welsh (ed.), *Humanitarian Intervention and International Relations* (Oxford University Press, 2004), pp. 52–68.

them, Yugoslavia, underwent dramatic political turmoil. The Yugoslavian state had encompassed several distinct ethnic groups, including Serbs, Croats, Bosniaks, Slovenes, and Albanians, and in the 1990s, as the political force of the central government weakened, the centrifugal force of their strong group identities came to the fore. Yugoslavia broke into several ethnically based states, and ethnic tensions were severe in some ethnically mixed areas that sought independence from the central government, controlled by the Serbs. A murderous civil war was fought in Bosnia between 1992 and 1995, including genocide and ethnic cleansing[5] on the part of the Serbs (and others) seeking to establish their own ethnic state within Bosnia. The war, which included an extended, murderous siege of the city of Sarajevo, dragged on for a number of months before the United States and Western Europe (under NATO, the North Atlantic Treaty Organization) got involved militarily, leading to an end to the conflict.

Another area of turmoil was Kosovo, a largely (80 percent) ethnic Albanian area which also sought independence, but which was still firmly under the control of the Serbian rulers of the rump state of Yugoslavia. In 1989, the president of this state, Slobodan Milošević, stripped Kosovo of the autonomous status it had been granted in 1974 by a former ruler of Yugoslavia. Milošević, playing to Serbian nationalism, but also responding to concern about the Albanian treatment of the minority Serbian population, stripped Kosovo of its autonomy and instituted a growing political repression, including efforts to force ethnic Albanians out of the country. In the early 1990s, the Kosovar Albanians responded to the repression nonviolently, staging peaceful protests and setting up alternative governmental and social institutions parallel to the official ones controlled by the Serbs.[6] Later in the decade, armed conflict between the Serb military and the Kosovo Liberation Army grew in intensity, and NATO began with increasing urgency to warn Serbia off of its militant, ethnically driven course. A Serb military offensive in 1998 killed 1,500 Kosovar Albanians

[5] Ethnic cleansing is forcing members of an ethnic group out of a given geographical area. It usually involves large-scale killing (and so may also be considered a form of genocide) in order to create the fear that will drive other members of the group out of the area as refugees.

[6] The nonviolent struggle was led by Ibrahim Rugova (1944–2006), known as the "Gandhi of the Balkans." In support of his movement's efforts, he asserted: "The Slaughterhouse is not the only form of struggle."

and drove thousands from the country. In the fall of 1998, the UN Security Council, in two resolutions, demanded that Serbia stop its assault against the civilian population of Kosovo, and NATO threatened air strikes. A brokered deal collapsed, and NATO began air strikes against Serbia on March 24, 1999 to force the Serbs to stop their ethnic repression. No NATO ground troops were used. The air assault included over 14,000 strike missions and lasted for eleven weeks, before Serbia agreed to withdraw from Kosovo. By the beginning of NATO's attacks, it is estimated that Serbia had forced about 200,000 ethnic Albanians out of Kosovo, but once the air attacks began, Serbia picked up the pace and viciousness of its ethnic cleansing. By the end of the war, roughly 750,000 Kosovars were international refugees.[7]

The Kosovo War was controversial for the way in which it was conducted, especially NATO's exclusive reliance on air power, which did great damage to the infrastructure of Serbia, seriously harming the civilian population. NATO justified deliberate attacks on infrastructure targets on the grounds that they were "dual use," meaning that they served military as well as civilian purposes. The reliance on air power allowed the Serbian forces within Kosovo, who could not be effectively attacked by high-flying aircraft, free rein to continue the ethnic cleansing while the war lasted. In addition, the war itself was fought without the backing of the UN Security Council, raising the criticism that it violated international law. (NATO did not put the war to a Council vote because it faced certain veto by China and Russia.) But fewer criticized the war *because* it was a humanitarian intervention. Many critics of the war accepted the moral principles on which it was fought. The war led to the first indictment of a serving head of state, Milošević, for crimes against humanity by the International War Crimes Tribunal in The Hague. He was eventually turned over to the Court by Serbia, but after engaging in extensive stalling tactics, he died in custody before the completion of his trial.

The humanitarian intervention exception seems firmly established in our contemporary understanding of the morality of war. But the exception appears to be inconsistent with the just cause criterion of the national defense paradigm. How is this to be explained? There are at least three lines of response.

---

[7] For this discussion, I drew in part from Adam Roberts, "NATO's 'Humanitarian War' over Kosovo," *Survival* 41, no. 3 (Autumn 1999), pp. 102–123.

(R1) The inconsistency is merely apparent; the humanitarian intervention exception can be accounted for through the national defense paradigm.

(R2) The inconsistency is real, and so the humanitarian intervention exception requires a new understanding of just cause and a new paradigm for *jus ad bellum*.

(R3) The inconsistency is real, but it is representative of a larger inconsistency that calls into question *jus ad bellum* as a whole.

We will examine each of these responses below, beginning with (R1).

4.2 The domestic analogy and state sovereignty

The moral foundation of the national defense paradigm is the *domestic analogy*. As one individual M is justified in attacking another, N, only if M is under attack by N (or is aiding someone who is under attack by N), a state S is justified in attacking another state T, only if S is under attack by T (or is aiding another state which is under attack by T). The analogy is between individual autonomy and state sovereignty.

State sovereignty is the moral value to which the domestic analogy refers.[8] But does sovereignty have the value thus attributed to it? The notion of state sovereignty is the problematic heart of the national defense paradigm. Sovereignty is related to the *non-intervention principle*, the rule that no state should intervene militarily in the affairs of other states, except in self-defense. Sovereignty is the discretionary power of a state to control what goes on within its borders. The idea is related to the well-known claim of the German sociologist Max Weber (1864–1920) that "the state is the form of human community that (successfully) lays claim to the *monopoly of the legitimate physical violence* within a particular territory." The state's ability to exercise sovereign discretion arises from the effective monopoly it has on violence. But the content of sovereignty goes beyond this. Weber continues: "The state is regarded as the sole source of the 'right' to use violence."[9] There is an ambiguity on the term *right*, suggested by Weber's

---

[8] Charles Beitz, *Political Theory and International Relations*, new edn. (Princeton University Press, 1999), p. 122.

[9] Max Weber, "Politics as a Vocation," reprinted in Michael Morgan (ed.), *Classics of Moral and Political Theory*, 4th edn. (Indianapolis, IN: Hackett Publishing, 2005), pp. 1213–1249, at pp. 1213–1214.

scare quotes. Is the state's discretionary right to use violence domestically merely a function of its power and its claims to legitimacy (might makes right), or is it a moral right?

There are two related aspects of state sovereignty. *Internal sovereignty* is a state's control of what goes on within its borders; it assumes *external sovereignty*, which is a state's freedom from external interference. The non-intervention principle is how external sovereignty is understood under the national defense paradigm. A sovereign state has territorial integrity and political independence. Absent its aggression, it is free to conduct its own internal affairs, free of forceful interference by other states. But under the regular war paradigm, as we saw in Chapter 2, external sovereignty represents a different form of discretion, a state's discretion to use its force abroad as it sees fit. Under this conception, the external sovereignty of one state is at odds with the internal sovereignty of another. Yoram Dinstein notes that: "State sovereignty has a variable content … The contemporary right to employ inter-state force in self-defense is no more 'inherent' in sovereignty than the discredited right to resort to force at all times."[10] External sovereignty can mean either *freedom from* external interference, as it does under the national defense paradigm, or *freedom to* interfere in the affairs of others, as it does under the regular war paradigm. The content of the idea of sovereignty is not constant, but changes with the historical context.

In the domestic analogy external sovereignty is understood as freedom from outside interference. In the analogy, the analogue of state sovereignty is individual autonomy. Autonomy represents the dignity of persons; it is what makes individuals morally important. It is their capacity for freedom, their power of choice, their ability to determine their own lives. It is the source of the idea that individuals have inalienable moral rights, which other people and all social and political systems are obligated to respect. Autonomy rights, also called *human rights*, do not depend on the political context in which a person exists or the political consequences of recognizing them. Human rights apply to everyone everywhere. Autonomy has intrinsic moral value; its value is not merely extrinsic or instrumental, not dependent on context. According to the domestic analogy, state sovereignty has analogous characteristics. But does it?

---

[10] Dinstein, *War – Aggression and Self-Defense,* 4th edn. (Cambridge University Press, 2005), p. 180.

Autonomy is the power of an individual to lead his own life. Defenders of the domestic analogy claim that states have the analogous power of *self-determination*. It is morally important that both individuals and states be able to chart their own destiny, and this is the moral grounding of both the non-intervention principle for states and the right of individuals to non-interference. In each case, a party is wronged when force is used against it (absent its aggression). Indeed, the self-determination of states is often seen as an important value in international affairs, and it is appealed to in opposition to various forms of control some states seek to exercise over others.

But there are problems with the idea of state self-determination.[11] For a state to be capable of self-determination, it must, in some relevant sense, be a *self*. An individual is a self because she has the power of choice, which makes her a responsible moral agent. Is the state a self in this sense? There are theorists who take this view. Emer de Vattel claims that a state "has her affairs and her interests; she deliberates and takes resolutions in common; thus becoming a moral person, who possesses an understanding and a will peculiar to herself, and is susceptible of obligations and rights."[12] Vattel sees the state as functioning like an individual, so being a determining self, and such a perspective seems necessary for the state to be appropriately similar to the individual, as required by the domestic analogy.

One rough way to understand the comparison between state and individual entailed by the analogy is in terms of the metaphysical concept of *holism*. An individual is a self because all of his parts are integrated into a whole, and this is necessary for a self to be a responsible moral agent. A self is a whole, more than the sum of its parts. Vattel sees the state in this way, but such a view is not readily sustainable. According to philosopher Douglas Lackey, states are "aggregates of persons [which] do not possess consciousness and 'make choices' only in a metaphorical sense," and speaking "of the 'right of nations' is like speaking about 'the average American family,' something that doesn't really exist, though rights exist and families exist."[13] If the state is not a whole in

---

[11] Beitz, *Political Theory*, pp. 92–95.

[12] Emer de Vattel, *The Law of Nations*, ed. Bella Kapossy and Richard Whatmore (Indianapolis, IN: Liberty Fund, 2008), p. 67.

[13] Douglas Lackey, *The Ethics of War and Peace* (Englewood Cliffs, NJ: Prentice-Hall, 1989), p. 38.

this sense, it cannot be self-determining in a way that an individual is self-determining.

If states are not wholes in this sense, then they have no moral status of their own. Their moral status, the respect they are owed by other states, derives from the moral status of their members, individual citizens. (To see the state in this way is to see it in *individualistic* rather than holistic terms.) On this view, states have only extrinsic moral value, not the sort of intrinsic moral value possessed by individuals. The value of state sovereignty and self-determination is extrinsic, and this value is derived from that of its members. The state has no intrinsic moral value. This opens up the idea that the moral status of sovereignty, the respect a state is due, depends on the moral respect it shows its own citizens, which would call into question the status of the non-intervention principle.[14]

But there may be other ways to apply the domestic analogy. Michael Walzer is a supporter of the national defense paradigm who advances this position through appeal to the domestic analogy. In his account, the analogue of the individual is not the state as such, but the community that the state normally represents. Speaking of that community, Walzer claims: "Over a long period of time, shared experiences and cooperative activity of many different kinds shape a common life." If aggression occurs, the protection the state provides to the community through defensive war "extends not only to the lives and liberties of individuals but also to their shared life and liberty, the independent community they have made."[15] Walzer distinguishes between two kinds of lives and liberties: (1) the *common life* of the community with its liberty and (2) individual lives of citizens with their liberty. The state may serve to protect them both. The common life is the product of individual decisions and interactions taken collectively, so that the state's defense of the common life is, Walzer argues, a defense of a special kind of individual right, the right of individuals to non-interference with the common life they have collectively created. Self-determination becomes the liberty of the community, not the state, to chart its own path. I will refer to such rights as *common life rights*. The obligation of a state not to engage in aggression is due to its need to respect the common life rights of the citizens of the would-be

---

14 Beitz, *Political Theory*, p. 69.
15 Michael Walzer, *Just and Unjust Wars* (New York: Basic Books, 1977), p. 54.

object of attack, as well as the more familiar kind of individual rights based on their individual lives and liberties. These latter, more familiar rights we will refer to as *liberal rights*. Liberal rights are held by individuals because they are individuals, not because they are participants in a common life. It is important to note that Walzer explicitly disavows any Vattel-like talk of the state as a moral person, and its holistic implications. "States are not in fact like individuals (because they are collections of individuals)."[16]

Walzer endorses the humanitarian intervention exception, but the question is how he does so, given his understanding of the domestic analogy. He argues that if we see the moral basis of the non-intervention principle as the need to respect common-life rights, the domestic analogy sometimes requires that its non-interventionary implications be suspended. Consider the sort of severe humanitarian crisis he argues could justify humanitarian intervention, involving rights violations within a state that "shock the moral conscience of mankind." In such a situation, "when a government turns savagely upon its own people," Walzer says, "we must doubt the very existence of a political community to which the idea of self-determination might apply."[17] It is not completely clear what Walzer means here. That idea seems to be that in a severe humanitarian crisis, the state no longer represents the common life of the community. When that is the case, the non-intervention principle no longer stands in the way of intervening with the actions of the state in order to protect the liberal rights of those under threat in the humanitarian crisis. Presumably, the common life rights remain in effect, but because the state no longer protects those rights (as evidenced by its massive violations of liberal rights), those rights no longer protect the state from interference. But one problem with this interpretation is that a military attack, due to the damage it would do, would probably violate common life rights, which means that they would still stand in the way of the intervention.

Walzer's account of the humanitarian intervention exception makes clear that the moral value of state sovereignty is derivative from the moral value of individuals. The value of state sovereignty is extrinsic, depending on the state's respect for the rights of its citizens, where the intrinsic value lies. The rights of states against intervention are derivative from the

[16] *Ibid.*, p. 72.   [17] *Ibid.*, pp. 101, 107.

individual rights of their citizens; they "derive ultimately from the rights of individuals, and from them they take their force."[18] But this picture is complicated for Walzer because of the different kinds of individual rights he posits, liberal rights and common life rights, which function differently in this regard. For Walzer, the rights of states against intervention derive directly from the common life rights of the community which the state represents. So long as the state represents the common life rights of the community, sovereignty stands inviolate, irrespective of whether the state respects its citizens' liberal rights. It is only when violations of liberal rights become massive, at levels that "shock the moral conscience of mankind," that the community's common life rights are no longer represented by the state and intervention may occur. Only then is there a moral opening for other states to act to protect the citizens' liberal rights. In this sense, respect for common life rights takes precedence over protection of liberal rights; common life rights are lexically prior to liberal rights. So, for Walzer, the state's respect for its citizens' liberal rights affects sovereignty only indirectly and at the margin, only when their massive violation by the state entail that the common life rights no longer protect the state. Only to this extent is the moral content of sovereignty conditional on the state's protecting the liberal rights of its citizens.

Because Walzer accepts some humanitarian intervention, state sovereignty may sometimes be violated, so that his theory is one of *conditional sovereignty*, but the conditions are very weak. In general, sovereignty is conditional when its ability to protect the state from outside interference is conditioned on (or limited by) the state's internal or domestic behavior, specifically. Absent the satisfaction of the condition, outside intervention may be justified. In general, theories of conditional sovereignty condition sovereignty on a state's respect for its citizens' liberal rights. The conditions in Walzer's theory are distinctive, and weaker, due to the priority he gives to common life rights over liberal rights. Among theories of conditional sovereignty, his is among the weakest.

In assessing Walzer's theory, it is helpful to note the distinction between *nations* and *states*. Nations are groups of people strongly connected by a common ancestry, history, and/or culture. The community that possesses common life rights for Walzer is similar to a nation. There is no one-to-

---

[18] *Ibid.*, p. 53.

one correspondence between states and nations because not all nations have states (for example, the Kurdish nation is spread among several states, including Turkey, Iraq, and Iran) and not all states encompass a single nation (for example, Britain includes the English, the Scots, and the Welsh). This lack of correspondence poses a problem for theories of sovereignty that condition the moral protection sovereignty provides on the nation. The American philosopher David Luban notes that "the concept of sovereignty systematically and fallaciously confuses a nation and its state, granting illegitimate states a right to which they are not entitled."[19] This should not count as a criticism of Walzer because he does not identify nation or community with state. But the wide-spread lack of correspondence between nations and states may raise a problem for him, namely, whether his theory of conditional sovereignty can have much relevance to the world given that few states could represent a single unified nation.

One criticism of Walzer is that common life rights are not really individual rights at all, so that his theory would not escape the criticisms of a holistic approach to sovereignty discussed earlier. There are different ways this is argued. One is to claim that these rights cannot be individual rights because individual rights serve to protect individuals in certain ways from the conduct of other individuals. For example, a person's right to life is her right that no other individual take her life. But common life rights lack this characteristic. They protect nothing of mine from other members of my society, but rather protect something which is partly mine (the common life) from external interference. Common life rights cannot protect me from other members of my society because it is my interactions with them that define what the common life is, what is to be protected. For Walzer, my common life rights stand in the way of efforts by outsiders to protect my liberal rights from encroachment by my state. Walzer seems to want to include common life rights as individual rights, along with standard liberal rights, in order to avoid commitment to a holistic perspective. But, on his view, an oppressive state can appeal to its citizens' common life rights to immunize itself from outside efforts to protect their liberal rights. Walzer's set of individual rights, including common life rights, is, in a sense, self-confounding, in that there is built-in opposition between

---

[19] David Luban, "Just War and Human Rights," *Philosophy & Public Affairs* 9, no. 2 (Winter 1980), pp. 160–181, at p. 169.

liberal rights and common life rights. While liberal rights may occasionally conflict with one another, they are not in systemic opposition as liberal rights and common life rights seem to be, given the prevalence of oppressive governments. Walzer endorses the apparent paradox that individuals "have a right to a state within which their rights are violated."[20]

A related criticism is a comment on Walzer's claim that, in the case of most authoritarian governments, we should recognize "a morally necessary assumption: that there exists a certain 'fit' between the community and its government and that the state is 'legitimate'."[21] The point is that oppressive governments may represent the common life of their communities because their stance toward liberal rights fits the traditions of the community. Charles Beitz argues that this assumption is often quite implausible, especially in the developing world, where it "appears quite clearly false that authoritarian regimes arose from indigenous political processes, reflecting widely shared, traditional values, and without significant external influences."[22] Adopting a different tack, Walzer at points presents his argument in epistemological terms, basing his general injunction against intervention on our *ignorance* of the internal workings of other societies. On this weaker version of his argument, the claim is not that most illiberal states are in fact legitimate, but rather that, given our ignorance, we should presume that they are unless their illegitimacy becomes "radically apparent," as in cases of genocide. But Beitz's point is that a basic understanding of political forces at work in the developing world makes illegitimacy radically apparent in a much broader range of cases than Walzer would allow.[23] It seems, in any case, that Walzer's shift to an epistemological argument is at odds with his basic idea of common life rights, according to which such rights hold, not simply that they should be *assumed* to hold, short of genocide.

These criticisms reveal the theoretical price that Walzer pays for attempting to defend, on grounds of individual rights, a position usually

---

[20] Michael Walzer, "The Moral Standing of States: A Response to Four Critics," *Philosophy & Public Affairs* 9, no. 3 (1980), pp. 209–229, at p. 226.

[21] *Ibid.*, p. 212.

[22] Charles Beitz, "Nonintervention and Communal Integrity," *Philosophy & Public Affairs* 9, no. 4 (1980), pp. 385–391, at p. 386, note 2.

[23] See also David Luban, "The Romance of the Nation-State," *Philosophy & Public Affairs* 9, no. 4 (summer 1980), pp. 392–397.

defended on the grounds of non-derivative state sovereign rights. By moving to a theory of conditional sovereignty, Walzer opens himself up to criticisms from proponents of other theories of conditional sovereignty. These theories typically place much stronger conditions on sovereignty because they do not have a category like that of common life rights, respect for which take precedence over defense of liberal rights. Walzer's attempt to explain the humanitarian intervention exception is theoretically problematic.

A shift from Walzer's theory to a theory that conditions sovereignty exclusively on a state's respect for liberal rights represents a shift from an (R1) response to an (R2) response. An (R2) response recognizes the need to move beyond the national defense paradigm in order to explain the humanitarian intervention exception. Charles Beitz characterizes this shift as a move from a *morality of states* to a *cosmopolitan morality*.[24] The national defense paradigm, following the domestic analogy, is a morality of states because it treats states as its basic moral units. An approach that conditions sovereignty on a state's respect for liberal rights, is, in contrast, a cosmopolitan approach, in that it would base justification on rights that are universal among individuals. Under such an approach, the wrongs that provide a just cause for war are wrongs to individuals, not directly to states. The effort to reconstruct *jus ad bellum* in terms of individual rights (without common life rights) requires a switch to what I will call the *human rights paradigm*.

4.3 Humanitarian intervention and the human rights paradigm

Consider the most basic liberal right, the right to life. States sometimes do a fair job of protecting this right for most of their citizens most of the time. Individuals have often had a better chance of having their right to life respected and protected by their own state than by trusting to the kindness of international strangers (not to say that their chances were that good in either case). Even those enslaved or oppressed were likely to fare worse at the hands of a foreign invader. The fact that aggression would generally

[24] Charles Beitz, "Bounded Morality: Justice and the State in World Politics," *International Organization* 33, no. 3 (Summer 1979), pp. 405–424, at p. 406. Also Beitz, *Political Theory.*

decrease the life prospects of the citizens of the target state could serve as a justification for defensive war. But in recent decades, this assumption has weakened in many parts of the world. In both capability and intention many states have become more oppressive and murderous toward their citizens. This, along with growth in the consciousness of the importance of human rights and an awareness of their violation through the media, has meant that states are now sometimes motivated to intervene to protect citizens of other states from the depredations of their own governments. As Walzer notes: "It isn't too much of an exaggeration to say that the greatest danger most people face in the world today comes from their own states, and the chief dilemma of international politics is whether people in danger should be rescued by military forces from the outside."[25]

The result is an increase in the occasions in which humanitarian intervention may be justified, and the resultant need to seek an understanding of *jus ad bellum* that takes account of this fact. The difficulties with Walzer's account of the humanitarian intervention exception gives us reason to abandon efforts to account for this exception in terms of the national defense paradigm. What we seem to require instead is an account of *jus ad bellum* grounded in individual liberal rights rather than the rights of states or common life rights as Walzer understands them. This is the human rights paradigm.

Here is an analogy that may help to explain the proposed switch in paradigms. Just war theory is now like physics was at the start of the twentieth century, when Einstein's theories of relativity replaced Newton's physics. Einstein recognized that Newton's physics explained the motion of objects in our experience, but Einstein's theory implied that objects behaved very differently at great velocities. Not until later in the century would tests be developed to observe that very fast-moving objects conformed to Einstein's rather than Newton's paradigm. These new experiences showed the need to switch to Einstein's paradigm.[26] This switch in paradigms is similar in some ways to the switch from the national defense paradigm to the human rights paradigm. In the past century we have been aware of situations where military intervention might plausibly be a better way to

---

[25] Walzer, *Just and Unjust Wars*, 3rd edn. (New York: Basic Books, 2000), p. xi.
[26] Einstein did not base his theory on such experience, but rather on theoretical considerations. The theory could not be tested on such objects until decades later.

protect individual rights than a blanket rule of non-intervention, but the old paradigm, the national defense paradigm, endorsed the blanket rule. Thus the need for a new *ad bellum* paradigm, the human rights paradigm. But as Einstein had to show that his theory could explain what Newton's did, in addition to the new experiences, we must show that the human rights paradigm can justify traditional defensive wars, as well as humanitarian intervention.

To introduce a discussion of the human rights paradigm, consider some further points about military intervention, in general, and humanitarian intervention, in particular.

The priority principle is the rule that a state should not be the first to use force against another state, and aggression is military force that violates that principle. This understanding would make humanitarian intervention, which violates the principle, a form of aggression. But humanitarian intervention, if it is sometimes justified, should not be seen as aggression because aggression is a *moralized concept*, meaning that any war labeled aggression is understood to be unjust.[27] Thus, we need to abandon the priority principle and admit that some wars involving the first use of force are justified. This requires an intermediate concept like *intervention* that lies between aggression and defense. Consider this list of moral categories of war: (a) defense; (b) intervention; and (c) aggression. The national defense paradigm recognizes only defense and aggression. The addition of intervention adds a morally relevant category to the way we think about *jus ad bellum*. Intervention is different from defense because it involves a first use of force, and it is different from aggression because it can sometimes be justified. In this list, (a) is justified, (c) is not, and (b) sometimes is and sometimes is not.

The distinction between intervention and aggression may be cast in terms of motive. Aggression typically exhibits the sort of negative or vicious motives that concerned Augustine, such as greed, lust, or desire to dominate. In contrast, behind intervention, whether justified or not, are generally neutral or virtuous motives, such as benevolence or fear (which is also a motive for defense). In the last chapter, we discussed *preventive intervention*, which we called preventive war, whose motive is fear

---

[27] On the idea of a moralized concept, see Darrel Mollendorf, *Cosmopolitan Justice* (Boulder, CO: Westview Press, 2002), p. 104.

of future attack. Preventive intervention is unjustified. Now we consider humanitarian intervention, whose motive is generally benevolence, and which is sometimes justified. Other forms of intervention are discussed in Chapter 7.

While the occasional justification of humanitarian intervention has only recently come to be generally accepted, in contrast to the way it is generally viewed under the national defense paradigm, it has a longer pedigree in the just war tradition. Hugo Grotius asks, "Whether we have a just Cause for War with another Prince, in order to relieve his Subjects from their Oppression under him?" He answers yes, because: "If the Injustice be visible … as no good Man living can approve of, the Right of human Society shall not be therefore excluded."[28] Indeed, we can trace the theoretical basis for humanitarian intervention back to Augustine, who argued that force should be used not in defense of oneself, but in defense of others.[29] Augustine and Grotius speak out of the just war paradigm, and this suggests that there may be some overlap between that older paradigm and the human rights paradigm. Each justifies a first use of force.

In a discussion of just war theory, Elizabeth Anscombe offers this criticism of the national defense paradigm: "The present-day conception of 'aggression' … is a bad one. Why *must* it be wrong to strike the first blow in a struggle? The only question is, who is in the right, if anyone is." Striking the first blow is not always wrong, as the priority principle would have it. To provide an example, she compares two military policies of Lord Palmerston (1784–1865), a nineteenth-century British politician and prime minister: the Opium Wars, intended to force China to open up to Western trade, and his efforts at the suppression of the Atlantic slave trade. Both of these policies involved the first use of force, but "there is no doubt that he was a monster in the one thing [the Opium Wars], and a just man in the other [suppressing the slave trade]."[30] His military actions against the slave

---

[28] Grotius, *Rights of War*, pp. 1159–1161. The phrase "as no good Man living can approve of" echoes the phrase used by Walzer, actions that "shock the moral conscience of mankind." *Just and Unjust Wars*, p. 107.

[29] Gregory Reichberg, "Jus ad Bellum," in Larry May (ed.), *War: Essays in Political Philosophy* (New York: Cambridge University Press, 2008), pp. 11–29, at p. 23.

[30] Elizabeth Anscombe, "War and Murder," in E. Anscombe (ed.), *Ethics, Religion, and Politics* (Oxford: Blackwell, 1981), pp. 51–61, at p. 52. Palmerston was reported to have said: "I will not talk of non-intervention, for it is not an English word."

trade were a form of humanitarian intervention, and morally justified despite being a first use of force.

Humanitarian intervention is a military response to a severe humanitarian crisis within another state, a response designed to ameliorate or end the human rights abuses that constitute that crisis. In addition to genocide and ethnic cleansing, human rights abuses may include deprivation of basic necessities, as in cases of mass famine. Humanitarian intervention is distinct from both *humanitarian assistance*, provision of welcomed aid in the case of natural disasters, and *humanitarian interference*, non-military forms of coercion, such as economic boycotts, meant to end human rights abuses. These three forms are sometimes mixed, for example, intervention and assistance can go together, as in the United States intervention in Somalia in 1992, where military force was used to create the order and stability necessary for the successful distribution of assistance to the starving. While humanitarian assistance is welcomed by the victims, it sometimes requires military force as well either because the situation is politically chaotic (as in Somalia) or because the government seeks to avoid the outside scrutiny that assistance would bring. One example of the latter is resistance to aid by the military government of Myanmar (formerly Burma), which suffered a devastating cyclone in 2008. The target of a humanitarian intervention can be a *normal state* (where the government is fully in control), an *inept state* (where the government is only partly in control), or a *failed state* (where there is little or no functioning central government). In recent years, humanitarian crises have been occurring more often in inept or failed states, where the crisis is usually due, in part, to the depredations of militia forces beyond the government's control.

Humanitarian intervention is a form of *rescue*, its goal being to rescue individuals caught in humanitarian crises. (Indeed, under the human rights paradigm, this is true of all justified wars, including defensive wars.) The purpose of the intervention is to prevent rights violations, not to punish a state for the violations it has already committed. The intervention must be undertaken in the midst of a crisis, when there are still violations to be avoided, not after it is over. Humanitarian intervention may involve either *mere rescue, rescue through regime change*, or *rescue through political reconstruction*. In the case of mere rescue, the rights violations may be ended without the need to overthrow the regime. In the case of rescue through regime change, the regime is removed as a necessary step in achieving the humanitarian ends. In the case of rescue through political reconstruction, sustained efforts at "nation building," beyond simple regime change, are required to end the abuses. If the state itself is the chief rights violator, often the only way to achieve rescue is to overthrow the regime, which is then likely to require subsequent efforts at political reconstruction.[31]

Argentine legal scholar Fernando Tesón offers a cosmopolitan account of humanitarian intervention elaborated in terms of individual rights.[32] According to Tesón, state sovereignty has no intrinsic moral value, only a derivative or instrumental value, dependent on the extent to which the state promotes the protection of individual rights. Morally acceptable humanitarian intervention is "the proportionate international use or threat of military force, undertaken in principle by a liberal government or alliance, aimed at ending tyranny or anarchy, welcomed by the victims, and consistent with the doctrine of double effect."[33] Some of the clauses deserve comment. "Tyranny" and "anarchy" are political conditions that tend to involve systematic violations of individual rights (though it would have been better had he used the idea of individual rights violations directly in the definition). The stipulation that humanitarian intervention must "cause more good than harm" is the requirement that it satisfy the proportionality criterion, which we discuss in the next section.[34]

That the intervention must be "welcomed by the victims" is, presumably, to ensure that the state conduct that justifies intervention is in fact a violation of rights. If the apparent victims would not choose to be spared the conduct that appears to victimize them, there would be no evidence that their rights were being violated. For Tesón, however, the consent in question is not actual consent, but *ideal consent*, meaning that it is determined by the answer to a hypothetical question: would the victims consent to the intervention, assuming that they were rational and aware of the risk that innocent persons, including themselves, could be killed in the war? Lastly, Tesón's stipulation that intervention must be in accord with

[31] Michael Walzer, "Regime Change and Just War," *Dissent* (Summer 2006), pp. 103–111.
[32] Fernando Tesón, "The Liberal Case for Humanitarian Intervention," in J. Holzgrefe and Robert Keohane (eds.), *Humanitarian Intervention: Ethical, Legal, and Political Dilemmas* (Cambridge University Press, 2003), pp. 93–129.
[33] *Ibid.*, p. 94.
[34] *Ibid.*, p. 114. Presumably by "good" here, Tesón means the avoidance of evil or harm.

the doctrine of double effect brings *jus in bello* into the discussion.[35] The doctrine permits *some* killing of innocent people, as long as their deaths are merely foreseen, not intended, as we discuss in Chapters 5 and 6.

Tesón's and Walzer's accounts of humanitarian intervention differ substantially in theory, as one represents the national defense paradigm and the other the human rights paradigm. According to Tesón, they also differ substantially in practice, as his theory would, in principle, allow humanitarian intervention in all cases of tyranny or anarchy, while Walzer would see many such cases as ones where the state is protected from intervention by its support for the common life rights of the community.[36] The reason for this difference is that common life rights play no role in Tesón's account. This raises the *scope question*, the question of the scope or range of cases in which humanitarian intervention would be justified. This is the question of where to draw the line between justified and unjustified humanitarian intervention. In answering the scope question, we must consider, as we do shortly, the proportionality criterion under the human rights paradigm.

The cosmopolitan approach provides a justification not only for humanitarian intervention, but for defensive war as well. This is why it represents a new *ad bellum* paradigm. Considered theoretically, humanitarian intervention is not an exception; it only appears so from the perspective of the national defense paradigm. Humanitarian intervention is simply one sort of case where the use of military force may be justified in terms of the general moral principle that a state may act to aid victims of human rights violations. So, the new approach needs to show how defensive war may be justified in these terms as well. The basic idea is that defensive war is justified by a state's protecting the rights of its own citizens. David Luban has advanced the more general position.[37] He argues that sovereignty is conditional on a state's respect for the rights of its citizens. As a result, "we should be able to define *jus ad bellum* directly in terms of human rights, without the needless detour of talk about states." This means that just cause should be formulated in terms of threatened human rights

---

[35] *Ibid.*, pp. 119–121, 115–117.

[36] *Ibid.*, p. 104. Tesón also says that intervention would be justified only in cases that are "beyond the pale" (p. 98), seeming to echo Walzer's limiting of intervention to cases that "shock the moral conscience of mankind."

[37] See Luban, "Just War and Human Rights."

violations rather than the sovereign rights of states.[38] With sovereignty being conditional, states drop out of the equation.

Based on these distinctions, Luban offers a definition of just and unjust war. (1) A just war is "(i) a war in defense of socially basic human rights (subject to proportionality); or (ii) a war of self-defense against an unjust war." (2) An unjust war is "(i) a war subversive of human rights, whether socially basic or not, which is also (ii) not a war in defense of socially basic human rights."[39] One problem with this definition is that, in separating the two clauses in (1), Luban does not make clear the unity behind the human rights paradigm, as (i) humanitarian intervention and (ii) defensive war are justified on the same grounds. Also his formulation suggests that proportionality applies to humanitarian interventions but not to defensive wars. In any case, Luban provides an initial sketch of an account of *jus ad bellum* in terms of individual rights, an account that puts the discussion of war in a cosmopolitan context of "universalist politics."[40]

The moral rights referred to in the human rights paradigm are *claim rights*, that is, rights that entail corresponding duties or obligations on the part of others. If a young child has a claim right not to be targeted in war, there is duty or obligation on the part of combatants not to target that child. A claim right is violated when the duty or obligation corresponding to that right has not been fulfilled.[41] When I speak of moral rights, I mean universal, nonconventional rights, rights that apply to everyone and must be respected by everyone, though moral rights may be conventionally recognized as well. (For example a person's moral right not to be killed is nonconventional, but it is also conventionally recognized in laws against murder.) In contrast with claim rights are *liberty rights*, which are permissions and lack any corresponding obligations on the part of others. When a state satisfies the criteria of *jus ad bellum*, it has a liberty right to go to war, which means simply that it is not wrong of the state to do so. (We discuss later whether humanitarian intervention is an exception to this claim.)

Human rights are a species of moral rights. Their grounding is the interest each of us has in our own autonomy, and they embody, in their

---

[38] Beitz, *Political Theory*, p. 55.   [39] Luban, "Just War and Human Rights," p. 175.

[40] Luban, "The Romance of the Nation-State," p. 392.

[41] The idea of a claim right was developed by Wesley Hohfeld (1879–1918). See David Rodin, *War and Self-Defense* (Oxford University Press, 2002), chapter 1.

corresponding obligations, the demand that autonomy be respected.[42] There are, we may say, two sorts of human rights: (1) rights that directly protect activities through which we exercise our autonomy, such as rights of association; (2) rights that protect the basis necessary for the exercise of autonomy, such as rights to basic security. Without security, we cannot exercise autonomy. The second category could be what Luban had in mind when he referred to socially basic rights.[43] Luban borrows the notion of basic rights from American philosopher Henry Shue. Moral rights, says Shue, are basic "only if enjoyment of them is essential to the enjoyment of all other rights."[44] Two important categories of basic rights are rights to physical security and rights to economic security (the latter are called *subsistence rights*). It is clear that without physical and economic security a person is not free to enjoy other rights. We all have duties and obligations to ensure that others have this security.

An important feature of Shue's account of basic rights is his emphasis on *default duties*. Like other claim rights, basic rights have associated duties, but these duties are more complex and far-reaching than might be supposed. "Every effective system of rights needs to include some default, or backup, duties – that is, duties that constitute a second-line of defense requiring someone to step into the breach when those with the primary duty that is the first-line of defense fail to perform it." Everyone not only has duties not to violate the rights of others directly, but also has additional, default duties in regard to the conduct of others who might directly violate those rights. This has important implications regarding our duties to people in other states, as "the rest of us are not free merely to leave human beings to their fate when it is impossible for their basic rights to be protected by national institutions."[45] Beyond the first-level duties corresponding to basic rights, there are two levels of default duties, yielding three levels of basic duties: (BD1) "Duties to *avoid* depriving;" (BD2) "Duties to *protect*

[42] This view of human rights is related to the moral theory of Immanuel Kant (1724–1804). See his *Grounding for the Metaphysics of Morals* (Indianapolis: Hackett Publishing, 1993).

[43] Luban, "Just War and Human Rights," pp. 166, 174.

[44] Henry Shue, *Basic Rights: Subsistence, Affluence, and US Foreign Policy*, 2nd edn. (Princeton University Press, 1996), p. 19.

[45] Henry Shue, "Limiting Sovereignty," in Welsh (ed.), *Humanitarian Intervention*, pp. 11–28, at pp. 16, 20.

from deprivation;" and (BD3) "Duties to *aid* the deprived."[46] In each case, the deprivation involved is that of basic physical and economic security. A violation of basic rights occurs whenever duties at any of the levels are not fulfilled by the persons or institutions that have those duties.

For example, a state T may violate the subsistence rights of its citizens either by: (1) *depriving* them of their means of livelihood, a failure to fulfill (BD1); (2) *not protecting* them from being deprived by others of their means of livelihood, a failure to fulfill (BD2); or (3) *not aiding* them when they have lost their means of livelihood due to a lack of fulfillment of duties (1) and (2), which is a failure to fulfill (BD3). (BD2) and (BD3) are default duties. But, because human rights are universal, individuals outside of T, acting through their states, may also have these duties toward citizens of T. The duties of citizens of state S, or of S itself, resulting from violation of the subsistence rights of citizens of T, are not mere matters of charity, but moral obligations. Shue's idea of basic rights and their complex of duties provides a theoretical foundation for justifying war, not only in the form of humanitarian intervention, but in the form of national defense as well.

We may refer to (BD1) as duties requiring *respect* for rights, and (BD2) and (BD3) as duties requiring *protection* of rights. Humanitarian intervention is an effort to *protect* against the violation of rights in another state when those rights are not being *respected*, usually by the government of that state. It is appropriate that one of the key UN documents setting out the case for humanitarian intervention is called "Responsibility to Protect."[47]

Here is the proposed formulation of the just cause criterion under the human rights paradigm.

> Just Cause (Human Rights Paradigm): a war waged by S against T must be a response to an ongoing policy of T that results in a substantial violation of basic rights of either: (1) citizens of S (or some third state), when T's use of force is unjustified (covering the national defense case); *or* (2) against T's own citizens (covering the humanitarian intervention case).[48]

---

[46] Shue, *Basic Rights*, p. 52.

[47] "Responsibility to Protect," The International Commission on Intervention and State Sovereignty, http://responsibilitytoprotect.org/ICISS%20Report.pdf, accessed January 4, 2011.

[48] In a more thorough elaboration, the formulation would include, as our earlier one did, reference to measures short of war, which might be justified in response to lesser humanitarian crises. See Walzer, "Regime Change and Just War."

This formulation seeks to cover both traditional defensive war and humanitarian intervention by understanding the justification of each to be a matter of avoiding the substantial violation of basic rights resulting from a failure to respect basic rights on the part of the state that is the object of attack. Both defensive war and humanitarian intervention are the fulfillment of duties to protect against such violations. (Whether the human rights paradigm makes war obligatory rather than merely permissible will be considered later.) The criterion may be understood in two ways: either it assimilates defensive war to humanitarian intervention by understanding each as a response to wrongs by a state against individuals (rather than against states); or it assimilates humanitarian intervention to defensive war by understanding each as a response to aggression by another state, whether the aggression is inter-state or intra-state. In either case, aggression is against individuals. The criterion abandons the priority principle, which views the justification for war as a threat against a state, not against individuals.

One way to see defensive war and humanitarian intervention as part of the "same underlying moral structure" is proposed by David Rodin. The traditional idea of national defense includes third-party defense, allowing S to go to war against T in order to aid citizens of R whose rights are being violated by T. Humanitarian intervention fits the same structure except that the rights of the citizens of R are not being violated by another state T, but by R itself.[49]

One important implication of this criterion is that a state under attack is not justified in a military response if the attack itself is justified. Under the state-centric national defense paradigm such a case could not arise because justified intervention is ruled out. But, under humanitarian intervention, a first use of force can be justified, and, when it is, a "defensive" response is not. This preserves the principle that only one side in an armed conflict can be just. According to Vattel, if an opponent waging war against us "has justice on his side, we have no right to make forcible opposition; and the defensive war then becomes unjust."[50] As a matter of fact, of course, the state that is the object of a justified humanitarian intervention may well respond with military force as if it were the victim of aggression, but it is not justified in doing so.

---

[49] Rodin, *War and Self-Defense*, pp. 130–131.   [50] Vattel, *Law of Nations*, p. 487.

The requirement that basic rights violations be *substantial* represents the idea that war should not be undertaken for minor reasons. This is largely implicit in the formulation of just cause under the national defense paradigm, since aggression against a state is almost certain to involve substantial individual rights violations, but it should be made explicit in the formulation covering humanitarian intervention because all states violate basic rights of their citizens to some extent. Without the qualification "substantial," any state would in theory have a just cause at any time for intervention in any other state. Of course, we have yet to consider the proportionality criterion for the human rights paradigm, which presumably imposes further restrictions of this sort on justification. Note that the appeal to basic rights in the formulation shows that the answer to the frequently raised question of whether humanitarian intervention may be undertaken to impose democracy is no. The rights that are violated by the fact that a government is not democratic are not basic rights; the citizens of a non-democracy may have all their security and subsistence rights respected and protected by their state.

To understand the wrong of inter-state aggression in terms of the violations of basic rights, we need simply to appreciate how a military attack violates those rights. First, citizens of the state attacked are deprived of their physical and economic security; they are killed and maimed and have the resources they need to survive taken from them. This violates their basic rights by the attacker's failure to fulfill its duties not to deprive those citizens of their basic rights. Second, the attacking state also fails to protect the basic rights of those citizens because it damages the capacity of the state attacked to protect those rights. The attacking state fails to observe its default duties to protect those rights. As Larry May observes, when a state that generally protects its citizens' basic rights is attacked, it is destabilized, undermining its ability to protect those rights.[51] It is this violation of basic rights of individuals, not an attack on the state as an entity, that constitutes the moral wrong of aggression. But we may note for future reference that any war, even a justified war, also entails such rights violations.

Earlier, we raised the scope question: what is the proper range of cases of humanitarian crisis where humanitarian intervention would be

[51] May, Larry, *Aggression and Crimes against Peace* (Cambridge University Press, 2008), p. 6.

justified? Part of the test for an adequate theory of *jus ad bellum* is that it gives a proper answer to the scope question. We may think in terms of the *threshold* of basic rights violations that would, other things being equal, trigger justified intervention. A good theory should be neither too permissive nor too restrictive in this regard; it should set the threshold at the proper point, neither too high nor too low. Consider two theories of humanitarian intervention we have considered so far: the theory of the national defense paradigm under Walzer's revised interpretation and the theory of human rights paradigm under Tesón's interpretation. Walzer's theory of the humanitarian intervention exception permits humanitarian intervention only in cases that "shock the moral conscience of mankind." This is fairly restrictive, setting the threshold for intervention quite high. Tesón criticizes Walzer for setting the threshold too high, but his own theory, which allows intervention to end anarchy or tyranny, may put the threshold too low. Under the human rights paradigm, it seems that the number of cases of justified border crossings under the banner of humanitarian intervention is potentially large, given that many states, at different times, are guilty of substantial violations of their citizens' rights. But Tesón does specify that any intervention must satisfy the criterion of proportionality, so perhaps if we had a clearer understanding of how this criterion should be understood under the human rights paradigm, we would have a theory that adequately addresses the scope question.

But before revisiting proportionality, we may briefly consider how the other *ad bellum* criteria should be understood under the human rights paradigm.

4.4 Other *ad bellum* criteria

The criterion of rightful intention is roughly the same under the new paradigm. The intervener must have the intention defined by the just cause, namely, to avoid the threatened rights violations. It may have other intentions, but only those that require no greater use of force than that needed to avoid those violations are acceptable. This addresses the frequently posed question of whether humanitarian intervention can be justified when the intervener's motives are not purely benevolent. Admittedly, pure benevolence is unlikely; a state will generally aid victims abroad only if it also foresees some resulting benefit to its national interest. But, as we saw earlier, singleness of motive is largely irrelevant. The criterion is in terms of *intentions*, which are in our control, not *motives*, which often are not. While intentions can also be multiple, this is handled by the provision that none can require greater use of force than that needed to avoid the rights violations.

Legitimate authority, as outlined in the last chapter, requires simply that a war be initiated by some person or group with legal or *de facto* authority within a large organization, apart from whether it or its organization has moral legitimacy. Many would argue that conditions on authority should be more restrictive in the case of humanitarian intervention, for example, that the only legitimate authority is the UN Security Council. We saw this controversy earlier in our discussion of the Kosovo War. The UN Charter itself makes no explicit provision for humanitarian intervention, though it allows the Security Council to authorize the use of force for the sake of "international peace and security," and this concept has been stretched to encompass humanitarian intervention.[52] But morality is not the same as law, despite their close relationship. Michael Walzer asserts that a UN authorized intervention may not be "any more just or timely" than that of a single state.[53] The Security Council may not be able to agree on an intervention when one is clearly morally warranted (as in the case of Kosovo) and, if approval does come, it may come too late.

There is another reason to think that stronger conditions on the legitimate authority may be needed, a reason that is more evident in the case of humanitarian intervention, but which applies also in the case of defensive wars. The concern is of war being initiated by private groups rather than states. Earlier, I said that individuals outside of a state, "by themselves or through their states," may have duties toward citizens of that state. A state can discharge such obligations through humanitarian intervention, but can individuals do so directly? Approaching this problem from a different angle, Cheyney Ryan has referred to it as the "sovereign symmetry problem."[54] The problem is that sub-state organizations may

---

[52] A stretch because a humanitarian crisis, if completely contained within a state's borders, may not pose a challenge to international peace and security.

[53] Walzer, *Just and Unjust Wars*, 3rd edn., p. xiii.

[54] Cheyney Ryan, "Moral Equality, Victimhood, and the Sovereign Symmetry Problem," in D. Rodin and H. Shue (eds.), *Just and Unjust Warriors: The Moral and Legal Status of Soldiers* (Oxford University Press, 2008), pp. 131–152.

seek to engage in humanitarian intervention (or defensive wars, for that matter), and the legitimate authority criterion, as formulated, would not stand in their way. Ryan speaks of a group of Irish immigrants at the end of the American Civil War who, in what might be considered an unusual form of humanitarian intervention, formed a private army to seize territory in Canada to broker for Irish independence from England.[55] But this may be a problem we are stuck with, for, as discussed in Chapter 7, making moral sense of intra-state wars requires giving legitimate authority to sub-state groups, which are often groups of private individuals. It seems likely, however, that other *ad bellum* criteria would rule much of this sort of privateering that would be morally objectionable.

Regarding reasonable chance of success, the formulation of this given earlier applies here as well, but an extra caution is in order. In the case of humanitarian intervention, success is ending the rights violations, and, as we mentioned, this may require, beyond mere rescue, regime change and political reconstruction. A successful military action may end the violations for the time being, but they may be reasonably expected to return immediately upon military withdrawal in the absence of regime change or political reconstruction.[56] The more ambitious agenda may make success much harder to attain, in terms of the difficulty of the task and the great patience it may require. Part of a judgment of reasonable chance of success should include reasonable expectations about the political staying power of the intervener in regard to the difficult reconstruction process that may be necessary.

The likely need for regime change deserves some comment. In wars of national defense, regime change is seldom necessary to achieve the defensive ends. Moreover it is, for that reason, generally not justified, as it would be a use of force beyond what is necessary to achieve the rightful intention. This point is emphasized by Michael Walzer, who argues that regime change is not justified in defensive wars, with Nazi Germany being an exception to this rule.[57] But in the case of humanitarian intervention, as we mentioned, removing the threat to the victims of a murderous regime often requires removing that regime. Otherwise, the regime is likely to

[55] *Ibid.*, p. 148.

[56] C. A. J. Coady, *Morality and Political Violence* (Cambridge University Press, 2008), p. 76.

[57] Walzer, *Just and Unjust Wars*, pp. 111–117.

resume the rights violations of its vulnerable victims as soon as the intervener leaves; the political dynamics that originally lead to the oppression
remain in place.

Finally, the earlier formulation again seems appropriate in the case of
last resort. The emphasis would be on the moral cost of delaying the intervention while peaceful resorts were tried. In the case of a humanitarian
crisis, the cost of delay is likely to be great.

4.5 Proportionality revisited

Many of the wrongs typical of aggression are not limited to aggression,
but characterize any attack by one state on another, justified or not. Any
attack violates basic rights. As we saw in the last chapter, the created evil
of a war cannot in practice be zero. Now, we need to investigate more
precisely the components of the created evil, which must be assessed as
part of the application of the proportionality criterion. This will help to
determine whether the human rights paradigm can provide an adequate
answer to the scope question.

Under the human rights paradigm, the criterion may be formulated as
it was under the national defense paradigm:

> Proportionality criterion (human rights paradigm): a war must be such
> that the significance of the created evil does not exceed the significance of
> the resisted evil.

The created evil, as before, refers to wrongs to individuals, but under the
human rights paradigm, the resisted evil does as well. We need to address
anew the three questions addressed in the previous discussion of the criterion: (a) What is the resisted evil? (b) What is the created evil? (c) How are
the two compared to determine whether war would be disproportionate?

Considering (a), the resisted evil under the human rights paradigm is
the threatened violation of individual rights, which provides a just cause
for war. In the case of defensive war, the aggressor violates the rights of
citizens of the state attacked.[58] In the case of humanitarian intervention,
a state violates the rights of its own citizens. These are evils that another

---

[58] And perhaps those of its combatants as well, an issue raised in the next two
chapters.

state may be justified in using military force to resist. Under the human rights paradigm, states themselves have no rights and cannot be wronged. Talk of the rights of states or of wrongs done to them is simply convenient shorthand for the rights of individuals or wrongs done to them. "Persons, rather than states," Beitz observes, are "the ultimate subjects of international morality."[59]

Turning to (b), the created evil consists of wrongs, specifically, the violation of individual rights, that the warring state with a just cause does to individuals in the state that it attacks. In practical terms the created evil cannot be zero. While not everyone who is harmed by military action is wronged, some who are harmed will be wronged because they are not liable to be harmed. To say that the created evil cannot be zero is to say that, in practical terms, a war cannot be fought without basic rights being violated, without serious harm being done to those not liable to be harmed. As we see in the later discussion of *jus in bello*, civilians in general are not liable to be harmed. When civilians are harmed, as many will predictably be, often they are wronged, their basic rights violated. Some civilians may be harmed intentionally, in violation of the *in bello* principle of discrimination, but even if this principle is adhered to scrupulously, some will be harmed unintentionally but foreseeably (some such harm being permitted under the *in bello* principle of proportionality). When civilians are harmed in either of these ways, they are wronged, and such wrongs will often be a violation of their basic rights. War inevitably produces much such harm.

The harm to civilians in violation of their basic rights may be to their person or to their important possessions. In IHL, such possessions are referred to as *civilian objects*. Civilian objects are "objects indispensable to the survival of the civilian population, such as foodstuffs, agricultural areas for the production of foodstuffs, crops, livestock, drinking water installations …"[60] Recall that the policy of the United States and its allies in both the Gulf War and the Kosovo War was morally controversial because it involved intentional attacks on civilian infrastructure, an important form of civilian object. The justification for these attacks was often that such infrastructure served a "dual use," that it had military as

---

[59] Beitz, "Bounded Morality," p. 409.

[60] 1977 Geneva Protocol I, in Adam Roberts and Richard Guelff (eds.), *Documents on the Laws of War*, 3rd edn. (Oxford University Press, 2000), p. 451.

well as civilian uses. But, because of their important civilian uses, destroying these objects was a violation of the basic duties states have to avoid depriving individuals of their security. Note that such civilian objects are best understood as a form of *collective or public property* of all individuals in a society, whatever their legal status.

While the usual examples given of civilian objects are of "material and tangible things,"[61] there is no reason that something intangible, such as an *institution*, if it played the same sort of indispensable role for civilians as tangible objects, could not count morally as a "civilian object." Indeed, tangible civilian objects are often valuable only in conjunction with institutions that exist to create and foster them and to distribute their product among the citizens; so respect for tangible objects entails respect for the affiliated institutions. Many social institutions are of basic value to individuals not only in this sort of extrinsic way, but intrinsically as well. They help to provide the members with cultural as well as physical sustenance. Moreover, social institutions, like tangible objects, can be damaged or destroyed in war, through disruption of normal social activities. Basic social institutions, like their tangible counterparts, are created over time by many members of the community, and, like them, can be said to be public property, the property of all individuals in the society.

The destruction of civilian objects, tangible or intangible, may be counted as a violation of individuals' basic rights, even though the objects are collective or public products. This makes individual rights against the damage or destruction of basic social institutions something like Walzer's common life rights. The common life of a society is composed in large part of its social institutions. This suggests that Walzer could have arrived at his account of common life rights through the idea of a civilian object. But if Walzer had taken this approach, he would have recognized that common life rights are different from those portrayed in his account and play a different and broader moral role.

The moral content of common life rights is captured in the moral force behind the claim, "it's none of your business." This complaint, understood morally, is a claim that outsiders should not intervene in the affairs of a group. It can be true or false, but when it is true, the outsiders have

---

[61] Yoram Dinstein, *The Conduct of Hostilities under the Law of International Armed Conflict* (Cambridge University Press, 2004), p. 84.

a strong moral reason not to intervene. Consider a mugger who tries to warn you away from interfering to protect her victim with the claim that it is none of your business. Here the claim would be patently false; it is your business. This is because mugger and victim, assuming them to be strangers, are not a group in a morally relevant sense. There would be no moral bar to your intervention on behalf of the victim, and, indeed, it may be your default duty (BD2) to intervene. Consider another case. One of the participants in a fist fight makes the moral claim that it is none of your business to warn you away from intervention to break up the fight. There are three possibilities here. The first is that, like the mugging, the fighters do not know each other and one is simply seeking to victimize the other, in which case the moral claim is false, at least when the one warning you away is the victimizer. In the second and third cases, the fighters are members of a fight club, so they form a social group in a morally relevant sense. Then the moral claim may be either true or false. In the second case, one of them is clearly taking unfair advantage of the other, in which case the claim may be false, and it may be appropriate for you to intervene, despite their being members of a group. In the third case, it is clear that the fight is a fair one which both participants agreed to participate in by being members of the club. In that case, the claim "it's none of your business" may be true, and you should not intervene.

When the claim "it's none of your business" is true, the members of the group or association have a common life right against intervention. Thus, common life rights, the rights individuals have against intervention in the activities of their groups, apply to individuals in all social groups, not just to those in states or nations. Their application in war, for example, in the right of individuals not to have their basic social institutions damaged or destroyed, is just a species of the larger genus. This is because the moral grounding of the rights, the moral content of the claim "it's none of your business," applies to all social groups. Any social group creates a common life, from which common life rights flow. By limiting common life rights to states or nations, Walzer fails to recognize their breadth. When individuals create groups, they construct a common life with their fellow members through the institutions that constitute the group, and the individuals have rights against those who would damage or destroy those institutions or, more generally, interfere in activities within the group. As individuals in states have common life rights against intervention by other states, individuals in associations in civil society have common life rights against legal intervention in their groups. In either case, the claims resulting from the common life rights can be overridden by other rights claims. This means that, despite such rights, it may be permissible for a state to engage in humanitarian intervention, as it is for it to force private clubs not to discriminate based on race. Like other rights, common life rights are *prima facie*, subject to being overridden in particular circumstances by considerations of competing rights. To justify the humanitarian intervention exception, one need not appeal to the ad hoc claim that the common life rights cease to exist if the state is engaged in massive rights violations against some of its own people.

So our conception of common life rights differs from Walzer's in two main respects. Common life rights apply to any social group or association, not only national communities, and they can be overridden by other rights claims. In fact, common life rights may be regarded as a form of liberal rights. Common life rights may be seen as flowing from *freedom of association*. In civil society, individuals have the freedom to gather into associations, which means that the state has a *prima facie* duty not to interfere in those associations. But, notes American philosopher Amy Gutmann: "Freedom of association may be limited for the same kind of reason that freedom of speech may be: it can conflict with other vital claims." She also notes: "Because freedom of association is neither morally nor constitutionally absolute, we cannot conclude that an intrusion into the internal structure is unjustified before we evaluate the purposes of the intrusion and compare the merits of intrusion with those of nonintrusion into an association's internal structure or affairs."[62] When other duties conflict with the duty not to interfere with freedom of association, as they often do, sometimes the other duties are weightier. As John Rawls notes, churches may be allowed to excommunicate heretics, but not to burn them at the stake.[63]

In any war, the social institutions of the state attacked will be damaged, and this counts as a violation of the common rights of the citizens of the state, whose association the state is. This is an important part of the created evil of a war, whether defensive or humanitarian. But the special

---

[62] Amy Gutmann, "Freedom of Association: An Introductory Essay," in Gutmann (ed.), *Freedom of Association* (Princeton University Press, 1998), pp. 3–32, at pp. 17, 11.

[63] John Rawls, *Justice as Fairness* (Cambridge, MA: Harvard University Press, 2001), p. 11.

relevance of this to humanitarian intervention lies in the frequency with which these wars require regime change and political reconstruction, processes which, however necessary to ending the murderous rights violations, involve the destruction, not simply the damaging, of major social institutions, amounting to serious violations of the basic rights of the entire population, which is dependent on those institutions. Major social institutions may be part of the war effort, but they are also of great importance to the population. They are *dual use* entities, a species of dual use infrastructure. They may be a mechanism through which humanitarian crises are perpetrated by states, but they are also the basis of the associational life of the population. If they are destroyed in the process of ending the humanitarian crisis, the resulting rights violations should be counted in the created evil of the war.

To consider the nature and extent of appropriate governmental intervention in associations in civil society, take family law. The family is generally treated in law as an intimate or primary association, rather than a secondary association, which means that intervention in the family faces higher legal hurdles than intervention in, say, the Junior Chamber of Commerce. But state intervention in the family is still legally permitted, more so now than in the past. Formerly, family law in the United States was governed by the doctrine of *oneness*, according to which the family was in some respects impervious to legal intervention. Oneness of the family is normatively analogous to the unconditional sovereignty of the state in the national defense paradigm. The family was treated as a unit, and its members, to that extent, were not treated as individuals. For example, one legal commentator notes: "Originally, the doctrine of 'oneness' of husband and wife precluded any lawsuit between spouses." Though this doctrine has now been largely abandoned, even today: "Taking into account the special nature of family relationships, the law of torts applies special immunities to disputes within the family."[64] Family members do not have the full protection from each other that they would have were they outside such an association. The rationale is that, were family members treated as individuals in their legal dealing with each other, this would "disturb family

---

[64] Harry D. Krause, *Family Law in a Nutshell*, 2nd edn. (St. Paul, MN: West Publishing, 1986), p. 116. Relations between parents and children raise additional complications not considered here.

harmony," and the family would not be able to function as the kind of group that its members want it to be.

Of course, another take on "oneness" is that it served simply to reproduce the patriarchal domination of men over women, and, indeed, much of the impetus for the move away from oneness in family law has been the demand that women be treated as the equals of men *as individuals*. For example, Rawls suggests that "special provisions are needed in family law (and no doubt elsewhere) so that the burden of bearing, raising, and educating children does not fall more heavily on women, thereby undermining their fair equality of opportunity."[65] Despite the attenuation of the idea of oneness, the law still respects common life rights against legal intervention in the family. In some cases, other rights carry the balance, and legal intervention is justified, while in others, common life rights carry the balance and intervention is not justified.

This is not to say that social groups within states are the same as national communities in all relevant respects. Perhaps the principal difference is that membership in a national community or political society is not voluntary, while membership in social groups within a state generally is voluntary.[66] But this difference does not seem to be relevant because individuals build a common life in the groups they are in even when their membership is non-voluntary. Moreover, membership in a national community may not be completely non-voluntary, given possibilities of emigration, and membership in social groups within a state may be significantly less than fully voluntary.[67] In addition, while states generally lack the *legal* authority to intervene in other states that they have to intervene in domestic groups, this is legally but not morally relevant to the question whether national communities and civic associations both generate common life rights that need to be considered.

As a result, the morality of humanitarian intervention must be considered in terms of its effects on institutions of the target state and the common life rights its citizens have that those institutions not be interfered with. Intervention to rescue victims of humanitarian crises, like defensive war, will damage the institutions of the community's common life

---

[65] Rawls, *Justice as Fairness*, p. 11.   [66] See *ibid.*, p. 20.

[67] See Michael Walzer, "On Involuntary Association," in Gutmann (ed.), *Freedom of Association*, pp. 64–74.

and violate common life rights. Judging whether an intervention is justified must take into account not only the rights violations the intervention would avoid, but also the common life rights the intervention would itself violate. The justifiability of some cases of humanitarian intervention shows that common life rights do not always take precedence. Moreover, as with family law, the balance between common life rights and other rights is changing over time in the light of our greater appreciation of the force of human rights. Indeed, the recent interest in humanitarian intervention represents a similar shift in the balance from emphasis on common life rights to greater concern for other basic rights.

Note three more points concerning the balance among rights violations in these sorts of situations. First, common life rights apply to all the members of a group, so interfering in the group to protect some members may violate the common life rights of the other members. This must be taken into account in the calculation of created evil. Second, members of a group generally have obligations to other members of the group, for example, based on the moral principle of reciprocity or fair play. Common life rights may, in part, reflect the obligations an outside intervener owes other members of the group not to intervene in ways that would let a member with such obligations off the moral hook, or simply in ways that, in rescuing individuals, would seriously damage the group. Third, consent to group membership is not always as relevant as it might seem to be. One might think that common life rights apply only when the relevant group members continue to consent to being in the group. But consent may be indeterminate, not just epistemologically, but inherently. For example, the victim of fraternity hazing may want both to endure the treatment in order to protect the group and his role in it and to escape it.

4.6 Comparing created evil and resisted evil

This brings us to the question (c): how the created evil and the resisted evil are to be compared. Consider again the question of whether it is possible to compare or weigh the resisted evil and the created evil against each other. Is it possible to justify a state's violating some rights (the created evil) in order to avoid rights violations by others (the resisted evil)? Our understanding of basic duties casts this question in a different light. Rights entail default duties, for example, the duty not to let a third party violate someone else's rights. We have obligations both to *respect* rights and to *protect* others from rights violations. When a person stops another from violating the rights of a third party, he not only does a morally good thing, but also fulfills a duty. But if he cannot fulfill that duty to protect from rights violations (resisted evil) without violating his duty to respect a right (created evil), his situation should be understood as a conflict of duties. The weighing of resisted and created evil becomes a matter of balancing conflicting obligations. So, we need to acknowledge some version of what we call the *trade-off approach*, according to which it is possible to compare duties regarding prospective rights violations and to determine an overall obligation in some situation based on that comparison.

One way to conceive of the trade-off approach is in terms of what American philosopher Richard Wasserstrom has called *a utilitarianism of rights*, according to which sets of rights violations can be compared to determine which set contains fewer violations. Wasserstrom proposed this idea as the basis of an account of humanitarian intervention alternative to that of Walzer's.[68] As David Koller expresses the position, "an action may be taken if the anticipated enjoyment of human rights by all individuals outweighs the anticipated human rights enjoyment of all alternative courses of action."[69] But it is misleading to refer to the sort of balancing required in weighing the created evil against the resisted evil as simply totting up the number of violations, or the number of unfulfilled duties, on each side of the equation. Some rights violations are more significant than others, and some duties are more stringent than others, so the significance of rights violations or duty non-fulfillments is just as important, if not more so, than the numbers of such.

To see how we should think about the weighing involved in the proportionality calculations, consider a case proposed by American philosopher Joel Feinberg, who offers the following domestic analogy (which I have slightly modified). A person is hiking in the mountains with her young child when an unexpected blizzard arises, threatening their lives, whereupon she stumbles upon a locked cabin with an absent owner. In a clear

[68] Richard Wasserstrom, review of Walzer's *Just and Unjust Wars*, in the *Harvard Law Review* 92, no. 2 (December 1978), pp. 536–545, at p. 544. Walzer rejects this alternative in "The Moral Standing of States."

[69] David S. Koller, "The Moral Imperative: Toward a Human Rights-Based Law of War," *Harvard International Law Review* 46, no. 1 (Winter 2005), pp. 231–264, at p. 255.

violation of the owner's property rights, she breaks in, uses the owner's food, and burns his furniture to keep them both alive.[70] When we compare the conflicting rights violations, it seems clear that the hiker is overall morally justified in destroying the property because her duty not to destroy the property is outweighed or overridden by her duty to save her child's life (and perhaps her own too). If she had to kill the owner, who refused to let her in, to save their lives, the weighing of the relevant duties might go in the other direction. Judging whether the resisted evil justifies imposing the created evil is a matter of weighing the conflicting duties that are involved.

This is what we do in applying proportionality. Consider a prospective war by S against T which has a just cause, but may or may not satisfy proportionality. The resisted evil is composed of the basic rights violations, including common life rights violations, that are threatened by T and would be avoided by the military efforts of S, whether the violations are against citizens of S (in the case of defensive war) or of T (in the case of humanitarian intervention). The created evil is composed of the basic rights violations, including common life rights violations, that S's military efforts would impose on those citizens of T not liable to be harmed. (In both cases we consider reasonable expectations of the violations occurring.) We then weigh the conflicting duties corresponding to avoiding these prospective rights violations.

We normally think of not fulfilling a duty (thereby violating the corresponding right) as wrongful behavior. But in a conflict of duties, not fulfilling those that come out on the short side of the balancing is not wrongful. The hiker does not do wrong in not fulfilling her duty to respect the owner's property rights because that duty is outweighed by the conflicting duty to save her child's life. American philosopher Judith Jarvis Thomson, using examples of the sort that Feinberg introduced, provides a helpful way of speaking about these cases. Switching from a discussion of duties to a discussion of the corresponding rights, she suggests that we recognize a contrast between *infringing a right* and *violating a right*.

> Suppose that someone has a right that such and such shall not be the case. I shall say that we infringe a right of his if and only if we bring about that

---

[70] Joel Feinberg, "Voluntary Euthanasia and the Inalienable Right to Life," *Philosophy & Public Affairs* 7 (Winter 1978), pp. 93–123, at p. 102.

> it is the case. I shall say that we violate a right of his if and only if *both* we bring about that it is the case *and* we act wrongly in so doing.[71]

This distinction between violating and infringing a right makes clear that it is misleading to say, when respect for rights has been overridden, that the rights have been violated. The hiker infringes the cabin owner's property rights, but does not violate them. According to Thomson, only some infringements are violations, so not all infringements are wrongful. Thomson rejects "the view that every infringing of a right is a violation of a right."[72] A violation is a wrongful infringement, and an infringement that is not wrongful is permissible.

The distinction between rights infringements and rights violations provides a way of making clear that rightful action in many cases, especially in choosing war, is a matter of weighing conflicting rights and duties. It is inevitable that some rights will be infringed and some duties unfulfilled. The distinction makes clear the response to the pacifist who argues, with the rights absolutist, that war is impermissible because it cannot be conducted without rights violations. As Daniel Montaldi asserts, "the possibility of just wars depends upon the possibility of there being permissible infringements of basic rights."[73] The proportionality calculation concerns the significance of sets of prospective rights infringements. We do not know which of the rights infringements are also rights violations until we have made the judgment of the side on which the greater significance lies. That judgment tells us which rights infringements would be wrongful. So we must modify the earlier claim that a failure to respect a right, or a failure to fulfill a duty, is always a wrong; when the failure is a mere infringement, it is not wrongful. What may seem in isolation like a rights violation may turn out to be a mere infringement in the context of the comparison of sets of prospective infringements.

Consider, finally, how this discussion of proportionality helps to address the question about whether the human rights paradigm gives a satisfactory answer to the scope question. This question arises primarily in regard to

---

[71] Judith Jarvis Thomson, *Rights, Restitution, and Risk: Essays in Moral Philosophy* (Cambridge, MA: Harvard University Press, 1986), p. 51.

[72] *Ibid.*, p. 40.

[73] Daniel F. Montaldi, "Toward a Human Rights Based Account of Just War," *Social Theory and Practice* 11, no. 2 (Summer 1985), pp. 123–161, at p. 126.

humanitarian intervention: does the human rights paradigm set the proper threshold for when a humanitarian crisis is sufficiently grave to justify intervention? Our earlier speculation was that Walzer's theory regarding humanitarian intervention may set the threshold too high, while Tesón's version of the human rights paradigm may set it too low. What I have added to our understanding of the human rights paradigm is a recognition of common life rights, and this recognition would raise the threshold implicit in Tesón's account. It adds to the plausibility of a theory of *jus ad bellum*, if it has a threshold for humanitarian intervention between those implicit in Walzer's and Tesón's theories, and a version of the human rights paradigm that recognizes common life rights is such a theory.

A theory that recognizes common life rights has different implications for humanitarian intervention than it does for defensive war. In defensive war, common life rights are generally infringed by both sides; both aggressor and defender fight on the other's soil, infringing common life rights. This means that common life rights infringements would tend to cancel each other out, so to speak, as they would be part of both the resisted evil and the created evil. But in the case of humanitarian intervention, common life rights are normally infringed by one side only, the side that intervenes.

In the case of defensive war, the issue is what the human rights paradigm implies about border crossings. Ordinary moral judgments about defensive war tend to agree with the priority principle that any border crossing (with significant military force) can justify defensive war. But the human rights paradigm may not have as clear an implication because a border crossing does not necessarily entail a serious infringement of individual rights, including common life rights. Border crossings, however, are usually a prelude to significant rights infringements.[74] As Walzer notes, "we assign a certain *presumptive* value to the boundaries that mark off a people's territory and to the state that defends it."[75] This suggests that any theory of defensive war may need in practice to make use of *presumptive principles*, and there is no reason why the human rights paradigm should not as well. Presumptive principles are rules of thumb, adopted as

---

[74] Larry May, "The Principle of Just Cause," in May (ed.), *War: Essays in Political Philosophy* (New York: Cambridge University Press, 2008), pp. 49–66, at p. 58.

[75] Walzer, *Just and Unjust Wars*, p. 57, emphasis added.

an expeditious way of approximating correct decisions in real-world, time-sensitive situations in which it is difficult to apply the moral principles that determine the correct decisions. Presumptive principles are *prima facie* and defeasible, which means they can and should be overridden by the correct moral principles in situations in which the latter can be clearly applied. The need to operate under presumptive principles is usually a drawback for a theory, but it seems that any theory that must account for humanitarian intervention as well as defensive war would need, for practical purposes, to make use of the priority principle as a presumptive principle. Use of the priority principle is recognition of the importance of common life rights. It would place the burden of proof on those who advocate not responding to aggression with defensive force and on those advocating engaging in humanitarian intervention.

Before leaving this discussion of the human rights paradigm, we should address the contrast between *permission* and *obligation*. Just war theory is understood as a theory of the permissibility of war; when the *ad bellum* criteria are satisfied, a state is justified or permitted to initiate war. But under the human rights paradigm, war is initiated because of rights violations, and avoiding rights violations, in general, is more a matter of *obligation*, not mere permission. This question is raised especially in regard to humanitarian intervention, with some commentators claiming it may be obligatory, but it applies to defensive war as well. Two points may help to explain this apparent discrepancy. First, there seems to be a difference in stringency between obligations to respect rights and obligations to protect others from rights violations. Protecting others from rights violations is connected with the idea of the "good Samaritan," and the requirement to be a good Samaritan assumes that being one is not too burdensome, for example, personally not too risky. The same may apply to the requirement that a state respond to a humanitarian crisis in another state, given what a state risks in blood and treasure from going to war. Second, a leader has obligations toward her own citizens (as the moralized realist emphasizes) that are outside the realm covered by just war theory, and which may be at odds with her initiating a war, again, especially in the case of humanitarian intervention.[76] These two factors do not logically imply that satisfying

---

[76] Allen Buchanan, "The Internal Legitimacy of Humanitarian Intervention," *Journal of Political Philosophy* 7 (1999), pp. 71–87.

jus ad bellum yields a mere permission rather than an obligation to go to war, but they may explain why, given the existence of forms of moral obligation impinging on leaders outside of just war theory, it is appropriate to treat going to war as a mere permission.

4.7 Is a moral defense possible?

Earlier in the chapter I suggested that there were three responses to the apparent inconsistency between the national defense paradigm and the humanitarian intervention exception. We have considered two of these. (R1) was represented by Michael Walzer's attempt to explain humanitarian intervention in a way consistent with the national defense paradigm. (R2) was represented by the replacement of the national defense paradigm with the human rights paradigm, explaining both humanitarian intervention and defensive war in terms of duties to respect and protect individual rights. Now we consider the third response. Advocates of (R3) take the position that the apparent inconsistency between the national defense paradigm and the humanitarian intervention exception reveals something deeper about the morality of war, calling into question not simply the national defense paradigm, but any version of *jus ad bellum*. Proponents of (R3) argue that war cannot be justified through either paradigm; the violation of rights, whether of states or of individuals, cannot justify war, or cannot justify it beyond a very limited number of possible cases, so that we may be effectively led to unconditional anti-war pacifism.

Richard Norman offers a version of (R3). Norman argues that the crucial moral fact about a war is that it involves killing, so war can be justified only if what is being defended is worth killing for. The attack of one individual on another may justify killing in self-defense, but it does not follow that the attack of one collectivity on another justifies individual members killing each other. Individual killing would be justified only if the threat was "literally, the lives of people in the victim community," in which case "only something like a defensive war of resistance to genocide could be justified." In the more usual sort of invasion, "if there were no resistance, [the enemy] could invade without having to take any lives."[77] This is a point also suggested by Rousseau, who asserted: "It is

---

[77] Richard Norman, *Ethics, Killing, and War* (Cambridge University Press, 1995), p. 135.

sometimes possible to kill the State without killing a single one of its members; and war confers no right that is not necessary to its end."[78] What would be lost in such an invasion, if it were not resisted with force, would be merely the political community, not individual lives. Norman asks: "Why does the life of a political community matter, and does it matter enough to justify killing in its defence?"[79] His answer is that, in general, it does not.

According to this line of argument, once we recognize that talk about defense of states is shorthand for talk about defense of individuals, we are forced to appreciate that most defensive wars are not justified. David Rodin, arguing in a similar vein, suggests that we might understand the relation between war and individual self-defense by viewing the state as having a right to defend its citizens "the way a parent has the right to defend his or her child."[80] In killing in a defensive war, combatants act for the state in carrying out its parent-like responsibility to protect its citizens. Against this approach to justifying war, Rodin raises two lines of arguments: what he calls the argument from humanitarian intervention and the argument from bloodless invasion.

In his argument from humanitarian intervention, Rodin claims that there is a tension between defensive war and humanitarian intervention: "When a state intervenes in another state on humanitarian grounds, one of the moral considerations weighed against this action is the defensive rights of the subject of the intervention." Thus, a right to humanitarian intervention entails that "the moral basis of the right of national defense can in certain circumstances be justly overridden, not [that] the right of humanitarian interventions [is], in some sense, an application of those moral considerations."[81] This is similar to our argument about the inconsistency between the national defense paradigm and the humanitarian intervention exception. But the argument does not have the anti-war implications Rodin assumes it does, partly due to his use of a bad analogy. In line with the social contract tradition, the relation between state and citizen is not like parent to child, but more like agent to client. The

---

[78] Rousseau, *The Social Contract*, quoted in Roberts, "The Principle of Equal Application of the Laws of War," in Rodin and Shue (eds.), *Just and Unjust Warriors*, p. 233.

[79] Norman, *Ethics, Killing, and War*, p. 137.

[80] Rodin, *War and Self-Defense*, p. 129.   [81] *Ibid.*, p. 131.

state serves as agent of its citizens in many different respects, including carrying out their moral obligations that require collective action. These obligations may include both defending our fellow citizens against rights violations from foreign aggression and also defense of non-nationals from rights violations by their own government. With the switch in the analogy, the tension Rodin finds between national defense and humanitarian intervention disappears. An obligatory defense of individual rights provides a foundation for both.

Rodin's argument from bloodless invasion is similar to Norman's argument. The argument poses the question of whether defensive war can be justified even when it would not avoid any deaths (because the attackers would kill only if there was armed resistance to their takeover). In such cases, they would claim, the created evil of the wrongs of a defensive war would be disproportionate to the resisted evil of the loss of political community. Canadian philosopher Thomas Hurka, following Norman, claims that defensive war "satisfies proportionality only if it protects rights of citizens that are important enough to justify killing."[82] Norman and Rodin argue that it does not. But their arguments are based on a misunderstanding of how the proportionality criterion applies. A state could never be sure in advance that its attacker, absent resistance, would not kill. This uncertainty must be taken into account in the proportionality calculation, in the reasonable expectations of unjust harms. Thus the resisted evil in the proportionality calculation will always include some killings by the aggressor, along with violations of other rights, because it reflects the range of probabilities concerning the number the unresisted aggressor would kill. That it might be zero in some cases does not allow the calculations to be run as if it were zero.

There are several other reasons why defensive war may be justified, even if an unresisted invasion would turn out to be bloodless. First, even without any killings, the takeover of a state certainly involves other serious rights violations, which might by themselves justify defensive killings. On analogy, in the case of individual self-defense, the victim is morally permitted to kill the attacker if this is the only way to stop him from

---

[82] Thomas Hurka, "Proportionality in the Morality of War," *Philosophy & Public Affairs* 33, no. 1 (2005), pp. 34–66, at p. 52.

imposing serious rights violations short of killing.[83] Second, the number of people whose lesser rights (lesser than right to life) would be infringed by the attacker is presumably greater than the number in the opponent's society whose right to life would be infringed in a defensive war, and there is no reason that the proportionality calculations should not take this into account, sometimes justifying defensive killing by balancing the greater numbers of less significant infringements against the lesser number of more significant infringements.[84] Third, even if the unresisted invaders kill no one, they would threaten to kill should there be resistance, and threats of death may sometimes justify defensive killing in response.[85] Fourth, Hurka argues that, even with a bloodless invasion, "it is a mistake to see the only rights of citizens threatened by aggression as rights of political self-determination; they also include the right to be secure in a political and cultural home." The analogy is to a person protecting her actual home, where the law, "on the ground that 'a person's home is his castle,' allows more force to be used … than in protecting other forms of property."[86] This is in the spirit of common life rights, and, indeed, when common life rights violations are included in the resisted evil, a further basis is provided for the conclusion that the created evil in a defensive war, even granting the possibility of bloodless invasion, need not be disproportionate to the resisted evil.

Rodin sees two different argument strategies at work in support of the claim that defensive war can be justified: the *analogical strategy* (based on an analogy between individual and state self-defense) and the *reductive strategy* (based on an attempt to reduce the right of a state to defend itself to the rights of individuals). The analogical strategy is a version of the argument from the domestic analogy under the national defense paradigm, and the arguments Rodin and Norman offer against it overlap with the arguments presented earlier against the national defense paradigm.[87]

---

[83] Jeff McMahan, "War as Self-Defense," *Ethics & International Affairs* 18, no. 1 (2004), pp. 75–80, at p. 78.

[84] This point, as well as the next two, are suggested by Hurka, "Proportionality," pp. 53–56.

[85] In contrast, Rodin and Norman argue that threats of death cannot, in general, justify self-defensive killings.

[86] Hurka, "Proportionality," pp. 55, 56.

[87] David Rodin outlines the two strategies in *War and Self-Defense*, p. 123, and offers his criticism of the analogical strategy in chapter 7 of that work. Richard Norman offers his criticism of the analogical approach in *Ethics, Killing, and War*, chapter 4.

But the arguments against the reductive approach, which, for Rodin, include the humanitarian intervention argument and the bloodless invasion argument, appear not to succeed. They fail to show that the human rights paradigm is not an adequate basis for *jus ad bellum*.

This completes the discussion of *jus ad bellum*. Next we consider *jus in bello*.

5 How should war be fought? Part one

> It is occasionally lawful to kill the innocent not by mistake, but with full knowledge of what one is doing … This is proven, since it would otherwise be impossible to wage war against the guilty, thereby preventing the just side from fighting.
>
> Vitoria[1]

> … for we know enough, if we know we are the king's subjects: If his cause be wrong, our obedience to the king wipes the crime of it out of us.
>
> William Shakespeare[2]

The morality of war is divided into two parts, *jus ad bellum*, concerning *when* a state may fight, the initiation (and continuation) of war, and *jus in bello*, concerning *how* it should fight, the conduct of war. The two parts are usually seen to represent a moral division of labor: *jus ad bellum* is relevant mainly to leaders, and *jus in bello* is relevant mainly to the combatants. The rules for leaders are the *ad bellum* criteria discussed in the last two chapters. In this chapter and the next, we consider the *in bello* criteria, the rules for combatants. There are three basic *in bello* rules: the principles of *discrimination*, *proportionality*, and *due care*. Each of these principles is a necessary condition, and a military action in war is justified only if it satisfies all three. A consequence of adherence to the *in bello* rules is the limitation of the violence of war, not only through reducing the extent of human suffering while war goes on, but also through facilitating the subsequent establishment of peaceful relations between

---

[1] Francisco Vitoria, "On the Law of War," in Anthony Pagden and Jeremy Lawrance (eds.), *Vitoria: Political Writings* (Cambridge University Press, 1991), pp. 293–327, at p. 315 (emphasis removed).

[2] William Shakespeare, *Henry V*, Act 4, Scene 1, *The Riverside Shakespeare* (Boston, Houghton Mifflin, 1974), p. 957.

the belligerents.[3] But some *in bello* rules may have a moral foundation independent of their efficiency in limiting the violence.

5.1 The war in Afghanistan: the Bala Baluk episode

Shortly after the terrorist attacks of September 11, 2001, the United States went to war against Afghanistan to overthrow the Taliban regime, then in power over most of the country, which had been harboring al-Qaeda, the organization responsible for the attacks. Working with insurgent forces already battling the Taliban, the United States and Britain quickly overthrew the regime. US forces remained in Afghanistan, joined by forces from other member states of NATO (North American Treaty Organization), to stabilize the new regime they helped to put in power. The occupation continued into the next decade, although the main focus of attention for the United States for much of that time shifted to the war in Iraq. The Taliban were never completely subdued, in part because they had safe haven next door in the "lawless" tribal regions of Pakistan, and their insurgency against the Afghan government grew. Because the number of NATO troops was relatively small, given the large size of the areas in which Taliban insurgents were active, the troops, in their engagements with the insurgents, relied heavily on *close support air strikes* (air strikes in support of ground troops in battle).

There were a large number of episodes in which Afghan civilians were killed by US close support air strikes. One of the worst occurred on May 4, 2009 in southwestern Afghanistan, in the Bala Baluk district of Farah province. According to local reports, endorsed by the Afghan government, over 140 civilians were killed by NATO air strikes, including 93 children and 25 women.[4] According to a preliminary investigation by the non-governmental organization Human Rights Watch, a large Taliban force entered a village in the Bala Baluk district on May 3. A firefight ensued between these forces and forces of the Afghan government and NATO. During that fighting close air support resulted in a reported six civilian deaths. In the early evening, according to villagers, most of the Taliban withdrew from the

---

[3] Michael Walzer, *Just and Unjust Wars* (New York: Basic Books, 1977), p. 132.
[4] Reuters Press, "List of 140 Afghan Killed in US Attack Includes 93 Children," www.informationclearinghouse.info/article22603.htm, accessed September 16, 2009.

village, but at 8:30, air strikes began again, with between eight and twelve bombs being dropped, killing most of the civilians who died.[5] While the precise details about the Bala Baluk episode are a matter of controversy, it seems clear that many civilians were killed by the air strikes at Bala Baluk. How might this attack be assessed in terms of the main principles of *jus in bello*?

(1) The focus on the deaths of civilians indicates that the most important moral criticism of the episode is that it violates the *principle of discrimination*, which requires that combatants discriminate in their attacks between combatants and civilians, attacking only the former. Combatants may neither (a) attack a target deliberately intending to kill civilians nor (b) attack a target indiscriminately, that is, in a way that makes no effort to distinguish between combatants and civilians. The US air strikes can be criticized in terms of this principle. While the United States presumably did not attack intending to kill civilians, there are strong indications that the attack was indiscriminate. The large number of civilian deaths suggests that the air attack was carried out without a serious effort to distinguish between combatants and civilians.

(2) The *principle of proportionality* of *jus in bello* differs in important respects from its *ad bellum* cousin. On one interpretation, *in bello* proportionality requires that the evil created by a particular military attack or engagement not be disproportionate when compared with the contribution of the attack to victory in the overall war. The principle requires weighing the moral wrong of an attack against the military advantage achieved. How does Bala Baluk fare in terms of this principle? The military advantage expected from these close support air strikes was (a) victory in the battle in which they are used, enhancing the overall chances of victory in the war, and (b) reducing casualties among NATO forces. But the contributions of the Bala Baluk air strikes to the overall chances of victory seem modest, at best. Some Taliban combatants were probably killed, although, according to reports, the bulk of the strikes occurred after a large portion of the Taliban had left the area. Nor is it clear that the strikes saved many,

[5] Human Rights Watch, "Afghanistan: US should Act to End Bombing Tragedies," www. hrw.org, accessed September 13, 2009.

if any, lives of NATO troops. On the other side, the civilian deaths from the strikes probably upset many Afghans and undermined their support for NATO's presence, representing a significant loss of military advantage.[6] There is, then, a strong argument that the air strikes at Bala Baluk violated *in bello* proportionality.

(3) The *principle of due care* requires that combatants make efforts to minimize the amount of harm to civilians their attacks cause. While *in bello* proportionality requires that the foreseeable civilian harm not be disproportionate to the military advantage of the operation, due care requires that civilian harm be kept as low as possible. This idea is sometimes expressed by requiring a *precautionary* approach, an approach of *constant care* in military operations to avoid civilian casualties, including gathering adequate intelligence, choosing the least harmful means and methods of attack, and timing the attack to minimize risk to civilians.[7] Clearly, these efforts may come at the cost of military advantage, for example, by increasing the risk to one's own forces, but this is a price that this principle requires be paid.[8] There is a strong argument that the air strikes at Bala Baluk violated due care. There seems to have been little effort, for example, to gather adequate intelligence about the situation, especially if it indeed is true that most of the Taliban had left the area before the strikes that killed the vast majority of the civilians. More generally, Bala Baluk seems to have been part of a general US and NATO policy then in effect of utilizing close air support in disregard of the increased risk to civilians in order to provide greater safety for their own forces, and, in broader terms, to avoid a need to increase the overall number of troops in the country, which would have lessened the need for air support to relieve outnumbered forces. The principle of due care puts a limit on the extent to which such a policy can be exercised, a limit that seems, in the case of Bala Baluk, to have been exceeded.

---

[6] Carlotta Gall and Taimoor Shah, "Civilian Deaths Imperil Support for Afghan War," *New York Times* (May 7, 2009).

[7] Human Rights Watch, "Troops in Contact: Airstrikes and Civilian Deaths in Afghanistan," www.hrw.org, accessed September 4, 2009, pp. 35–36.

[8] Walzer, *Just and Unjust Wars*, especially p. 156, uses the notion of "due care," emphasizing the need to increase military risks in order to decrease civilian risk.

Two other aspects of the Bala Baluk episode deserve comment. First, the Taliban clearly violate *jus in bello* on a large scale, for example, with suicide bomb attacks aimed at civilians. In 2008, according to one estimate, two-thirds of the civilians killed in the Afghan conflict were killed by the Taliban.[9] In the case of Bala Baluk, the US military charged that the Taliban had herded civilians against their will into some of the structures that were attacked in the air strikes.[10] This brings up an important moral question: if one side seeks military advantage by attacking civilians or using them as shields, should the other side be allowed to relax the protection it provides for enemy civilians? If one side abandons the principles, it may seem only fair that the other side may do so as well. Otherwise the other side would be fighting with "one hand tied behind its back." This raises a deep issue about the nature of the *in bello* rules, namely, whether they are based simply on convention and reciprocity, or, instead, have deeper moral foundations. We discuss this question in the next chapter. Many believe that violation of *in bello* rules by one side does *not* give the other side license to violate them as well. The Human Rights Watch report claims: "Serious violations of the laws of war by one side do not absolve the other side from its obligation to refrain from unlawful acts."[11]

The other aspect is that Bala Baluk is part of a war that is importantly different from most of the wars we have discussed so far. The Afghanistan War is not between two states, but between a state (Afghanistan), with the support of other states (the United States and other members of NATO), and a non-state entity, the Taliban insurgency. Subsequent to its overthrow, the Taliban became an insurgent group fighting a guerrilla war, and the Afghan state and NATO are fighting a war of *counterinsurgency*. The armed conflict is an intra-state or civil war, in that its primary aspect is a struggle between two forces within a state, with the added dimension of outside states coming to the aid of one of the sides. Since World War II, most of the world's armed conflicts have been intra-state, and taking account of them is an important challenge for just war theory. This is addressed in Chapter 7.

---

[9] Golmar Motevalli, "Analysis – Civilian Deaths Mount as the Afghan War Deepens," Reuters, www.reuters.com, accessed September 13, 2009.

[10] Reuters Press, "List of 140."

[11] Human Rights Watch, "Troops in Contact," p. 5.

The *in bello* assessment of the Bala Baluk attack has made no reference to the question of whether the Afghanistan War is *ad bellum* just. This omission suggests that *in bello* judgments are not dependent on *ad bellum* judgments. In the next chapter, extending our discussion of dependence in Chapter 3, we consider whether *jus in bello* is dependent on *jus ad bellum*.

5.2 The war convention

Jus in bello is normally understood to encompass a wide range of rules for the conduct of war, a much wider range than is represented by the principles of discrimination, proportionality, and due care. Michael Walzer refers to the set of rules constituting *jus in bello* in this wider sense as the *war convention*. The war convention is "the set of articulated norms, customs, professional codes, legal precepts, religious and philosophical principles, and reciprocal arrangements that shape our judgments of military conduct."[12] The war convention includes a large number of specific conventions, mainly set forth in IHL, the component of international law concerning war. IHL (along with international law, more generally) is primarily composed of international agreements, such as the Geneva Conventions, which most states have adopted.

A convention, speaking generally, is a norm of behavior within a group, a rule that governs the interactions of members of the group. A convention exists, first, when the rule it represents is adhered to by most of the group's members most of the time and, second, when the members take a *critical attitude* toward behavior in relation to the rule, that is, when they tend to assess their own and others' behavior in terms of the rule.[13] Conventions are sometimes formally agreed to, as the Hague or Geneva Conventions were, but often there is no formal adoption of a convention; the agreement is implicit, consisting simply in general conformity and the taking of a critical attitude toward behavior in relation to the rule, as is the case with the conventions of etiquette. If adherence to a convention falls off sufficiently, the convention ceases to be, as a language, which is composed of conventions, dies out when it loses its speakers.

---

[12] Walzer, *Just and Unjust Wars*, p. 44.
[13] H. L. A. Hart, *The Concept of Law* (Oxford University Press, 1961), pp. 55–56.

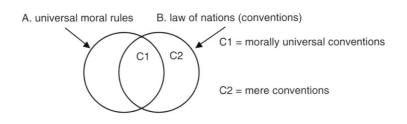

Figure 5.1   *Jus in bello* rules

There is a distinction made by many in the just war tradition between two groups of *in bello* conventions. Consider Grotius' distinction between the *law of nature* and the *law of nations*. Rules of conduct, he asserts, may be "either a correct deduction from the principles of our nature, or some general agreement. The former means that it is a law of nature, the latter that it is a law of nations."[14] Grotius was one of the first to develop the idea of international law. The law of nature is composed of *universal moral rules*, and the law of nations is composed of the conventional rules of international society (including the rules of the war convention). The universal moral rules embody respect for human rights, the claim rights discussed in the last chapter.

Most of the rules of the war conventions are part of the law of nations, but some are also identical with or directly derived from universal moral rules. Using Grotius' terms, the law of nations and the law of nature partly overlap. For example, the rule that combatants should not attack innocent civilians is part of the law of nations and is also a universal moral rule embodying respect for human rights. This suggests two categories of *in bello* conventions, as represented in Figure 5.1:

(C1) those identical with or directly derived from universal moral rules; and

(C2) those *not* identical with or directly derived from universal moral rules.

[14] Hugo Grotius, *The Rights of War and Peace*, ed. Richard Tuck (Indianapolis, IN: Liberty Fund, 2005), Prolegomenon, p. 1756.

Those in (C2) are part of the law of nations only, that is, they are *merely conventional*. Many rules of the war convention fall into this second category. For example, consider this provision of the Geneva Conventions: "The wearing [by prisoners of war] of badges of rank and nationality, as well as of decorations, shall be permitted."[15] This convention is clearly not derived from a universal moral rule. Let us say that conventions in (C1) are *morally universal conventions*, while those in (C2) are, in contrast, *mere conventions*, conventions without the backing of universal moral rules.

The two categories are represented in the words of Justice Joseph Story in his opinion in *United States* v. *La Jeune Eugenie*, a famous 1822 case concerning the African slave trade: "Now the law of nations may be deduced, first, from the general principles of right and justice ... or, secondly, in things indifferent or questionable, from the customary observances and recognitions of civilized nations; or, lastly, from the conventional or positive law, that regulates the intercourse between states."[16] Story's "general principles of right and justice" correspond to our universal moral rules. His first point is that some of the laws of nations are also in this category. His second and third points are that some of the laws of nations are conventions of international society not derived from universal moral rules, some customary (second point) and some of positive law (third point). Story's claim that the *in bello* conventions may be either "indifferent or questionable" from the perspective of "the general principles of right and justice" suggests that mere conventions may be divided into those that are inconsistent with universal moral rules (those that are "questionable") and those that are neutral in relation to universal moral rules (those that are "indifferent"). Thus (C2) may be divided into:

(C2a) conventions neutral in relation to universal moral rules; and

(C2b) conventions inconsistent with universal moral rules.

An example of (C2a) would be the convention mentioned above allowing prisoners of war to wear badges and decorations. A hypothetical example of (C2b) would be a convention allowing the punishment of the families of enemy combatants.

---

[15] "Geneva Convention III Relative to the Treatment of Prisoners of War," Adam Roberts and Richard Guelff (eds.), *Documents on the Laws of War*, 3rd edn. (Oxford University Press, 2000), p. 260.

[16] *United States* v. *La Jeune Eugenie*, 26 Federal Cases 832 (1822), pp. 846–848.

An interesting aspect of the contrast between (C2a) and (C2b) conventions is suggested in a remark on a different topic by American philosopher Thomas Scanlon. Writing on free speech, Scanlon asserts: "It seems clear to me that our (or at least my) intuitions about freedom of expression involve both natural and artificial elements. An adequate account of the subject should make clear whether these two kinds of intuitions represent rival views of freedom of expression or whether they are compatible or complementary."[17] On analogy, the natural elements of our view of the morality of war are the (C1) conventions and the artificial elements are the (C2) conventions. If the natural and artificial elements are *rival* views of the morality of war, many *in bello* rules would be (C2b) conventions, those inconsistent with universal moral rules. But if the natural and artificial elements are *compatible* or *complementary*, most or all of the artificial elements would be (C2a) conventions. We should keep this contrast in mind as we further explore the war convention in this and the next chapters.

Consider now categories analogous to (C1) and (C2) in domestic law. In distinguishing the categories of domestic law, we can use Aristotle's distinction between legal justice and natural justice, mentioned in Chapter 2. Natural justice, like Grotius' law of nature, is composed of universal moral rules, rules that are the same everywhere. In contrast, legal justice is composed of the conventional legal rules of particular societies, which collectively constitute, as we might call it, the *law convention* of those societies. (1) Some of the conventional legal rules will be derived from rules of natural justice, such as laws against murder; (2) some may be inconsistent with rules of natural justice, similar to those in (C2b), such as laws denying suffrage based on race or sex; and (3) some may be neither derived from nor inconsistent with rules of natural justice, similar to those in (C2a), such as legal rules requiring that automobiles be driven on the right-hand side of the road. Traditionally, behavior prohibited by laws in (1) is referred to as *malum in se*, behavior that is wrong in itself, not wrong simply because it is illegal, while behavior prohibited by laws in (2) and (3) is referred to as *malum prohibitum*, behavior that is wrong simply because it is illegal. Analogously, in *jus in bello*, we may regard behavior prohibited by (C1)

---

[17] Thomas Scanlon, "A Theory of Freedom of Expression," *Philosophy & Public Affairs* 1, no. 2 (Winter, 1972), pp. 204–226, at p. 206.

conventions as *malum in se*, and behavior prohibited by (C2) conventions as *malum prohibitum*.

Consider Vitoria's response to the question of whether enemy combatants taken prisoner may be executed: "I reply that, in itself, there is no reason why prisoners taken in a just war ... should not be killed, so long as common equity is observed. But as many practices in war are based on the law of nations, it appears to be established by custom that prisoners taken after a victory ... should not be killed, [and] this law of nations should be respected."[18] Vitoria here asserts that the law of nations prohibiting the killing of prisoners is a mere convention, in category (C2).[19] So it concerns behavior which is *malum prohibitum*.

The view that the war convention is composed of both mere conventions and morally universal conventions is similar to Walzer's view of *jus in bello*. The war convention, he asserts, is "a set of restrictions that rest in part on the agreements of states but that also have an independent foundation in moral principle." By including agreements of states as part of the war convention, he suggests that not all *in bello* conventions are morally universal. Indeed, some of the rules in the war convention "are susceptible to the transformations brought about by social change, technological innovation, and foreign conquest," as could be the case for those that are mere conventions.[20] One question for later is whether the main *in bello* conventions, especially the principle of discrimination, are (C1) or (C2) conventions.

Although (C2) conventions are not derived from universal moral rules, adherence to them usually has moral value *in terms of consequences*. There is a moral reason to have some of these conventions, even though they do not represent universal moral rules. This contrast reflects the distinction, discussed in earlier chapters, between a deontological moral perspective, represented by the universal moral rules behind (C1) conventions, and a consequentialist moral perspective, which judges the value of an action or a rule in terms of consequences. Grotius draws an analogy between domestic law and international law in terms of the role of consequences: "But just as the laws of each state consult the utility of that state, [there are

---

[18] Vitoria, "On the Law of War," pp. 321–322.

[19] Note that this law-of-nations rule does not contradict Vitoria's law-of-nature rule because the latter *allows*, but does not require, that prisoners be killed.

[20] Walzer, *Just and Unjust Wars*, pp. 131, 42.

laws] which consult the utility not of the individual societies but of their totality. This is what is termed 'the law of nations,' in so far as we distinguish that from the law of nature."[21]

The beneficial consequences of adherence to (C2) conventions lie in reducing the destructiveness of war. They are rules for *limiting* war, and, in general, the more limits observed in war, the less destructive it is. Moreover, the conventions tend to continue in existence through expectations of reciprocity. *Reciprocity* is a form of mutual adherence to a rule, where adherence by one side encourages adherence by the other. Each party adheres in reasonable expectation that the other party will follow suit. In the case of a convention between M and N, for example, M's adherence generally *directly* benefits N. But the idea of reciprocity is that M's adherence encourages N to adhere, and N's adherence directly benefits M. So M's adherence *indirectly* benefits himself because it, in turn, encourages N's adherence. So, a main motivation for adherence to a convention is that this reinforces expectations of reciprocity. M does not benefit unless N adheres, but M's adherence is generally a necessary condition for N's adherence. Expectations of reciprocity stabilize a convention, promoting its continued existence. Moreover, expectations of reciprocity serve to coordinate social behavior within a group, which is valuable for all because it permits individuals to predict what others will do, allowing them to pursue their own goals accordingly. Of course, in terms of benefits of adherence, some conventions are better than others.

At the international level, the same dynamic of reciprocity applies. States want other states to adhere and they recognize that they cannot reasonably expect this, if they themselves do not. As an example of this, consider reactions to the United States government's policy of using torture in the interrogation of terrorist suspects after the September 11, 2001 terrorist attacks. Torture violates rules of the war convention. Fear of another terrorist attack led to support for torture, but, despite such fear, there was considerable domestic opposition to violating the torture convention, and some of this was expressed in terms of reciprocity. For example, General John Vessey argued that torture by the United States "could give opponents a legal argument for the mistreatment of Americans being held prisoner

---

[21] Grotius, *Rights of War*, Prolegomenon, pp. 1749–1750.

in time of war."[22] The United States would benefit from the convention against torture (not having its own troops tortured) only if there was an expectation of reciprocity, which would require US adherence.

Thus, adherence to the (C2) conventions is generally *morally beneficial*, even though these conventions are not derived from universal moral rules, as (C1) conventions are. But, the moral value of (C2) conventions, since it is consequentialist, depends on the circumstances, while the moral value of (C1) conventions, because they are derived from universal moral rules, does not. There is always moral value in adhering to them.

5.3 The principle of discrimination: civilian immunity

According to the principle of discrimination, combatants are allowed to attack only enemy combatants. This principle (also called the *principle of distinction*) naturally divides into two component principles, the *principle of civilian immunity*, which stipulates that civilians may not be attacked, and the *principle of combatant liability*, which holds that enemy combatants may be attacked. The principle of civilian immunity is that civilians are not morally liable to attack, while the principle of combatant liability is that combatants are not immune from attack. In the everyday sense of the terms, *combatants* are members of the military, and *civilians* are not.[23] But, as we seek a justification for these principles, it will become clear, speaking more strictly, that some civilians are liable to attack, and some combatants are immune from attack.

In this section we consider civilian immunity. Combatant liability will be discussed later. The principle of civilian immunity has taken a beating in the past century. Civilians have become an increasing portion of the increasingly larger number of casualties of war. As mentioned earlier, a century ago, the ratio of combatant to civilian deaths in war was approximately eight to one, whereas by the end of the twentieth century the ratio had reversed and was roughly one to eight.[24] The twenty-first century

---

[22] www.humanrightsfirst.info/pdf/06914-etn-vessey-geneva-ltr.pdf, accessed October 11, 2009.

[23] *Combatant* is a general term for a uniformed member of the military. Other terms may be too specific, as in the United States military, where a different term is used for combatants in each military branch: soldiers, sailors, marines, and airmen.

[24] See Mary Kaldor, *New and Old Wars*, 2nd edn. (Stanford University Press, 2006), p. 9. Aaron Xavier Fellmeth finds that the proportion of civilian casualties was between 5

does not seem to have offered any improvement in this dismal trend.[25] This unprecedented slaughter of civilians poses perhaps the greatest contemporary challenge to just war theory, calling into question its practical ability to bring about effective limitations in war.[26] The greatest orgy of civilian destruction, in terms of numbers, occurred mid-century in World War II, where an estimated 35 million civilians were killed. Many of these were killed in the deliberate bombing of cities, especially by the Allies, a moral issue considered in the next chapter. The initial formulation of the principle is:

> *Principle of civilian immunity*: civilians are immune from attack in war.

The principle of civilian immunity prohibits attacks on civilians, but civilians can be attacked in different ways. The prohibition covers not only *deliberate attacks* but also *indiscriminate attacks*, which are attacks undertaken with no effort to distinguish between combatants and civilians. Indiscriminate or reckless attacks are those "not directed at a specific military objective."[27] Some claim that respect for civilian immunity should be cost-free from a military perspective because there is generally little or no military advantage in killing civilians. But part of the plausibility of this claim lies in thinking of deliberate attacks on civilians. While such attacks may be of little military value, indiscriminate attacks may have military value because they often are a less costly way of destroying military targets as, for example, they allow quicker action and expose the attackers to less risk. Moreover, some have challenged the claim that deliberate attacks on civilians have no military value. Advocates of both *strategic bombing* (the deliberate bombing of population centers), widely practiced in World War II, and nuclear deterrence, widely practiced since 1945, claim that

---

and 10 percent in World War I and between 75 and 90 percent in the 1990s. "Questioning Civilian Immunity," *Texas International Law Journal* 43, no. 3 (Summer 2008), pp 453–501, at p. 455.

[25] In the 2003 Iraq War, combatants comprised less than 18 percent of the deaths. Fellmeth, "Questioning Civilian Immunity," p. 457.

[26] The recent extent of civilian deaths has led some to suggest that civilian immunity may no longer be an existing convention. George Mavrodes, "Conventions and the Morality of War," *Philosophy & Public Affairs* 4, no. 2 (Winter 1975), pp. 117–131, at p. 128.

[27] Geneva Conventions, Additional Protocols 1, article 51(4), in Roberts and Guelff, *Documents*, p. 449.

bombing or threatening to bomb civilians can achieve important military objectives. These issues are explored in the next chapter.

It may be helpful to begin by considering some arguments *against* the principle of civilian immunity. The English essayist George Orwell (doubtless with some irony) criticized those opposing the World War II British policy of strategic bombing. He argued: "Why is it worse to kill civilians than soldiers," for to attack only soldiers "picks out and slaughters all the healthiest and bravest of the young male population."[28] His argument may be based on considerations of distributive justice, on the idea that the suffering of war should be spread more equally in society.[29] In a related argument, Michael Green criticizes the principle of discrimination as a hold-over from earlier, pre-democratic forms of political organization, where most of the population lacked political authority. In a democracy, in contrast, political authority, and so responsibility for national policy, including war, is shared among the population.[30] As a result, there is no reason that the pain of war should not also be shared. Orwell and Green suggest that moral liability to attack in war should fall on civilians as well as combatants. To criticize these arguments effectively, we need to find some characteristic that distinguishes combatants from civilians, an *immunity-overriding characteristic*, so to speak, which combatants have, but civilians lack.

Orwell probably assumes that what makes someone liable to attack in war is that she is *morally responsible* for the war, and this seems to be Green's view as well. This is suggested by Orwell's endorsing the idea of shared suffering with the comment that this would lead to the sight of "a jingo with a bullet hole in him."[31] A jingo is a chauvinistic civilian who strongly advocates for a belligerent foreign policy for his state.[32] A jingo, sharing moral responsibility for a war, should, in fairness, share its suffering. This line

---

[28] Orwell, quoted in Richard Norman, *Ethics, Killing, and War* (Cambridge University Press, 1995), p. 163.

[29] Igor Primoratz, "Civilian Immunity in War: Its Grounds, Scope, and Weight," in Primoratz (ed.), *Civilian Immunity in War* (Oxford University Press, 2007), pp. 21–41, at pp. 22–23.

[30] Michael Green, "War, Innocence and Theories of Sovereignty," *Social Theory and Practice* 18 (1992), pp. 39–62, quotation at p. 44.

[31] Orwell, quoted in Primoratz, "Civilian Immunity in War," p. 23.

[32] This argument works only if the war to which the jingo leads his state is an unjust war, but I ignore this complication here.

of thinking is bolstered by commentators creating portraits of a hypothetical pair of contrasting individuals. The first is a war-mongering civilian (a
jingo) who provides strong support to the political party advocating war,
and the second is a poor, uneducated, hapless conscript, who finds himself
on the battlefield unwillingly. The principle of discrimination would allow
attack on the hapless conscript, but give immunity to the jingoistic civilian, and this does not seem fair or morally correct.[33]

The idea seems plausible that someone is liable to attack only if he
is morally responsible for some unjust harm that the attack is meant to
avoid. Moral responsibility of the targets is what justifies attacks in war.
Accordingly, the guilty (the morally responsible) are liable to attack and
the non-guilty, the innocent (the morally non-responsible) are immune.
This implies that some civilians, such as the jingo, are liable to attack, and
some combatants, such as the hapless conscript, are not, which contra-
dicts the principle of discrimination. The distinction between innocence
(responsibility) and guilt (non-responsibility) cuts across the distinction
between combatant and civilian, since the jingo is guilty, and the hapless
combatant is innocent. This lies at the base of Orwell's and Green's criticisms of the principle of discrimination.

Noting this point, American philosopher George Mavrodes argues that
labeling civilians as innocent and combatants as guilty results in "divest-
ing [innocence and guilt] of the moral significance which they require if
they are to justify the moral import of the distinction itself."[34] Because
liability to attack should result from moral responsibility for a war, the
standard division between civilians and combatants leaves the principle
of discrimination without moral support. The principle would be justified only if liability to attack is separate from moral responsibility for the
war. Mavrodes poses an interesting solution to this problem; he offers
"different grounds" for the moral relevance of the distinction between
combatant and civilian. He proposes that our moral obligation not to
attack civilians is the result of a mere convention, and so is a "convention-
dependent" obligation rather than an obligation resulting from universal moral rules. He is saying that the principle of discrimination is a (C2)
rather than a (C1) convention, and its obligations exist only because the
convention itself does. The principle of civilian immunity "is best thought

[33] Mavrodes, "Conventions and the Morality of War," p. 122.   [34] *Ibid.*, p. 124.

of as a convention-dependent obligation related to a convention which sub-stitutes for warfare a certain form of limited combat."[35] The principle of civilian immunity is a mere convention adopted to make war less destruc-tive, not one derived from a universal moral rule.

American philosopher Robert Fullinwider criticizes Mavrodes' argu-ment. According to Fullinwider, liability to attack may be viewed from two moral perspectives, "the point of view of self-defense and the point of view of punishment." The punishment perspective, which Mavrodes adopts, concerns moral responsibility, innocence and guilt. But the self-defense perspective provides support for the principle of discrimination in terms of a universal moral rule. Fullinwider claims that "the moral relevance of the distinction in war between combatants and noncombat-ants" is based on the *principle of self-defense*, according to which individuals may be attacked if they are putting the life of another "directly and imme-diately in mortal jeopardy" and force is necessary "to end that threat."[36] The self-defense principle provides a basis, apart from mere convention, to separate moral liability to attack from moral responsibility for a war, and it gives a moral reason why the hapless conscript may be subject to attack while the jingo is not, namely, that the conscript but not the jingo poses a threat which may justify self-defense. If we assume that the principle of self-defense is a universal moral rule, a liberty that all individuals have to protect themselves (or others) from a deadly threat, we may view the prin-ciple of discrimination, contra Mavrodes, as a (C1) convention.

The idea that self-defense justifies civilian immunity goes back at least to Grotius. He argued that there is a "Right of Self-Defense" not based on the "Injustice or Crime of the Aggressor" that is applicable in war, implying that combatants may be liable to attack even if they are not mor-ally responsible for the threat they pose. Even "if the Person be no Ways to blame, as for Instance, *a Soldier who carries Arms with a good Intention*; or a Man that should *mistake me* for *another*; or one *distracted* or *delirious* (which may possibly happen) I don't therefore lose that *Right* that I have of *Self-Defence*."[37] Correspondingly, civilians would be immune from attack because self-defense does not justify attacks against them. Colm McKeogh

---

[35] *Ibid.*, p. 127.

[36] Robert Fullinwider, "War and Innocence," *Philosophy & Public Affairs* 5, no. 1 (Autumn 1975), pp. 90–97, at pp. 92, 93.

[37] Grotius, *Rights of War*, Book II, chapter 1, section 3, p. 397.

observes that, in the case of *jus ad bellum*, Grotius abandons "the concepts of guilt and innocence, central to the attempt to justify war for more than a thousand years." A focus on moral responsibility as the operative moral consideration had led to the idea that a just war is essentially *punitive*, a form of punishment. Grotius "famously declared the punitive justification of war to be at an end."[38] This shift in thinking led to the abandonment of the medieval notion that a just war is punishment of the aggressor state and to the modern idea that just war is a defense against rights violations threatened by the aggressor. Grotius extended his insight to *jus in bello*. Because military attacks are justified in terms of defense, civilians cannot be attacked because they are not posing the kind of direct and immediate threat that justifies defensive force.

Liability is a general purpose moral and legal notion; a person who is liable or has liability is subject to certain sorts of restraints or impositions at the hands of others. In tort law, for example, a person may be liable for paying damages to those injured in an accident he caused. In *jus in bello*, the issue is liability of individuals to attack in war. The two justifications for attack in war, punitive and defensive, correspond to two forms of liability. The form of liability associated with a punitive justification may be called *fault liability*, liability to attack due to being at fault, being morally responsible for some wrong or harm. In contrast, the form of liability associated with a defensive justification is *threat liability*, liability to attack due to posing a threat of immediate and serious harm. Fault liability results from a person's being responsible for (being at fault in regard to) some unjust harm his actions cause or threaten, and it justifies punitive force (or punishment). In contrast, threat liability results from a person's posing an imminent threat of serious harm, and it is the justification for defensive force. (A person with fault liability is also often *culpable*, or deserving of punishment, while a person with threat liability is liable to attack, but not deserving of being attacked.) The two forms of liability are not necessarily exclusive, as one may be liable on both defensive and punitive grounds. For example, if one attacks an aggressor in self-defense, the aggressor usually, but not always, has fault liability as well as threat liability. But some aggressors, like the hapless conscript,

---

[38] Colm McKeogh, "Civilian Immunity in War: From Augustine to Vattel," in Primoratz (ed.), *Civilian Immunity in War*, p. 73.

have threat liability without having fault liability.[39] The extent of force to which a person is liable depends upon which form of liability she has. Threat liability makes one liable to the amount of force necessary to put an end to the threat, while fault liability (when coupled with culpability) makes one liable to the amount of force corresponding to the degree of punishment the person is owed.

Fullinwider's proposal implies that the principle of civilian immunity is based on the principle of self-defense, not on moral guilt. Civilians are immune from attack because they lack threat liability, even though, like the jingo, they might be morally responsible for the war and so have fault liability. One reason that liability to attack in war cannot be based on moral responsibility or guilt is that fault liability cannot, in practice, be assessed in the immediacy of war. Determining guilt involves determining a person's mental state, and this can effectively be evaluated only through a judicial proceeding. The jingo might be guilty of war crimes and be liable for prosecution and punishment for them outside the context of the war, but not liable for attack in the midst of war. In contrast, the lack of threat liability is fairly easy to determine. Without the need to assess his mental state, a person's behavior is generally sufficient to show that he does not pose an immediate threat. Moreover, the extent of force justified follows the same pattern. The degree of fault liability, and so the degree of appropriate punishment, cannot be assessed in the midst of war, and, in the case of a combatant, may not be sufficient to justify the punishment of death. In contrast, threat liability justifies killing, if killing is the only way to avoid the lethal threat. (There is one apparent problem with this use of threat liability to establish combatant liability: many combatants liable to attack are not posing at that moment an immediate threat of the sort needed to bring the self-defense principle in to play. We discuss this later in the chapter.)

The four possibilities for combinations of threat and fault liability are set out in Table 5.1. Those who have fault liability are *responsible*, and those who lack it are *non-responsible*, while those who have threat liability are *threats*, and those who lack it are *non-threats* (also called *bystanders*).

---

[39] In fault liability innocence means *not morally responsible for harm*, while in threat liability it means *not directly causing harm*. Primoratz, "Civilian Immunity in War," p. 30.

Table 5.1. *Forms of individual liability*

		Individuals and threat liability	
		have	lack
Individuals and fault liability	have	(a) person is a responsible threat	(b) person is a responsible non-threat
	lack	(c) person is a non-responsible threat	(d) person is a non-responsible non-threat

Civilians are in categories (b) and (d); they may or may not be fault liable. The principle of civilian immunity is that no one in these categories is liable to attack in war. Civilians in (b) who are fault liable, as the jingo may be, cannot be attacked in war. Force, in the form of punishment, may be used against them only as the result of a judicial proceeding outside the context of war. Examples of punishment of civilians with fault liability are provided by some of the cases heard at the Nuremberg War Crimes Trials after World War II. The Nazi defendants at these trials included not only government decision makers and high-ranking officers, all of whom could be considered combatants, but also civilians. One was Julius Streicher, a virulently anti-Semitic magazine editor and propagandist for the Holocaust under the Nazi regime. Though there was no evidence that he participated in any wartime decision making, including decisions about the Holocaust, he was tried and convicted of crimes against humanity at Nuremberg.[40] But despite his guilt, it would not have been permissible to attack him as part of the war effort because he lacked threat liability. Combatants are in (a) and (c). They may be attacked in war, but they may not be punished (if captured).

But combatants can also have fault liability and so be subject to punishment if they have committed *war crimes*. War crimes are actions in war that violate major provisions of the war convention, the *in bello* rules. An example of this resulted from a Vietnam War episode in which a large number of civilians were deliberately killed by US combatants in the village of My Lai, an episode known as the My Lai (pronounced "me lie") Massacre.

[40] See "The Nuremberg Trials," at www.law.umkc.edu/faculty/projects/ftrials/nuremberg/nuremberg.htm, accessed October 28, 2009.

The main task of the American military effort in that war was to uproot the Viet Cong insurgent forces operating from the South Vietnamese countryside. This involved many operations where US forces entered rural villages seeking to capture or kill the insurgents thought to be based there. On March 16, 1968, a platoon of US soldiers, led by Lieutenant William Calley, entered My Lai, following up on a report that Viet Cong were operating from the village. No Viet Cong were found, and the platoon met no military resistance. The American combatants shot to death most of the civilian residents, approximately 500 in number.[41]

Because the villagers, as civilians, had immunity from attack, their killers were their murderers, who thus had fault liability and were subject to punishment. Though the massacre was covered up for a period of time, it became publically known over a year afterwards, and there were calls for legal justice. Amidst great controversy, Calley was eventually convicted for his role in the massacre, but he was the only one. He served a short portion of his sentence before it was commuted by then-president Richard Nixon. One moral and legal issue that arises from the episode is that of *command responsibility*, that is, whether Calley's superiors shared responsibility with him for the actions of his platoon. They were not in fact prosecuted. There was at least one hero of the My Lai episode, Warrant Officer Hugh Thompson, who, witnessing the massacre from an observation helicopter, landed and confronted Calley, saving the lives of several of the villagers. For many years, Thompson was shunned by the military, but in 1998 he received vindication, being awarded the Soldier's Medal by the government. Part of Thompson's vindication was that his story was given attention by the US military academies, where he was presented to the cadets and midshipmen as a model to be emulated.

5.4 Double effect

An apparent implication of the principle of civilian immunity, however, is that it implies unconditional anti-war pacifism. It appears that the criterion cannot be satisfied in war, making war morally impermissible. Consider the following statements:

---

[41] William Eckhardt, "My Lai: An American Tragedy," www.law.umkc.edu/faculty/projects/ftrials/mylai/ecktragedy.html, accessed November 1, 2010.

(1) morally, civilians cannot be attacked in war;

(2) war cannot be fought without civilians being attacked.

(1) is the principle of civilian immunity. (2) seems clearly true, given that modern war involves weapons of great destructive power against military forces not always sharply separated from civilians. Even when combatants take great caution to attack discriminately, civilians often die. (Such civilian deaths are labeled *collateral damage*.) But (1) and (2) together imply that war cannot morally be fought.[42]

Can just war theory avoid this implication? The solution to the puzzle is to recognize that a person can cause harm to another with different states of mind, and that these correspond to different degrees of stringency in the moral assessment of his action. The idea is that the degree to which a person is morally responsible for some harm he causes depends on whether the harm was intended or not. Consider the distinction between causing harm intentionally and causing it accidently. Morally, an agent is judged more harshly for intentional harm than for accidental harm. For example, the child will be held to greater moral account if he breaks the window deliberately than if he breaks it accidently. This opens the possibility of understanding the principle of civilian immunity in terms of this sort of difference. The way that this solution is embodied in the just war tradition is the *doctrine of double effect*, referred to in our discussion of Aquinas in Chapter 2. The "double" in "double effect" refers to the distinction between effects caused intentionally and effects caused unintentionally. Intentionally caused harm is held to stricter moral standard. The principle of civilian immunity applies only where civilians are killed or harmed intentionally. In contrast, when civilians are killed or harmed unintentionally, the combatant may still be held to moral account, but in terms of the other *in bello* principles, proportionality and due care, as we discuss later. Thus, (1) must be revised: morally, civilians cannot be *intentionally* attacked in war. With this revision, (1) and (2) imply pacifism only if (2) reads: war cannot be fought without civilians being *intentionally* attacked. But this new version of (2) is not obviously true in the way that the old version is. It is possible, though it may not often occur, that

---

[42] See Robert Holmes, *On War and Morality* (Princeton University Press, 1989), especially chapter 6.

war can be fought where all the civilians who are harmed are harmed unintentionally.

So, the new version of the principle of civilian immunity, in accord with the doctrine of double effect, is:

> *Principle of civilian immunity* (revised): civilians are immune from intentional attack in war.

But where precisely is the line to be drawn between intentional and unintentional civilian harm? Consider this passage from Grotius: "Thus a Ship full of Pirates, or a House of Thieves, may be sunk and fired, tho' within the Ship, or the House, there may be Children, or Women, or other innocent Persons."[43] This is consistent with Vitoria's statement at the beginning of this chapter: "It is occasionally lawful to kill the innocent not by mistake, but with full knowledge of what one is doing [for] it would otherwise be impossible to wage war against the guilty." In determining how the distinction between intentional and unintentional attacks is to be drawn, an important notion is *foresight*, that is, a combatant's knowledge or reasonable belief about the harm likely to result from his actions. Clearly, unforeseen harm is unintended, but not all foreseen harm is intended. Grotius and Vitoria make clear that some foreseen civilian deaths are permitted. Not only is war morally impossible without civilian deaths; it is also morally impossible without foreseen civilian deaths. Australian philosopher C. A. J. Coady remarks that "the conduct of war in contemporary circumstances is morally impossible unless warriors are allowed knowingly to put noncombatants at risk in certain circumstances."[44] This means that harm that is foreseen may also be unintentional.

This is how the doctrine of double effect is understood. Among unintended effects are some that are foreseen. While all intended effects are foreseen, not all foreseen effects are intended. For example, the pirate ship may be fired despite the attacker's foreseeing that it is likely that civilians will be killed in the process because the civilian deaths in that case though foreseen do not count as intended. There are various ways to tell whether a foreseen effect is intended or not. The basic idea is that an effect, foreseen

---

[43] Grotius, *Rights of War*, Book III, chapter 1, section 4, p. 1188.

[44] C. A. J. Coady, *Morality and Political Violence* (Cambridge University Press, 2008), p. 136.

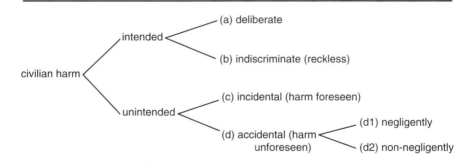

Figure 5.2   Modes of civilian harm in the doctrine of double effect

or not, is unintended when it is not part of the agent's plan. This would be the case if she either wishes the effect would not have occurred (or is indifferent to its having occurred) or would have taken the action even if she did not foresee the effect. The civilian deaths in the firing of the pirate ship are unintended because the attacker, we assume, does not wish the civilians' death and would still have taken the action even if the civilians were not present. The purpose was to kill the pirates, not the civilians. So, unintended effects may be either foreseen or unforeseen. Likewise, there are two categories of intended effects. As discussed earlier, the principle of civilian immunity rules out both deliberate and indiscriminate (or reckless) civilian harm. This creates a four-way distinction, as indicated in Figure 5.2. In war, a combatant may intentionally cause civilian harm either (a) deliberately or (b) indiscriminately (or recklessly), and he may unintentionally cause civilian harm either (c) *incidentally* or (d) *accidently*. Incidental harm is foreseen, while accidental harm is not foreseen.[45] (More on (d1) and (d2) shortly.)

The doctrine of double effect counts among intended effects both ends and means, both effects that are the purpose or ends of an action and effects that are adopted as means to those ends. The means are the effects on the casual chain from the action to the end or purpose. This is in accord with the saying that *he who intends the end intends the means*. For example, if someone breaks a valuable piggy bank in order to steal its contents, the

---

[45] The terms "incidental" and "accidental" are borrowed from *ibid.*, p. 134. But ordinarily the terms are not always used in this way, as an effect may be called incidental even when it is not foreseen.

breaking is intentional even though the purpose of the action is the theft. Contrast two scenarios, one where a combatant throws a grenade to destroy an enemy machine-gunner while foreseeing that this will also kill a nearby civilian, and the other where a combatant drops a grenade into the bag of an unsuspecting civilian walking by, expecting that the grenade will explode just as the civilian reaches the enemy combatant. In the latter scenario, but not the former, the civilian's death would be a means to the end of the enemy combatant's death. According to the doctrine of double effect, only in the latter scenario would the civilian's death be regarded as intended, and the action prohibited by the principle of civilian immunity.

The doctrine of double effect has its critics, who claim that it is too permissive. They would cite the scenarios just sketched as an example of this. In their view, there is no morally relevant difference between how the deaths were brought about in the two scenarios, and the principle of civilian immunity should apply in both cases. Indeed, the principle should prohibit *all* foreseen civilian harm. The line between harm falling under the principle and that not falling under the principle should be drawn between the accidental and the incidental, rather than between the intended and the unintended. This corresponds with the way that foreseen effects are generally classified in domestic law.[46] Colm McKeogh endorses the idea that no foreseen civilian harm should be permitted.[47] But he goes further, arguing that the prohibition should also extend to unforeseen or accidental civilian harm that is the result of negligence, our category (d1). Roughly speaking, harm is caused negligently when, though it is unforeseen, it *should have been foreseen*. Negligent harm is the result of carelessness, of a combatant's not attending to a battle situation closely enough to recognize the obvious evidence that her actions would put civilians at serious risk of harm. McKeogh would presumably allow only civilian harm in (d2). Of course, as suggested by Grotius and Vitoria, the more expansive one's interpretation of the scope of civilian immunity, the more difficult it becomes to wage war justly. McKeogh's position may imply pacifism.

---

[46] Following the legal maxim that one is presumed to intend the natural consequences of his or her actions. H. L. A. Hart, *Punishment and Responsibility* (Oxford University Press, 1968), pp. 119–120.

[47] McKeogh, "Civilian Immunity in War," p. 83.

The doctrine of double effect also specifies the role of the other *in bello* criteria. One part of the doctrine prescribes that the intended effects of a military action should be assessed in terms of the principle of civilian immunity. But another part concerns moral constraints on the unintended harm of an action as well. Consider Grotius' pirate ship. The first part of the doctrine shows that the principle of civilian immunity does not stand in the way of sinking the ship, despite the expected harm to the civilians, because that harm is unintended. The second part concerns the moral assessment of the incidental harm and it raises questions such as: (1) how many civilians are on board; and (2) are there other ways to attack the pirates that would impose less risk to the civilians? These questions bring the principles of proportionality and due care into the picture. We discuss these criteria in the next chapter.

Two other points should be made about civilian harm. First, civilian harm may be foreseen either as *certain* to occur or merely as *likely* to occur. Indeed, it is more common for combatants to foresee a *risk* to civilians from their actions, that is, a possibility or likelihood short of certainty. Information available to combatants in battle is often meager, and though it frequently indicates some risk of civilian harm, it is often insufficient to indicate the degree of certainty of that harm. As with other aspects of just war theory, we need to think about foreseen civilian harm in terms of reasonable expectations of the effects of an attack. Second, though we often have spoken of civilian harm mainly in terms of death, *jus in bello* is concerned with all serious civilian (lethal or non-lethal) harm to bodies, psyches, or property (civilian objects).

To see the sometimes stark demands of civilian immunity, consider a June 2005 episode from the Afghanistan War, involving a group of four members of the Navy's Special Operations forces ("Seals") on a mission ("Operation Redwing") to capture a leader of the insurgent forces known as the Taliban.[48] The Seals were deposited in a remote part of Afghanistan, and several hours into their mission the team encountered three Afghan civilians, two adult males and a boy. Given the nature of the mission, the team could not take the civilians prisoner, and if they were let go, there was a good chance that they would notify the Taliban of the team's presence. Should the team kill the civilians? The Seals chose, in respect of the

---

[48] See Laura Blumenfeld, "The Sole Survivor," *Washington Post*, June 11, 2007.

principle of civilian immunity, to let them go. An hour later, the team was attacked by a large Taliban force. The resulting two-hour firefight left three of the four members dead, along with sixteen other combatants in a rescue helicopter shot down by the Taliban. Many Taliban were killed as well. The only survivor of the team was Marcus Luttrell. (Interestingly, Luttrell was saved by an Afghan villager, who found the American gravely wounded and took him into his care, helping Luttrell recover and protecting him from the Taliban in the vicinity.) The principle of civilian immunity is clear: killing the civilians would have been wrong. Luttrell himself seems to affirm this judgment when he said later of his decision to spare the Afghans, "I'm not a murderer." But given what was at stake, and the impossibility of holding the civilians as prisoners, should the principle have been ignored? This case raises, at the *in bello* level, the issue of *military necessity*, the idea that combatants are morally permitted to do what is necessary from a military point of view, regardless of the *in bello* rules. Some would say that military necessity would permit the killing of the Afghans in those circumstances. We consider military necessity further in the next chapter.

Another important issue is that of *innocent shields*. States at war sometimes use civilians as "shields" either by placing military forces in their midst (in a residential neighborhood, for example) or by placing the civilians in the midst of the forces, so that the forces cannot be attacked without great harm to the civilians. In doing this, states seek to shield their forces from attack by counting on the enemy's reluctance to launch attacks that would harm civilians. The use of innocent shields is a familiar tactic in war, and familiar too from bad Westerns, where the outlaw grabs a bystander to hold in front of him for protection. An example from World War II is the Nazi practice of forcing civilians in occupied countries to ride on the front of locomotives to discourage resistance fighters from blowing up the trains. Shields represent a serious moral difficulty. Coady remarks: "The innocent shield problem represents an inescapable aspect of moral prohibitions: namely, the way in which the unscrupulous can exploit the adherence of the scrupulous to moral standards."[49] The shields in question are innocent, not simply because they are civilians, but because they have little or no say in their becoming shields. Sometimes shields may be

---

[49] Coady, *Morality and Political Violence*, p. 149.

voluntary, but this would be exceptional. One possible example is Serbian civilians in the Kosovo War who stationed themselves on bridges over the Danube that were expected targets of NATO bombers, some wearing shirts with targets printed on the back.

When there are innocent shields involved, is the opponent morally bound, in the light of the principles of proportionality and due care, not to attack the shielded targets (as the users of the shields hope)? We could think of the question in this way: when one side coerces its civilians to become shields, it violates an obligation it has towards them that is similar (or related) to an *in bello* obligation it has towards the opponent's civilians not to impose such a risk on them. One egregious example of a violation of such an obligation is the reported practice of Iran during the Iran–Iraq War (1980–1988) of sending human waves of its own citizens, sometimes children, to clear minefields laid by the Iraqis.[50] If state behavior in using shields is seen in this way, the question of whether states should attack shielded targets then becomes a version of the more general question raised earlier, namely, whether one side's violation of its *in bello* obligations relieves the other side of its corresponding obligations. Perhaps, when one side uses shields, the other side is morally permitted to attack the shielded targets anyway, ignoring its otherwise applicable *in bello* obligations. Walzer notes: "When we judge the unintended killing of civilians, we need to know how those civilians came to be in the battle zone in the first place." Later he notes, speaking of the German use of innocent shields in the Franco-Prussian war, that "the responsibility for their deaths, even if these deaths were actually inflicted by the French, lay with the German commanders."[51] Or perhaps, as Walzer suggests elsewhere, responsibility for harm to the shields is shared by both sides, a view supported by Australian theorist Hugh White, who argues that, in the case of the use of innocent shields, the obligations the opponent normally has to avoid civilian harm would be weakened, though not suspended entirely.[52] This is a difficult issue, but I will suggest in the next chapter reasons to think that *in bello* principles apply undiminished even when innocent shields are involved.

[50] Global Security, "The Iran–Iraq War," www.globalsecurity.org/military/world/war/iran-iraq.htm, accessed July 1, 2010.

[51] Walzer, *Just and Unjust Wars*, pp. 159, 174n.

[52] Hugh White, "Civilian Immunity in the Precision-Guidance Age," in Primoratz (ed.), *Civilian Immunity in War*, pp. 182–200, at pp. 195–196.

Before exploring the principle of combatant liability, we consider further who should count as a civilian and who as a combatant.

5.5 Civilians and combatants

Earlier, I raised the point that *some* civilians may have threat liability and *some* combatants may not. Having explored the moral foundation of the distinction between combatants and civilians, we are now in a position to discuss this point further. The characteristic that makes combatants generally liable to attack, threat liability, may in fact be present in some civilians and lacking in some combatants.

The difficulty in the view that all civilians lack threat liability is that some civilians are part of the war effort, broadly understood. When a state goes to war in the modern era, the effort involves the mobilization of large numbers of civilians. Indeed, some modern wars have been referred to as *total wars*, in the sense that large portions of the population and much of the state's economy are mobilized for war. Weapons need to be fashioned, combatants fed, and it is largely civilians who do these things. Indeed, some civilians may make more of a contribution to the fight than some combatants. Perhaps, then, some civilians are a threat liability. In the case of combatants, it seems that some uniformed personnel have no direct part in the fighting, for example, medical personnel and cooks, and these individuals may lack threat liability.

Let us refer to individuals who have threat liability as the *threat liable*, and those lacking it as the *non-threat liable*. The threat liable are mostly combatants, but may include some civilians, while the non-threat liable are mostly civilians but may include some combatants. The question is: how should the distinction between the threat liable and the non-threat liable be drawn, given that it may depart somewhat from the distinction between combatants and civilians? Here, as elsewhere, the line drawing is difficult because there is "a participation continuum that runs from general support for the war effort to the conduct of combat operations."[53]

One idea is that the threat liable are those who directly participate in *hostilities*, the actual fighting, while those who simply participate in the

[53] Michael N. Schmitt, "Humanitarian Law and Direct Participation in Hostilities by Private Contractors or Civilian Employees," *Chicago Journal of International Law* 5, no. 2 (Winter 2005), pp. 511–546, at p. 532.

larger *war effort* by supporting those who participate in the hostilities are non-threat liable.[54] But this may draw the category of the threat liable too narrowly. Consider this example. If Jones is under armed attack by Smith, and a third person, Winston, is supplying Smith with the ammunition Smith needs to continue the attack, it seems a reasonable application of the principle of self-defense that Jones should be allowed to defend herself by shooting Winston to stop the flow of ammunition to Jones (assuming that Winston could not be disabled in a non-lethal way). Analogously, it seems reasonable that the principle of self-defense, as applied to war, would allow each side to attack those civilians on the other side who are supporting the war effort in a way similar to the way Winston is supporting Smith's attack. Now, imagine a fourth person, White, who is supplying Smith with the food he needs to keep up his strength for the continuing assault on Jones. While White is, along with Winston, part of Smith's "attack effort," it does not seem as plausible that the principle of self-defense would justify Jones' attacking White.

Elizabeth Anscombe suggests a way to understand the difference between Winston and White. She asserts that combatants are allowed to attack "supply lines and armament factories" of the opponent, but not to attack those who support combatants "by growing crops, making clothes, etc."[55] Walzer expresses the difference nicely: "The relevant distinction is not between those who work for the war effort and those who do not, but between those who make what soldiers need to fight and those who make what they need to live, like the rest of us."[56] Civilians who make (and supply) what the soldiers need to fight (like Winston) would, like combatants, be threat liable, while those who make (and deliver) what combatants need to live (like White) would have immunity. It is also important to keep in mind that even under conditions of total war, many civilians do not work for the war effort in either capacity. Indeed, many will not be involved in economic production at all (children, the disabled, the elderly).

[54] David Kretzmer, "Civilian Immunity in War: Legal Aspects," in Primoratz (ed.), *Civilian Immunity in War*, pp. 90–91.
[55] Elizabeth Anscombe, "War and Murder," in E. Anscombe, *Ethics, Religion, and Politics* (Oxford: Blackwell, 1981), pp. 51–61, at p. 53.
[56] Walzer, *Just and Unjust Wars*, p. 145. Also Paul Christopher, *The Ethics of War and Peace*, 2nd edn. (Upper Saddle River, NJ: Prentice-Hall, 1999), pp. 97–98.

The civilians who make (and supply) what soldiers need to fight have traditionally been known as *munitions workers*. Customarily, however, munitions workers have only *partial* threat liability, in that they can be attacked only in their work activity, not outside of that context.[57] Combatants, on the other hand, customarily have full threat liability, in the sense that they can be attacked at any time or place. So, the threat liability of munitions workers puts them in a sort of moral halfway house between combatants, who are always subject to intentional attack, and other civilians, who never are.

Do civilian leaders of a state involved in directing a war have threat liability? May they be assassinated? These leaders are, in effect, at the top of the military chain of command, and there seems to be little moral difference between them and top members of the uniformed military, who, as combatants, have threat liability.[58] Whether or not it is morally permissible to attack them, it seems like it would not be wise to do so. To end a war and establish a durable peace, a state must negotiate with its top leaders. A good example of this is the American Civil War, at the end of which Confederate General Robert E. Lee offered full surrender of the Confederate forces. At the time, many in the Confederacy wanted to prolong the struggle through guerrilla warfare, a position Lee opposed, and he effectively put an end to that prospect by his formal surrender. If the Union had earlier assassinated Lee, there is a good chance it would have had to endure years of guerrilla struggle against Confederate forces.[59] Assassinating top leadership can create disarray in the opponent's military effort, but it may hinder the goal of peace, which is the overall point of war. Another example is the plan entertained by both sides during the Cold War that, in the event of war, it would immediately "decapitate" the enemy's leadership by the nuclear destruction of its capital. But carrying out this plan would surely have been unwise. While it might have seemed attractive militarily, its enactment could have made it impossible to limit the resulting nuclear war.

---

[57] Should makers of protective armor be considered munitions workers?

[58] If it is *in bello* justified to attack civilian leaders, this is due to their command role in the ongoing fighting, not due to their role in having initiated the war.

[59] Alan T. Nolan, *Lee Considered: General Robert E. Lee and Civil War History* (Chapel Hill, NC: University of North Carolina Press, 1996), p. 122.

But it seems more than unwise to assassinate the opponent's top leaders. It is in fact morally wrong. Top leaders should be considered non-threat liable. The reason is made clear by Michael Walzer.[60] Because one of the goals of a just war is to establish a just peace, and because the establishment of a just peace generally depends on a belligerent's ability to negotiate with its opponent's top leaders, just war theory implies that top leaders should be treated as among the non-threat liable.

Another group of civilians who have threat liability is those who "pick up the gun," who participate in the fighting without being members of the military. Some isolated individuals do this, but many who pick up the gun are now employees of private military contractors, which have had a significant and controversial role to play in the US wars early this century in Afghanistan and Iraq. One commentator notes that "in modern warfare in developed states, civilian contractors are increasingly used to perform training, logistics, intelligence, detention, and other military functions."[61] The trend toward greater use of private contractors to perform functions traditionally performed by the uniformed military has been referred to as the "civilianization" of war.[62] In the United States, this trend has been part of a more general trend toward the outsourcing of traditionally governmental functions. Military analyst Peter W. Singer notes that the trend is "the corporate evolution of the age-old profession of mercenaries," those who fight for money. Indeed, the employees of these corporations are often former members of the military. There are, Singer observes, three categories of such contractors: (1) military provider firms, which offer military, including combat, assistance; (2) military consulting firms, which offer strategic advice and military training; and (3) military support firms, which provide logistics and maintenance services, such as providing food, to the military.[63] It seems that many of those in (1) would be counted as direct participants in hostilities, and so have full threat liability, while some of those in (2) and (3) would be involved in making

---

[60] Michael Walzer, "Terrorism and Just War," *Philosophia* 34 (2006), pp. 3–12, at p. 10.

[61] Fellmeth, "Questioning Civilian Immunity," p. 459.

[62] Schmitt, "Humanitarian Law," p. 511. The term could also be used to characterize the tendency for wars to include a growing proportion of civilian casualties.

[63] Peter W. Singer, "Outsourcing War," *Foreign Affairs* 84, no. 2 (March 2005), pp. 119–132, at pp. 120–121.

"what soldiers need to fight," and so, like munitions workers, have partial threat liability.

Two other moral issues arise regarding private military contractors. First, their threat-liable employees may be morally worse off than combatants. Not only do they have threat liability like regular combatants, but according to IHL they may be classified as *unlawful combatants*. If captured, they would lack privileges normally afforded combatants, such as *prisoner of war status*. They may, unlike combatants, be treated as criminally responsible for their participation in the war, as fault liable as well as threat liable.[64] The moral justification for this aspect of IHL would be that civilian fighters, lacking a uniform or insignia to identify them as fighters, gain an unfair advantage over their opponents by not being identifiable to them.

The second issue regarding private contractors is the way they put at risk one of the key features of war, as we defined it, which is that war is conducted by groups with hierarchical authority structures. This helps to ensure that the individuals involved have some accountability for the violence they perpetrate, so that the violence will be controlled toward the achievement of some end, rather than being random. In contemporary military parlance, forces in war must be subject to *unity of command*.[65] When military contracting firms, with their separate structures of authority, participate in war, they may disrupt accountability and undermine unity of command. The contractors "remain private businesses and thus fall outside the military chain of command and justice systems." An illustration of this was the role of private contractors in the torture of detainees in Abu Ghraib prison in Iraq during the early stages of the Iraq War.[66] In addition, private contractors allow a government to "accomplish public ends through private means," undermining public control. For example, early in this century, the use of private contractors allowed the executive branch of the United States to involve itself in Columbia's armed civil conflict without having to respect Congressional limits on such involvement.[67]

---

[64] Schmitt, "Humanitarian Law," pp. 519–520. See also Yoram Dinstein, *The Conduct of Hostilities under the Law of International Armed Conflict* (Cambridge University Press, 2004) pp. 33–44.

[65] Schmitt, "Humanitarian Law," p. 516.

[66] At Abu Ghraib 36 percent of the proven incidents of torture involved employees of private contractors. Singer, "Outsourcing War," pp. 124, 127–128.

[67] *Ibid.*, p. 125.

In this way, the use of private contractors can lead to a war's failing to satisfy the *ad bellum* criterion of legitimate authority.

Having considered civilians who are threat liable, we now consider combatants who may not be. The main group of combatants immune from attack are those who are *hors de combat*, "out of the fight," a category covering combatants who are unable to fight either because they are in the hands of the enemy (prisoners of war) or have indicated a choice to surrender, or because they are too injured or sick to fight.[68] According to IHL, combatants who are *hors de combat* cannot be attacked or punished (unless they are convicted through a judicial proceeding of violating the war convention), and they are entitled to certain privileges, such as, in the case of prisoners, "benign quarantine." IHL also recognizes at least two categories of uniformed combatants who lack threat liability: medical personnel and military chaplains.[69] The moral reason for regarding these groups as immune is the same as that for regarding farmers as immune, namely that they supply combatants with what they need to live (medical attention and spiritual guidance) rather than what they need to fight. This in turn suggests that military personnel who cook the food and provide similar services to other combatants should also be immune, though this is not at the moment legally recognized.

One other category of combatant to consider is the *child soldier*. An unfortunate reality of contemporary warfare is the presence, in large numbers, of children among combatants, especially in armed civil conflicts. Peter W. Singer, writing in 2006, notes: "In over three fourths of the armed conflicts around the world, there are now significant numbers of children participating in active combat." Moreover: "Eighty percent of these conflicts where children are present include fighters under the age of fifteen."[70] Should child soldiers be considered non-threat liable, so immune from attack? This is a difficult case for the theory that views threat liability as the criterion of combatant liability. Recall that the hapless conscript is threat liable, despite good reason to regard his presence in battle as non-voluntary (resulting from coercion and/or ignorance). The same, it seems, may be said about the child soldier. A combatant has a defensive justification for attacking all enemy combatants, even underage combatants.

---

[68] Dinstein, *Conduct of Hostilities*, p. 145.   [69] *Ibid.*, pp. 146–148.

[70] Peter W. Singer, *Children at War* (Berkeley, CA: University of California Press, 2006), pp. 6, 29.

But there is a difference between the child soldier and the hapless conscript, in that the child's participation in war is more profoundly non-voluntary than the hapless conscript's, especially since the children are often drugged before battle. This difference should make some difference in how combatants approach battle with child soldiers, and this will be reflected in our later discussion of the due care criterion.

In rough summary, then:

> The *threat liable* are: (1) those who participate directly in hostilities, including most combatants (excepting those *hors de combat* and those providing services that combatants need to live), as well as individuals who "pick up the gun," whether as individuals or as employees of private military contractors; and (2) those civilians who supply those in category (1) with what they need to fight (munitions workers).

The *non-threat liable* are those who are not threat liable. The characterization of the non-threat liable in this negative way (those not threat liable) follows IHL.[71] From now on, unless otherwise indicated, when I speak of combatants and civilians, I will be speaking in this special sense: *combatants as those who are the threat liable* and *civilians as those who are the non-threat liable*. In this special sense, of course, combatants include some civilians in the traditional sense (such as munitions workers), and civilians include some combatants in the traditional sense (such as military chaplains).

The combatant–civilian distinction also applies in the area of *property*. Not only are civilians immune from attack, but so is their property. Like the distinction between civilians and combatants, there is a distinction between *civilian objects* and *military objects*. As discussed in Chapter 4, civilian objects include tangible property and intangible property, such as key social institutions. A problem raised earlier is that some civilian objects are dual-use facilities, having military uses as well. Electrical grids, for example, may provide electricity for both civilians and for the military. In recent wars fought by the United States, such as the Gulf War and the Kosovo War, extensive targeting of dual-use facilities was part of the strategic plan. The US military view is that civilian economic facilities may be attacked so long as they "indirectly but effectively support and sustain the enemy's war-fighting capability."[72] In the Gulf War (1991), the United

---

[71] Schmitt, "Humanitarian Law," p. 523. Dinstein, *Conduct of Hostilities*, p. 114.

[72] US Navy's *Commander's Handbook on the Law of Naval Operations*, quoted in Fellmeth, "Questioning Civilian Immunity," p. 470.

States determined "that the economic infrastructure of Iraqi society – all of it – was a legitimate target: communication and transportation systems, electric power grids, government buildings of every sort, water pumping stations, and purification plants."[73] It is estimated that in the immediate aftermath of the Gulf War over 100,000 Iraqis, primarily children, died from disease, lack of medical care, and malnutrition that were, at least in part, due to the destruction of Iraqi infrastructure in the war.[74]

The targeting of dual-use facilities seems to be illegal under IHL.[75] In addition, there are good moral reasons to regard dual-use facilities as being immune from attack. First, the civilians who are killed as a consequence of the destruction of the infrastructure, especially those who die from the delayed health effects, are not supplying combatants with "what they need to fight," so they are not in the category of munitions workers. Indeed, many of the facilities destroyed, and the civilians killed directly in those attacks, are supplying members of the military with "what they need to live," such as power and water.[76] Second, the civilian deaths from such targeting may be intended, which would violate the principle of civilian immunity. The main purpose in these attacks may be not to degrade the opponent's military capability, but to overthrow its regime. If so, the civilian deaths are intended, according the doctrine of double effect, because they are a means to the goal of regime overthrow, not incidental to it. Such attacks are, indeed, terrorism, as we discuss in the next chapter. Third, even if the targeting does not violate civilian immunity, because the civilian deaths are incidental rather than intended, it would surely in many cases represent a violation of the *in bello* criteria of proportionality and due care, discussed in the next chapter.

Are the conventions involved in the distinction between combatants and civilians in the category of (C1), morally universal conventions, or (C2), mere conventions? Because the distinction is fundamental, but has changed over time, it seems clear that both sorts of conventions contribute

---

[73] Walzer, *Just and Unjust Wars*, 2nd edn., p. xx.

[74] Beth Daponte, "A Case Study in Estimating Casualties from War and Its Aftermath: The 1991 Persian Gulf War," *Medicine and Global Survival* 3, no. 2 (1993), www.ippnw. org/MGS/PSRQV3N2Daponte.html, accessed January 13, 2010.

[75] See Henry Shue and David Wippman, "Limiting Attacks on Dual-Use Facilities Performing Indispensable Civilian Functions," *Cornell International Law Journal* 35 (2002), pp. 559–579.

[76] Walzer, *Just and Unjust Wars*, 2nd edn., p. xx.

to it. Note Michael Walzer's point that there are two clusters of rules in the war convention, those concerning: (1) *whom* combatants can kill; and (2) *how and when* combatants can kill. We may refer to these as the *who-aspect* and the *when-aspect* of the distinction between the threat liable and the non-threat liable. Our discussion so far has focused mostly on the who-aspect. Bringing in the when-aspect indicates that threat liability may be a function not necessarily of the more general status of the person (combatant of civilian), but of what she is doing at the moment. Walzer observes that the who-aspect is "crucial to the idea of war as a moral condition," as it is "more closely connected to universal notions of right and wrong."[77] This suggests that the who-aspect of the distinction is largely derived from (C1), morally universal conventions. In contrast to the relative constancy of the who-aspect, the when-aspect has changed over time. The current view, for example, is that combatants can be attacked anytime, anywhere (except for the partial immunity of munitions workers), but the view used to be that combatants could *not* be attacked when they were resting, eating, or sleeping, or even when they were standing guard. This suggests that the when-aspect of the distinction is derived largely from (C2), mere conventions.

Walzer argues that the main reason for the shift in the when-aspect regarding threat liability is the pressure from weaker belligerents in *asymmetric armed conflicts* (armed conflicts in which the military capabilities of the belligerents differ greatly). The weaker side seeks to expand the time and place they can attack to make up for their relative weakness.[78] We may refer to this change in the content of the category of liability as *rule creep*, a creeping increase in the scope of what the combatant liability part of the rule covers. Expanding the when-aspect gives greater sway to stealth, ambush, and deception, tactics which generally benefit the weaker party in a struggle. What had been "unfair" fighting became fair fighting. Asymmetric armed conflicts will be discussed in Chapter 7.

The American Revolution is an example of an asymmetric conflict. The Continental Army, being the militarily weaker party, used tactics that British regarded as unfair, such as firing at lines of advancing "redcoats" from behind trees and raiding an enemy encampment on Christmas Eve when the combatants were partying (George Washington's famous "crossing of the Delaware"). Despite the British view of such tactics, the Colonists

[77] *Ibid.*, p. 43.   [78] *Ibid.*, p. 143.

regarded them as appropriate, and subsequent history has regarded them so as well. If would have been different if Washington had adopted the tactic of rounding up civilian hostages and executing them, as this would have impinged on the who-aspect of the scope of threat liability, which is morally universal, so not subject to legitimate change. Contemporary terrorism, in its deliberate attacks on civilians, pushes for major changes in the who-aspect, and so is morally unacceptable. But the terrorists' motivation is, in part, the same as those, such as Washington, who pushed the envelope in regard to the when-aspect; the terrorists, in part, are trying to even out an armed conflict that, in their case, is extremely asymmetric. It should be pointed out, however, that it does not require asymmetry for belligerents to engage in terrorism. During World War II, which was a symmetric armed conflict, the Allies adopted a policy of deliberate attacks on civilians. Terrorism, whether by non-state actors or by states, is discussed in the next two chapters.

Now we turn to the other half of the principle of discrimination, the principle of combatant liability.

5.6 Principle of discrimination: combatant liability

The principle of combatant liability denies certain individuals (combatants) immunity from attack, allowing them to be targeted in war. This principle stands in greater need of moral justification than the principle of civilian immunity, which simply asserts the normal moral background assumption against killing, absent special circumstances. It is liability to attack rather than immunity to attack that needs to be justified. As Walzer notes: "the theoretical problem is not to describe how immunity is gained, but how it is lost. We are all immune to start with; our right not to be attacked is a feature of normal human relationships."[79] The principle of combatant liability, like the other key rules of the war convention, is understood to be *symmetric*, meaning that it applies to combatants whether the war they are fighting is just or unjust. So, as an initial formulation, we have:

> *Principle of combatant liability*: combatants are liable to be attacked by enemy combatants in war.

The claim that this principle is symmetric is a matter of controversy.

[79] *Ibid.*, p. 145n.

Initially, the basic justification of combatant liability seems to be the same as that for civilian immunity. Both principles are grounded in the notion of threat liability, based on the principle of self-defense, as set out earlier. Threat liability provides a moral foundation for the distinction between combatants and civilians, explaining both why combatants may be attacked and why civilians may not. Because combatants are engaged in attacking, the principle of self-defense justifies their being attacked in defense. But there is a problem: many cases to which the principle of combatant liability is applied seem not to be cases of self-defense at all, raising doubts about whether the principle of self-defense can justify attacks on combatants.

One aspect of this problem is most attacks on individual combatants seem not to be cases of self-defense because the targets are not *then* posing a threat of the sort that justifies self-defense. *At the time* that most combatants are attacked, they are not posing a direct and immediate threat to their attacker, or anyone else, so that it is hard to see how the principle of self-defense could justify the attacks. Self-defense is understood as *individual* defense. For Fullinwider, as we saw, the principle of self-defense applies when an individual is placing the life of another "directly and immediately in mortal jeopardy."

Richard Norman observes that the principle of self-defense applies only when "there is a forced choice of lives." But the killing of enemy combatants is seldom a forced choice of lives. If "killing in war is morally permitted only in individual self-defense, in the literal sense, [then] combatants can kill enemy combatants only when it was necessary to save their own lives (or perhaps the lives of others)."[80] The principle of combatant liability, as now understood, is, of course, much broader than this, permitting combatants to attack any enemy combatant at any time. Even if the principle were understood more narrowly, as it was at earlier points in history, it would still be too broad to be justified by the principle of self-defense. Even in the midst of battle, individual combatants are not killed in situations that represent a forced choice of lives. A principle of combatant liability that was justified on grounds of individual self-defense would so shrink in application that the practical result would be pacifism. David Rodin offers a similar argument against combatant liability, arguing that

---

[80] Norman, *Ethics, Killing, and War*, p. 121.

we cannot justify killing in war in terms of individual self-defense, taken as "an application, *en masse*, of the familiar right of individuals to protect themselves and others from unjust lethal attack." He continues: "Self-defense is the right to use necessary and proportionate lethal force against an imminent unjust threat to life. Yet soldiers fighting a defensive war are permitted to use violence against persons who pose no imminent threat to anyone."[81]

One response is to regard defense in war as *collective* rather than individual. If there were a principle of collective defense, analogous to the principle of individual defense, then attacks on the opponent's military forces, including all its combatants, would be permitted because collective defense requires degradation of the enemy's military forces, which is achieved by attacking combatants whether they are posing an imminent threat or not. Fullinwider at one point seems to adopt this approach: "From the point of view of self-defense, only those are justifiably liable to be killed who pose the immediate and direct jeopardy. In the case of war, it is the nation's armed forces which are the agents of jeopardy."[82] Through this collectivization of defense, individual combatants may be attacked not because they pose an immediate threat as individuals, but because they are members of a group that collectively poses a threat. This approach justifies combatant liability through a principle of collective, not individual, self-defense.

The collectivist approach is endorsed by Israeli philosopher Noam Zohar. He asserts: "Where the basic analogy to self-defense does function is on the collective level, justifying defensive war itself despite its necessary cost in innocent lives." In contrast, an effort "to make sense of warfare as though it were an aggregate of individual confrontations can only produce moral vertigo." It is only through a collectivist perspective "that we can appreciate the moral force of the war convention, without a dubious conscription into moral service of individual self-defense."[83] A principle of collective defense seems necessary to justify combatant liability.

---

[81] David Rodin, *War and Self-Defense* (Oxford University Press, 2002), p. 127.

[82] Fullinwider, "War and Innocence," p. 94.

[83] Noam Zohar, "Collective War and Individualistic Ethics: Against the Conscription of 'Self-Defense'," *Political Theory* 21, no. 4 (November 1993), pp. 606–622, at pp. 615, 619.

But in the case of *jus ad bellum*, we rejected a collectivist approach, represented by the national defense paradigm, in favor of an individualist approach, represented by the human rights paradigm. There is good reason to reject a collectivist approach at the *in bello* level as well. Under a collectivist approach, individual rights do not have priority. Treating individual combatants collectively determines their threat liability not in terms of the threat each is immediately posing, but in terms of their status as part of the collective war effort. Combatants are thus treated as means, as instruments, not as ends, and so their individual rights are disregarded. Liability to attack, as Colm McKeogh notes, becomes a *sortal* property, one based on the group to which an individual belongs, not a *scalar* property, one based on each individual's particular behavior.[84] The question is whether we can avoid a collectivist approach by providing a moral justification for the principle of combatant liability in individualist terms. Can we, contra Zohar, adopt an individualist perspective without suffering moral vertigo?

It seems that we can. The collectivization of defense involved in war may be different from that suggested above, and consistent with an individualist approach. Jeff McMahan argues: "The morality of defense in war is continuous with the morality of individual self-defense. Indeed, justified warfare just is the collective exercise of individual rights of self- and other-defense in a coordinated manner against a common threat."[85] The idea, as we might say, is that war is more a matter of a collective effort than the effort of a collective. Citizens pool their individual rights to defend themselves against a common attack, since only a collective effort would be effective. Because this defense is against the collective military effort of the other side, the individual agents of that effort would be subject to attack, even when they are not posing an individual threat.

Even if this objection has been met, however, there is another reason to think that combatant liability is not justifiable in terms of a principle of self-defense. Because self-defense is a morally *asymmetric* principle, it cannot justify attacks by combatants on both sides of an armed conflict.

---

[84] McKeogh, "Civilian Immunity in War," p. 76. Larry May recommends that we focus on an individual's behavior rather than on his status as a combatant; *War Crimes and Just War* (Cambridge University Press, 2007), chapter 8.

[85] Jeff McMahan, "The Ethics of Killing in War," *Ethics* 114 (July 2004), pp. 693–753, at p. 717.

Self-defense could justify attacks only by a side fighting a just war, not attacks by a side fighting an unjust war. Self-defense could justify attacks by *just combatants* (combatants fighting in a just war) against *unjust combatants* (combatants fighting in an unjust war), but not conversely. In a case of defensive war when S defends itself against T, T cannot then justify, on grounds of self-defense, the use of force in response to S's defensive efforts. Thus, the principle of self-defense justifies only half of the principle of combatant liability, the half that assigns liability to unjust combatants. Just combatants retain their immunity. Unjust combatants cannot attack because they have no legitimate targets. Lionel McPherson argues that "legitimate targets are available only for combatants on the side of a just war."[86] C. A. J. Coady notes: "There is a clear sense in which those who are waging an unjust war are not entitled to kill the troops who are justly in the field against them."[87] According to the principle of self-defense, you are *not* allowed to protect yourself against an attacker who is *justified* in attacking you, as when the attack on you is a self-defensive response to your aggression. An aggressor cannot extend its act of aggression because the defense against its original aggression now poses a threat to it.

In contrast, the principle of discrimination, along with other key rules of the war convention, is of *equal application*. Dinstein notes: "The *jus in bello* applies equally to all Parties to an international armed conflict, notwithstanding their disparate standing pursuant to the *jus ad bellum*."[88] There is a *moral symmetry of combatants*. "In our judgments of the fighting," Walzer observes, "we abstract from all consideration of the justice of the cause." Combatants on opposing sides "face one another as moral equals."[89] To illustrate this *in bello* symmetry, Walzer points to the moral differences between unjust combatants and bank robbers.[90] A bank robber who shoots a guard is guilty of assault, even if the guard was at the time trying to shoot him. The robber cannot claim self-defense; because he is engaged in an unjust action, the principle of self-defense does not apply to him. The guard is not threat liable. But the just combatant is threat liable, for the

---

[86] Lionel McPherson, "Innocence and Responsibility in War," *Canadian Journal of Philosophy* 34, no. 4 (December 2004), pp. 485–506, at p. 486.

[87] Coady, *Morality and Political Violence*, p. 122.

[88] Yoram Dinstein, "Comments on War," *Harvard Journal of Law & Public Policy* 27, no. 3 (Summer 2004), pp. 877–892, at pp. 881–882.

[89] Walzer, *Just and Unjust Wars*, p. 127.   [90] *Ibid.*, pp 127–128.

unjust combatant, despite being engaged in an unjust war, is permitted to attack him. There are *in bello* rules of war, but, Walzer notes, no rules of bank robbery.[91] There is a difference between *warring* and *policing*. In policing the moral relation between the contestants is asymmetric – guards are allowed to attack robbers, police are allowed to attack law breakers, but not vice versa. But in warring, unjust combatants are allowed to attack just combatants.[92]

But the question remains: if combatant liability is symmetric, how can it be justified in terms of the asymmetric principle of self-defense? All that the principle of self-defense could justify would be a different, asymmetric version of combatant liability.

> *Principle of combatant liability* (asymmetric version): in war, unjust combatants are liable to attack by just combatants, but just combatants remain immune from attack.

If we seek to continue to accept the symmetric version of this principle, but it cannot be justified in terms of self-defense, there are three possibilities.

> (R1) A kind of moral symmetry can be shown to hold between just and unjust combatants by applying the notion of invincible ignorance.

> (R2) The symmetric principle of combatant liability cannot be morally justified in terms of universal moral rules, but can be accepted as a mere convention.

> (R3) A symmetric principle of combatant liability can be morally justified, but on different grounds from self-defense.

(R2) is a view argued recently by American philosopher Jeff McMahan and others. We will consider each of these responses, the first in the remainder of this chapter and the other two in the next chapter.

5.7 Symmetry through invincible ignorance

One simple version of (R1) is based on the idea, mentioned earlier, that there is a moral division of labor in just war theory, that *ad bellum* and *in bello*

---

[91] *Ibid.*, p. 128.

[92] *Ibid.*, p. 41. Jeff McMahan objects, claiming that "just war *is* police action of a sort while unjust war is criminal action of a sort." "Liability and Collective Identity: A Response to Walzer," *Philosophia* 34 (2006), pp. 13–17, at p. 13.

judgments are made by different people, leaders and combatants. The argument takes this as implying that the respective judgments have no moral relevance to those who do not make them. The quotation from Shakespeare at the head of the chapter could be read in this way. When the English soldier asserts that, should the war be unjust, "our obedience to the king wipes the crime of it out of us," he may be implying not only that it is the moral job of leaders, not combatants, to make *ad bellum* judgments, but also that combatants are free of responsibility for the leaders' decision. One version of this idea is represented by Augustine's assertion that "one who owes a duty of obedience to the giver of the command does not himself 'kill' – he is an instrument, a sword in its user's hand."[93] Having no complicity in *ad bellum* judgments, combatants have no reason not to regard combatant liability as symmetric. Combatants on each side find themselves under attack by those on the other and act justifiably in their own defense.

But this abrogation of responsibility is morally unacceptable. A combatant fighting an unjust war cannot deny her complicity in the injustice simply because she had no role in the *ad bellum* decision. The crime is not so easily wiped away. To claim otherwise is akin to appealing to the notoriously discredited defense offered by Nazi defendants at Nuremburg that they were "only following orders." Challenging the division of moral labor argument, Lionel McPherson asserts that "the moral judgment that the unjust side cannot fight reaches to the unjust combatants themselves, and not exclusively to political leaders."[94] The contrary view, C. A. J. Coady suggests, is "based in part upon a surprisingly narrow view of political obedience," that a combatant "is merely a servant of the state and is not responsible for its wars."[95]

But a modified version of this argument is not so easy to dismiss. Consider the historical development of *jus in bello*, as rehearsed in Chapter 2. *Jus in bello* emerged from under the shadow of *jus ad bellum* when the regular war paradigm suggested that *jus in bello* should be thought of as symmetric. The development of the regular war paradigm and *in bello* symmetry were mutually supported by Vitoria's concept of *invincible ignorance*. Not only do unjust combatants mistakenly believe their war is just, but also

---

[93] Augustine, *City of God*, in May *et al.* (eds.), *The Morality of War: Classical and Contemporary Readings* (Upper Saddle River, NJ: Prentice-Hall, 2006), p. 15.

[94] McPherson, "Innocence and Responsibility," p. 500.

[95] Coady, *Morality and Political Violence*, p, 125.

their ignorance is invincible, not their fault. Given their circumstances, they could not reasonably be expected to be able, on their own, to correct their mistaken view. According to Dan Zupan, ignorance of the injustice of their wars is a "common feature" of unjust combatants: "Being under orders, trusting in his superiors, focusing on the mission at hand are such a part of the ordinary experience of being a soldier that 'knowing' his or her war to be unjust turns out to be something he or she literally cannot do."[96] Normally, combatants are fed official propaganda about the justice of their war, do not have access to information that might show otherwise, and are unskilled in the ability to sort out the various arguments involved, arguments that sometimes divide even intellectuals.

Because this argument appeals to what combatants know or believe, it may be referred to as an *epistemological argument*. The argument concludes not that the principle of combatant liability is symmetric, but rather that there is a moral symmetry among combatants at a different level. Unjust combatants who are invincibly ignorant *lack moral responsibility* for violating the asymmetric principle of combatant liability; in attacking just combatants, unjust combatants violate the principle, but they are not responsible for doing so. Grotius remarks that "there are many Things done without Right, when at the same Time no Blame can be charged on the Agent, on account of an inevitable Ignorance."[97] Under an assumption of invincible ignorance, what is morally symmetric is the judgment, applicable to just and unjust combatants alike, that they lack responsibility for violating a moral rule (namely, the asymmetric principle of combatant liability) – unjust combatants because they violate it but lack responsibility for doing so and just combatants because they do not violate it. The result is not a symmetry of justification but of blamelessness.

This argument is based on the familiar distinction between an action's being *justified* and its being *excused*. An action is justified when, as a type of action, it is generally wrongful (such as killing a person), but, given the circumstances, is not wrongful in the given instance. An example is self-defense. In contrast, an action is excused when it is wrongful, but the agent, given the circumstances, is not responsible or to blame for it. Unjust

---

[96] Dan Zupan, "A Presumption of the Moral Equality of Combatants: A Citizen-Soldier's Perspective," in David Rodin and Henry Shue (eds.), *Just and Unjust Warriors: The Moral and Legal Status of Soldiers* (Oxford University Press, 2008), pp. 214–225, at p. 218.

[97] Grotius, *Rights of War*, Book II, chapter 23, section 13, p. 1131.

combatants are not responsible for their wrongful behavior in attacking just combatants, if they have an *exculpatory excuse*. Ignorance is a leading excuse from responsibility for wrongful action, and when the ignorance is invincible, the excuse is exculpatory. To take a familiar example from the law, a defendant would be found not guilty of a charge of criminal trespass if the court were to determine that she did not believe she was trespassing and there were good reasons for her ignorance, that is, her ignorance was invincible. Another excuse is duress, and one could argue as well that unjust combatants are not responsible on its grounds.[98] The pressure, social and/or legal, on individuals to join the military and fight may be sufficiently intense that, were the war unjust, they would, as with invincible ignorance, have an exculpatory excuse for their wrongful behavior. But we will focus on the excuse of ignorance rather than duress.

One objection to the epistemological argument is that it is unjustifiably selective in the rule violations it excuses. Often, defenders of this argument, while they may regard combatants as not responsible for fighting in an unjust war, want to hold them responsible for violating the principle of civilian immunity.[99] But, the objection goes, this is inconsistent. Invincible ignorance should excuse both kinds of violations or neither. Lionel McPherson argues that combatants are often in no better position to judge a military situation in terms of the *in bello* rules than in terms of the *ad bellum* rules.[100] But, pace McPherson, combatants are, in general, in a much better situation to judge their behavior in *in bello* terms rules than in *ad bellum* terms. A combatant generally has much more information on which to judge whether those he is attacking are civilians than to judge whether the war he is fighting is unjust.

But there are strong criticisms of the epistemological argument. First, even if the argument were sound, the symmetry in blamelessness is not the right kind of symmetry. We seek to justify a symmetric principle of combatant liability, not simply a symmetric lack of responsibility for rule violations. One reason is an account of *jus in bello* should be action-guiding for combatants; they should be able to consult the account to determine what their moral obligations are. For unjust combatants to be told that if they are invincibly ignorant of the injustice of their war, this ignorance

---

[98] See Walzer, *Just and Unjust Wars*, pp. 39–40.   [99] *Ibid.*, p. 40.
[100] McPherson, "Innocence and Responsibility," p. 496.

will exculpate them, does not show them what to do. Second, the claim that unjust combatants are invincibly ignorant does not apply to all of them. Many unjust combatants would be aware of the injustice of their war, as is demonstrated by the existence of conscientious objectors, declared or undeclared.[101] Third, for many who are ignorant of the injustice of their war, their ignorance is not invincible, so not exculpatory. Rather, their ignorance is a matter of negligence, and, though this may *mitigate* their responsibility for fighting in an unjust war, it is not strong enough to *exculpate* them. As Vitoria notes, there are "arguments and proofs of the injustice of war so powerful, that even citizens and subjects of the lower class may not use ignorance as an excuse for serving as soldiers."[102]

The epistemological argument seeks to show some kind of moral symmetry between just and unjust combatants. But it gives the wrong kind of symmetry, and the argument may not work in any case. We need to consider another response. One move at this point would be to go back to Mavrodes' idea that the principle of discrimination is a convention with no inherent moral basis, that it is in category (C2), a mere convention. This is response (R2), which we turn to at the beginning of the next chapter.

---

[101] *Ibid.*, pp. 494–495.   [102] Vitoria, "On the Law of War," p. 308.

6   How should war be fought?
Part two

We are not only fighting hostile armies, but a hostile people, and must make old and young, rich and poor, feel the hard hand of war, as well as their organized armies.

General William T. Sherman[1]

The world will note that the first atomic bomb was dropped on Hiroshima, a military base. That was because we wished in this first attack to avoid, insofar as possible, the killing of civilians.

President Harry S. Truman[2]

In my judgment, this new paradigm renders obsolete Geneva's strict limitations on questioning of enemy prisoners.

Alberto Gonzales, White House Counsel[3]

The chapter continues our discussion of *jus in bello*. We begin by completing the discussion from the last chapter about the justification of the *in bello* principle of combatant liability, the principle that in war all combatants, just and unjust, are liable to attack by enemy combatants. The United States policy of torturing terrorist suspects, referred to by Alberto Gonzales in the above quotation, figures into this discussion. Then we examine the other main *in bello* criteria, proportionality and due care, and later discuss terrorism and *in bello* restraints on weapons in war. We open the chapter with a discussion of an event and a policy that challenge our understanding of *jus in bello* in the new century.

[1] Union General William T. Sherman, www.brotherswar.com/Civil_War_Quotes_4i. htm, accessed July 30, 2010.
[2] President Harry S. Truman, radio address, August 9, 1945, www.trumanlibrary.org/ publicpapers/index.php?pid=104&st=&st1=c, accessed July 2, 2010.
[3] White House Counselor Alberto Gonzales, referring to the Geneva Conventions, in a 2002 memorandum to US President George W. Bush. www.hereinreality.com/alberto_ gonzales_torture_memo.html, accessed June 17, 2010.

6.1 Terrorism and torture

On the morning of September 11, 2001, two commercial airliners flew into the twin towers of the World Trade Center in New York, setting them ablaze with thousands of gallons of jet fuel; ninety minutes later the two buildings collapsed. A third plane crashed into the Pentagon in Washington, DC, and a fourth, intended for another target in Washington, crashed into a field in Western Pennsylvania. Altogether almost 3,000 people, the great majority of them civilians, were murdered in the buildings and on the planes. This was an attack undertaken by members of the terrorist group al-Qaeda. The planes had been commandeered by the terrorists and deliberately flown into the buildings.[4] The United States was in a state of shock.

In response to the terror attacks, the administration of President George W. Bush initiated a "global war on terror." One of the first efforts in this policy was the Afghanistan War, launched in October 2001. The Taliban regime in Afghanistan harbored the leadership of al-Qaeda and allowed terrorist training camps on its soil. The regime was quickly overthrown, though the leaders of al-Qaeda escaped across the border into tribal areas of Pakistan. As a result of this war, a number of terrorist suspects were detained and moved, beginning in January 2002, to a US military base at Guantanamo Bay, Cuba, where some of them were interrogated under torture. The interrogation techniques approved for use at Guantanamo included the stress positions, detention in isolation, deprivation of light and auditory stimuli, removal of clothing, and using detainees' individual phobias (such as fear of dogs) to induce stress. In addition, detainees at Guantanamo were "waterboarded," a form of simulated drowning. These techniques violated International Law, including the Geneva Conventions.[5]

Regarding this interrogation policy, Alberto Gonzales, then White House Counsel, issued a memorandum containing the above quotation. In referring to the Geneva Conventions as "obsolete," Gonzales presumably

---

[4] See the 9/11 Commission Report, *Final Report of the National Commission on Terrorist Attacks upon the United States* (New York: Norton, 2004).

[5] United Nations Commission on Human Rights, "Situation of Detainees at Guantánamo Bay," (February 15, 2006), http://news.bbc.co.uk/2/shared/bsp/hi/pdfs/16_02_06_un_guantanamo.pdf, accessed June 27, 2010.

meant that the provisions of the Conventions regarding treatment of military captives had been rendered out-of-date by the phenomenon of contemporary terrorism and so should be abandoned. The claim that the rules of the Geneva Conventions could be rendered moot by changing circumstances suggests that they are *mere* conventions. In opposition to this is the view that international conventions against torture, as well as other basic *in bello* conventions, are derived from basic moral rules, that they are morally universal conventions. Many see rules against torture, for example, as grounded in universal human rights. The view that rules against torture, as well as other basic *in bello* rules, such as symmetric combatant liability, are mere conventions is known as *conventionalism*. We begin by examining conventionalism. The issue of terrorism, reflected in General Sherman's tactics and the bombing of Hiroshima, is taken up later in the chapter.

6.2 Conventionalism

The rules of the war convention, combatant liability among them, are symmetric, meaning that they apply equally to both just and unjust combatants. This is how they are represented in IHL. For example, the Geneva Conventions assert that their provisions "must be fully applied in all circumstances to all persons who are protected by these instruments, without any adverse distinction based on the nature or origin of the armed conflict or on the causes espoused by or attributed to the Parties to the conflict."[6] Combatants on each side are liable to attack by combatants on the other, whichever side's war is just. Combatants are to that extent in a morally symmetric relation. The same applies to their immunity to torture. The question of the foundation of the basic *in bello* rules is pressed on us because the principle of self-defense, which was thought to justify a symmetric principle of combatant liability, turns out to be problematical; because it is asymmetric, it seems not to apply to both sides in an armed conflict. This undermines the argument that a principle of self-defense could justify symmetric combatant liability, leaving the principle without a direct moral foundation. Neither fault liability nor threat liability

---

[6] Additional Protocol I to the Geneva Conventions, in Adam Roberts and Richard Guelff (eds.), *Documents on the Laws of War*, 3rd edn. (Oxford University Press, 2000), pp. 422–423.

can ground symmetric rules. While many of the rules of the war convention are mere conventions, the main rules, especially the three main *in bello* criteria, have been understood to be morally universal conventions. Now that view seems under challenge. One option at this point is to admit that symmetric combatant liability has no direct moral foundation and to return to the view of George Mavrodes that discrimination is a mere convention. This is response (R2), mentioned toward the end of the last chapter. The approach, as mentioned previously is *conventionalism*, and we begin by exploring it. Another approach (R3), taken up later, seeks an alternative moral foundation to ground a symmetric principle of combatant liability.

Conventionalism is the view that the main *in bello* rules, if not all of them, are mere conventions. The general template for conventionalism was laid by earlier thinkers in the just war tradition. One example is Emer de Vattel, who distinguished between the *necessary law of nations*, which is part of *intrinsic justice*, and the *voluntary law of nations*, which is a set of conventions among states that govern the morality of war in practice.[7] Despite the fact that it may depart from intrinsic justice, the voluntary law of nations should govern our behavior in war because general adherence to it will bring about better results than adherence to the rules of intrinsic justice. Adherence to the voluntary law of nations is "for the very safety and advantage of the great society of mankind." The reason, in part, is that these rules "are more certain and easy in their application" than the rules of intrinsic justice. Were we to attempt to follow intrinsic justice instead, war would become "more bloody, more calamitous in its effects, and also more difficult to terminate."[8] Following the voluntary law of nations yields better results overall than following the necessary law of nations. The conventions of the voluntary laws of nations, rather than the rules of intrinsic justice, should be the rules applied in practice.

Jeff McMahan echoes Vattel and Mavrodes by distinguishing between what he calls "the 'deep' morality of war," which is composed of universal moral rules, and "the laws of war," composed of mere conventions. The deep morality of war roughly corresponds to Vattel's intrinsic justice, and the laws of war to Vattel's voluntary law of nations. McMahan applies

---

[7] Emer de Vattel, *The Law of Nations*, ed. Bella Kapossy and Richard Whatmore (Indianapolis, IN: Liberty Fund, 2008), pp. 589–591.

[8] *Ibid.*, p. 590.

this idea specifically to the principle of combatant liability, which is asymmetric in the deep morality of war, but symmetric in the law of war. It "permit[s] what is immoral," because the corresponding principle of deep morality is asymmetric.[9] He argues that the laws of war are "conventions established to mitigate the savagery of war," which serve "to make the best of a bad situation by seeking to minimize the human costs." Their value lies in the better results of adherence to them. As Christopher Kutz puts it, "whatever moral deficits symmetric privileges display or moral costs they entail … they are pragmatically justified by the net death and destruction they prevent."[10] One reason that adherence to the conventions has better results is unjust combatants' ignorance (vincible or invincible) about the injustice of their war. Both sides tend to believe that they are fighting a just war, and, given this symmetry of belief, better consequences result if the rules followed are "neutral between just combatants and unjust combatants," as the laws of war are. While the principle of discrimination "is false as a criterion of moral liability to attack in war, it ought nevertheless be upheld as a convention to which all combatants are bound." McMahan notes: "The laws of war, in effect, are conventions in Mavrodes' sense that are justified by their utility."[11] The conventionalist asserts (using our terms) that general adherence to the main *in bello* rules has *indirect* or consequentialist moral value, despite lacking *direct* moral value, which it would have, if the conventions derived from universal moral rules.

To explain his view, Vattel draws an analogy between the voluntary law of nations and domestic law. For the sake of effectiveness, domestic law is sometimes at odds with morality. Vattel speaks of "alterations which the civil law makes in the rules of the law of nature, with a view to render them more suitable to the state of political society, and more easy and certain in their application."[12] Similarly, McMahan points out that while domestic law often has the same content as morality, it "cannot simply

---

[9] Jeff McMahan, "Innocence, Self-Defense, and Killing in War," *Journal of Political Philosophy* 2, no. 3 (1994), pp. 193–221, at p. 209.

[10] Christopher Kutz, "Fearful Symmetry," in David Rodin and Henry Shue (eds.), *Just and Unjust Warriors: The Moral and Legal Status of Soldiers* (Oxford University Press, 2008), pp. 69–86, at p. 70.

[11] Jeff McMahan, "The Ethics of Killing in War," *Ethics* 114 (July 2004), pp. 693–753, at p. 730; and "Innocence, Self-Defense," p. 209.

[12] Vattel, *Law of Nations*, p. 590.

restate the principles of individual morality, because the declaration and enforcement of laws have effects that must be taken into account in the formulation of the law."[13] To better serve its purposes, domestic law must sometimes depart from and indeed conflict with what basic moral rules recommend.

Consider the legal doctrine of strict liability, according to which conviction for some offenses does not require a *mens rea* element, or a showing of responsibility. One example is the strict liability offense prohibiting the sale of adulterated milk, for which shopkeepers may be convicted even if they did not know, indeed could not have known, that their milk was adulterated. The law goes against the moral principle that no one should be punished for a harm for which he was not at fault, but it serves interests of public health by reducing the presence of adulterated milk in the market. It is presumed that shopkeepers will be more vigilant because they would not be able to avoid punishment by claims of ignorance. A symmetric principle of combatant liability is, analogously, also a form of strict liability. Combatants, like shopkeepers, are strictly liable to be attacked or for selling adulterated milk, the moral fault of the individual being irrelevant. One disanalogy, however, is that strict liability offenses are a marginal phenomenon in domestic law, while the symmetric principle of combatant liability is a central feature of the law of war.

Conventionalism may seem our only option, given the lack of a direct moral justification for a symmetric principle of combatant liability. But some objections to conventionalism are worth considering.

The first objection to conventionalism focuses on the implications of the role of reciprocity in ensuring general adherence to mere conventions. As discussed earlier, the positive consequences of mere conventions lie in general adherence, and a reasonable expectation of reciprocity is effectively necessary to achieve this. McMahan notes regarding the laws of war that in the absence of reciprocity, "it may cease to be rational or morally required for the other side to persist in its adherence to them."[14] Douglas Lackey observes: "If the laws are merely conventional, one is not bound to keep the rules when fighting against opponents who consistently ignore

---

[13] Jeff McMahan, "Killing in War: A Reply to Walzer," *Philosophia* 34 (2006), pp. 47–51, p. 47.

[14] McMahan, "Ethics of Killing in War," p. 38.

them."[15] The objection is that this is not how the main *in bello* rules are understood; they are seen as creating obligations regardless of how the other side behaves. The obligations created by the rules seem to be convention-independent rather than convention-dependent. The *in bello* prohibition of torture illustrates this, and suggests the mistake in the remark by Alberto Gonzales. Universal moral rules, such as rules against torture, create obligations that do not depend on whether others adhere to them. This is how *in bello* rules are understood in international law. One commentary notes: "The obligation to respect and ensure respect for international humanitarian law does not depend on reciprocity."[16]

A second objection is that unless a convention has independent moral backing, beyond having positive consequences, it would not have the plausibility to gain general adherence. Michael Walzer observes: "No limit is accepted simply because it is thought that it will be useful. The war convention must first be morally plausible to large numbers of men and women; it must correspond to our sense of what is right."[17] Richard Norman makes a similar point. Speaking of Mavrodes' idea that the principle of discrimination is a mere convention, he asserts that that norm would be accepted only if "it has some independent moral weight," that is, "there must be something independently wrong in killing non-combatants."[18] This point would carry greater force in the case of conventions that are not merely morally neutral, but are inconsistent with morality, such as the conventionalists believe the symmetric principle of combatant liability to be.

A third objection focuses especially on the principle of civilian immunity, which McMahan also views as a mere convention. The objection is that a mere convention protecting civilians does not recognize what is morally at stake in the protection of civilians. As Igor Primoratz puts it: "The consequentialist view of civilian immunity is exposed to objections on two

---

[15] Douglas Lackey, *The Ethics of War and Peace* (Englewood Cliffs, NJ: Prentice-Hall, 1989), p. 62.

[16] Jean-Marie Henckaerts and Louise Doswald-Beck, *Customary International Humanitarian Law*, vol. 1, *Rules*, International Committee of the Red Cross (Cambridge University Press, 2005), p. 498. See also Adam Roberts, "The Principle of Equal Application of the Laws of War," in Rodin and Shue (eds.), *Just and Unjust Warriors*, pp. 226–254.

[17] Michael Walzer, *Just and Unjust Wars* (New York: Basic Books, 1977), p. 133.

[18] Richard Norman, *Ethics, Killing and War* (Cambridge University Press, 1995), p. 165.

counts: the protection it offers to civilians is too weak, and the ground provided for it indicates a misunderstanding of the moral issue involved."[19] A mere convention protecting civilians would be too weak because, as a mere convention, it could be too easily overridden by, for example, pursuit of a just cause.[20] Under the view that civilian immunity is a mere convention, as Primoratz notes, "The fact that they are civilians, in itself, counts for nothing."[21] Civilians are due greater protection than this.

Finally, conventionalism could be criticized on the grounds that its key assumption, that adherence to the main rules of *jus in bello* would produce better results, may not be true. An alternative view is based on two claims: that the best way to limit harm in a war is to end it as quickly as possible and that attacking civilians helps to end a war more quickly. If these claims are true, then general adherence to the war conventions would bring about worse results, in which case, there would no moral reason to adhere to them. Moreover, even if general adherence to the convention of civilian immunity would limit the harm in a particular war, the fact that wars are less harmful in this way may make them more frequent because states might then be less cautious about embarking on them. In that case, more frequent less harmful wars may lead to greater harm overall than less frequent more harmful wars.

Together these objections make a strong case against conventionalism. While the third and fourth objections apply specifically to the rule of civilian immunity (which is a prohibition), rather than to the rule of combatant liability (which is a permission), all support a general case against conventionalism.

6.3 Morality *in extremis*

Given these problems with conventionalism, we should take another look at whether there may be a direct moral justification for a symmetric principle of combatant liability. This is the approach taken under response (R3).

---

[19] Igor Primoratz, "Introduction," and "Civilian Immunity in War: Its Grounds, Scope, and Weight," in Primoratz (ed.), *Civilian Immunity in War* (Oxford University Press, 2007), pp. 1–41, at p. 25.

[20] Lackey, *Ethics of War and Peace*, p. 62.   [21] Primoratz, "Civilian Immunity," p. 26.

Discussions of the ethics of war often point to the extreme conditions of battle, and the need for morality to adjust itself to them. David Rodin claims that war represents "morality *in extremis*," morality applied in an extreme situation.[22] Michael Walzer asserts: "*Jus in bello* represents an adaptation of morality to the circumstances of combat, to the heat of battle."[23] The rules of war seem to be very different from the moral rules of everyday life. Behavior that is permitted in war is strongly condemned in peacetime. In war a person is not only allowed, but also encouraged, to kill other people. Think of how shocking it is when combatants return from war and, due to such conditions as Posttraumatic Stress Disorder, commit moral outrages of the sort that in war are morally acceptable. The question is: what are we to make of this moral difference between war and peace? The conventionalist response is that moral behavior in war is governed by mere conventions, adopted because of the good results of adherence to them in that context, which are at odds with the universal moral rules that apply outside of war. But the response we now investigate, what I call the *in extremis* view, is that the basic rules of war are genuine moral rules, not mere conventions, however different their content is from those applied in everyday life.

There are two ways to develop an argument for the *in extremis* view. The first proposes that the main *in bello* rules are the universal moral rules applicable in everyday life *as modified due to* the extreme circumstances of war. The *in bello* rules appear different from the moral rules in everyday life, but this is due simply to the difference in circumstances between war and peace. This seems to be the view of Michael Walzer in the previous quotation. Henry Shue, in criticizing McMahan's distinction between the deep morality of war and the law of war, observes: "The circumstances of war are so different from the context of ordinary life that even when the same fundamental moral touchstones are the reference, the differences in the circumstances yield different specific guidelines." The proper conclusion is that "morality is all of a piece," not that there are "two separate moralities, one inside war and one outside."[24] There are, instead, two

---

[22] David Rodin, *War and Self-Defense* (Oxford University Press, 2002), p. 1.

[23] Michael Walzer, *Thinking Politically: Essays in Political Theory* (New Haven, CT: Yale University Press, 2009), p. 277.

[24] Henry Shue, "Do We Need a 'Morality of War'?" in Rodin and Shue (eds.), *Just and Unjust Warriors*, pp. 87–111, at pp. 87, 88.

separate areas of application of the same morality based on the different circumstances. This perspective may be represented by the idea of *parametric universalism*, a notion introduced by Thomas Scanlon in an effort to support moral universalism in the face of the challenge of moral relativism. The idea is that "variations in what is right" can result from "applying a fixed set of substantive moral principles to varying circumstances."[25] The universal moral rules remain the same, but have a different content in their application to situations where the circumstances vary greatly.

In bello rules must take account of a variety of moral factors impinging on decisions made in battle, given the circumstantial differences between war and everyday life. According to Shue: "The laws that should govern war are the morally best laws of war," which "have taken as much account as reasonably can be taken of fundamental moral considerations."[26] Given that war involves a radically different kind of human interaction, it would not be surprising that the application of the moral universals yields in the case of war rules with a different content. Most importantly, a chief moral concern of everyday life, that infliction of harm requires fault liability, cannot be the rule in war because "ought presupposes can." Individual fault cannot be assessed in the heat of battle, so this circumstance of war leads to moral rules of war that do not (because they cannot) respect moral fault. As a result: "The human rights of combatants cannot be respected during war."[27] Shue claims that his approach is not an appeal to consequences, which would make his position closer to conventionalism, but "an observation about what is possible."[28] It is not that individual rights, which support the concern with fault liability, disappear, but that other moral considerations hold sway when individual fault cannot be determined.

The second way to develop an argument for the *in extremis* view is to propose that there are indeed two separate, non-conventional moralities, not one. Both McMahan and Shue maintain that there is only one such morality, McMahan arguing that the rules of war are not a part of it because they differ from everyday moral rules, and Shue arguing the rules of war

---

[25] Thomas Scanlon, *What We Owe to Each Other* (Cambridge, MA: Harvard University Press, 1998), p. 329.

[26] Shue, "Do We Need a 'Morality of War'?" p. 90.

[27] Henry Shue, "Laws of War," in S. Besson and J. Tasioulas (eds.), *The Philosophy of International Law* (Oxford University Press, 2010), pp. 511–527, at pp. 519, 521.

[28] Shue, "Do We Need a 'Morality of War'?" pp. 99–100.

are part of it despite their difference from everyday moral rules. The idea that there are different non-conventional moralities is developed by John Rawls, who proposed that the morality that applies to interpersonal inter- actions is different from the morality that applies to basic social institu- tions. Rawls developed a theory of justice for the basic structure of a society, the set of institutions that significantly determined the life prospects of its members, and the rules of justice of that theory are different from the moral rules that govern individual interactions. According to Rawls: "The principles of justice for institutions must not be confused with the prin- ciples which apply to individuals and their actions in particular circum- stances. These two kinds of principles apply to different subjects (basic institutions) and must be discussed separately."[29] The principles of social justice concern their own subject and are not a matter of "applied moral philosophy."[30] Adopting this approach, we could say that peacetime and the institutions of war are "different subjects" to which different moral rules apply.[31] The reason for treating wartime as a different subject for morality is similar to the reason Rawls has for treating the basic structure as a different subject. Each is an all-embracing institutional system that determines the major life prospects of individuals, with individuals hav- ing little or no impact on their operations. Under this view, we could reject the conventionalist view of *jus in bello* as a mistaken effort to treat conduct in war as "applied moral philosophy."

In political and legal philosophy, the question is sometimes asked: *what is the difference between the gunman and the taxman?* Each coerces money from others, yet the coercion may be morally permissible in the one case while it is not in the other. In Rawlsian terms, the difference is that the taxman in a just society is operating under the rules of justice that apply to the basic structure, and the coercion she applies to extract money is permitted, while the gunman, operating under rules of interpersonal interaction, is not permitted to engage in such coercion. The analogous question for us is: *what is the difference between the combatant and the murderer?* Each kills

---

[29] John Rawls, *A Theory of Justice* (Cambridge, MA: Harvard University Press, 1999), p. 47.

[30] John Rawls, *Justice as Fairness* (Cambridge, MA: Harvard University Press, 2001), p. 14.

[31] For an application of this Rawlsian idea to issues of global justice, see Thomas Nagel, "The Problem of Global Justice," *Philosophy & Public Affairs* 33, no. 2 (2005), pp. 113–147, at pp. 122–126.

others who lack moral fault, yet one killing may be permitted and the other not. The analogous answer is that the combatant acts under *in bello* rules that permit such killings, while the murderer acts under a different set of moral rules which prohibits such killing.

How do we determine or provide a justification for the different moral rules that apply in war? Rawls determines the rules of justice for the basic structure through a version of *social contract theory*. The idea is that the rules of justice for a society are the rules that would be agreed on by individuals in a hypothetical choice situation under "a veil of ignorance" in which they know nothing of their own characteristics and circumstances, but have general knowledge of the situation in which the rules would be applied. Under the veil of ignorance, they would confront each other as free and equal individuals. David Rodin proposes a version of this hypothetical choice method in order to choose moral rules that would apply in wartime. The choosers "know about the political, sociological, psychological and technical aspects of war and conflict, and they know that on occasion their own state will be involved in war, but they do not know whether they will be soldiers or civilians, whether they will be members of the winning or the losing side, or the just or the unjust side of a given conflict." Without developing a detailed argument in this regard, Rodin says that it may be assumed that the rules chosen would be "generally in conformity with standard current interpretations."[32] The reason for this, in general outline, should be clear. If the hypothetical chooser does not know whether she is a combatant or civilian nor which side she might be fighting on, she would choose to be permitted to defend herself if a fighter under attack and not to be attacked at all if she were not herself fighting, thus yielding symmetric principles of civilian immunity and combatant liability. The principle of combatant liability would be, as we earlier proposed, based on self-defense, but it would be a special symmetric form of self-defense, unlike the asymmetric principle of self-defense operative outside of war.[33] American legal theorist Paul Kahn refers to the symmetric principle as *reciprocal self-defense*. Unlike an asymmetric principle of individual self-defense, reciprocal self-defense "does not support

---

[32] David Rodin, "The Moral Inequality of Soldiers: Why *jus in bello* Asymmetry is Half Right," in Rodin and Shue (eds.), *Just and Unjust Warriors*, pp. 44–68, at p. 57.

[33] Rodin argues, on the contrary, that the hypothetical choosers would opt for a limited *in bello* asymmetry.

the moral autonomy and dignity of the individual [but] stands as its own first principle within a circumscribed context in which individuals are in politically compelled roles."[34]

This approach leads naturally to a distinction between an *in-war morality* and an *out-war morality*. The in-war and out-war morality distinction tracks the distinction between *jus in bello* and *jus ad bellum*. The decision to go to war is a decision made outside of war where different moral rules apply than in war and reflects the independence of *jus ad bellum* and *jus in bello*. Specifically, as the *ad bellum* criterion of just cause illustrates, decisions to go to war are morally governed by an idea of moral fault, and, as a result, *jus ad bellum* is morally asymmetric. But under the different moral system governing *jus in bello*, the rules are symmetric and moral fault is not considered. Different individual rights characterize in-war and out-war morality. The rights of the human rights paradigm that inform *jus ad bellum* are the human rights of everyday morality and they are closely connected with fault liability, in that the rights hold only for individuals who are not relevantly at fault. But these rights, we have just argued, do not apply at the *in bello* level. There are, however, individual rights that characterize war. Among the most important of these are the rights that combatants have should they become prisoners of war, such as a right to humane treatment, a right not to be punished for fighting (unless they have violated the *in bello* rules), and a right to be detained only for the duration of the war.

It is plausible that the main rules defining the rights of prisoners of war are among the rules that would be chosen in the hypothetical choice situation under a veil of ignorance, as described above. In the last chapter, we saw that Vitoria claimed that there is no moral reason why prisoners of war should not be slain, though he recommended following what he took to be an international law against such treatment. He was thus treating the rights of prisoners of war to humane treatment as mere conventions rather than as morally universal conventions. On the contrary, there is good reason to see such rights as a matter of basic morality in an in-war context.

---

[34] Paul Kahn, "The Paradox of Riskless War," in Verna Gehring (ed.), *War after September 11* (Lanham, MD: Rowman and Littlefield, 2003), pp. 37–49, at p. 40, italics omitted.

6.4 **Proportionality and due care**

The two main *in bello* criteria in addition to the principle of discrimination are proportionality and due care. These two are also morally symmetric principles, applying equally to both sides. Recall Grotius' example of firing on a pirate ship known to contain civilians. Assuming that the attack was directed at the pirates, any harm to the civilians would be incidental (foreseen but unintended), so the attack on the ship would satisfy the principle of civilian immunity. Still, there are moral doubts about the attack, doubts that turn on the particular details of the situation. First, if there were a large number of civilians on the ship, the attack might be morally unacceptable due to the civilian toll it would take. Such a judgment would be an application of the *in bello* principle of proportionality. Second, if there were some way to attack the pirates without putting the civilians at risk (for example, when they have gone ashore in search of treasure), an attack on the ship might be morally unacceptable. Such a judgment would be an application of the criterion of due care.

The Geneva Conventions, in Protocol 1, prescribe the following restrictions on military attacks:

(1) The civilian population as such, as well as individual civilians, shall not be the object of attack.
(2) Those who plan or decide upon an attack shall refrain from deciding to launch any attack which may be expected to cause incidental loss of civilian life, injury to civilians, damage to civilian objects, or a combination thereof, *which would be excessive in relation to* the concrete and direct military advantage anticipated.
(3) In the conduct of military operations, *constant care* shall be taken to spare the civilian population, civilians and civilian objects; *all feasible precautions* [shall be taken] in the choice of means and methods of attack with a view to avoiding, and in any event to minimizing, incidental loss of civilian life, injury to civilians and damage to civilian objects.[35]

Clause (1) represents the principle of civilian immunity, (2), *in bello* proportionality, and (3), due care. We look now at proportionality.

---

[35] This language is adapted from Articles 51 and 57 of the Protocol, with emphasis added. Roberts and Guelff, *Documents*, pp. 448, 452–453.

Ad bellum proportionality applies to a war as a whole, while *in bello* proportionality applies to particular actions, battles, or attacks within a war. (As *in bello* proportionality concerns combatant conduct, I will refer to it as *conduct proportionality*.[36]) But it would be a mistake to think that the only difference between the two levels of proportionality is in scope of application. Conduct proportionality, we are assuming, is symmetric. But *ad bellum* proportionality is asymmetric because it depends on the just cause criterion, which is asymmetric. Without a just cause, as we saw in Chapter 3, there is no resisted evil to balance against the created evil. Thomas Hurka rejects the idea that conduct proportionality is symmetric. He argues that a calculation of conduct proportionality, like one of *ad bellum* proportionality, must, in our terms, compare the created evil with the resisted evil. This has "the radical implication that no act by soldiers on a side without a just cause can satisfy proportionality."[37] In the words of Henry Shue: "A fighting force with no justification for the resort to war can engage in no conduct that is objectively proportional because it accomplishes no good that could possibly outweigh the civilian losses it inflicts."[38]

Can conduct proportionality be understood as symmetric? Proportionality, in general, is a comparative criterion, involving a relation of the expected negative results of an attack (or a war) with a counterbalancing good (or avoidance of an evil). If conduct proportionality is symmetric, the second term of this comparison would have to be available to both just combatants and unjust combatants and neutral between them. What could this be? The Protocol language cited above provides the answer. For conduct proportionality, the harm that would result from a military action should be compared with "the concrete and direct military advantage anticipated" from the action. This allows symmetry in application because "military advantage" is neutral between just and unjust sides – it is something both sides pursue. The second term in *ad bellum* proportionality is a measure of moral value (evil resisted), while the second term in

---

[36] From a suggestion by Henry Shue, "Indiscriminate Disproportionality," www.allacademic.com//meta/p_mla_apa_research_citation/3/1/3/9/2/pages313921/p313921-1.php, accessed August 16, 2010, p, 3, note 8.

[37] Thomas Hurka, "Proportionality in the Morality of War," *Philosophy & Public Affairs* 33, no. 1 (2005), pp. 34–66, at p. 45.

[38] Henry Shue, "Indiscriminate Disproportionality," p. 7. Shue states this view to argue against it.

conduct proportionality is military value.[39] As Douglas Lackey notes, *ad bellum* proportionality is *political* while conduct proportionality is *military*.[40] Hurka's argument that conduct proportionality is asymmetric is similar to McMahan's argument that combatant liability is asymmetric. Hurka is likely to follow McMahan in endorsing conventionalism, arguing that in war we should follow symmetric *in bello* principles for the sake of good consequences and the restraint on overall harm that adherence to them provides, while recognizing that they are mere conventions at odds with the relevant asymmetric universal moral rules. But we have already seen good reasons to reject conventionalism.

How, more specifically, might the criterion of conduct proportionality be applied? What is the first term of the comparison, the evil created, and how is this to be weighed against the military advantage the action would achieve? Consider the example of a proposed military action to destroy an enemy armaments factory. The reasonable expectation, let us say, is that the attack will kill several hundred civilian workers in the factory and several dozen civilians who live in the neighborhood, families of the factory workers. The created evil would be mainly the deaths of the neighborhood civilians, assuming that the munitions workers count as combatants, at least while they are working. So, the deaths of the civilians outside the factory are to be balanced against the concrete and direct military advantage which is reasonably expected from the strike. That advantage might include, for example, the weakened ability of the enemy to pursue its war due to shortages of armaments, perhaps leading to its earlier defeat. The example makes clear how difficult such a comparison is, both because of the inherent uncertainty in determining terms of comparison and because of the apparent incommensurability of these terms.

> *Principle of conduct proportionality*: a military attack must be such that the created evil reasonably expected from the attack is not of greater significance than the concrete and direct military advantage it is reasonably expected the attack would achieve.

The difficulties with conduct proportionality have led many to regard it, in practice, as a weak criterion with little bite in application and meager

---

[39] *Ibid.*, p. 9.   [40] Lackey, *Ethics of War and Peace*, p. 59.

ability to provide restraint. It is easy for combatants to convince themselves or others that the results come out the way they want.

Apart from the practical weakness of conduct proportionality, this principle does not tell the whole moral story. Imagine that the attack on the armaments factory could be mounted either on a day when many civilians would be outside the factory or on a day when few civilians would, and that the military advantage would be roughly the same in either case. If we assume that both attacks would satisfy proportionality, the criterion gives us no basis for preferring the latter to the former. This seems wrong. Conduct proportionality is by itself too permissive. The *principle of due care* provides a remedy for this.

The *doctrine of double effect* offers a schema for the application of the *in bello* principles of civilian immunity and proportionality, as well as due care. First, it prohibits intentional attacks on civilians or civilian objects, thereby incorporating civilian immunity. Second, an attack's incidental harm to civilians and civilian objects is subject to the requirements of conduct proportionality – the incidental harm must not be disproportionate to the reasonably expected military advantage from the attack. Third, due care also applies to the incidental harm. While proportionality is a comparative measure, due care has a strong non-comparative component. Proportionality requires that harm be kept below a level defined by the expected military advantage of an attack, but due care requires that the harm be minimized regardless of the end the attack would achieve.

To begin the discussion of due care, consider its relation to *military necessity*. Military necessity means different things to different theorists. Perhaps its most central characteristic, speaking roughly, is the idea that situations may force or require a military response, which is said to be necessary. Earlier we discussed *ad bellum* necessity as the idea that a state is forced to go to war, for example, because it is under attack. Being under attack, it has no choice. This is the basis of the distinction between *wars of necessity* and *wars of choice*. Two Israeli wars are often contrasted in this way. The 1973 Yom Kippur War, in which Israel responded to an attack by Egypt and Syria, is regarded as a war of necessity, while the 1982 Lebanon War, a war Israel initiated to root out anti-Israel guerrillas in Lebanon, is regarded as a war of choice. This idea of *ad bellum* necessity at least partly conforms to the principles of *jus ad bellum*, in that wars of necessity generally have defensive justifications while wars of choice often do not.

In contrast, *in bello* necessity has two different meanings. The first meaning partly corresponds to the idea of *ad bellum* necessity in the sense that it endorses actions said to be militarily required. But it is also partly at odds with *ad bellum* necessity in that it often stands in opposition to what morality prescribes.[41] Combatants might claim that military necessity forces them to do what the rules prohibit, for example, executing prisoners of war. This places prudence over morality. For example, recall the lone survivor case discussed in the last chapter, where the combatants had to decide whether to execute the civilians they encountered on their special mission in Afghanistan. Some would argue that they should have done so out of military necessity, despite this being prohibited by the *in bello* rules. But such pleas of military necessity can come too easily. Grotius asserted: "Advantage does not confer the same right as necessity."[42] Not everything that is militarily advantageous is militarily necessary, despite what combatants often claim. But it is hard to know where to draw the line between military necessity and military advantage short of necessity, or whether to give this form of *in bello* necessity any weight at all when it stands in opposition to *in bello* rules.

The second meaning of *in bello* necessity sees it not as standing outside and often in conflict with *in bello* rules, but as one of those rules, as an *in bello* criterion in its own right. Douglas Lackey makes clear the difference between two ideas of necessity, one outside and the other inside *jus in bello*: "Notice that the principle does not say that whatever is necessary is permissible, but that everything permissible must be necessary."[43] When "whatever is necessary is permissible," necessity is a sufficient condition for action and is outside of the moral rules, while when "everything permissible must be necessary," necessity is a necessary condition for permissibility and it is internal to the moral criteria. When, in the latter case, necessity is an inside condition of *in bello* morality, military action must be directed at achieving a direct and concrete military advantage (the action must be necessary *for* something). It excludes gratuitous harm, harm not related to a military goal. Military force must not be wasted. As Shue notes, "the principle of necessity is fundamentally a principle of efficiency."[44]

---

[41] Paul Christopher, *The Ethics of War and Peace*, 2nd edn. (Upper Saddle River, NJ: Prentice-Hall, 1999), p. 158.

[42] Grotius quoted in *ibid.*, p. 159.   [43] Lackey, *Ethics of War and Peace*, p. 59.

[44] Shue, "Indiscriminate Disproportionality," pp. 20–21.

This idea of necessity within *jus in bello* is part of the due care criterion, but there are other parts. One is *least harm*, the idea that expected civilian harm must be minimized. It is this part that requires that the factory attack occur on the day that there would be fewer civilians about, even if proportionality does not require this. Least harm is analogous to the *ad bellum* criterion of last resort, in that it allows an action be taken only if there is no less harmful action that could be taken instead to achieve the same military objective. Least harm is represented in the language of the Geneva Conventions Protocol 1, under (3) above. The idea of least harm includes the idea that military forces take *constant care* to spare the civilian population, and that they take all feasible precautions to avoid or minimize incidental harm to civilians. This last aspect is sometimes referred to as *the principle of precaution*.[45] The requirement of precaution is captured in the contrast between *not trying to harm* civilians and *trying not to harm* civilians.[46] The former is all that civilian immunity requires; due care requires the latter.

Another part of due care is *risk assumption*, which concerns how far combatants should go to minimize civilian harm. The care that combatants show for civilians must be what the civilians are due, but how much care is this? Here due care becomes partly comparative and the issue of military costs plays a role. For example, it may be that attacking the armaments factory when there are fewer civilians around (say at night) may lessen the likelihood of the success of the mission. The same may be the case if a less powerful bomb is chosen in order to reduce expected civilian damage. But due care requires that some such costs be incurred in order to reduce the risk to civilians. Reducing civilian risk may require not only accepting a lessened likelihood of military success, but also a greater expenditure of military resources, including, most importantly, combatants themselves. Combatants must assume some increased risk to themselves to reduce risk to enemy civilians. Michael Walzer notes that "if saving civilian lives means risking soldier's lives, the risks must be accepted."[47] The assumption of such risks is part of what due care requires. Walzer endorses this

---

[45] On the idea of precaution, see David Kretzmer, "Civilian Immunity in War: Legal Aspects," in Primoratz (ed.), *Civilian Immunity*, pp. 102–105.

[46] Judith Lichtenberg, "War, Innocence, and the Doctrine of Double Effect," *Philosophical Studies* 74 (1994), pp. 347–368, at p. 355.

[47] Walzer, *Just and Unjust Wars*, p. 156.

idea under the label *double intention*: combatants must act not only with the intention to achieve the military objective, but also with a second intention to reduce the risk of civilian harm, which may include the assumption of an increased risk to themselves.[48] Considering again the attack on the armaments factory, bombing from a low altitude might be an alternative to bombing from a high altitude. The low altitude strike may put the lives of the pilots at greater risk, but, if the increased accuracy would reduce the risk to civilians, it may be what due care requires.

For some, increased risk assumption is unacceptable, as it flies in the face of the requirements of *force protection*, the idea that belligerents should do all they can to protect their own forces from harm. Canadian Forces Colonel J. G. Fleury claims that Walzer's notion of risk assumption "conflicts with military logic and the psychology of command." He argues: "Nobody has a right to ask more from soldiers who are putting their lives on the line." The reason is that "soldiers do not have the same positive duty to protect innocents among the enemy population, as they have to protect their own population, although they have an obligation not to harm innocents intentionally regardless of their nationality."[49] Fleury's argument is based on an appeal to the idea of *moral partiality*, a form of moral asymmetry, which implies that a combatant in fighting is permitted to give greater consideration to members of her own group than to members of other groups. She is permitted to be partial to her compatriots in comparison with outsiders. While moral partiality may be acceptable in some cases, it is not in this case. Fleury's argument from partiality assumes that the protected status of enemy civilians results from their being *enemy* civilians rather than enemy *civilians*. The moral rights of civilians results from their status as human beings, irrespective of their nationality. All civilians lack threat liability. There is a floor of respect that combatants owe equally to all civilians, including the enemy's, and this floor includes some risk assumption.[50] Consider a domestic analogy used earlier. A parent may be morally partial toward his own child, so that, for example, if several children are starving, the father of one of them is entitled to save

---

[48] *Ibid.*, p. 155.

[49] J. G. Fleury, "*Jus in Bello* and Military Necessity," Advanced Military Studies Course 1 (Department of National Defense, Canada, 1998), pp. 5, 6, 7, www.cfc.forces.gc.ca/papers/amsc/amsc1/fleury2.pdf, accessed June 29, 2010.

[50] There may be some room for moral partiality above this threshold.

his child over the others, if he cannot save them all. But he also has a general moral obligation to respect the rights of all children equally. So, he is not permitted to steal food for his child from other starving children.

How much care is due civilians? How much are combatants required to lessen the chances of their mission's success, including increasing risk to themselves, in order to lessen the risk to enemy civilians? The answer depends on the importance of the military objective, the urgency of the attack, the military cost of the alternatives, and the degree to which the alternative would lessen civilian risk.[51] The risk assumption we expect of combatants, and they should expect of themselves, is a matter of weighing these factors in concrete situations. Walzer proposes a helpful domestic analogy to understand such judgments.[52] He suggests that the care due to enemy civilians is similar to the care due to civilians in domestic society on the part of responsible authorities dealing with an emergency, say a lifeguard confronted by a floundering swimmer. As part of his job, the lifeguard has an obligation to take some risk on himself to minimize the risk to the swimmer. But we do not expect him to put himself at great risk.

Putting all of these points together yields this formulation:

> *Principle of due care*: a military attack must be such that: (a) it has a direct bearing on a concrete military objective (*necessity*); (b) it is the least harmful of the available alternatives to achieve that objective (*least harm*); and (c) it involves the assumption by combatants of a due degree of risk (*assumption of risk*).

So far, we have focused on what *in bello* rules require for the treatment of civilians. But many *in bello* conventions apply to the treatment of combatants, such as rules regarding prisoner-of-war status mentioned earlier, and some of these may be morally universal conventions, not mere conventions. These may include the requirement that enemy combatants *hors de combat* are subject to what is called in international law "benevolent quarantine."[53] Combatants *hors de combat* have certain rights that should be recognized by those holding them, such as rights to adequate food and shelter, to necessary medical care, and to repatriation at the end of the war, and the right not to face punishment for having fought, so long as the fighting was in accord with *in bello* rules.

---

[51] This shows that due care has some overlap with proportionality.
[52] Walzer, *Just and Unjust Wars*, p. 156.   [53] *Ibid.*, p. 46.

Does the due care criterion apply to enemy combatants as well civilians? It seems so. Consider the element of necessity, which prescribes the avoidance of gratuitous harm. Combatants can be killed only if necessary to achieve a military objective and only as many as must be killed to achieve that objective. In regard to assumption of risk, consider that one of the protections of combatants *hors de combat* is the prohibition of "double tapping," the practice of killing a wounded combatant in battle to guarantee that he no longer poses a danger.[54] By adhering to this rule, a combatant would assume some extra risk, for example, of being shot by the wounded combatant. Risk assumption may also be the proper response to the issue of child soldiers, raised earlier. The participation of child soldiers in war is more profoundly non-voluntary than that of hapless conscripts, and this morally relevant difference could be accommodated by combatants taking greater risks to avoid having to kill them than they would in the case of adult combatants.

The least harm element of due care also restricts behavior toward enemy combatants. Moral consideration should be given not just to the killing of combatants, but to their suffering as well. Consider the 1868 St. Petersburg Declaration, an early document in IHL. The Declaration sought to fix "the technical limits at which the necessities of war ought to yield to the requirements of humanity." The Declaration prohibited the use of explosive bullets, a then new military technology. It states that "the only legitimate object which States should endeavour to accomplish during war is to weaken the military forces of the enemy; ... for this purpose it is sufficient to disable the greatest possible number of men; ... this object would be exceeded by the employment of arms which uselessly aggravate the sufferings of disabled men, or render their death inevitable."[55] The *killing* of enemy combatants is justified only if this is the only way to stop them from attacking, and all that is strictly required for this end is their disablement, not their death. A similar reasoning applies to individual self-defense, where the defender is allowed to kill the attacker only if this is the only way the defender can avoid being killed. If wounding the assailant is sufficient for this purpose, killing would be wrong. This point may

---

[54] Nicholas Fotion, "Reactions to War: Pacifism, Realism and Just War Theory," in Andrew Valls (ed.), *Ethics in International Affairs: Theories and Cases* (Lanham, MD: Rowman and Littlefield, 2000), pp. 15–32, at p. 26.

[55] Roberts and Guelff, *Documents*, pp. 54–55.

not often be relevant in war because attempting to kill is usually the only effective form of disablement. But when killing is necessary, it should be as humane as possible.

6.5 Weapons and war

The three *in bello* principles imply limitation on the weapons that may be used in war. Conventional limitations on weapons are almost as old as warfare itself. For example, the ancient Hindu code known as the Laws of Manu prohibited the use of poison arrows.[56] A number of the provisions of the War Convention concern limitations on weapons, and the project of weapons limitations was a major impetus to the development of IHL. The 1868 St. Petersburg Declaration prohibiting explosive bullets was, as mentioned, one of the first treaties to become part of IHL. After the experience with the use of poison gas in World War I, the 1925 Geneva Protocol prohibited the use of such weapons, as well as bacteriological weapons. More recently, the 1997 Ottawa Convention prohibited the use of anti-personnel mines.[57] The pace of development of weapons technology is constantly creating new moral issues regarding limitations on weapons, and the challenge to just war theory has, in some cases, been profound.

Consider first weapons posing special risks to civilians. Perhaps most lethal to civilians in our era are *small arms*, such as assault rifles. The world is awash in such weapons, an estimated 600 million, and they are the weapons of choice in intra-state conflicts, which claim the most civilian lives. Such weapons "that fall into the wrong hands often become tools of oppression, used to commit violations of human rights and international humanitarian law."[58] In this case the appropriate limitation is not prohibition, but restrictions on the transfers of such weapons to armed groups that are likely to use them intentionally to kill civilians. Another category of such weapons is *cluster munitions*, which are bombs that upon explosion release a large number of submunitions or bomblets. Many of the bomblets do not immediately explode, but remain on the ground for months or

---

[56] Roberts and Guelff, *Documents*, p. 53.
[57] For a discussion of treaties concerning weapons limitations, see *ibid.*
[58] Alexandra Boivin, "Complicity and Beyond: International Law and the Transfer of Small Arms and Light Weapons," *International Review of the Red Cross* 87, no. 859 (September 2005), pp. 467–496, at pp. 467–468.

years, often killing or injuring farmers or children who come in contact with them after the conflict is over. A final category is *anti-personnel mines*, subject of the Ottawa Convention mentioned above. These are small mines laid on the ground, intended to kill enemy combatants. As with the cluster munitions bomblets, many of these are not detonated during the conflict but only afterwards when they kill civilians. Rules of IHL to limit or prohibit such weapons have been enacted or proposed.

At the cutting edge of weapons technology in our era is a set of advances collectively referred to as the *revolution in military affairs* (RMA), which includes the application of miniaturized electronics, computers and sensors, to create new weapons systems. These include weapons delivery systems with much greater accuracy, *precision guided munitions*, such as cruise missiles. These may be of obvious moral value because they allow a further minimization of incidental civilian harm. But they have moral drawbacks as well. These weapons were developed for their military effectiveness, not for the moral effectiveness, and they are used for their military effectiveness, whether that takes advantage of their moral potential or not. They allow greater discrimination, but they may not always be used discriminately. For example, cruise missiles have allowed more effective attacks on economic infrastructure or dual-use targets, which we earlier found morally problematic, and they have been used in this way by the United States in recent wars.[59] A second moral drawback is that these weapons can lead to more frequent wars. Because of their effectiveness and low cost, they may lead their possessors to engage in wars they would not have otherwise waged, "encouraging them to resort to armed force more often, for less reason."[60] For example, it is questionable whether the United States would have fought the Kosovo War or the 2003 Iraq War if these weapons had not made it possible for the wars to be fought with fewer combatants and fewer combatant casualties. Another possibility, though as yet unrealized, is the development of chemical weapons that could induce

[59] Henry Shue, "Targeting Civilian Infrastructure with Smart Bombs: The New Permissiveness," *Philosophy & Public Policy Quarterly* 30 (Summer/Fall 2010), pp. 2–8. Michael Schmitt, "Asymmetrical Warfare and International Humanitarian Law," *Air Force Law Review* 62 (2008), pp. 34–35, www.thefreelibrary.com/Asymmetrical+warfare +and+international+humanitarian+law.-a0188490581, accessed August 17, 2010.

[60] Hugh White, "Civilian Immunity in the Precision Guidance Age," in Primoratz (ed.), *Civilian Immunity*, pp. 182–200, at p. 185.

unconsciousness without injury.[61] This development could, in theory, put an end to death in war, but, at the same time, it could allow strong powers to easily subdue weaker powers, making an unjust peace impossible to overcome.

There are many other robotic weapons systems potential in the RMA. Possibilities, in the realm of science fiction, include tiny flying sensors the size of insects, and robot fighters. In addition there is information warfare, which can include the destruction of social and military infrastructure through computer hacking.[62] But consider another existing weapons system made possible by this technology. The United States has been using *drone* aircraft not only for surveillance, but also for attack, for example, in hunting members of al-Qaeda and the Taliban in the tribal regions of north-west Pakistan.[63] The drone's weapons are fired by members of the CIA in the United States, sitting before computer screens using joysticks as if playing computer games. The use of drones for killing raises *in bello* issues. For example, it is not clear that the attacks are permitted under the law of war, given that they are not carried out by members of the uniformed military, but by CIA operatives. This creates, for example, a problem of accountability, given the secret nature of the CIA and its presence outside the military chain of command. Without accountability, there is no way anyone outside the CIA can know whether the drone strikes satisfy *in bello* principles.

But, more profoundly, such military technologies can create a basic moral quandary for just war theory, undermining its very logic, a quandary Paul Kahn refers to as the *paradox of riskless warfare*.[64] Most wars occurring over the past couple of decades have been militarily asymmetric, meaning that the military capability of one of the belligerents far exceeds that of the other, and this asymmetry is due in large part to the more powerful belligerent having high-tech weapons systems the other lacks. Its technological edge may allow the superior side to fight with little or no risk to its own combatants. One example is the Kosovo War, where, as

---

[61] See David Fidler, "The Meaning of Moscow: 'Non-lethal' Weapons and International Law in the Early 21st Century," *International Review of the Red Cross* 87, no. 859 (September 2005), pp. 525–552.

[62] Steven Metz, "The Next Twist of the RMA," *Parameters* (Autumn 2000), pp. 40–53.

[63] Jane Mayer, "The Predator War," *New Yorker* (October 26, 2009).

[64] Kahn, "Paradox."

we have noted, no NATO combatants died. The war was fought exclusively from the air, and the accuracy of the technologically enhanced bombs allowed the planes to fly high enough to avoid being shot down. Riskless war is a policy that pushes force protection to the limit, and so appears to ignore rules requiring some assumption of risk.[65]

But the paradox arises from some deeper implications of riskless war. Michael Walzer notes: "When the world divides radically into those who bomb and those who are bombed, it becomes morally problematic."[66] Kahn argues that the moral underpinnings of *jus in bello* are a reciprocal risk between the opposing combatants.[67] With riskless war, however, the idea of reciprocal self-defense at the heart of combatant liability loses its hold on military reality. The point may be put in this way: if combatants of the weak belligerent pose no risk to combatants of the strong belligerent, then the former to that extent lack threat liability, and attacks on them may not be justified. In practical terms, riskless warfare replaces combatant liability for the strong side to *combatant immunity*.[68] Riskless warfare replaces the symmetry of *jus in bello* with *de facto in bello* asymmetry. This makes riskless war closer to policing than to war as neither the police nor the strong side in riskless war have threat liability, the police for moral reasons and the strong side for technological reasons. But, Kahn notes, the preconditions for policing, namely, a legitimate central authority, do not exist. In riskless war, might becomes like right. On the assumption of *in bello* symmetry, the paradox of riskless war poses a challenge to the coherence of *jus in bello*.

There is a second technologically generated moral paradox, this one arising from *nuclear weapons*. Nuclear weapons are often classed together with chemical and biological weapons as *weapons of mass destruction* (WMD). WMD are *inherently indiscriminate*, or indiscriminate by nature, due to their effects. They cannot in general be used in a discriminate way, in a way that avoids causing great civilian harm. The use of these weapons is not consistent with *in bello* rules. As the International Court of Justice said in its

---

[65] On "riskless war," see also Martin Shaw, "Risk Transfer Militarism, Small Massacres and the Historical Legitimacy of War," *International Relations* 16, no. 3 (December 2002), pp. 343–360.

[66] Walzer, *Just and Unjust Wars*, 2nd edn., p. xxi.

[67] Kahn, "Paradox," p. 37.

[68] Primoratz, "Introduction," in Primoratz (ed.), *Civilian Immunity*, p. 4.

opinion on the legality of nuclear weapons: "States must never make civilians the object of attack and must consequently never use weapons that are incapable of distinguishing between civilian and military targets."[69] Other weapons can be used either discriminately or indiscriminately, depending on the choices of their users, but WMD cannot be used discriminately. This creates a paradox, however, only if the weapons are used.

The special paradox of nuclear weapons arises even when they are not being used in war. It arises from a feature of nuclear weapons, namely, their ability to create a condition known as *mutual assured destruction* (MAD).[70] The weapons are so destructive that when they are possessed in sufficient numbers by two nuclear opponents, they guarantee that in any nuclear war, each side can destroy the other. This possibility of mutual destruction is new in history; in all previous military confrontations, the possibility of destruction was only one-sided, the victor being able to destroy the vanquished (as Rome destroyed Carthage), but not the reverse. But the policy of *nuclear deterrence* that each side in a MAD relationship practices is morally unacceptable, a violation of *in bello* rules. Nuclear deterrence under MAD is a threat to destroy the opponent's society, and the intention this threat involves is incompatible with the principle of civilian immunity. The quandary is that while nuclear deterrence is *in bello* unjustified, it is *ad bellum* permissible, given that it is a form of self-defense against the opponent's threat to destroy one's own society. The logic of just war theory seems torn apart, *jus ad bellum* and *jus in bello* put irremediably at odds with one another. Walzer observes: "Nuclear weapons explode the theory of just war. They are the first of mankind's technological innovations that are simply not encompassable within the familiar moral world."[71]

6.6 Does *jus in bello* depend on *jus ad bellum*?

The differences between conventionalists and supporters of the *in extremis* view of discrimination have sometimes been extended into a discussion of a dependence relation between *jus ad bellum* and *jus in bello*. The debate over

---

[69] International Court of Justice, "Advisory Opinion on the Legality of the Threat or Use of Nuclear Weapons," *ICJ Report 1996*, pp. 226–267, at paragraph 78, p. 257.

[70] See Steven P. Lee, *Morality, Prudence, and Nuclear Weapons* (Cambridge University Press, 1992).

[71] Walzer, *Just and Unjust Wars*, p. 282.

conventionalism has been partly in response to Michael Walzer's advocacy of the *independence theses*, that each of the two levels of just war theory is independent of the other. In Chapter 3, we introduced two dependence theses:

(DT1) A war is *ad bellum* just, only if it is *in bello* just (the *ad bellum* dependence thesis).

(DT2) A war is *in bello* just, only if it is *ad bellum* just (the *in bello* dependence thesis).

Walzer claims that both are false, though in Chapter 3 we argued that he implicitly accepted a version of (DT1) in accepting what we called the justly winnable version of the *ad bellum* dependence criterion. Having discussed the *ad bellum* dependence thesis in Chapter 3, we now consider the *in bello* dependence thesis, the idea that *jus in bello* is dependent on *jus ad bellum*.

Walzer's view is that (DT2) is false. Conventionalists, in general, regard (DT2) as true. McMahan's view, as we have seen, is that the deep morality of war does not allow unjust combatants to attack just combatants (though the mere conventions of the law of war permit this); hence if a war is *in bello* just (in terms of deep morality), it is also *ad bellum* just. This dependence is implied by the asymmetric relation between just and unjust combatants. In contrast, those holding *in extremis* views tend to regard (DT2) as false. Because they regard the symmetric *in bello* rules as morally universal conventions, they do not believe that *ad bellum* injustice implies *in bello* injustice. Indeed the second *in extremis* position sketched earlier, the one that views *jus in bello* as a separate moral realm from *jus ad bellum*, implies that because of this separation, there is no basis for a dependence of one level on the other.

If (DT2) is true, it could be represented by a modification in the *in bello* criteria, most likely, as in the conventionalist's view, by substituting an asymmetric criterion of combatant liability for the symmetric one; only unjust combatants would be liable to attack. This makes it morally impossible for unjust combatants to fight at all. But there are other, weaker versions of *in bello* asymmetry that do not prohibit unjust combatants from fighting. These weaker versions recognize asymmetries between just and unjust combatants that are less encompassing than the asymmetry in combatant liability recognized by conventionalists like McMahan. These versions would require unjust combatants to fight under *in bello* rules more restrictive than those for just combatants, such that either: (a) the *in bello* rules for just combatants are less restrictive than the standard set of *in bello* rules; or (b) the *in bello* rules for unjust combatants are more restrictive than the standard set of *in bello* rules. In either case, *jus in bello* would depend on *jus ad bellum*, but (DT2) would not hold. An example of (a) is what Walzer refers to as the *sliding scale*, according to which the *in bello* rules that apply to just combatants are less restrictive than the standard set, which continues to apply to unjust combatants. As Walzer puts it: "The greater the justice of my cause, the more rules I can violate for the sake of the cause – though some rules are always inviolable."[72] David Rodin offers an example of (b), which he calls *restrictive asymmetry*, according to which unjust combatants must fight under a more restrictive set of *in bello* rules, while just combatants must adhere to the standard set of *in bello* rules. In both cases, unjust combatants are still entitled to fight, and the asymmetry lies in the fact that they are under a more severe set of *in bello* restrictions than just combatants.[73]

One special version of (a) is what Walzer calls *supreme emergency*. In rejecting the sliding scale, Walzer argues, consistent with *in bello* symmetry, that both just and unjust combatants must generally adhere to the same set of *in bello* rules. But under a rare set of circumstances, the just side may ignore at least some of the rules. A supreme emergency exists when a political community is under imminent threat of destruction, that is, "when our deepest values and our collective survival are in imminent danger."[74] As an example of supreme emergency, Walzer cites the imminent threat posed by Nazi Germany to Britain in 1940. A German invasion of Britain seemed imminent, which entailed the prospect not simply of military conquest, but of the destruction of the basic values that the political community of Britain stood for, given the extreme racist, anti-liberal values of the Nazis. Moreover, there was no military response available to Britain except the bombing of German cities. The supreme emergency, Walzer argues, justified that military response, despite the wholesale violation of civilian immunity involved.[75] Interestingly, the supreme emergency exception to (DT2) partly parallels Walzer's exception to (DT1),

---

[72] *Ibid.*, p. 229. Walzer does not himself endorse the sliding-scale view.
[73] Rodin, "Moral Inequality of Soldiers," pp. 56–64.
[74] Michael Walzer, *Arguing about War* (New Haven, CT: Yale University Press, 2004), p. 33.
[75] Walzer, *Just and Unjust Wars*, pp. 251–263.

discussed in Chapter 3. As *jus ad bellum* depends on *jus in bello* in those rare cases in which a war cannot be fought to victory in a just way, *jus in bello* depends on *jus ad bellum* in those rare cases in which a political community faces the imminent threat of destruction. We have more to say on supreme emergency later.

There is an even stronger version of (DT2). According to this version, *ad bellum* justice is not only a necessary condition for *in bello* justice, but a sufficient condition as well. If *ad bellum* justice is only a necessary condition for *in bello* justice, just combatants may still fight unjustly, for example, by attacking civilians. But in the stronger, *unrestricted version*, any war that is *ad bellum* just is also *in bello* just, whatever tactics are used. Whatever just combatants do in war is not *in bello* unjust. The just side may use any means necessary to win; it faces no *in bello* restrictions beyond efficiency, the usefulness of its military force in achieving its just end.[76] *Ad bellum* right knows no *in bello* limits. In the unrestricted version, *jus in bello* disappears as a separate set of restrictions on the just side.

> (DT2, unrestricted version): a war is *in bello* just *if and only if* it is *ad bellum* just.

It is not clear if anyone has ever actually held the unrestricted version, though it is suggested in a remark by the seventeenth-century theorist Samuel Pufendorf. He observes that to secure justice in war "it is permissible to use whatever means I think will best prevail against [the enemy], who, by the injury done me, has made it impossible for me to do him an injury, however I may treat him."[77] The unrestricted version may also, to some extent, be seen in the writings of American Civil War General William T. Sherman, quoted at the beginning of the chapter.[78] Sherman attacked civilian targets in the Confederacy seeking military advantage for the Union. In 1864 he famously set the torch to Atlanta and engaged

---

[76] *Ibid.*, p. 230.

[77] Samuel Pufendorf, *The Law of Nature and Nations*, in Gregory Reichberg *et al.* (eds.), *The Ethics of War: Classic and Contemporary Readings* (Oxford: Blackwell Publishing, 2006), p. 461. Pufendorf may be referring to combatants, not civilians. On his view, see Reichberg, "Just War and Regular War: Competing Paradigms," in Rodin and Shue (eds.), *Just and Unjust Warriors*, p. 212.

[78] Walzer, *Just and Unjust Wars*, p. 230.

in a "march to the sea" through Georgia, destroying civilian infrastructure as he went. One commentator notes that his army "destroyed or confiscated vast quantities of agricultural produce, crops, and livestock; destroyed huge numbers of railroad ties, rendering the Southern railroads unusable; destroyed factories and burned warehouses."[79]

Before burning Atlanta Sherman ordered the City's evacuation; his method was to destroy civilian objects but not civilian lives. When the Atlanta city council asked him to withdraw the order to burn the city, he rejected the request in these words:

> War is cruelty, and you cannot refine it; and those who brought war into our country deserve all the curses and maledictions a people can pour out. I know I had no hand in making this war ... You might as well appeal against the thunder-storm as against these terrible hardships of war. They are inevitable, and the only way the people of Atlanta can hope once more to live in peace and quiet at home, is to stop the war, which can only be done by admitting that it began in error and is perpetuated in pride.[80]

Sherman often claimed that "war is hell," and Michael Walzer refers to the argument represented by this quotation as the "war is hell" argument.[81]

Sherman's words are worth a few comments. By claiming that war cannot be refined, Sherman seems to be implying that there is no point in attending to *jus in bello*, understood as an attempt to refine war, and this is consistent with the implication of the unrestricted version of (DT2) that *jus in bello* disappears as a separate level of moral consideration (though Sherman did respect civilian immunity regarding lives, if not property). In addition, Sherman surprisingly denies that he is to blame for the anti-civilian action he is about to undertake in burning Atlanta, and he claims that the fault for his actions lies with the Confederacy. Because they started the war, they are the unjust side, and only their choosing to end the war can stop him. Sherman's denial of his own responsibility is

---

[79] Rachel Neuwirth, "The Hard Hand of War," *American Thinker*, www.americanthinker.com/2007/06/the_hard_hand_of_war.html, accessed July 30, 2010.

[80] William T. Sherman, Letter to Mayor of Atlanta, 1964, http://freepages.genealogy.rootsweb.ancestry.com/~josephkennedy/Sherman_1864.htm, accessed July 1, 2010.

[81] Walzer, *Just and Unjust Wars*, pp. 32–33.

evident when he compares the complaints by Atlanta's City Council with an "appeal against the thunder-storm."[82]

Consider these remarks in conjunction with his words from the head of the chapter, which suggest a direct moral justification for his anti-civilian tactics. It is not only the Confederate Army that is hostile, but its people as well, and the justification for attack lies in that hostility. This, in fact, is a version of fault liability and a rejection of threat liability: both combatants are civilians are at fault (due to the injustice of their war), so it is justified to attack both. The quotation also suggests a consequentialist justification for attacking civilians, namely, that the war cannot end until their hostile spirit is broken, not until they, along with their combatants, "feel the hard hand of war." (This is a standard justification offered for terrorism.) The consequentialist justification is strengthened by another of Sherman's well-known comments regarding war: "the crueler it is, the sooner it will be over." Thus, ignoring *in bello* rules is justified because it will reduce overall suffering by bringing the war to a quicker end. This is the same sort of justification as offered by conventionalists for following the conventions rather than the deep morality of war: doing so would bring about better results overall. But Sherman takes this line of argument a step further: combatants should follow neither deep morality *nor* the law of war because better results can be expected if *in bello* rules, including civilian immunity, are ignored. Though Sherman continues to uphold respect for civilian life, it is but a short step to use this sort of argument to justify disregard of life as well as property.

Earlier in the book, I remarked on an apparent pattern holding between historical understandings of *jus ad bellum* and *jus in bello*, as represented in Figure 2.1. *Jus ad bellum* and *jus in bello* tended to be both symmetric or both asymmetric. This was the case under both the just war paradigm (both asymmetric) and the real war paradigm (both symmetric). This pattern was broken by the emergence after World War II of the asymmetric national defense paradigm, paired with a symmetric *jus in bello*. The success of the conventionalist arguments for *jus in bello* asymmetry (at the

---

[82] Recall Walzer's argument that realists (and Sherman may be seen as a moralized realist), when they claim that their wartime actions are *necessary*, are equivocating on this term, between the meanings of "inevitable" and "indispensable." *Ibid.*, p. 8.

level of basic morality) would re-establish the pattern.[83] But if the arguments of this chapter against *in bello* dependence and conventionalism are correct, the pattern would remain broken, with an asymmetric human rights paradigm and a symmetric *jus in bello*.

6.7 The overall judgment of *jus in bello*

The idea of an overall judgment of *jus ad bellum* was discussed in Chapter 3. Can we make an overall judgment of the *jus in bello*, and, if so, how should this be done? The legal scholar Aaron Fellmeth notes: "[J]us in bello does not merely determine the legality of a single decision of a state; it governs innumerable decisions by military commanders at multiple levels of the chain of command in every kind of pre-combat, combat, and occupation situation."[84] As noted earlier, the relation between a war and *ad bellum* judgment is one-to-one, while the relation between a war and *in bello* judgment is one-to-many. *Jus ad bellum* is characterized by a single decision, to initiate war, while *jus in bello* may cover hundreds of thousands of decisions by tens of thousands of combatants, or more, over the course of a war.

So an overall *in bello* judgment involves surveying across a myriad of decisions made by many individual combatants. Given the involvement of so many individuals, no war could, in practice, be perfectly *in bello* just, any more than a large society could be without crime. So, we should perhaps speak of a war at the *in bello* level as *substantially*, rather than completely just (or unjust). For this, it may help to appeal to a distinction between occasional and systemic *in bello* violations. Gentili suggests a contrast between *in bello* offenses that are "for the moment" (so occasional) and those that "are successive and continuous" (so systemic).[85] Systemic violations are largely under the control of the administrative hierarchy, the military exercising command responsibility, while occasional violations largely escape such control. A war can be judged as substantially *in bello* just only when the state has made serious and successful efforts to control and suppress *in bello* violations, which is the case when the violations that

---

[83] Reichberg, "Just War and Regular War," p. 210.

[84] Aaron Xavier Fellmeth, "Questioning Civilian Immunity," *Texas International Law Journal* 43, no. 3 (Summer 2008), pp 453–501, at p. 461.

[85] Gentili quoted in Theodore Meron, "Shakespeare's Henry the Fifth and the Laws of War," *American Journal of International Law* 86 (January 1992), pp. 1–45, at p. 18.

do occur are occasional rather than systematic. By its pronouncements and disciplinary policy, a military command should establish within the military a culture of respect for the *in bello* rules, and when it does not do this, its war is substantially unjust at the *in bello* level.

One of the main mechanisms military commanders have for avoiding systemic *in bello* violations is the setting and enforcing of proper *rules of engagement*. Rules of engagement specify the conditions under which combatants are entitled to use force. A state fights a war justly when the leadership sets rules of engagement that minimize *in bello* violations. Another factor determining the likelihood of *in bello* violations is whether a state has committed forces sufficient to fight a war justly. States have a tendency to try to fight wars "on the cheap" (economically as well as morally). They fail, for political reasons, to commit sufficient forces to allow a war to be fought successfully with rules of engagement that promote respect for *in bello* rules. We have seen this in two cases discussed earlier. One was the Bala Baluk episode in the Afghanistan War, where the high toll of unintended civilian deaths resulted from a reliance on close air support, which is a tactic adopted, in part, because of the relatively small number of forces committed to the war. Another was the Kosovo War, where civilian casualties were high due to the exclusive reliance on a policy of bombing to win the war. The main reason for this policy was political, in that the leaders of the United States and the military coalition did not believe that they could sustain domestic political support for the war were there to be a high casualty rate among their combatants. This example raises the interesting question of whether states may sometimes need to choose between fighting a war unjustly or not fighting it at all, given that domestic political support for the war may require fighting it on the "moral cheap."[86]

6.8 Terrorism

Terrorism is a military tactic involving systematic violation of civilian immunity. Belligerents are guilty of terrorism when they adopt as a policy attacks on enemy civilians. Terrorism is the worst *in bello* crime a belligerent can commit. Recall that combatants can violate the principle of

---

[86] Such a war is justly winnable, but only with the commitment of a level of resources that domestic politics makes impossible.

civilian immunity through either deliberate or indiscriminate attacks on civilians. Terrorism occurs when civilian attacks are deliberate and also systematic, part of a policy, not isolated acts. In terrorism, civilian harm is imposed as a means to an end. Understanding the nature of terrorism is understanding this means–end relationship.

Consider the use of the atomic bomb, referred to in the quotation from President Truman at the beginning of the chapter. The bomb, developed by the United States during World War II, was a thousand times more powerful than the largest non-nuclear (or conventional) explosive. It was first tested in July of 1945, after Germany had surrendered, but while Japan continued to fight. The first bomb was dropped on Hiroshima on August 6, 1945, the second three days later on Nagasaki, and Japan surrendered shortly thereafter. The atomic bombings continued an Allied policy that had begun with the British bombings of German cities in 1940. This was a policy of *strategic bombing* (bombing aimed at the destruction of civilian targets) rather than tactical bombing (bombing in direct support of the military effort on the ground). Often whole cities were destroyed through firebombing, including Hamburg, Dresden, and Tokyo. The atomic bombings represented the culmination of this trend.

This was a policy of terrorism. The bombings were systematic attacks on civilians. As Walzer notes of the early British bombings of German cities: "The purpose of the raids was explicitly declared to be the destruction of civilian morale."[87] In this respect, the quotation from President Truman at the beginning of the chapter represents a double lie. First, it was a lie that the bombing of Hiroshima was an effort to avoid the killing of civilians. No one destroys a major city in an effort to avoid killing civilians. Second, it was a lie that the bombing had the tactical purpose of destroying "a military base." The effort was, as Walzer said of the British city raids, to destroy civilian morale and thereby force the Japanese government to surrender. The atomic bombing "was surely an act of terrorism: innocent men and women were killed in order to spread fear across a nation and force the surrender of its government."[88]

A definition of terrorism should make clear the means–end relationship that characterizes the policy. Terrorism may be defined as a policy of the

[87] Walzer, *Just and Unjust Wars*, p. 256.
[88] Michael Walzer, "Terrorism and Just War," in *Philosophia* 34 (2006), p. 5.

use of military force that (1) involves deliberate attacks on civilians and civilian targets, (2) in order to terrorize a general population and thereby weaken its morale, (3) in order to bring about some political change.[89] In terrorism, the creation of terror is an expected causal intermediary between the civilian attacks and desired political change, usually forcing the other side to surrender or withdraw from the conflict. The policy is called *terrorism* because terror plays this expected causal role. The assumption behind the means–end relationship of terrorism is that random attacks that create terror in the civilian population can put pressure on the state to concede. This assumption is based on a set of empirical claims about how civilian populations react to terrorist attacks, which may or may not be true in particular cases. On the one hand, consider Sherman's anti-civilian tactics, his application of "the hard hand of war," in an effort to weaken civilian morale. His terrorism seems to have worked, bringing about a swifter Union victory.[90] On the other hand, some argue that terror campaigns often fail due to a contrary psychological effect, namely, that the attacks deepen the population's hatred of the enemy and strengthen its resolve in support of its regime.[91] In any case, the moral status of terrorism is not dependent on whether it works.

Terrorism is not a new tactic. One of its earlier forms was the siege of cities, and later the blockade of states, designed to enforce suffering on the civilian population under siege or blockade, to force surrender. More people died in the siege of Leningrad in World War II than died in the city bombings of Hamburg, Dresden, Tokyo, Hiroshima, and Nagasaki combined.[92] Britain imposed a naval blockade of Germany during World War I that led to the deaths through malnutrition and disease of an estimated

---

[89] The three features of this definition capture what is prominent in most definitions of the term. The definition covers all actors, state and non-state alike, and implies that the claim that "one person's terrorist is another person's freedom fighter" is false.

[90] It also may have helped win the war in an indirect way. Some historians speculate that Lincoln would not have won the 1864 election without Sherman's successes in Georgia, and a Democrat elected instead might have sued for peace preventing the reuniting of the nation.

[91] Robert Pape, *Bombing to Win: Air Power and Coercion in War* (Ithaca, NY: Cornell University Press, 1996).

[92] On the anti-civilian tactics of siege and blockade, see Walzer, *Just and Unjust Wars*, chapter 10. The Leningrad statistic is cited on p. 160.

800,000 civilians.[93] Blockades and severe economic sanctions can be applied by states outside of war, and there is no reason not to regard these as terrorist policies, when they are intended to force political change on the leadership of the targeted state through imposing suffering on its civilians. Mass rape has become a practiced form of terrorism.[94] Rape has always been a source of violations of civilian immunity in war, but in some recent wars, such as those in the former Yugoslavia and in Central Africa, it has become a systematic policy, hence a form of terrorism.

Terrorism in war is sometimes the result of a significant military asymmetry between the belligerents, with the weaker side resorting to terrorism because of its weakness, often believing that, given its military inferiority, it has no other option but to use terror. Civilians are, after all, "soft targets," easier to attack than military targets. Walzer's example of supreme emergency is an instance of this dynamic. In 1940, Britain was asymmetrically weak in its military relationship with Germany, and all it could do to keep fighting was to bomb German cities. This *terrorism of the weak* is related to a topic discussed in the last chapter, namely, the shift over time in the precise content of the war convention, what we called *rule creep*. As we saw, over time, a larger portion of combatants (or combatants over a larger portion of the time they are combatants) has come to be regarded as threat liable, until we have reached the current *in bello* understanding that any combatant not *hors de combat* can be attacked at any time. This shift, as we discussed, has largely resulted from pressure from weaker belligerents who, to make up for their weakness, sought to expand when and where their opponent's combatants could be targeted. With the current *in bello* understanding, we have reached the limit of what this pressure can achieve through an expansion of the scope of combatant liability (short of allowing attacks on combatants *hors de combat*). The only place for the pressure to go, so to speak, is to breach the distinction between combatants and civilians and make civilians targets; and terrorism represents this breach. This breach is a more serious matter because the earlier rule creep involved largely a change in the merely conventional content

---

[93] Primoratz, "Introduction," p. 3.

[94] On terrorist rape, see Sally Scholz, "War Rape's Challenge to Just War Theory," in Steven P. Lee (ed.), *Intervention, Terrorism, and Torture* (Dordrecht: Springer, 2007), pp. 273–288.

of combatant liability, while terrorism involves an extension that violates the universal moral rule underpinning the principle of discrimination.

Terrorism can also be a foreign policy practiced by states outside of war, as in the case of economic sanctions mentioned above, and also a domestic policy of states against their own population (where the political goal sought is the maintenance of the regime's power). Moreover, terrorism can be a policy of non-state agents. In fact, when people think of terrorism they are likely to think not of state terrorism, but of non-state terrorism, such as the attacks on the World Trade Center on September 11, 2001. The definition of terrorism should be neutral between state actors and non-state actors because attacks on civilians raise the same moral issues in either case. There is something morally constant in the phenomenon of terrorism whether it is practiced in or out of war, by states abroad or against their own citizens, or by states or by non-state agents. Moreover, wherever terrorism occurs, it can be morally analyzed in the same terms. The basic moral defect of terrorism is the serious abuse of innocent people as a means to achieving some political end, and this is what the *in bello* principle of civilian immunity prohibits. Joseph Boyle notes that "terrorist actions are wrong because those who do them seek to affect others' behavior and decisions by directly or indirectly harming people whom they have no right to harm."[95]

Can terrorism be justified? Note that it is an implication of the neutrality of the definition of terrorism that if it can be justified for states, it can, in principle, be justified also for non-state agents. C. A. J. Coady remarks that if terrorism is "allowed to states, it seems mere consistency to allow it to non-state agents on the same terms."[96] From a moral perspective, it does not matter who the agent is, though features of the context in which states and non-state agents act may make it more likely that state or non-state agents can meet the conditions on justifiability (if there are any). Robert Fullinwider points out that terrorists sometimes seek to justify their attacks on civilians by putting their actions in the context of alternative moral theories, such as communalist theories assigning collective

[95] Joseph Boyle, "Just War Doctrine and the Military Response to Terrorism," *Journal of Political Philosophy* 11, no. 2 (2003), pp. 153–170, at p. 157.

[96] C. A. J. Coady, "Terrorism, Just War, and Supreme Emergency," in C. A. J. Coady and Michael O'Keefe (eds.), *Terrorism and Justice* (Melbourne University Press, 2002), pp. 8–21, at p. 15.

guilt to a population or perfectionist theories justifying the use of violence to bring about the human ideal.[97] But in terms of the human rights paradigm, such theories are simply mistaken and contrary to the values that animate a correct moral understanding of the world.

Walzer's doctrine of supreme emergency is the view that in rare cases state terrorism is morally acceptable (or at least excusable, as he argues that its perpetrators are still murderers[98]). His discussion of terrorism by non-state agents usually dismisses the idea that their terrorism could ever be excusable, though he does on occasion admit the possibility that it would be excusable were it to be in response to a supreme emergency.[99] His skepticism about excusable terrorism for non-state agents likely reflects his assumption that they would never be in a position to avoid the destruction of a political community, which is the only situation in which attacks on civilians could be excused. While he believes that a state may use terrorism to save the political community it represents, an individual cannot, analogously, attack innocent bystanders to save his own life. Walzer's claim that "self-defense cannot be made morally impossible" applies to political communities, not individuals.[100] The lives of political communities are of higher value than the lives of individuals, giving communities "different and higher prerogatives."[101]

Walzer's argument that deliberate attacks on civilians are sometimes acceptable or excusable depends on his view that political communities have categorically greater moral value than individuals. While this view is compatible with the national defense paradigm, it is inconsistent with the human rights paradigm. While there are common life rights, they apply to any human association, not only national political communities, and they are not rights of a categorically higher value than other rights. Under the human rights paradigm, Walzer's justification for supreme emergency fails to get off the ground. Nor are we free to weigh rights infringements, as we do in applying the human rights paradigm, in an attempt to justify

---

[97] Robert Fullinwider, "Understanding Terrorism," in Larry May, Eric Rovie, and Steve Viner (eds.), *The Morality of War: Classical and Contemporary Readings* (Upper Saddle River, NJ: Prentice-Hall, 2006), pp. 306–315, at p. 312.

[98] Walzer, *Just and Unjust Wars*, p. 323.   [99] Walzer, *Arguing about War*, p. 54.

[100] Michael Walzer, "Responsibility and Proportionality in State and Non-State Wars," *Parameters* 39 (Spring 2009), pp. 40–52, at p. 48.

[101] Walzer, *Just and Unjust Wars*, p. 254.

attacks on civilians in a supreme emergency. This is precluded by the independence of *jus ad bellum* and *jus in bello* and by the different moral rules that apply at each level. It may be best to consider the situations of supreme emergency in terms of the domestic analogue of individual self-defense. Walzer is right to note that from a moral perspective an individual cannot harm an innocent bystander to save his own life. The same is the case for states facing a supreme emergency. If an individual does harm an innocent bystander as the only way to save his own life, we would understand such a decision as putting self-interest or prudential considerations ahead of moral demands. This is how we should understand a state which attacks civilians as the only way to overcome a supreme emergency. The only difference is that when a state acts against innocents to avoid destruction much more is prudentially at stake than when an individual acts against innocents to save her own life. The state's action may be understandable, but it is not morally acceptable.

Our discussion now switches to an examination of armed conflict within a state, an arena in which insurgent forces challenging an established government often resort to terrorist tactics due to asymmetric military weakness.

7 Civil wars

A civil war breaks the bands of society ... [and] produces in the
nation two independent parties [which stand] in precisely the same
predicament as two nations ... This being the case, it is very evident
that the common laws of war ... ought to be observed by both
parties in every civil war.

Emer de Vattel[1]

US Colonel Harry Summers: "You know, you never defeated us on
the battlefield."

Vietnamese Colonel Tu: "That may be so, but it is also irrelevant."

Conversation in Hanoi about the Vietnam War, 1975[2]

For the asymmetrically powerful to insist on the maintenance
of the combatant/noncombatant distinction has the appearance of
self-serving moralizing.

Paul Kahn[3]

Whether we bring our enemies to justice, or bring justice to our
enemies, justice will be done.

President George W. Bush[4]

Most of the armed conflicts occurring in the past sixty years have been
within states, and most of the deaths in war, especially of civilians, have

---

[1] Emer de Vattel, *Law of Nations*, vol. 3, secs. 293–94, ed. John Chitty (Philadelphia: T. &
J. W. Johnson, 1883), www.constitution.org/vattel/vattel.htm, accessed June 15, 2011.

[2] A conversation about the Vietnam War between two participating military officials,
an American (Summers) and a Vietnamese (Tu). Widely reported; see, for example,
www.slate.com/id/2171510, accessed July 5, 2010.

[3] Paul Kahn, "The Paradox of Riskless War," in Verna Gehring (ed.), *War after September
11* (Lanham, MD: Rowman and Littlefield, 2003), pp. 37–49, at p. 45.

[4] George W. Bush, Address to Congress Following the 9/11 Attacks, September 20, 2001,
www.guardian.co.uk/world/2001/sep/21/september11.usa13, accessed June 15, 2011.

occurred in those conflicts. From 1945 to 1999, there were roughly five times as many armed conflicts within states, and five times as many people killed in those conflicts, as there were international armed conflicts and resulting deaths.[5] Armed conflicts within states are referred to in International Law as "armed conflicts not of an international character." We will refer to them as *armed civil conflicts*, and to each side's involvement in such conflicts as *civil wars*. For example, the American Civil War was in our terms an armed civil conflict in which the Union and the Confederacy each fought a civil war against the other. The term *civil war* is often used to refer to what I call armed civil conflicts, but consistent with the commitment to keep this distinction clear, I will use the term *civil war* to refer to each side's involvement rather than to the larger armed conflict. Armed civil conflicts often have an international component because other states intervene in support of one or another side, but the principal focus of these conflicts is internal, involving primarily a struggle between different groups within a state. There are many kinds of civil wars, including secessionist wars, tribal and ethnic struggles, proxy and client wars, efforts at ethnic cleansing and genocide, guerrilla war, anti-colonial and anti-occupation struggles, wars of national liberation, bloody coups, revolutions, and resource wars.[6]

Armed civil conflicts have continued to be the dominant form of warfare following the end of the Cold War in 1991, though their character has changed. Prior to the 1990s, the Cold War between the United States and the Soviet Union influenced and shaped the politics and conflicts within many states in what was then called the Third World. With the decline of that influence, ethnic and other tensions within states have come to the fore to shape internal conflicts. These conflicts have been referred to as *new wars*,[7] and what characterizes many of them, as British philosopher Paul Gilbert notes, is that they are "a continuation of the politics of identity." Many of the wars are fought in the name of ethnic identity, and they "arise in communal or sectarian violence between small numbers of people from opposed identity groups."[8] The state then may get involved on

---

[5] James Fearon and David Laitin, "Ethnicity, Insurgency, and Civil War," *American Political Science Review* 97, no. 1 (February 2003), pp. 75–90, at p. 75.

[6] A given civil war may fit more than one of these categories.

[7] Mary Kaldor, *New and Old Wars*, 2nd edn. (Stanford University Press, 2006).

[8] Paul Gilbert, "Civilian Immunity in the 'New Wars'," in I. Primoratz, *Civilian Immunity in War* (Oxford University Press, 2007), pp. 201–216, at pp. 202, 204.

one side or the other, often as demagogues seek political advantage from championing an ethnic cause.[9] As Gilbert notes, the principle of civilian immunity is often ignored in such conflicts because the opposing ethnic group becomes defined as the enemy.[10] This feature of armed conflicts in our era has led to genocides, episodes of ethnic cleansing, and the need for humanitarian interventions.

An armed civil conflict may be defined roughly as a large-scale armed clash occurring mainly within a state between large organized groups of that state, though often with the involvement of outside forces.[11] An armed civil conflict, including those originating in ethnic strife, is usually a clash between a group out of political power and a group in political power; it is a struggle between the forces of the internal political status quo and those seeking to change that status quo. But not all internal violence against a state counts as a civil war, and a sharp line cannot be drawn in this regard. The Second Protocol of the Geneva Conventions, designed to cover armed civil conflicts, applies the rules of the Geneva Conventions to conflicts between the armed forces of a state and "dissident armed forces or other organized armed groups which, under responsible command, exercise such control over a part of its territory as to enable them to carry out sustained and concerted military operations and to implement this Protocol." Excluded are "situations of internal disturbances and tensions, such as riots, isolated and sporadic acts of violence and other acts of a similar nature."[12]

Internal groups that take up arms against a political status quo are generally referred to as *insurgents*, and their civil war as an *insurgency*. The civil war of their opponents, designed to defend the status quo, is sometimes called a *counterinsurgency*. A counterinsurgency is a kind of war designed to address the special challenge of fighting an insurgency, involving special tactics and strategy. Our era has been referred to as the age of insurgency. The increased prevalence of insurgencies is likely due to an increase in the

---

[9] For example, Slobodan Milošević rode Serbian identity politics to power in the former Yugoslavia and set the stage for the Kosovo war.

[10] Gilbert, "Civilian Immunity," p. 205.

[11] On the definition, see Nicholas Sambanis, "What Is Civil War?" *Journal of Conflict Resolution* 48, no. 6 (2004), pp. 814–858.

[12] In Adam Roberts and Richard Guelff (eds.), *Documents on the Laws of War*, 3rd edn. (Oxford University Press, 2000), p. 484.

factors that feed insurgencies. Among these factors, according to Steven Metz and Raymond Millen, are

> mounting global discontent arising from globalization; the failure of economic development to keep pace with expectations; the collapse of traditional political, economic, and social orders; widespread anger and resentment; environmental decay; population pressure; the presence of weak regimes; the growth of transnational organized crime; and the widespread availability of arms.

Added to this is "an inability to ameliorate these through legitimate political means."[13] This last factor connects the discussion of civil wars with the so-called *right of revolution*, a traditional topic in political theory.

More traditional armed civil conflicts are of three main kinds. (1) The conflict may be between the government of a state and an internal insurgent group seeking to take over the government, examples being the French Revolution and the Cuban Revolution. (2) The conflict may be a struggle of a group within a state against the government of that state to establish an independent state for that group on part of the territory of the larger state, an example being the American Civil War. (3) The conflict may be an insurgent struggle against an occupying power (as in the American Revolution) and (often) the local government that power has installed or supports, a puppet regime of that power (as in the Viet Cong War against the South Vietnamese government propped up by the United States).[14] The anti-colonial struggles of the third quarter of the twentieth century, often referred to as national liberation struggles, are examples of this third kind. We may refer to these three kinds of insurgencies respectively as civil wars (1) for control of the central government, (2) for secession, and (3) for national independence.

The "new wars" of the post-Cold War period constitute a fourth kind of armed civil conflict, which may overlap with any other of the three. (4)

---

[13] Steven Metz and Raymond Millen, "Insurgency and Counterinsurgency in the 21st Century: Reconceptualizing Threat and Response," Carlisle, PA: Strategic Studies Institute, 2004, pp. 1, 12, www.strategicstudiesinstitute.army.mil/pdffiles/PUB586.pdf, accessed August 24, 2010.

[14] In the third kind, unlike the first two, the insurgents battle an outside force. Still, the insurgents are battling an internal political status quo, though one established and defended, by a foreign power.

Ethnic wars are armed conflicts that originate with tensions between different national, ethnic, and religious groups, often based in long-standing grievances regarding historical relations of domination and oppression between the groups. Examples of ethnic wars include the 1990s conflicts in the former Yugoslavia and the more recent conflicts in Central Africa, mainly the Congo. Ethnic wars sometimes break the pattern typical of the traditional civil wars in that none of the parties may be in control of a state, not because the state has not taken a side but because there is no effective central government. Such conflicts occur within a *failed state*. Any of the four kinds may involve military intervention by other states.[15] Foreign intervention may *internationalize* an internal conflict, but it usually remains principally local and internal.

The question is whether just war theory can provide an adequate explanation of the moral dimensions of civil wars. In our case, the question is whether theories developed earlier in the book, the *ad bellum* human rights paradigm and the *in extremis* view of *jus in bello*, can make sense of civil wars. There is, of course, the possibility that international armed conflicts and armed civil conflicts require different versions of just war theory. Asa Kasher suggests that "deep differences between such conflicts [may] warrant the introduction and application of different standards."[16] But, before accepting this conclusion, we should see if a unitary just war theory covering both internal and external war is possible. I will argue, first, that the standard account of *jus ad bellum*, the national defense paradigm, has trouble accounting for civil war, just as it has trouble accounting for humanitarian intervention, and that the human rights paradigm can better explain civil war, the way it is able better to explain humanitarian intervention. Second, I will argue that the standard symmetric account of basic *in bello* rules, as represented in the *in extremis* view, can account for morality in the fighting of civil wars. Before considering these arguments, we should examine an unfortunate contemporary case of an armed civil conflict.

[15] If foreign involvement comes to dominate the civil war becomes a *client war* or a *proxy war*, wherein contending outside powers support opposing sides.

[16] Asa Kasher, "The Principle of Distinction," *Journal of Military Ethics* 6, no. 2 (2007), pp. 152–167, at p. 158.

7.1 The Congo civil wars

Beginning in 1998, largely ignored by the outside world, a series of armed conflicts in the Democratic Republic of the Congo left millions dead, mostly civilians. Estimates put the number of deaths at 5.4 million; most of the deaths were due not directly to the military violence, but to starvation and preventable diseases brought about by the wars.[17] It is the deadliest conflict since World War II. As one observer noted, "as moral beings, we cannot help but be gravely concerned with the unspeakable human suffering that has resulted from the recent war, as well as Congo's other postcolonial traumas."[18]

The Congo is a large, resource-rich state at the heart of Africa. Prior to receiving its independence in 1960, it was exploited and left undeveloped by its colonial master Belgium. Upon independence, the country was immediately caught up in the Cold War struggle for influence between the United States and the Soviet Union. Its initial leader, Patrice Lumumba, who was seen as sympathetic to the Soviet Union, was assassinated. From 1965 to 1997, the Congo was ruled by Mobutu Sese Seko (who in 1971 renamed the state Zaire), with support of the West. Mobutu plundered the state for his own financial gain and drove it further into economic ruin. The decline of Mobutu's power in the 1990s set the stage for the armed civil conflict shortly to follow. Laurent Kabila, who had been involved for some years in a guerrilla struggle against Mobutu, mounted a major challenge to Mobutu's forces in 1996.[19]

The resulting conflict had international involvement from the start. Rwandan forces had entered Congolese territory in the aftermath of the Rwandan genocide. As discussed earlier, militant ethnic Hutus in Rwanda slaughtered up to 1 million ethnic Tutsis and moderate Hutus in 1994. The

---

[17] The death figure is for the period 1998–2007. Benjamin Coghlan *et al.*, "Mortality in the Democratic Republic of Congo," International Rescue Committee, www.theirc. org/sites/default/files/resource-file/2006-7_congoMortalitySurvey.pdf, accessed July 12, 2010.

[18] John F. Clark, "Introduction: Causes and Consequences of the Congo War," in John F. Clark (ed.), *The African Stakes of the Congo War* (New York: Palgrave Macmillan, 2002), pp. 1–10, at p. 1.

[19] Jermaine O. McCalpin, "Historicity of a Crisis: the Origins of the Congo War," in Clark (ed.), *African Stakes*, pp. 33–50.

genocide ended with a Tutsi-dominated rebel movement coming to power in Rwanda. Hutus responsible for the genocide then fled into Zaire, where they caused mischief by cross-border raids and were pursued by Tutsi military forces. Forces from Rwanda as well as Uganda assisted Kabila's rebellion. After Kabila seized power, he ordered his foreign supporters out of the country, but they refused to leave and instead backed an anti-Kabila guerrilla force. Kabila survived this challenge with the assistance of outside forces from Angola, Zimbabwe, and Namibia. Fighting continued for the next several years, with the horrendous civilian toll referred to above. Even after a peace agreement (the Lusaka Accord) was reached in 2002, the fighting and civilian deaths continued through the first decade of this century. Much of the impetus for the continuation of the conflict is the natural resources, or "conflict minerals," that the various guerrilla movements were able to extract to support and enrich themselves. Resources include diamonds, gold, tin, copper, and columbite-tantalite, a mineral used in advanced electronics, including cell phones.[20]

There were some calls during the Congo crisis for humanitarian intervention, but given that the West did nothing in the Rwandan genocide, it was not likely to do something in the Congo, where the costs would have been greater and the chances of success less, so much so that such an intervention may not have been justified. A UN peacekeeping force was deployed to parts of the conflict zone as a result of the Lusaka Accord, but it was not of a sufficient size to make much of a difference. There were, however, short of military intervention, actions other states could have taken to mitigate this humanitarian tragedy, and this will form part of the theme for the next chapter. Meanwhile, we must turn to ask whether just war theory can make moral sense of civil wars, such as those in the Congo.

7.2 Civil wars and *jus ad bellum*

In terms of its logic, the national defense paradigm has little to say about civil war. Under this paradigm the right of a state to go to war is due to the violation of its sovereignty by an outside aggressor. The sovereignty that is violated is *external sovereignty*, the right of a state not to be attacked by other

---

[20] Information from www.globalsecurity.org/military/world/war/congo.htm and www.globalissues.org/article/87/the-democratic-republic-of-congo, accessed July 12, 2010.

states. But civil war is a matter of *internal sovereignty*, the right of a state to control what goes on within its borders. Because the national defense paradigm bases the moral status of wars on considerations of external sovereignty, civil war does not count morally as war. In an armed civil conflict, neither side is defending a state from outside aggression, and absent this, the paradigm offers no way to assess civil wars in moral terms. The national defense paradigm regards what goes on internally as a matter of policing, not a matter of warring. When an armed civil conflict exists, the paradigm has nothing relevant to say about the justice of the parties.

For much of its history, IHL was not regarded as applying to civil wars. From the perspective of IHL, armed civil conflict was basically a *morality free zone*. The reason is that IHL is largely an embodiment of the national defense paradigm. Legal scholar James E. Bond notes: "Traditionally, international law did not tell sovereign states how they could treat their own nationals; and nations dealt with bandits, rebels, and other malcontents largely as they wished."[21] International law has more recently sought to fill this legal gap by treating groups conducting insurgencies, in some cases, as if they were states. This was accomplished initially through the legal doctrine of *recognition of belligerency*, according to which an insurgent group satisfying certain conditions could be recognized legally as a belligerent. So recognized, the insurgency could be treated as an entity to which the laws of war would apply, and the behavior of and toward its combatants would be governed by *in bello* rules. The conflict would be regarded "as if it were an international one."[22] The conditions put forth for an insurgency to achieve recognition of belligerency, as suggested in the language of the Second Protocol, are that it (a) has a responsible government, (b) controls territory, and (c) has a military able to follow the laws of war. When insurgents satisfy these conditions, they have, Bond notes, "become in effect a *de facto* government." As a result: "The doctrine of the sovereign equality of states, which remains a fundamental building block of the international legal order, rather than the demand of humanity, dictated applying the laws of war to belligerencies."[23] The approach of international law is to

---

[21] James E. Bond, *Rules of Riot: Internal Conflict and the Law of War* (Princeton University Press, 1974), p. 3.

[22] Adam Roberts and Richard Guelff, "Introduction," in Roberts and Guelff (eds.), *Documents*, p. 23.

[23] Bond, *Rules of Riot*, pp. 53, 51.

encompass armed civil conflicts by extending the honorary status of a state, as a kind of legal fiction, to insurgent groups satisfying the proper conditions.

But the doctrine of recognition of belligerency, while appropriate as a legal device to bring civil wars under *in bello* rules, does not represent an adequate foundation for an *ad bellum* perspective on civil wars. In assigning an artificial status of sovereignty to a sub-state group, in treating the insurgency as if it were a state, the doctrine ignores the moral basis of the national defense paradigm. In his discussion of civil wars, Michael Walzer seeks to correct this defect in a way similar to the way he sought to correct the defect in the national defense paradigm regarding humanitarian intervention. In effect, Walzer connects the legal doctrine of recognition of belligerency with his notion of *political community*. In Chapter 4 we saw how he used the notion of political community in seeking to incorporate the humanitarian intervention exception into an account of *jus ad bellum*. For Walzer, moral value belongs to the political community, not the state as such, and this moral value is the basis of the principle of non-intervention. Walzer formulates this principle as: "always act so as to recognize and uphold communal autonomy." He asserts that "non-intervention [in a state] is most often entailed by that recognition, but not always."[24] While a political community is usually represented by a state, it may not be.

In a justified humanitarian intervention, on Walzer's account, there is a state that does not represent a political community, while in an armed civil conflict an insurgency *may* represent a political community not represented by a state. When an insurgency represents a political community, it has the moral status of sovereignty. An insurgency may show that it represents a political community when "it has rallied its own people and made some headway in the 'arduous struggle' for freedom." This statement reflects the legal conditions for recognition of belligerency, especially the control of territory. Insurgents may be taken to represent a political community when they "establish control over some substantial portion of the territory and population of the state." Control of territory is an indirect indicator that an insurgency represents a political community because such control requires the insurgency's success in fighting among

---

[24] Michael Walzer, *Just and Unjust Wars* (New York: Basic Books, 1977), p. 90.

the people. When the insurgents hold territory, "it is best to assume that they have some serious political support among the people."[25]

What Walzer's account implies about the *ad bellum* status of a civil war may be seen by considering his account of justified military intervention. First, consider the justifiability of involvement in an ongoing international armed conflict. Third parties may involve themselves, but only on the just side. Coming in on the side of a state that is *ad bellum* just is itself *ad bellum* just, and coming in on the side of a state that is *ad bellum* unjust is itself *ad bellum* unjust. A state aiding another state's defense is itself a defender, while a state aiding another state's aggression is itself an aggressor. If we apply this general principle to the case of intervention in an armed civil conflict, the implication is that intervention is permitted only if the civil war of the party supported is *ad bellum* just. But when we consider what Walzer has to say about intervention in armed civil conflicts, we see that the justifiability of intervention has nothing to do with factors that we are inclined to regard as relevant to determining *ad bellum* justice. For Walzer, the justifiability of intervention is based on different, non-moral grounds.

Under a traditional understanding of the national defense paradigm, the non-intervention principle holds, and intervention is not permitted. This is one of the problems with the national defense paradigm, since some forms of intervention should be permitted. One permissible form, as we saw, is humanitarian intervention.[26] Walzer permits some forms of intervention under what he calls "rules of disregard," as exceptions to "the legalist paradigm," which is a traditional understanding of the national defense paradigm. Walzer uses the notion of a political community to distinguish permissible from non-permissible forms of intervention. Humanitarian intervention is permissible; it is not interference in a political community because the state at that point does not represent the political community. Regarding intervention in armed civil conflicts, Walzer divides these conflicts into two sorts of cases, corresponding to the first two of the four kinds of civil wars discussed earlier: (1) struggles for control of a central government and (2) struggles for secession. He

---

[25] *Ibid.*, pp. 93, 96, 185.

[26] We also discussed one impermissible form, preventive intervention, or preventive war.

prohibits intervention in (1) but sometimes permits it in (2).[27] The problem is that the factors in his account determining the justifiability of intervention (and the side on which it should occur) make no reference to the justice of the civil war on the side on which intervention occurs.

Central to Walzer's views on the justification of intervention are the related ideas of *self-help* and *self-determination*. Self-help is a kind of "rugged individualism" for states. It is the idea that states are on their own, so to speak, in the international system; they have to look out for themselves and their own security.[28] Self-help has a negative side and a positive side. The negative side is that no state can expect other states to come to its assistance in an hour of need, and the positive side is that states are free of outside interference in their affairs. The positive side is self-determination, the idea that a state (or the political community it represents) has a right to make its own governance decisions through its own chosen political processes. Walzer's claim is that intervention in an armed civil conflict needs to respect the self-determination of political communities. In (1) struggles for control of a central government, intervention is not allowed because that struggle itself represents an unresolved process of self-determination by the political community.[29] In (2) struggles for secession, intervention may be allowed on the side of the secessionists (once they have satisfied the conditions for recognition of belligerency) because a secessionist civil war is part of a self-determination process of the political community seeking to secede. Recall that from the perspective of the human rights paradigm self-determination has some moral value in that it represents common-life rights of the political community, as the self-determination of a family has moral value. But in either case that value can be overridden by other rights considerations, such as threatened rights violations within the group.

Regarding struggles for control of a central government, Walzer's account of intervention may be roughly represented by Table 7.1. At (a), when the insurgency is beginning, the state is entitled to treat the rebellion as a criminal matter, as a matter of policing and law enforcement,

---

[27] Walzer, *Just and Unjust Wars*, pp. 91–101.

[28] On self-help, see Yoram Dinstein, *War – Aggression and Self-Defense*, 4th edn. (Cambridge University Press, 2005), pp. 175–176.

[29] Walzer, *Just and Unjust Wars*, pp. 91–101. However, Walzer (p. 97) allows *counter-intervention*, that is, intervention to balance prior intervention by another state, so long as it does not exceed the prior intervention.

Table 7.1. *Walzer's view of justified civil-war intervention*

status of insurgency:	a. beginning	b. recognition of belligerency	c. victory
intervention permitted:	on side of the state	on neither side	on side of the state

however brutal; other states are entitled to assist the state in an attempt to suppress the insurgency, but not to assist the insurgency.[30] Once the insurgency has reached (b) recognition of belligerency, the state must treat the insurgency as a war in terms of applicable *in bello* rules, but no other state may intervene on either side because the conflict has become an internal matter of self-determination. At (c), the insurgency has won control of the state and has become the central government, self-determination has been achieved. As at the beginning, another state may aid it in suppression of any remaining opposition forces, which now are insurgents, and may not aid the new insurgency. At no point can insurgents be aided, regardless of the *justice* of their side.

The moral objection to this approach is that the justice or injustice of intervention should not depend on the outcome of the internal military struggle. This approach, in essence, involves an assumption that might makes right. The objection can be run at two different levels. The first level accepts the moral force of self-determination, but sees self-determination as having moral relevance only if it is roughly democratic in form. Walzer views self-determination as having a role for military force; he puts weight on the outcome of a military struggle because he believes that military success indicates the support of the people, of the political community. But, as David Rodin notes, the "outcome of a civil war reflects far more than the support of a majority of the population." It also depends on "access to armaments and military training" and on ruthlessness, "the preparedness to use brutality and terror, all too often against members of the civilian population." It is a mistake to think that "a military outcome can serve as an accurate proxy for a normative process such as self-determination."[31] If anything, forces representing an

---

[30] *Ibid.*, p. 96.
[31] David Rodin, *War and Self-Defense* (Oxford University Press, 2002), pp. 157–158.

oppressive group are more likely to be ruthless than forces representing a liberal or democratic group. David Luban has similar concerns. He refers to the "apolitical technology of violence" used in armed civil conflicts, and he accuses Walzer of "a blindness to the threat physical repression poses to political processes" and a failure to recognize that "repression is itself an attempt to restrict, or rather, to eliminate the political process."[32] The conclusion of Rodin and Luban is that the result of an armed civil conflict may not be self-determination in a morally relevant sense.[33]

The second level of the objection comes out of the human rights paradigm and calls attention to the gap between self-determination, however achieved, and respect for human rights, viewing respect for human rights as being the more important moral consideration. The moral value of self-determination is derivative from the moral value of respect for human rights. If our moral concern in intervening in an armed civil conflict is respect for human rights, and it should be, then self-determination may sometimes have to be ignored. A state should not intervene on the side of oppression, even when the oppression is an expression of self-determination. As we know, a majority may democratically choose to oppress a minority. Popular leaders can be oppressive autocrats.

This criticism supports the claim that the national defense paradigm, and Walzer's defense of it in terms of the notion of political community, is unable to explain the *ad bellum* justice of parties in an armed civil conflict, and it can be further supported by criticisms of the specific moral claims Walzer makes about intervention in armed civil conflicts, as represented by Table 7.1. Walzer's focus on self-determination allows him to endorse intervention on the unjust side in an armed civil conflict and prohibit intervention on the just side. British philosopher Simon Caney notes: "Surely, whether one can intervene or not in support of one participant in a conflict should depend in part on their moral legitimacy."[34] Consider

---

[32] David Luban, "The Romance of the Nation-State," *Philosophy & Public Affairs* 9, no. 4 (Summer 1980), pp. 392–397, at pp. 394, 397.

[33] Self-determination may not involve armed struggle when the culture a political community seeks to preserve is one of non-violence. If Tibet has such a culture, judging a Tibetan secessionist movement by its military success against China would miss the point. (Thanks to Leanne Place and Rachel MacElhenney on this point.)

[34] Simon Caney, *Justice beyond Borders: A Global Political Theory* (Oxford University Press, 2005), p. 247.

the beginning of an insurgency, where, for Walzer, the state's side of the struggle can be supported through intervention, but the insurgent's side cannot. On the contrary, if the insurgency is fighting an *ad bellum* just war and the state is not, it may be permissible to intervene on the side of the insurgency and impermissible to intervene in support of the state.[35] In defense of his position, Walzer remarks that "intervention is not justified whenever revolution is."[36] Indeed, the fact that revolutionaries have justice on their side is not sufficient to justify intervention on their behalf, in that such an intervention may fail to satisfy *ad bellum* criteria other than just cause. But, *contra* Walzer, if the insurgents have justice on their side, intervention would at least satisfy just cause. Similar points can be made concerning points (b), where neutrality is prescribed,[37] and (c), where intervention is permitted: Walzer would permit intervention when he should not and prohibit it when he should not.

The same criticism applies to Walzer's account of secessionist struggles. Walzer's view is that the two sides involved represent different political communities since the secessionists are fighting to establish a state separate from that of the main state. The main state is aggressing against the fledgling state, by seeking to destroy it in the cradle. The secessionists are exercising self-determination, and intervening on their side is morally the same as aiding a state in its defense against external aggression. (In contrast, in wars for control of a central government, there is only one political community, the control of which awaits the outcome of the internal struggle, so that respect for self-determination requires non-intervention.[38]) But not all secessionist struggles are just.[39] For example, the Confederacy's civil war was unjust because it had as a main purpose the preservation of slavery. It would have been morally impermissible for Britain to aid the secession of the South, as it apparently considered doing. Walzer treats civil

---

[35] This assumes, with Table 7.1, that the struggle of an insurgent group can count as a war even before it achieves recognition of belligerency status.

[36] Walzer, *Just and Unjust Wars*, p. 89.

[37] Walzer claims that "this kind of neutrality is a feature of all the rules of war." ("The Moral Standing of States: A Response to Four Critics," *Philosophy & Public Affairs* 9, no. 3 (1980), pp. 209–229, at p. 217.) But this is true only of *in bello* rules, and the rule in question is an *ad bellum* rule.

[38] With the exception of counter-intervention to balance a third-party intervention.

[39] On secession, see Allan Buchanan, *Secession: The Legitimacy of Political Divorce from Fort Sumter to Lithuania and Quebec* (Boulder, CO: Westview Press, 1991).

wars against an occupying power and the regime it supports as morally like secession because they are expressions of self-determination of a political community.[40] The same criticism applies. Not all struggles for national liberation are just, as in the case where an occupying power is protecting a minority within the state that the revolutionaries would persecute.

The view we should adopt on armed civil conflict is closer to that expressed by Vattel: "Whenever therefore matters are carried so far as to produce a civil war, foreign powers may assist that party which appears to them to have justice on its side. He who assists an odious tyrant, or he who declares for an unjust and rebellious people, violates his duty."[41] The justice of intervention in armed civil conflict should conform to the principles of justice of involvement in international wars: parties that are *ad bellum* just may sometimes be aided with military force, and parties that are *ad bellum* unjust may not. Connecting *ad bellum* justice with a response to the violation of state sovereignty, as the national defense paradigm does, does not allow an adequate theory of armed civil conflict.

The human rights paradigm provides a better explanation of the morality of armed civil conflict than does the national defense paradigm. We have gotten an indication of how this works in our discussion of intervention. Just as the defense of human rights provides a better explanation for the humanitarian intervention exception (showing it not to be an exception), so it provides a better explanation of when it is appropriate to intervene on the side of a party fighting a civil war. The account the paradigm provides of intervention in armed civil conflict depends on the justice of the civil war itself on the side of which intervention occurs. How do we determine whether a civil war is just? Here, the main virtue of the human rights paradigm lies in its notion of just cause. According to the paradigm, what gives a war a just cause in general is that it is a response to systematic, ongoing human rights violations. This is the way we judge where justice lies in armed civil conflicts. Some have a moral prejudice against insurgency. This prejudice is like the prejudice against humanitarian intervention in that each represents a bias in favor of sovereignty, external

---

[40] Walzer, "Moral Standing of States," p. 217.

[41] Vattel, *Law of Nations,* in *The Law of Nations,* ed. Bella Kapossy and Richard Whatmore (Indianapolis, IN: Liberty Fund, 2008), pp. 290–291. Vattel recommends, however, that states abide by the voluntary law of nations, which precludes intervention.

sovereignty in the case of humanitarian intervention and internal sovereignty in the case of insurgency. But both prejudices should be discredited; an insurgency, as well as a humanitarian intervention, can have a just cause and be a just war. This is due to the fundamental role of respect for human rights.

To encompass cases of armed civil conflict, the formulation of the just cause criterion should be revised. R, S, and T are states or large organized groups.

> Just cause (human rights paradigm, revised): a war waged by S against T must be a response to a substantial ongoing policy of violations of basic rights on the part of T either: (1) against the members of S or R, when T's use of force is unjustified (which covers national defense, third party defense, civil wars, and civil war interventions); or (2) against the members of T (which covers humanitarian intervention).

Civil war interventions are akin to a state aiding another state under attack (third-party defense). Note that in international conflicts, the side starting the war is usually the unjust side (the exception being humanitarian intervention), but this is not necessarily the case with armed civil conflicts. The insurgent side is usually the side that starts the conflict, but this should not prejudice the judgment of its justice in doing so.

Whether a civil war is *ad bellum* just depends not only on the just cause criterion, but also on the other *ad bellum* criteria. The other criteria apply to civil wars and civil-war interventions roughly as they apply to international wars. Rightful intention in all wars requires that the intention with which the war is waged is defined by the just cause. The parties must intend to avoid the expected rights violations the threat of which constitutes the just cause (and not to intend anything else that would involve the use of a greater amount of force than that necessary to achieve the rightful intention). In the case of last resort, feasible alternatives to war need to be attempted first, taking into account the moral costs of delaying the war while the alternatives are attempted. If the resort to violence comes too soon, even with a just cause, the war fails the last resort criterion. Non-violent forms of political protest, and political action more generally, are especially important as alternatives to an insurgency because the political processes within an oppressive state may be open enough to serve as a vehicle for ending the oppression. Indeed, there is often a conflict between factions within an incipient insurgency about whether to keep their struggle against government oppression at the political level, including non-violent resistance, or to move to violence and civil war with the state. Insurgencies often divide themselves into a political wing and a military wing, as did the Irish Republican Army in its civil war against British occupation of Northern Ireland in the twentieth century.

A civil war, like an international war, must have a reasonable chance of success. Measuring reasonable chance of success for insurgencies may be especially difficult because the forces of insurgency gamble on their ability to enlist popular support, to win the "hearts and minds" of the population, needed for eventual victory against the superior military forces of the state. Legitimate authority requires that a war be initiated by some person or group with legal or *de facto* authority within a hierarchical organization that would control the military effort, apart from whether that person or group has moral legitimacy. (Though, if the authority lacks moral legitimacy, other of the criteria may not be satisfied.) It is helpful in thinking about legitimate authority for insurgencies to consider the argument of Aquinas for his more stringent interpretation of the criterion. For him, legitimate authority applied only to the sovereign head of a state because any authorities below the sovereign who sought to represent a group threatened with injustice that might otherwise constitute a just cause for war could appeal to the sovereign for redress, obviating the need for war.[42] But if the sovereign is unresponsive to requests for redress or, more likely, is the agency of the oppression for which redress is sought, the implication of Aquinas' argument is that legitimate authority would devolve to lower levels.

The *ad bellum* criterion of proportionality requires that a war be such that the significance of the created evil does not exceed the significance of the resisted evil. Under the human rights paradigm, the created and resisted evils are wrongs to individuals, and the criterion, so understood, applies to civil wars as well. As in other kinds of wars, proportionality may serve as a significant restraint, as least in theory, on wars because there would often be cases where a prospective war would satisfy just cause but fail proportionality. One important consideration in applying

---

[42] Aquinas, *Summa Theologica*, in Larry May *et al.* (eds.), *The Morality of War: Classical and Contemporary Readings* (Upper Saddle River, NJ: Prentice-Hall, 2006), p. 27.

proportionality to civil wars is that many rights violations can be brought about by the political instability the war may cause within the state. This is especially evident in the Congo civil wars, where most of the deaths, as we saw, have been due to starvation and disease resulting from the breakdown in social order caused by the war. Note that a developed state considering intervention in an armed civil conflict in a developing state will sometimes recognize the negative impact of a potential increase in political instability the intervention would bring and seek to ameliorate this prospect (making the intervention more likely to satisfy proportionality) by planning to rebuild the society after the war, to engage in what is called *nation building*. This is a laudable goal, but it is important that the intervener recognize, in calculating reasonable expectations of success, what a difficult task nation building usually is. Even if it is achievable, its high cost may make the state unable to maintain the political support of its own public necessary for such a mission to be carried to completion.

The relation of just war theory to armed civil conflict is discussed by William O'Brien. He focuses on one kind of civil war, what he calls revolutionary war, roughly our category (3), wars of national independence. He agrees that just war theory should be extended to such wars, because "revolutionary war remains war, with material characteristics essentially identical to international conflict," and "all war is subject to the conditions of just war doctrine."[43] While acknowledging that some revolutionary wars can satisfy *jus ad bellum*, his view seems to be that most cannot.[44] Revolutionaries have trouble satisfying proportionality because they often have as their goal the achievement of "an open-ended utopia." The promise of this utopia, the lack of which is included on the resisted-evil side of the proportionality calculation, makes them willing to engage in wars in which the reasonable expectation of created evil is inordinately high.[45] But Uwe Steinhoff points out some problems with O'Brien's argument.[46] The fact that insurgents make mistaken calculations of proportionality does not show that an insurgency cannot satisfy proportionality. O'Brien is not condemning insurgency so much as criticizing the way that

---

[43] William V. O'Brien, *The Conduct of Just and Limited War* (New York: Praeger, 1981), p. 163.

[44] *Ibid.*, pp. 158–166.   [45] *Ibid.*, p. 164.

[46] Uwe Steinhoff, "In Defense of Guerrillas," *Diametros* 23 (March 2010), pp. 84–103, at pp. 99–100.

proportionality calculations are often made by its proponents. In addition, the status quo forces in armed struggle with the insurgents are subject to a corresponding excess of vision, as they often claim that the success of the revolutionaries would be the end of civilization as we know it, for example, as a victory for the international communist conspiracy, and they use such an assumption in their own proportionality calculations.

7.3 Civil wars and *jus in bello*

In some respects, armed civil conflict may pose a greater challenge to *jus in bello* than it does to *jus ad bellum*. This is due to the disparity in military capability that generally exists between an insurgency and those making war in support of the political status quo. (I will refer generally to the latter war as counterinsurgency, whether or not it employs the sort of tactics or strategies associated with the idea of counterinsurgency.) Armed civil conflict is usually *asymmetric warfare* in terms of size and the quality of the fighting forces of the opposing belligerents. An insurgency marshals fewer combatants (at least initially) and is poorer in firepower and weapons technology than the counterinsurgency. The military inferiority of the insurgents may lead them to adopt strategies and tactics that run afoul of *in bello* rules. The International Committee of the Red Cross notes: "Asymmetric warfare is characterized by significant disparities between the military capacities of the belligerent parties," and as a result, such warfare "specifically affects compliance with the most fundamental rules of the conduct of hostilities."[47] Given this, the question is whether the *in bello* rules, which developed in the context of international war, are adequate for armed civil conflict. Toni Pfanner poses the objection: "It is debatable whether the challenges of asymmetric war can be met by the current law of war."[48]

Consider first asymmetric warfare. Earlier we discussed *moral* asymmetry in war, including the moral asymmetry between the belligerents at the *ad bellum* level and the question whether such asymmetry also applies

---

[47] International Committee of the Red Cross, "International Humanitarian Law and the Challenges of Contemporary Armed Conflicts," *International Review of the Red Cross* 89 (September 2007), pp. 719–757, at p. 732.

[48] Toni Pfanner, "Asymmetrical Warfare from the Perspective of Humanitarian Law and Humanitarian Action," *International Review of the Red Cross* 87 (March 2005), pp. 149–174, at p. 158.

at the *in bello* level. Here we are discussing *military* asymmetry, that is, differences in military capability between opposing sides in armed conflict. Military asymmetry is not itself a moral concept, but it may have moral implications. Most armed civil conflicts are militarily asymmetric, and some international armed conflicts are as well. Our observations about militarily asymmetric armed civil conflicts should apply to such conflicts at the international level as well. Since the end of the Cold War, the United States has been the preeminent military power on the planet. The United States far exceeds other nations in military expenditures; for example, in 2009 it spent 43 percent of total global military expenditures.[49] It has no peer competitor, meaning that there is no state that would be its near military equal in an international armed conflict. An armed conflict between the United States and any other state would be militarily asymmetric.[50]

Militarily asymmetric warfare is referred to as *unequal combat*. In unequal combat, the militarily weaker side seeks to make up for its relative weakness by adopting strategies and tactics that give it an advantage over its stronger opponent, in an effort to level the playing field. In trying to make the combat more equal, the militarily weaker side may fight in a different way, often adopting a non-traditional paradigm of warfare. The classical example of this is the biblical story of David and Goliath, where the "battle of champions" between the two was militarily asymmetric due to Goliath's great size and strength.[51] David, seeking to equalize the combat, adopted the sling shot to give him a technological advantage, and he defeated Goliath. It would not be surprising if the Philistines, whose champion Goliath was, viewed the sling shot as violating the existing war convention. Clearly, the attempt by insurgents to equalize the combat sometimes works because sometimes the militarily weaker side wins.

The problem, as David Rodin notes, is that the traditional paradigm of warfare has moral as well as strategic elements, so when insurgents adopt a different strategic paradigm, this raises the prospect that their behavior will be at odds with traditional *in bello* rules.[52] Michael Schmitt observes

---

[49] *SIPRI Yearbook 2010*, Stockholm International Peace Research Institute, p. 203, www.sipri.org/yearbook/2010/05, accessed July 28, 2010.

[50] With the exclusion of a nuclear war between the United States and Russia.

[51] 1 Samuel, chapter 17.

[52] David Rodin, "The Ethics of Asymmetric War," in Richard Sorabji and David Rodin (eds.), *The Ethics of War: Shared Problems in Different Traditions* (Farnham, UK: Ashgate Publishing, 2006), pp. 153–168, at p. 154.

that "the internal logic of technological asymmetry can drive the weaker party into tactical choices involving a violation of *jus in bello*."[53] Earlier, we discussed the phenomenon of *rule creep*, using as our example the historical expansion in the scope of combatant liability in terms of when combatants may be attacked. Rule creep, as we said, is usually motivated by the weaker side in an asymmetric conflict seeking more equal combat. The conflicting paradigms of warfare at work in an asymmetric conflict are evident in the exchange between the American Colonel Summers and the Vietnamese Colonel Tu, quoted at the beginning of the chapter. Summers was thinking in terms of the traditional paradigm of warfare when he pointed out that in the Vietnam War the Vietnamese never defeated the Americans in battle; he seems to be expressing puzzlement over how, if this was the case, the United States could have lost the war. Tu, speaking from the perspective of a different paradigm, specifically, guerrilla warfare, observed that winning battles was irrelevant. In asymmetric warfare, Michael Schmitt notes, "one must distinguish victory on the conventional battlefield from victory in the conflict more generally."[54]

Given that the insurgents, by changing the traditional paradigm of warfare, seek to equalize what is unequal combat, they are searching for some way in which they are asymmetrically advantaged over their militarily stronger opponent. As Rodin observes, "asymmetry is, so to speak, itself a symmetrical concept."[55] In other words, each side has asymmetric strengths, and effective fighting is discovering what those are and using them effectively. "The fundamental aim of asymmetrical warfare," Toni Pfanner notes, "is to find a way round the adversary's military strength by discovering and exploiting, in the extreme, its weaknesses."[56] It involves "leveraging your own strengths and exploiting the enemy's weaknesses."[57]

Insurgents in armed civil conflicts are often referred to as *guerrillas* or guerrilla fighters, engaged in *guerrilla war*, as in the case of the Vietnamese

---

[53] Michael Schmitt, "21st Century Conflict: Can the Law Survive?" *Melbourne Journal of International Law* 8 (2007), pp. 443–478, at p. 465.

[54] Michael Schmitt, "The Vanishing Law of War: Reflections on Law and War in the 21st Century," *Harvard International Review* 31, no. 1 (Spring 2009), pp. 64–68, at p. 66.

[55] Rodin, "Ethics of Asymmetric War," p. 155.

[56] Pfanner, "Asymmetrical Warfare," p. 151.

[57] Schmitt, "21st Century Conflict," p. 468.

against the Americans. Guerrilla war is often referred to as *irregular war*, suggesting that it is war fought outside the regular paradigm of war. The guerrilla fighters perhaps best known to Americans are the combatants in their own revolution. As mentioned earlier, the Continental Army often refused to meet the British "Redcoats" in set-piece battles involving large concentration of forces meeting on a battlefield, but attacked them in unconventional ways. A major impetus for twentieth-century insurgencies has been the doctrine of "People's War," an influential strategy for insurgency promulgated by the Chinese Communist Revolutionary leader Mao Tse-Tung.[58]

The paradigm of warfare adopted by guerrillas differs from the standard paradigm in two main ways: (1) the use by the guerrillas of different ways of engaging the enemy combatants, such as ambush and hit-and-run attacks, seeking to wear them out; and (2) the guerrillas' exploitation of civilians and of their opponents' adherence to the principle of civilian immunity. The first of these, though it involves some rule creep, is generally consistent with universal moral element in the principle of discrimination. The second puts guerrillas in direct opposition to the principle of civilian immunity. Consider each of these.

(1) Guerrillas adopt tactics that take advantage of their mobility to harass and weaken their powerful opponents. They are mosquitoes in their battle with large animals. What the mosquito lacks in strength, it makes up for in maneuverability and stealth. Guerrillas substitute skirmishes for mass battles. They take advantage of their nimbleness and mobility to harass the large and cumbersome forces of their opponent, picking off small groups of enemy combatants and attacking their supply lines. Nimbleness and mobility are *their* asymmetric advantage. Guerrillas refuse to "come out and fight," frustrating their opponents, because the guerrillas know that if they did they would be playing to the advantages of their opponents and stand little chance. A guerrilla force must avoid being swatted. It seeks the death of its powerful opponent by a thousand cuts. Often it cannot hope to defeat the opponent in military terms, as with the Vietnamese failure to win battles against the Americans; rather it seeks to wear the opponent out, forcing it eventually to quit the fight.

---

[58] Metz and Millen, "Insurgency and Counterinsurgency in the 21st Century," pp. 8–9.

(2) Civilians play an important role in guerrilla warfare. Each side seeks to woo them, to win their "hearts and minds," recognizing that therein lies the path to ultimate victory. At the same time, each side, especially the insurgents, sees military advantage in exploiting them. There are three main ways in which guerrillas seek to exploit civilians.

(2a) First, guerrillas exploit civilians by directly attacking civilians, such as city dwellers, who generally have allegiances to the counterinsurgency. Civilian targets are usually "soft" targets, much easier for guerrillas to attack than protected military targets. Such attacks are terrorism, and the guerrillas hope to get the sorts of benefits from the practice of terror that have lead states to engage in terrorism in international armed conflicts. The goal of the terrorist, as discussed in the last chapter, is to use the terror he creates among the civilian population to force political changes from the enemy's leadership, winning concessions or winning the war. In addition, the ethnic character of many contemporary insurgencies provides, from the attacker's perspective, an intrinsic reason, not simply an instrumental one, for attacking civilians.

(2b) The second way that guerrillas exploit civilians to advance their movement is by provoking their opponents to attack civilians. As Walzer notes, guerrillas "invite their enemies" to attack civilians by living among civilians, by melting away into the civilian population between attacks. The guerrillas "depend upon the counter-attacks of their enemies to mobilize" the population to the insurgency.[59] The guerrillas seek to justify their struggle by claiming that the status quo forces are oppressive, and they seek to make that apparent (and make it true) by provoking the counterinsurgency to attack civilians. The guerrillas can then present themselves as the people's protectors. The psychological situation in which the insurgency puts the counterinsurgency is interesting. In part, the guerrillas are depending on their opponents to overreact, to respond with too heavy a hand, to lash out inappropriately and counterproductively at a challenge to their power. The guerrillas have laid a trap into which their opponents often readily fall. At the same time, the counterinsurgents are concerned to maintain their power, and they recognize that their power lies largely in the credibility of their threats to maintain order by force. They fear a diminution of that credibility and a slow erosion of their power should

---

[59] Walzer, *Just and Unjust Wars*, p. 180.

they respond with too light a hand. The heavy hand may be as much a cal-culation as an instinctual lashing-out. In any case, the guerrillas in this way exploit civilians by making then more vulnerable to attack by the other side.

(2c) The third way that guerrillas exploit civilians is to use them for pro-tection. By hiding among the people, guerrillas seek not only to provoke a heavy-handed reaction, as in (2b), but also to avoid being attacked. Even if the heavy hand falls, guerrillas are much safer disguised as civilians than they would be if naked in their status as combatants. The military weakness of the insurgency makes guerrillas highly vulnerable, and living among civilians gives them a place to hide. Living among civilians provides the guerrillas with cover; the guerrillas rely on their opponents' generally respecting the principle of civilian immunity (while also expecting some exercise of the heavy hand). As David Rodin puts it, the guerrillas seek to "operationalize the moral dispositions of the enemy by using the reluc-tance of the enemy to target civilians as a source of strategic advantage."[60] These dispositions become a source of "weakness" on the part of the coun-terinsurgents that the guerrillas can exploit. Charles Dunlap refers to this strategic approach as *lawfare*. "Lawfare describes a method of warfare where law is used as a means of realizing a military objective." It involves "a cynical manipulation of the rule of law and the humanitarian values it represents." Instead of "seeking battlefield victories, *per se*," the guerrillas "try to destroy the will to fight by undermining the public support" that the counterinsurgency needs to maintain its part of the struggle.[61]

Strategy (2a) involves attacking civilians and so is a direct violation of the principle of discrimination. But in the case of (2b) and (2c) it is not the guerrillas who do the attacking. Instead, the opponent is invited or provoked by the insurgency to attack civilians by the insurgents adopting a civilian guise. But this also can be seen as a violation of the principle of discrimination, if the principle is more broadly understood. As we have seen, the principle requires that each side in their attacks distinguish between combatants and civilians on the other side. But this is possible

---

[60] Rodin, "Ethics of Asymmetric War," p. 158.

[61] Charles Dunlap, "Law and Military Interventions: Preserving Humanitarian Values in 21st Century Conflicts," Carr Center for Human Rights Policy Workshop Paper, Harvard Kennedy School (2001), www.hks.harvard.edu/cchrp/Web%20Working%20 Papers/ Use%20of%20Force/ Dunlap2001.pdf, accessed August 22, 2010, p. 11.

only if it is clear who the combatants and civilians are. So an implication of the principle is that each side distinguish the combatants and civilians within its own population. Discrimination applies symmetrically, and implicit in this is a kind of reciprocity where each belligerent must distinguish between its own combatants and civilians in order to enable the other side to distinguish them. Walzer remarks that it is the purpose of the *in bello* rules "to specify for each individual a single identity; he must be either a soldier or a civilian."[62]

The distinction between (1), the use of stealth, mobility, and surprise, on the one hand, and (2b) and (2c), adopting the guise of civilians, on the other, is the difference between *ruse* and *perfidy*.[63] According the Additional Protocol 1 of the Geneva Conventions, "ruses are acts which are intended to mislead an adversary or to induce him to act recklessly but which infringe no rule of international law applicable in armed conflict and which are not perfidious because they do not invite the confidence of an adversary with respect to protection under that law."[64] Perfidy is "the feigning of protected status in order to kill or injure the enemy."[65] A ruse would be, for example, "a combatant [camouflaging] himself by wearing foliage to blend into a woodland background," while perfidy would be "feigning civilian, and therefore protected, status."[66] As Walzer puts it, guerrillas may seek the "natural cover" of the jungle or forests or the "political or moral" cover of life among civilians, but which of these they choose is morally relevant.[67] Seeking the former is a ruse, while seeking the latter is perfidy. Other examples of perfidy are feigning injury, using a false flag of truce, and giving a false indication of surrender. In (2b) and (2c), guerrillas engage in perfidy by feigning civilian status. A recent example of perfidy is the use of suicide bombers to attack combatants in cases where the bomber feigns civilian status in order to get close enough to her target to destroy it. In the case of perfidy we see again the role of reciprocity in observance of the

---

[62] Walzer, *Just and Unjust Wars*, p. 179.

[63] Yoram Dinstein, *The Conduct of Hostilities under the Law of International Armed Conflict* (Cambridge University Press, 2004), pp. 198–208.

[64] *1977 Geneva Protocol 1*, Article 37(2), in Roberts and Guelff (eds.), *Documents*, p. 442.

[65] Schmitt, "The Vanishing Law of War," p. 66.

[66] A. P. V. Rogers, "Unequal Combat and the Law of War," *Yearbook of International Humanitarian Law* 7 (2004), pp. 3–34, at p. 11.

[67] Walzer, *Just and Unjust Wars*, p. 176.

in bello rules; S can effectively observe the rules only if T does not seek an advantage by exploiting S's disposition to observe the rules.

The question is whether insurgency can be conducted without the use of the anti-civilian tactics represented by (2b) and (2c). Some might say that it cannot, adopting the slogan: no insurgency without perfidy. They would endorse Paul Kahn's remark at the beginning of the chapter that the counterinsurgency's insistence that the insurgency adhere to the principle of discrimination "has the appearance of self-serving moralizing." The point is not that insurgents will as a matter of course be perfidious, but that it is practically impossible to run an insurgency with any hope of success without adopting (2b) and (2c) tactics. If so, then a symmetric *jus in bello* is inadequate to explain civil wars.

There have been some legal efforts to accommodate the requirements of insurgent civil wars. In recognition of the special nature of insurgency, IHL has added some elements to the war convention that are of special advantage to insurgents. The four Geneva Conventions of 1949 contain a common Article 3, which specifies certain general humanitarian safeguards that were to apply in the case of "armed conflict not of an international character."[68] This idea was further developed in the 1977 Protocols to the Geneva Conventions, where the law was modified in a significant way to take account of insurgency. According to the Protocols, insurgents need not distinguish themselves from civilians at all times. Rather they are, in Adam Roberts' words, "entitled to hide among the population, being only required to put on uniforms or insignia immediately before engaging in acts of military resistance."[69] Indeed, Protocol 1 asserts that in some cases, all that is necessary is that the combatant "carries his arms openly" in deployment for or in the midst of a military engagement. Insurgent acts consistent with these requirements "shall not be considered as perfidious."[70]

These concessions to insurgency seem to be another example of rule creep. But they may be understood as a change to those aspects of the

---

[68] Roberts and Guelff, *Documents*, pp. 24, 198.

[69] Roberts, "Principle of Equal Application," in David Rodin and Henry Shue (eds.), *Just and Unjust Warriors: The Moral and Legal Status of Soldiers* (Oxford University Press, 2008), p. 241.

[70] Roberts and Guelff, *Documents*, pp. 444, 445.

war convention that are merely conventional, not a change to those aspects that represent morally universal rules. Our earlier example of rule creep concerned historical changes in how and when combatants may be attacked. Those changes affected the scope of combatant liability, which is merely conventional, but not its morally universal element, what we called the who-aspect, which is its foundation in the idea of threat liability. Like that earlier example of rule creep, this example affects mainly the when-aspect of discrimination, not the who-aspect. Both of these forms of rule creep facilitate the ability of insurgents to engage in ruse.

These changes, however, seem to be inconsistent with a symmetric *jus in bello*, as they advantage insurgents rather than the counterinsurgents. But, in fact, symmetry remains intact in that the revised rules apply *in theory* to both sides, even though they apply *in practice* only to the insurgency. Because of the military superiority of the counterinsurgents, it would be of little use for them to hide among the civilian population. The new rule would permit them to do so, so the rule is formally symmetric, but they have little military reason to do so. Their strength lies in their massed force and in their separation from civilian society. The support the civilian population provides for them does not come directly, as it does for the insurgents, but indirectly, through provisions provided by the state through the taxation of the population. There are other rules of the war convention like this, rules that are theoretically symmetric, in that they formally favor neither side, but which are in practice asymmetric, in that they end up benefitting one side more than the other. We may refer to such rules as *effectively asymmetric*. Many such rules are of practical benefit to the stronger side rather than the weaker side. For example, various conventions regarding the required treatment of prisoners of war are much easier for the stronger side to comply with than the weaker side. The resources of the weaker side are less adequate to the task. So the addition of rules like those of the Protocol do not violate symmetry, and, in a larger sense, they balance the war convention out somewhat by offsetting existing rules that are effectively asymmetric to the advantage of the stronger side, the counterinsurgents.

Consider now the counterinsurgency and its policies in terms of the *in bello* rules. In mounting a counterinsurgency, the defenders of the status quo may adopt strategies and tactics specifically designed to defeat an insurgency. Thus a counterinsurgency, like an insurgency, may depart from the traditional paradigm of war, and the question is whether this departure may also involve violation of the *in bello* rules. On the one hand, it may seem that a counterinsurgency, because it has the clear military advantage, "has little incentive to violate international humanitarian law." On the other hand, if the insurgency ignores *in bello* rules, the counter-insurgency may "begin to perceive the *jus in bello* as an obstacle to oper-ational success," and ignore the rules as well.[71]

Counterinsurgency doctrine has varied considerably over time. In 1974 James E. Bond provided an account of counterinsurgency doctrine as it was then understood, much as it was put into practice by the United States in the Vietnam War. Included were policies such as the relocation of citi-zens into "strategic hamlets," the defoliation of crop land and natural cover, treating captured insurgents as criminals rather than combatants, summary trials and executions, arbitrary detentions, torture, and denial of humanitarian relief.[72] Clearly, many of these policies violate *jus in bello*. But more recent conceptions of counterinsurgency doctrine seem to focus more on "winning hearts and minds" than winning battles. Perhaps in the twenty-first century, the United States has taken to heart the lesson taught by Colonel Tu. Michael Schmitt notes that "the restrictions imposed on counterinsurgency operations typically surpass those found in the law of war." He observes that the law of war is meant to "balance military neces-sity against humanitarian considerations," and that with current counter-insurgency doctrine "we may be witnessing an emergent, and promising, confluence of the two – where humanitarian considerations can enhance military operations, rather than limit them."[73] But it is military necessity that tends to be in the driver's seat, and any confluence between it and humanitarian considerations may be accidental and temporary.

What *apologia* do insurgents (and their supporters) offer for their sys-tematic *in bello* violations? Adam Roberts notes they base their arguments, to the extent that they offer any, "on a mixture of *jus ad bellum* and *jus in bello* considerations," specifically, "that a virtuous cause under the *jus ad bellum* entitles belligerents to ignore aspects of the *jus in bello*."[74] This is an instance of the weaker form of the *in bello* dependence thesis discussed in the last chapter, another example being Michael Walzer's "sliding

[71] Schmitt "21st Century Conflict," pp. 462, 471.

[72] Bond, *Rules of Riot*, pp. 102–136.

[73] Schmitt, "Vanishing Law of War," pp. 67, 68.

[74] Roberts, "Principle of Equal Application," p. 242.

scale." The *ad bellum* justice of one's cause allows one to cut *in bello* corners. But this sort of reasoning is also used by defenders of the status quo. An example related to the "war on terrorism" is indicated in the quotation from Alberto Gonzales at the beginning of Chapter 6. We have rejected the idea of *in bello* dependence, agreeing with Michael Schmitt, who is concerned about the "erosion of the heretofore impenetrable wall between the *jus in bello* and the *jus ad bellum*." This is, he says, a trend that "that must be resisted."[75] There is no more reason to accept *in bello* dependence in the case of civil wars than in the case of international wars.

But a rejection of efforts by insurgents to justify their actions through appeal to an *in bello* dependence thesis begs the question raised earlier: is it possible for insurgents to fight successfully without systematic violations of *in bello* rules? David Rodin takes up this question, seeking "to assess the adequacy of the norms embodied in the just war theory themselves to the phenomena of asymmetric and unequal war."[76] Speaking in general of the problem faced by the weaker side in asymmetric military conflicts, he claims that it is unfair for the weaker belligerent to be unable to pursue its legitimate war aims, including self-defense, due to *in bello* constraints.

> If (as just war theory assumes) war is a morally appropriate remedy to redress certain kinds of injustice, then fairness ought to dictate that it be a remedy open to the weak as well as the strong. Indeed, it is precisely the weak who have most need of the protection provided by the norm of self-defence.[77]

Jus ad bellum allows groups to press their case for justice through force of arms. It is unfair, Rodin believes, that some groups should not be able to avail themselves of this remedy. He suggests that there is a conflict between fairness at the *ad bellum* level and symmetry at the *in bello* level. This recalls Walzer's comment that "self-defense cannot be made morally impossible."[78] Rodin rejects two possible solutions to this conflict: (1) to accept the *ad bellum* unfairness (thus making self-defense sometimes morally impossible for the weaker side); or (2) to weaken the *in bello* requirements for the weaker side (what, for example, Walzer did with the doctrine

---

[75] Schmitt, "21st Century Conflict," pp. 472, 473, 474.
[76] Rodin, "Ethics of Asymmetric War," p. 156.   [77] *Ibid.*, p. 159.
[78] Michael Walzer, "Responsibility and Proportionality in State and Non-State Wars," *Parameters* 39 (Spring 2009), pp. 40–52, at p. 48.

of supreme emergency). His solution is (3) to strengthen the *in bello* requirements for the stronger belligerent.[79] While this solution, like (2), abandons
in bello symmetry, it does not do so in a way that lowers the basic moral
standards of civilian immunity, since these still set a moral floor for both
sides. Instead the stronger side must adhere to stricter standards.

There are two objections to Rodin's proposal. First, it may not be necessary, in the sense that what he seeks to achieve may already hold under
a symmetric *jus in bello*.[80] The argument is that the changes in the rules
Rodin recommends to make *jus in bello* more restrictive for the stronger side
simply point out the effective asymmetry of existing rules. For example,
Rodin proposes that the strong side be required to have a higher level of
certainty about the military status of a target before it may be attacked.[81]
But this requirement is already represented in the due care criterion, in
that the degree of care that is due is partly a function of the capabilities of
a belligerent to exercise care. Because the strong side is superior in such
capabilities, the degree of care it is required by *in bello* rules to exercise
would be greater than that required of the weaker side. Michael Schmitt
makes this point: "Of course, the legal standard that applies to belligerents is a constant. However, because they have greater ability to exercise
precautions in attack, advanced militaries are held to a higher standard as
a matter of law."[82]

The second objection comes from the other direction: is Rodin's proposal, despite the advantages it offers to insurgents, sufficient to make
it morally possible for them to fight successfully; is it sufficient to make
self-defense morally possible? Rodin's proposal, along with the Protocol
rules allowing combatants to distinguish themselves as combatants only
when deploying and fighting, represent effectively asymmetric rules that
benefit the insurgents, but are these sufficient to make insurgent victories
possible? If not, the tension would remain between *jus ad bellum* and *jus in
bello*, along with the temptation on the part of insurgents to appeal to the
in bello dependence thesis to justify asymmetric *in bello* rules favoring the
insurgency. This would support the suspicion that a symmetric *jus in bello*

---

[79] Rodin, "Ethics of Asymmetric War," pp. 160–162.
[80] Rodin himself alludes to this objection. *Ibid.*, p. 165.   [81] *Ibid.*, p. 162.
[82] Michael Schmitt, "Asymmetric Warfare and International Humanitarian Law," *Air
Force Law Review* 62 (2008), pp. 1–42, at p. 36.

is inadequate to explain civil wars. The corresponding argument is sometimes made on the side of the counterinsurgency. For example, Charles Dunlap, commenting on the American confrontation with rogue states, argues: "We need a new paradigm when using force against societies with malevolent propensities. We must hold at risk the very way of life that sustains their depredations."[83] This argues for the *in bello* dependence thesis in the same way that Sherman did when he claimed that civilians in the South must be made to feel "the hard hand of war." But in Dunlap's view, it is the strong that need this advantage.

Can insurgencies (or counterinsurgencies) fight effectively (that is, with a chance to succeed) under the traditional symmetric *jus in bello*? The historical trend in civil wars may be away from adherence to these rules, but can this trend be resisted consistent with the possibility of military effectiveness for the belligerents? Dunlap's suggestion that counterinsurgencies cannot be conducted effectively without advantageous *in bello* asymmetries seems implausible, and certainly less plausible than the parallel claim regarding insurgencies. Counterinsurgencies have much greater resources at their disposal. Assuming they have the support of the people, there is no reason they cannot win within the constraints of traditional *in bello* rules. It may be more costly for them to do so, but costliness is not impossibility. Moreover, as some contemporary theorists of counterinsurgency assert, their path to victory lies through scrupulous adherence to *in bello* rules, for only in this way can they get and keep the people on their side.

The case is harder for insurgencies. Recall our distinction between two categories of tactics often employed by guerrillas, (1) stealth, mobility, and surprise, and (2) exploitation of civilians. The distinction between (1) and (2) follows the distinction between ruse and perfidy. Tactics under (1) do not raise problems with traditional *jus in bello*, if we grant the acceptability of the sort of rule creep we have discussed, but tactics under (2) do. So the question can be put like this: can guerrillas get by on ruse without resorting to perfidy? The story of David and Goliath represents the idea that ruse can be sufficient for victory. In making their case for violating *in bello* rules, insurgents appeal to their weakness in relation to the state, but, as Michael Walzer notes, there are different sorts of weakness that may be involved: "the weakness of the movement vis-à-vis the opposing

---

[83] Charles Dunlap, quoted *ibid.*, p. 31.

state and the movement's weakness vis-à-vis its own people."[84] The second sort of weakness may make terror and perfidy seem the only option, but if the insurgency is not weak in this sense, there is much less reason to think it cannot overcome the counterinsurgency's military advantages by relying simply on ruse and the support of the people. It seems that either side in a civil war can win, consistent with adherence to traditional *in bello* rules, if it has the support of the people. So, we should conclude with Uwe Steinhoff: "There is no reason in principle why guerrillas should not be able to fight within the constraints of *jus in bello*."[85] If so, a unitary theory of *jus in bello* is possible, and the account of *jus in bello* laid out in the last chapter would apply to both international wars and civil wars.

7.4 Global terrorism

Insurgencies are generally local, occurring within a state. Occasionally they may be regional if an oppressed group waging the civil war is located in an area straddling the borders of contiguous states (like a Kurdish insurgency might encompass areas of Iraq, Iran, and Turkey). But some authors have suggested that the rise of global terrorism represents something new, a *global insurgency*.[86] A number of states, developed and developing, have in the past twenty years been subject to terrorist attacks (such as the 9/11 attacks in the United States) perpetrated by individuals who claim to be part of one or more international organizations, such as al-Qaeda, the militant Islamist group. The conflict between these organizations and various states may be described as an armed conflict "not of an international character" because, though it is transnational, it is not between states. It is *global* rather than international. Moreover, if an insurgency is defined as "a popular movement that seeks to change the status quo through violence and subversion," as David Kilcullen proposes, then a movement that seeks to do this globally can be counted as a global insurgency.[87] Such an insurgency would no longer be a civil war, in the way we have defined it, but we

---

[84] Michael Walzer, *Arguing about War* (New Haven, CT: Yale University Press, 2004), p. 55.

[85] Steinhoff, "In Defence of Guerrillas," p. 98.

[86] Metz and Millen, "Insurgency and Counterinsurgency," p. 24.

[87] David Kilcullen, "Countering Global Insurgency," *Small Wars Journal* (2004), http://smallwarsjournal.com/documents/kilcullen.pdf, accessed June 9, 2010, p. 15.

could enlarge our understanding of insurgency to include the use of force on a global scale. The more basic question, however, is whether the global violence perpetrated by such organizations, as well as the response to it, is a war at all. The view of the United States and others is that it is a war. They have referred to their own efforts to thwart global terrorist organizations as a "war on terrorism," thereby giving the status of an armed conflict to struggle in which they are engaged.[88]

If the terrorist campaign of a global organization and the struggle by states against it are not wars, what are they? The alternative model to warring is, of course, policing. On the alternative model, the terrorist campaign is crime, and the struggle against it is police action. The alternative model of policing should, in some respects, be appealing to opponents of global terror because of the moral asymmetry it implies. As criminals, the agents of terrorist organizations have no legitimacy, while those who struggle against them, the police, have legitimacy. In contrast, on the war model, the agents of the terrorist organization are combatants, and, as such, according to *in bello* symmetry, are the moral equals of the combatants in the war against them, despite the terrorists' acting contrary to *in bello* rules. As noted in a report by the International Committee of the Red Cross, to say that a "war is being waged against groups such as Al-Qaeda would mean that, under the law of war, their followers should be considered to have the same rights and obligations as members of regular armed forces."[89]

Is it more appropriate to regard the global terrorist campaign as war or as crime? Does the struggle of the states opposing the terrorist organization better fit the model of warring or policing? Recall the definition of war from Chapter 1: war is the use of force for political purposes by one side in a large-scale armed conflict where both (or all) sides are states or other large organized groups. The terrorist campaign may fit this definition, if we assume that the violence may be sufficiently connected with a large organized group. In the view of the 9/11 Commission, global terrorist attacks beginning in 1998 were "planned, directed, and executed by al-Qaeda," the group responsible for the terrorist attacks of September 11, 2001, which is "a hierarchical top-down group with defined positions,

---

[88] As has been noted, the phrase "war on terrorism" is an oxymoron because terrorism is a tactic; one goes to war against an organization, not a tactic.

[89] International Committee of the Red Cross, "International Humanitarian Law," p. 725.

tasks and salaries."[90] Another feature suggesting that the terrorist campaign is war rather than crime is noted by legal theorist Noah Feldman. In war, typically the parties engaged in conflict deny the legitimacy or sovereignty of their opponents, if not completely, at least in regard to whatever is contested in the war, while in crime, the criminal generally does not reject the legitimacy or sovereignty of the state whose rules she breaks. Al-Qaeda clearly denies the legitimacy or sovereignty of the states it attacks, suggesting it is engaging in war rather than crime.

On the other hand, a case can be made that the campaign of the global terrorists is crime rather than war. Toni Pfanner observes: "Unlike classic guerrilla movements, such terrorist organizations do not even tactically depend on the population's support," suggesting that the "struggle against such groups is … more reminiscent of the battle against organized crime than of a classic war."[91] Legal theorist Anne-Marie Slaughter concurs on the comparison between global terrorism and organized crime, pointing out an important feature they share, one not shared with the traditional notion of war, namely lack of finality. Wars typically end with a formal conclusion, such as a peace treaty, while struggle against global terrorism, like the fight against crime, is of indefinite length.[92] Another reason for regarding global terrorism as crime rather than war may be gleaned by considering one of the criteria of IHL for recognition of belligerency, namely, that the organization's fighters be able to follow the laws of war, such as abiding by the principle of civilian immunity. This does not seem possible for the global terrorists, that is, given the nature of their campaign, they are terrorists by necessity not choice. It is not simply that the degree of military asymmetry between the terrorists and their opponents is so great, but that the terrorists, attacking far from their home base, do not have much of an option to use the insurgent tactics of ruse to attack the opponent's military forces. A local guerrilla force can usually choose either to attack military forces through ruse or to engage in perfidious attacks on civilians. Global insurgents become global terrorists because in practice lack the former option.

---

[90] 9/11 Commission Report, *Final Report of the National Commission on Terrorist Attacks upon the United States* (New York: Norton, 2004), p. 67.

[91] Pfanner, "Asymmetrical Warfare," p. 155.

[92] Anne-Marie Slaughter, "Tougher than Terror," *The American Prospect* (January 2002).

But the question of war or crime is often asked in a different way, not whether the war or crime model is more appropriate, but whether the struggle against the terrorist campaign is *more effective* if waged by treating the campaign as war or treating it as crime. Some have argued that the struggle against global terrorism is more effective if carried on as police work rather than as war. For example, the British military historian Michael Howard argues that declaring "war on terrorists immediately creates a war psychosis that may be totally counterproductive to the objective" because it undermines "qualities needed in a serious campaign against terrorists – secrecy, intelligence, political sagacity, quiet ruthlessness, covert actions that remain covert, above all infinite patience." He also argues that "the terrorists have already won an important battle if they can provoke the authorities into using overt armed force against them."[93] It is like the guerrilla tactic of building the movement by getting the state to overreact to its military efforts. Journalist Ted Koppel notes: "The goal of any organized terrorist attack is to goad a vastly more powerful enemy into an excessive response." This is what the American war on terrorism has been. Much of what al-Qaeda has achieved "we have done, and continue to do to ourselves."[94]

But, given the contrast between the two models, war and crime, the United States has sought to have it both ways. Feldman notes that one way to contrast war and police work is to note that generally criminals may not be killed by their pursuers but are subject to punishment once captured, while combatants can be killed, but if captured may not be punished. But US policy treats "international terrorists as war adversaries while they are being pursued and as criminals of some sort after they are captured."[95] It mixes the two models, taking from each what is most advantageous to itself. This approach mixes threat liability with fault liability, making the terrorist fighters liable in both senses. It is not clear that this is coherent. This analysis is developed by David Luban, who labels as the "hybrid

---

[93] Michael Howard, "It Was a Terrible Error to Declare War," *The Independent* (November 2, 2001).

[94] Ted Koppel, "Nine Years after 9/11, Let's Stop Fulfilling bin Laden's Goals," *Washington Post* (September 12, 2010), p. B1.

[95] Feldman, "Choices of Law, Choices of War," *25 Harvard Journal of Law & Public Policy* 457 (2002), p. 458.

model" the mixture adopted by the United States: "By selectively combining elements of the war model and elements of the law model, Washington is able to maximize its own ability to mobilize lethal force against terrorists while eliminating traditional rights of a military adversary, as well as the rights of innocent bystanders caught in the crossfire." On this last point, the hybrid model takes advantage of the acceptability of collateral damage among civilians. Luban makes a theoretical objection and a moral objection to the hybrid model. The theoretical objection is "that the law model and the war model each comes as a package, with a kind of intellectual integrity." The hybrid model risks incoherence. The moral objection is the way in which the hybrid model tramples human rights.[96]

But there is another way to approach the struggle against global terrorism, one which avoids the hybrid model without relying exclusively on either the crime model or the war model, that is, without combining the two in the way just described. Given current global conditions, perhaps the best we can do is to divide the struggle into discrete aspects, applying the war model to some and the crime model to others. This contrasts with the hybrid model, which applies both the war and crimes models across the board. Despite her support for the crime model, this is the "twin track" approach recommended by Anne-Marie Slaughter. She advocates using both "the full power of the United States' legal system" by trying individual terrorist operatives in federal courts and utilizing "military force to destroy terrorist bases and to deter the governments that sponsor them."[97] The conditions may not now be adequate to bring the whole of the struggle against global terrorism under the crime model. But, given the arguments for the benefits of the crime model, and the suffering inevitable in war, we may hope that the time will come when conditions will be adequate for this, and perhaps, more generally, for obviating the need for war altogether. This prospect is explored in the next chapter.

---

[96] David Luban, "The War on Terrorism and the End of Human Rights," in Gehring (ed.), *War after September 11*, pp. 51–62, at pp. 53, 56.

[97] Anne-Marie Slaughter, "Beware the Trumpets of War," *Harvard Journal of Law and Public Policy* 25, no. 3 (Summer 2002), pp. 965–976, at p. 976.

8 Justice at the end of war

It is well that war is so terrible, lest we grow too fond of it.

General Robert E. Lee[1]

War does not determine who is right, only who is left.

Bertrand Russell[2]

Perhaps my factories will put an end to war sooner than your congresses.

Alfred Nobel[3]

With malice toward none, with charity for all, with firmness in the right as God gives us to see the right, let us strive on to finish the work we are in … to do all which may achieve and cherish a just and lasting peace among ourselves and with all nations.

Lincoln, Second Inaugural Address[4]

We have spoken little so far of the end of war, but war's end raises issues that are part of the ethics of war. The aspect of just war theory that considers the end of particular wars is *jus post bellum*, justice at the end of war. It is about what justice requires after the shooting has stopped, and it concerns such matters as settlements, peace treaties, reparations, reconstruction, and the like. But the phrase *the end of war* is ambiguous. While it may refer to the end of a particular war, it also may refer to *the general*

[1] Robert E. Lee, Comment at Battle of Fredericksburg on December 13, 1862, http://en.wikiquote.org/wiki/Robert_E._Lee, accessed June 14, 2011.

[2] Widely attributed to Bertrand Russell, e.g., www.famous-proverbs.com/Russell_Quotes.htm, accessed June 15, 2011.

[3] Alfred Nobel, in an 1891 letter to Bertha von Sutter, http://nobelprize.org/alfred_nobel/biographical/articles/tagil/, accessed August 24, 2010.

[4] Abraham Lincoln, *Second Inaugural Address*, www.loc.gov/rr/program/bib/ourdocs/Lincoln2nd.html, accessed June 15, 2011.

end of war, of all war, the end of war as a human practice. In this chapter, we consider justice at the end of war in both of these senses, beginning with the ending of particular wars. But before we can consider *jus post bellum*, there is a prior set of moral issues that need attention concerning when and how a war should be brought to an end. Because these issues arise in the midst of war, they should be considered first. To begin, however, we examine a historical case that raises questions about the end of war in both senses.

8.1 World War I: the war to end war

The twentieth century was the bloodiest in human history, and the bloodshed began in earnest with World War I. On June 28, 1914, an heir to the Austro-Hungarian Empire was assassinated in Sarajevo by an ethnic Serb opposed to Austrian rule in the Balkans. This led Austria to declare war on Serbia, and through the interlocking system of alliances existing among European states at the time, this resulted in the involvement of Russia, Germany, and France. Russia had mobilized its forces in the light of its alliance with Serbia, and Germany followed suite due to its connections with Austria. France mobilized as a result of its alliance with Russia. Given the plans that the great powers had for mobilization, each felt pressure to begin mobilization once its opponents had, lest it be unprepared for war. The shooting began on August 3, when Germany declared war on France and invaded neutral Belgium on its way to France. Britain, in alliance with Belgium, declared war on Germany. Other fronts opened in Eastern Europe and in other areas, and the conflict became true to its designation as a *world war*. The United States entered the conflict on the side of the Allied Powers against Germany in April of 1917, partly due to attacks on US shipping carried out by Germany in an effort to blockade Britain.

Many people in Europe welcomed the war. Europe had been largely at peace since 1870, and the horrors of war were not part of the experience of most of those alive in 1914. The British philosopher Bertrand Russell, who was jailed for his pacifist activities during the war, recalls encountering cheering crowds in London on August 4, the day that Britain declared war on Germany. He notes: "During this and the following days I discovered to my amazement that average men and women were delighted at the prospect of war."[5] Most Europeans thought that the war would be short. "When war broke out in August 1914 it was commonly expected that the combatants would be home by Christmas."[6] But the military technology of the time gave the advantage to the defense, producing a long-drawn-out struggle. The German advance into France was halted, and the conflict on the Western Front settled into stagnant trench warfare. The war would last for four more years, with a total of 9 million combatants killed and many more maimed in body and mind.

By mid 1918, the Allies had retaken much of German-occupied France, and Germany, suffering grievously from a British blockade of its ports, soon requested an armistice, which put an end to the fighting on November 11, 1918. In early 1919, the victorious allies met to formulate a treaty to formally end the war. In early 1918 US President Woodrow Wilson announced his ideas for the design of the post-war peace in a document referred to as the *fourteen points*. The points included a call for open diplomacy (point one), a criticism of European colonialism (point five), and a call for a "general association of nations," what would become the League of Nations (point fourteen). The Germans at the end supported a peace based on the fourteen points, seeing in them "the concept of a 'just' rather than a punitive peace."[7] In the treaty, Germany was labeled the guilty party in the war and was required to pay reparations, mainly for damage done by Germany in Belgium and northern France. Germany is today regarded as the state most responsible for the war, so in retrospect these treaty provisions seem just. But in the aftermath many Germans perceived the treaty as more punitive than just. Criticism of the treaty figured heavily in right-wing German politics in the 1920s and was a factor, though not the principal one, leading to the rise of the Nazis in the 1930s. Historian Margaret Macmillan notes: "In my view Germany could and should have made reparations for its aggression in World War I – but was the risk of renewed war worth forcing it to do so?"[8]

[5] Bertrand Russell, *Portraits from Memory and Other Essays* (New York: Simon and Schuster, 1963), p. 27.

[6] René Albrecht-Carrié, *The Meaning of the First World War* (Englewood Cliffs, NJ: Prentice Hall, 1965), p. 39.

[7] *Ibid*. The Fourteen Points are reproduced on pp. 84–85.

[8] Margaret MacMillan, "Ending the War to End All Wars," *New York Times* (December 25, 2010), www.nytimes.com/2010/12/26/opinion/26macmillan.html?scp=1&sq=marga ret%20MacMillan&st=cse, accessed January 13, 2011.

Wilson referred to the conflict as a war to "make the world safe for democracy," but this result was not achieved; political regimes in Europe after the war turned authoritarian in Italy, Russia, and Germany. He also referred to the war as "a war to end war" and as leading to "the final triumph of justice."[9] The war clearly did not achieve these results either, and they seem to be results that war cannot achieve. A war may serve justice, which is an assumption of *jus ad bellum*, but only in a limited way, and, as we shall see, the idea that war can serve more morally lofty goals increases the danger that it will be fought without the sort of restraint that the *in bello* rules demand.

World War I also had a profound social impact in Europe, and it fostered what is sometimes called the *modernist* view of war, the view that war has no moral meaning, that the deaths in war have no moral meaning, that the dead die in vain.[10] The modernist view may be part of a radical critique of war (and society) that understands armed conflict as being instigated by ruling groups exclusively for their own advantage with little or no benefit for the ordinary citizen, the people who die on the battlefield or suffer on the home front. While such a view made sense in the age of aristocracy, when wars were the result of personal conflicts between individual rulers, it is still alive today in our age of democracy. In the view of some, modern Western societies, despite their democratic patinas, are plutocracies, ruled by economic elites for their own advantage, sometimes sought through war. One recent example of this way of thinking is the claim that the 2003 Iraq War was primarily an effort to benefit corporate oil interests. World War I fostered the modernist view in part because the Wilsonian rhetoric in support of the war greatly overpromised what that war or any war could achieve.

World War I helps to illustrate two of the topics discussed in this chapter. The Versailles Treaty is an important example of the ending of a particular war. In addition, World War I shows how war cannot be expected to bring an end to war in general, despite the rhetoric at the time. War seems simply not to be a way of creating social conditions that reliably end the prospect of future war. War cannot, by itself, produce the conditions for

---

[9] Kathleen Hall Jamieson, *Eloquence in an Electronic Age: The Transformation of Political Speechmaking* (New York: Oxford University Press, 1990), p. 99.

[10] Walzer, *Just and Unjust Wars* (New York: Basic Books, 1977), pp.109–110.

lasting peace, which Augustine saw as its main purpose. If there is to be a general end of war, it must come from another quarter; it cannot come from war itself.

8.2 Keeping war just: *jus extendere bellum*

The moral dimension of mid-war decisions about whether to continue or end a war may be referred to as *jus extendere bellum*, justice in the continuation of war.[11] In the midst of war, leaders must choose to continue a war or to end it, and these decisions have a moral dimension. In deciding whether to continue a war, leaders need to consider whether the war continues to satisfy the conditions morally required for its initiation. The principles of *jus extendere bellum* are an extension of the principles of *jus ad bellum*, especially just cause and rightful intention, applied not to the initiation of war, but to its continuation. The *ad bellum* criteria do not cease to be relevant once a war is under way. Joseph Boyle notes this when he refers to *jus ad bellum* as "the moral permissibility of going to war (or continuing in fighting a war already begun)."[12] Events occurring during a war may change the context of the original decision to go to war in a morally relevant way, requiring that the question of the war's morality be revisited *in media res*.

The basic nature of *jus extendere bellum* is implicit in a passage from Aquinas, who observes that "it is lawful to repel force by force, provided one does not exceed the limits of a blameless defense."[13] If a war, which begins as just, exceeds what defense morally allows, the fighting is no longer blameless; the war has become unjust, a war of aggression. (In that case, the opponent's war, which began as unjust, may become just.) The notion of *jus extendere bellum* is meant as a reminder that the moral status of a war needs to be monitored at the *ad bellum* level throughout its course. (This is in addition to its continuing assessment at the *in bello* level.) If a just

---

[11] *Jus extendere bellum* partly overlaps with what Darrel Mollendorf refers to as *jus ex bello*, in "Jus ex Bello," *Journal of Political Philosophy* 16, no. 2 (2008), pp. 123–136.

[12] Joseph Boyle, "Just War Doctrine and the Military Response to Terrorism," *Journal of Political Philosophy* 11, no. 2 (2003), pp. 153–170, at p. 158.

[13] Aquinas, *Summa Theologica*, in Reichberg *et al.* (eds.), *The Ethics of War: Classic and Contemporary Readings* (Oxford: Blackwell Publishing, 2006), p. 190. Aquinas is speaking of individual self-defense, but the idea is applied here to defensive war.

war becomes unjust, it should be ended or scaled back to the point where it is just. The *ad bellum* criteria may cease to be satisfied due either: (1) to the belligerent's ignoring the limitations to which it is committed by the fighting of a just war; or (2) to unanticipated changing circumstances.

Regarding (1), rightful intention may cease to be satisfied when leaders change their minds and adopt different intentions from those they held at the beginning of the war. Grotius notes that "a war may be just in its origins, and yet the intentions of its authors may become unjust in the course of its prosecution."[14] This may happen in a deliberate way, as when a state fighting an initially just war chooses to use the opportunity to seek some unjustified gain from its opponent, a rightful intention being replaced by a wrongful intention. The just war of defense then becomes an unjust war of aggression. Clausewitz suggests that this is typical: "When one has used defensive measures successfully, a morally favourable balance of strength is usually created; thus, the natural course in war is to begin defensively and end by attacking."[15] Typical or not, it is not morally acceptable. Note, however, that the switch to an unjust intention may not result from a single deliberate choice, but may come to be through a series of strategic augmentations, what is sometimes called "mission creep," that may amount over time to a switch to a wrongful intention. The Korean War is an example where a change in intention arguably turned a just war into an unjust war. In that war, the United States came to the assistance of South Korea, which had been invaded by North Korea. The forces of the United States (and other members of the UN) pushed the North Korean forces back to the border between the two Koreas, but then kept going until they occupied virtually the whole of the North. What began as a war of defense had become a war of aggression.[16]

When the rightful intention behind a war changes to a wrongful intention, just cause ceases to be satisfied as well. The war acquires a new cause, an unjust one. But there are ways other than a belligerent's choice by which a war can acquire an unjust cause. For example, this may occur in the case of a reasonable mistake (reasonable, otherwise the war would not

---

[14] Hugo Grotius, *The Rights of War and Peace*, trans. A. C. Campbell (Washington, DC: M. Walter Dunne, 1901), p. 273.

[15] Carl von Clausewitz, *On War*, quoted in David Rodin, *War and Self-Defense* (Oxford University Press, 2002), p. 120.

[16] On the Korean War, see Walzer, *Just and Unjust Wars*, pp. 117–121.

have been just). If S reasonably believes that the missiles striking its territory were fired by T, then it may have a just cause to go to war against T. Imagine, however, that the missiles were in fact fired by R. If S discovers this in the midst of its war against T, S no longer has a just cause for that war, and the war must cease. In a very different sort of case, a war begun without a just cause may acquire an unanticipated just cause.[17] Some think that the 2003 Iraq War is an example of this. On this understanding, the war was unjust at its beginning, but part way through it became clear (a reasonable expectation) that ending the war immediately would result in an all-out sectarian civil war within Iraq, causing much more harm than continuing the war would. If this is a correct understanding, then the unjust war acquired a just cause, avoiding a sectarian bloodbath (interestingly, a humanitarian justification), which it lacked at the beginning. This may be so even though it was the unjust war itself that created the conditions making its continuation just.

Regarding (2), changing circumstances in the midst of war, especially when they change in a way that would not have been reasonably expected at the beginning of the war, may lead to other *ad bellum* criteria no longer being satisfied. Consider proportionality. War is not a static thing in terms of its reasonably expected costs. William O'Brien observes, "either the situation or the belligerent's perception of it may change." The effort needed to win the war may grow beyond what was reasonably expected at the beginning, causing proportionality no longer to be satisfied. World War I may be an example of this. As a result, calculations of proportionality must be made "periodically throughout a war to reevaluate the balance of good and evil that is actually produced by the war."[18] Something like this applies for some of the other *ad bellum* criteria as well. This is obvious in the case of reasonable chance of success. If the war, contrary to reasonable expectations at its beginning, comes to seem a hopeless cause, it should be ended. This could even apply in the case of last resort. If there is a peaceful resort that was overlooked at the beginning of the war, or one the war itself has created, then it should be pursued while the fighting is held in abeyance.

---

[17] This is emphasized by Mollendorf in "*Jus ex Bello.*"

[18] William O'Brien, *The Conduct of Just and Limited War* (New York: Praeger, 1981), pp. 36, 28.

But there are great moral complications in *jus extendere bellum*. For example, ending or scaling back a war that, for whatever reason, no longer satisfies *ad bellum* criteria may entail additional harm, and this may affect the decisions one should make about discontinuation, how and when the discontinuation should occur. A sudden ending could bring about more harm than a phased ending or a temporary continuation. The Iraq War, on the understanding discussed just above, may be an example of this. Relevant here is what C. A. J. Coady calls "extrication morality," which is a recognition that other moral factors may play a role in when and how a person should extricate himself from an immoral situation in which he is complicit.[19] In general, there are two opposing moral tendencies at work in discontinuation decisions. One is the idea that it is morally important to continue a war in order to honor the combatants who have already died in the war, that they "not have died in vain." It is hard to know how much moral weight this idea should have, or if it should have any at all, but it is a sentiment often strongly felt in a state at war. It is, in part, a focus on the moral importance of adhering to commitments. The opposing tendency, in favor of discontinuation, is represented by the moral equivalent of sayings such as "don't throw good money after bad" or "if you find yourself in a hole, stop digging." This approach recommends cutting moral losses, so to speak, focusing on avoiding future harm rather than honoring past commitments.

Not all agree that a just war can become unjust in a way that requires that it be ended or scaled back. According to Yoram Dinstein, "There is no support in the practice of states for the notion that [*ad bellum*] proportionality remains relevant – and has to be constantly assessed – throughout the hostilities in the course of war. Once war is raging, the exercise of self-defence may bring about [the total defeat of the enemy] regardless of the condition of proportionality."[20] International law seems largely to view the issue in the same way.[21] Even Grotius, quoted for support earlier in this section, asserts that when intentions become unjust in the midst of

[19] C. A. J. Coady, "Escaping from the Bomb: Immoral Deterrence and the Problem of Extrication," in Henry Shue (ed.), *Nuclear Deterrence and Moral Restraint* (Cambridge University Press, 1989), pp. 163–226.

[20] Yoram Dinstein, *War – Aggression and Self-Defense*, 4th edn. (Cambridge University Press, 2005), pp. 237–238.

[21] Rodin, *War and Self-Defense*, pp. 111–112.

war, the new intentions, though "blamable ... do not render the war *itself* unjust, nor invalidate its conquests."[22] Despite these views to the contrary, however, it seems crucial to the ethics of war to ensure that a war be morally required not only to begin as just, but to continue as just.

The next question is one broached in Chapter 3: assuming that a war begins with just cause, how far can it go before it exceeds the amount of force that the just cause permits? When does the fighting "exceed the limits of a blameless defense"? When would the cause for which the war is being fought change from just to unjust? Consider again the Korean War. Given the North Korean aggression, it seems clear that the US forces were permitted to do more than merely push the North Korean forces back to their border with the South, but that they exceeded the limits of a blameless defense when they pushed the North back to its border with China. One possible answer to our question is that a state with a just cause is entitled to fight up to the point at which it has restored the status quo ante, the situation before the opponent's aggression. But in the Korean War, the status quo ante would be the North Korean forces pushed back within their own borders, and doing more than this seems to be permitted.

What beyond restoring the status quo ante would be permissible? For example, is a state fighting a just war permitted to *punish* its opponent? Does punishment provide a just cause, and so support a rightful intention? Under the old just war paradigm, punishment was a just cause, and a rightful intention could be punitive. For example, Vitoria asserts that "even after the victory has been won ... it is lawful to avenge the injury done by the enemy, and to teach the enemy a lesson by punishing them for the damage they have done."[23] But this idea was discredited under the national defense paradigm. One reason, suggested by Larry May, is that military force is not an effective mechanism to achieve punishment, as it paints with "too broad a brush," and "it is too likely that those who deserve to be punished will not be, and those who do not deserve to be punished will be."[24] This criticism is consistent with the human rights paradigm,

---

[22] Grotius, *Rights of War and Peace*, p. 273.

[23] Francisco Vitoria, "On the Law of War," in Anthony Pagden and Jeremy Lawrance (eds.), *Vitoria: Political Writings* (Cambridge University Press, 1991), pp. 293–327, at p. 305, emphasis omitted.

[24] Larry May, *Aggression and Crimes against Peace* (Cambridge University Press, 2008), pp. 106–107.

and it assumes, as the just war paradigm does not, that the proper object of the punishment is individuals, not states. This point is endorsed by Douglas Lackey, who argues that the measures imposed on the losers in a war "must not violate the rights of the citizens of the losing nation or the rights of third parties."[25] A more basic reason why punitive intentions are wrongful, Joseph Boyle argues, is that "leaders lack the authority to punish outsiders" because leaders' authority to punish extends only to their own citizens. Leaders have authority to attack others only to defend their own citizens, which they exercise in a defensive war."[26] Richard Norman observes that the authority to punish would belong only to "an independent judicial authority at the international level."[27]

But what the national defense paradigm rejects is *retributive* punishment, harm done out of a punitive intention to "pay back" a state for wrongful action. But instead of retribution, punishment can seek deterrence. *Deterrent* punishment is imposed for the sake of influencing future state behavior, and it need not involve a punitive intention. Boyle observes that "punishment can be a means to defense, insofar as it deters some from actions for which punishments are prescribed." When understood as deterrence rather than retribution, punishment is a form of long-term, preventive defense, in contrast with the short-term defense of repelling the immediate attack. Thus, aggressor states can be punished if the goal is deterrence, and that can be a justification for the use of force beyond the restoration of the status quo ante. But note that the impermissibility of preventive war implies that deterrent punishment by itself is not a justification for war, though it may be an acceptable justification *in conjunction with* immediate self-defense.[28]

Walzer adopts something like this view. He argues that the relevant status quo ante is not the situation that existed immediately before the

[25] Douglas Lackey, *The Ethics of War and Peace* (Englewood Cliffs, NJ: Prentice-Hall, 1989), p. 44.

[26] Boyle, "Just War Doctrine," pp. 161–162. We should add, leaders are also entitled under the human rights paradigm to defend citizens in other states. Vitoria disagrees with Boyle, claiming that leaders have the authority to punish others under both the law of nations and natural law. "On the Law of War," p. 305.

[27] Richard Norman, *Ethics, Killing, and War* (Cambridge University Press, 1995), p. 190.

[28] Thomas Hurka, "Proportionality in the Morality of War," *Philosophy & Public Affairs* 33, no. 1 (2005), pp. 34–66, at p. 41. This is how it is with punishment in domestic society.

aggression, but the one that existed before the threat from the aggressor began to build. This means that the defender is entitled not only to push the aggressor back to its own borders, but to further degrade its military capability. He claims that "war aims legitimately reach to the destruction or to the defeat, demobilization, and (partial) disarming of the aggressor's armed forces," an idea he refers to as "restoration plus" and as "resistance, restoration, reasonable prevention."[29] Referring to the distinction between retributive and deterrent punishment, Walzer asserts that while the permissible goals of defense fall "short of the 'punishment of aggression,' it has to be said that military defeat is always punishing and that the preventive measures … are also penalties."[30] He cites the Gulf War, where a ceasefire was called by the United States, even though some urged that the war continue with a march to Baghdad and the overthrow of the Iraqi government. Walzer argues that such an overthrow would not have been a permissible goal of the war, that it would have gone beyond what the just cause allowed.[31]

So a state fighting a just war is permitted not only to reverse the opponent's aggression, but also to inflict additional military damage to serve as a deterrent (but not retributive) punishment. But this is as far as the defender is allowed to go; this is all the just cause allows. "To press the war further than that is to recommit the crime of aggression." More generally, under the idea of *jus extendere bellum* a defender must monitor its war for continuing adherence to the *ad bellum* criteria lest the war turn from just to unjust. If the war becomes unjust, it must be returned to a state of justice or ended. On the other hand, "wars can end too soon."[32] If the just cause of a just war is sufficient to justify the use of force, the war should, granting that the other *ad bellum* criteria remain satisfied, be pressed until the rightful intention has been achieved.

8.3 Justice at the end of a war: *jus post bellum*

Jus post bellum applies after the guns have fallen silent, and though this is the end of the war in the usual way of speaking, there is a broader sense

---

[29] Walzer, *Just and Unjust Wars*, 2nd edn. (New York: Basic Books, 1992), pp. xvii, xx, 121.
[30] *Ibid.*, pp. 116, 121.   [31] *Ibid.*, pp. xvii, 110–117.   [32] *Ibid.*, pp. 268, 123.

in which the war continues. The immediate aftermath of a shooting war is a time in which the victorious party can fully achieve its war aims by being in a position to determine the peace settlement. *Jus post bellum* concerns the justice of the actions of the victorious party in that immediate aftermath. Assume that the victorious state's war is *ad bellum* just, both initially and through its course. Then the state may act, consistent with *jus post bellum*, to fully achieve its rightful intention, but no more. The general point is that some of what the state is entitled to achieve by the just war (its just aims for the war) may be achieved not in the fighting itself, but in the terms or arrangements made after the shooting stops. If a war is *post bellum* just, those terms will be a fulfillment of the rightful intention with which the war began. Pressing a just war to victory means, in part, a state's fighting the war to the point where it is in a position to guarantee that the post-war arrangements achieve the war's rightful intentions, though not more than this. The arrangements are constituted by such policies and devices as the terms of the peace treaty, the occupation of the defeated state, and perhaps the political reconstruction of the regime of the defeated state.

Though the just war tradition has recently begun taking *jus post bellum* seriously, there is considerable work on this topic (though not under that name) by classic just war theorists, such as Suarez, Grotius, Vattel, and Kant.[33] The idea was largely ignored in the nineteenth and the twentieth centuries, but is now getting renewed attention.[34] An increasing portion of IHL is relevant to *jus post bellum*. Of the post-war instruments prescribed in IHL, one is the *truce* or *ceasefire*, which stops the shooting but gives no guarantees that it will not resume. Fighting is suspended but not terminated. Another instrument is the *armistice*, which was used to end the fighting in World War I. Then there is the *peace treaty*, which makes a formal end of the conflict by the establishment of terms that both sides accept.[35]

---

[33] Brian Orend, *War and International Justice* (Waterloo, Canada: Wilfred Laurier Press, 2000), and Carsten Stahn, "*Jus ad bellum, jus in bello … jus post bellum*? Rethinking the Conception of the Law of Armed Force," *European Journal of International Law* 17 (2006), pp. 921–943, at pp. 933–935.

[34] Carsten Stahn, "*Jus Post Bellum*: Mapping the Discipline(s)," *American University International Law Review* 23 (2008), pp. 311–347, at p. 314.

[35] Dinstein, *War*, pp. 34–59.

In the discussion of peace in Chapter 1, we drew a distinction between a positive social order, in which basic rights were generally respected, and a negative social order, in which they were not. Recall Cicero: "Wars, then, ought to be undertaken for this purpose, that we may live in peace, without injustice."[36] This theme was later picked up by Augustine in his proclamation that *the aim of a just war is a just peace*. Joseph Boyle observes that armed conflict "can be justified only on the narrow grounds that war justly serves peace."[37] Michael Walzer notes: "Implicit in the theory of just war is a theory of just peace."[38] The peace of a positive social order is often referred to as a *positive peace* or a *just peace*, and that of a negative social order as a *negative peace* or an *unjust peace*. A positive peace is the appropriate aim at the *post bellum* stage, as it is at the *ad bellum* stage. British legal theorist Carsten Stahn sees growing interest in *jus post bellum* as a turn away from understanding peace simply as negative, as merely the termination of conflict, to understanding it as positive, as the result of *peacemaking*.[39] *Jus post bellum* represents the moral responsibilities of belligerents to use their victory to build a positive peace. Yoram Dinstein observes that "a treaty of peace is not just a negative instrument (in the sense of the negation of war); it is also a positive document (regulating the normalization of friendly relations between the former belligerents)."[40] Friendly relations among states are, of course, a main element of a just peace.

Over the past several decades there has been a change in understanding of what a peace treaty should be. Stahn notes that there was "a time when peace settlements were conceived as mutual bargaining processes among states over post-war rights and obligations." Increasingly, however, "peacemaking has moved beyond the borders of inter-state bargaining within the confines of self-interested or bilateral dispute settlement [to] become part of a normative framework."[41] If peace making is strictly bilateral, a transaction between victor and vanquished, the best we can hope for in

---

[36] Cicero, *On Duties*, in Reichberg *et al.* (eds.), *Ethics of War*, p. 52.
[37] Boyle, "Just War Doctrine," p. 164.
[38] Michael Walzer, "Terrorism and Just War," *Philosophia* 34 (2006), pp. 3–12, at p. 4.
[39] Carsten Stahn, "*Jus ad Bellum – Jus in Bello – Jus post Bellum*: Toward a Tripartite Conception of Armed Conflict," European Society for International Law, available at www.esil-sedi.eu/fichiers/en/Stahn__838.pdf, accessed August 26, 2010, pp. 1–2.
[40] Dinstein, *War*, p. 38.
[41] Stahn, "*Jus ad Bellum – Jus in Bello – Jus post Bellum*," pp. 3, 5–6.

terms of achieving a positive peace is that the victors have the attitude recommended by Lincoln: "with malice toward none, with charity for all." Because this attitude is rare, a more common result was not a just peace, but "victor's justice." Instead of counting on the goodwill of the victors, peacemaking is now seen as falling under universal standards binding on the parties. Stahn observes: "The regulation of substantive components of peace-making is not merely determined by the discretion and contractual liberty of the warring factions, but is governed by certain norms and standards of international law."[42] Peacemaking should be seen "not only as a political process, but also a legal phenomenon." What was a practice of mutual bargaining has now become regularized under a set of rules, the moral dimension of which is *jus post bellum*.

Jus post bellum, like *jus extendere bellum*, is an extension of *jus ad bellum*. Several authors seem, at least in part, to agree. Canadian philosopher Brian Orend remarks that the aims that should characterize a state adhering to *jus post bellum* are those set by the just cause criterion of *jus ad bellum*.[43] Stahn notes: "The case for a *jus post bellum* is to some extent inherent in the conception of *jus ad bellum*."[44] According to Gary Bass: "*jus post bellum* is connected with *jus ad bellum*."[45] *Jus post bellum* does have some moral content of its own, different from that of *jus ad bellum*, but that content is animated by the basic moral principles the two share. The difference in the moral content of *jus post bellum* (apart from a few exceptions discussed below) results from the need to apply the principles it shares with *jus ad bellum* to the circumstances of war's immediate aftermath. To take an example, the least harm principle applies at both levels. In *jus ad bellum*, this principle grounds the last resort criterion, while in *jus post bellum*, it grounds, for instance, the convention that reparations are to be minimized. Last resort is not a concern of *jus post bellum*, and reparations is not a concern of *jus ad bellum*, but conventions regulating each of these matters flow from the same moral principle.

---

[42] Stahn, "*Jus ad bellum, jus in bello… jus post bellum?*" p. 937.

[43] Brian Orend, "Jus Post Bellum," *Journal of Social Philosophy* 31, no. 1 (Spring 2000), pp. 117–137, at p. 123.

[44] Stahn, "*Jus Post Bellum*," p. 328.

[45] Gary Bass, "*Jus Post Bellum*," *Philosophy & Public Affairs* 32, no. 4 (2004), pp. 384–412, at p. 386.

The shooting and its immediate aftermath are stages of the process of a war. They are distinguished by whether the guns are firing, but the morally relevant features of war are common to both stages across the boundary between them. Both involve a use of force, applied force when the guns are firing and threatened force in the aftermath. A belligerent can achieve some of its war aims directly through the fighting and others indirectly by bringing about a cessation of the shooting that puts it in a position to exact them from the opponent, for example, through a peace treaty. The latter aims are still achieved through force because the victor, through its militarily superior position, may dictate terms by threatening to resume the war. In its most general form, the basic moral issue lying behind just war theory is: what is a state permitted to do through the use of military force to those outside its borders (or those inside, in case of civil war)? What may military force be used to achieve? This question remains after the shooting stops, which is why *jus post bellum* is an extension of *jus ad bellum*. After the shooting ceases, the victor uses its military position to exact concessions from the other side. The victor can achieve its war aims both through the actual fighting and through its threats to resume fighting after the fighting has stopped. The *ad bellum* question continues to apply in the immediate aftermath of the war: does the state use (or threaten to use) force with a just cause?

Consider how this might work in the case of victory in a just war. The just aims of war, as discussed earlier, include reversing the aggressor's gains plus applying some deterrent punishment, for example Walzer's "resistance, restoration, reasonable prevention." During the shooting phase of the war, the state fighting a defensive war succeeds in driving the aggressor back across its border, reversing its gains and partially destroying its military capability; this achieves the aims of resistance and restoration, and part of the aims of reasonable prevention. Imagine then that the aggressor, realizing it has lost, offers to accept a ceasefire. The defender has a choice whether to accept the offer. If it believes that it could achieve the remainder of its just aims in the *post bellum* stage, it has an obligation to accept the offer. If, on the other hand, it believes that it would not have a strong enough hand to achieve these aims should the fighting end now, it is permitted to refuse the offer. If the offer is accepted, the belligerents enter the stage of *jus post bellum*, when the victorious state is entitled to use the threat to resume fighting to achieve the balance of its just aims. In this case, imagine that the opponent's demobilization and partial disarmament would fulfill the remainder of the victor's just aims, completing the goal of reasonable prevention. The victor may then apply coercive policies necessary to achieve these, which might include military occupation of the defeated aggressor, refusing to return sovereignty to the defeated state until it meets the victor's just demands. Occupation would be *post bellum* just should it be necessary to get the aggressor to demobilize and partially disarm. The balance of the victor's aims may be achieved in a peace treaty, but the victor, to remain just, cannot demand treaty provisions beyond the just aims which permitted it to go to war in the first place. What may not be achieved through use of force, may not be achieved through threat of force. This shows the way in which *jus post bellum* is a continuation of *jus ad bellum*.

Someone might object that because states use the threat of force against other states all the time, not only in the immediate aftermath of war, the claim that threats of force characterize *jus post bellum* would erase the distinction between war and peace. Military threats for the sake of deterrence are a feature of the relations of adversaries in war and peace. But, while there is a continuous background threat of force between adversaries for the sake of *deterrence*, in the immediate aftermath of a war, the victorious side exercises the threat of force for the sake of *compellence* in achieving its aims. Compellence is the threat of force to exact positive concessions from an opponent, that is, to get the opponent to give up something it values; in contrast, deterrence is a state's threat of force to get an opponent to refrain from positive action against the interests of the state.[46] Deterrence seeks only something negative from the opponent, to stop it from aggression, while compellence seeks something positive, its surrender of something it values. Compellence says, "I will use force if you don't give me what I want," while deterrence says, "I will use force if you seek to take something from me by force." If a state seeks to use compellence against an opponent in peacetime, this would be an act of war, even if the threat of force has yet to be carried out.

One practical reason to recognize that *jus post bellum* is an extension of *jus ad bellum* (and *jus extendere bellum*) is that it is often difficult to distinguish between a shooting war and its aftermath. The move from one to

---

[46] Successful compellence can serve as a deterrent against future attacks.

the other may be a transitional process rather than something occurring all at once. The shooting may die down gradually. The boundary may be blurred.[47] This is especially the case in our era in which civil wars predominate because insurgencies, though under the control of a hierarchy, often do not have the tight unity of command that makes it possible for its leadership to enforce a ceasefire. The continuity between *jus ad bellum* and *jus post bellum* allows the same moral principles to be applied whatever the state of the war. But my argument for the continuity does not depend on this empirical point, but rather on the moral point that the just aims of a war, as defined by *jus ad bellum*, govern what is permissible over the course of the war, including its immediate aftermath when military force for compellence is still in play.

Much of the recent discussion of *jus post bellum* has focused on the topic of regime change and political reconstruction ("nation building"). Under the national defense paradigm, these ideas played little role. This is due to the fundamental role of national sovereignty under that paradigm. When Walzer speaks of legitimate just war aims as "resistance, restoration, reasonable prevention," he does not think of these as including regime change. He remarks that the "theory of ends in war is shaped by the same rights that justify the fighting in the first place" (which suggests that *jus post bellum* is an extension of *jus ad bellum*), but he goes on to say that "the most important of these rights" is "the right of nations, even enemy nations, to continued national existence."[48] This view is reflected in his opposition to demands for unconditional surrender, an opposition that has its source in the importance he places on the notion of political community.[49] To demand unconditional surrender is tantamount to a demand that the political community cease to be. The vanquished cannot, Walzer claims, be put under "political tutelage."

This perspective changes when the human rights paradigm replaces the national defense paradigm. The moral value of state sovereignty is derivative from that of individual human rights, and regime change is no longer seen as inherently morally problematic. Recognition of this has come with the recent attention to humanitarian intervention. In Chapter 4, we saw

---

[47] Stahn, "*Jus Post Bellum*," p. 322.   [48] Walzer, *Just and Unjust Wars*, p. 123.

[49] *Ibid.*, pp. 111–117. Unconditional surrender is a permissible demand, however, in the defeat of Nazi Germany, which rejected fundamental human values.

that humanitarian interventions may require not simply mere rescue, but rescue through regime change and political reconstruction. Walzer recognizes the need for regime change in the case of humanitarian intervention: "It isn't only aggressiveness then, but also murderousness that makes a political regime a legitimate candidate for forcible transformation." It may even be permissible to impose democracy on a state, though a lack of democracy can never by itself be a just cause for war.[50] Political transformation is a just aim only in conjunction with the need to remove a regime as a necessary step to avoid a threat of massive human rights violations. If there is a humanitarian intervention in response to such a threat, the intervener may need to destroy the offending regime to remove the threat. If the regime must be destroyed, there may be a further obligation to help build another, to construct a new regime as part of a nation-building project. This is an implication of the so-called Pottery Barn rule: "If you break it, it's yours." If you break a regime you have an obligation to bear the cost of building another. Rescuing the victims of severe human rights violations may require not simply removing the murderous regime, but replacing it with another.

An important aspect of *jus post bellum* is the conduct of war-crimes trials. The charges in such trials may include violations of international law that reflect *ad bellum* rules, for example, charges related to engaging in aggressive war. But crimes prosecuted should also include violations of *in bello* rules. Those charged with *in bello* violations should include all those responsible whether victors or vanquished; otherwise the trials would be a one-sided exercise in "victor's justice."[51] Because the trials would prosecute *in bello* offenses, *jus post bellum* is not exclusively an extension of *jus ad bellum*; it is also, in part, an extension of *jus in bello*. As Carsten Stahn observes: "Some of the very concepts of *jus post bellum* are designed to remedy previous violations of *jus ad bellum* or *jus in bello* – state responsibility, individual criminal responsibility, compensation, etc."[52] Another feature of *jus post bellum* that represents an extension of *jus in bello* is the repatriation of prisoners of war. The rules of the war convention include provisions for the post-war repatriation of prisoners.

---

[50] Michael Walzer, "Regime Change and Just War," *Dissent* (Summer 2006), pp. 103–111, at p. 104.
[51] Orend, "*Jus Post Bellum*," p. 127.   [52] Stahn, "*Jus Post Bellum*," p. 344.

The difficult issue of justice in compensation or reparations by the vanquished involves some considerations that are *ad bellum* (was the vanquished fighting an unjust war?) and some that are *in bello* (what individuals should be made to bear the burden of the reparation payments?). Brian Orend suggests that compensation be taken from the fortunes frequently held by the military and political elites of the vanquished aggressor, or, failing that, from a modest tax imposed on the aggressor's population.[53] Stahn observes: "Contemporary developments in international law point to the emergence of a rule that prohibits the indiscriminate punishment of a people through excessive reparation claims or sanctions."[54] The concern, of course, is to avoid collective punishment, a concern that reflects the foundation of just war theory in the human rights paradigm rather than the national defense paradigm. We would like the jingoes to pay, but there is no effective way to separate them from the general population. In regard to our example of the First World War, there is debate among historians about the justness of the post-war reparations demanded of Germany, and the further, more prudential issue of whether the reparations, even if just and justly apportioned, were a wise move, given their effect on German politics.

There is another aspect of *jus post bellum* that illustrates the shift to the *ad bellum* human rights paradigm. New Zealand philosopher Jeremy Waldron argues that "in a world where many nation-states have their origins in conquest, occupation, the aftermath of war, or the resolution of colonial possession[,] *jus post bellum* should be understood at least as much in the light of our general theory of good governance as in the light of laws relating specifically to warfare." He speaks of the continuity between *jus post bellum* and political theory more generally and observes that "it would be wrong to think that there is no criterion of minimally good government apart from self-determination."[55] In a similar vein, Walzer observes: "Democratic political theory, which plays a relatively small part in our arguments about *jus ad bellum* and *in bello*, provides the central principles" of an account of *jus post bellum*.[56] The shift from the national

---

[53] Orend, "*Jus Post Bellum*," p. 125.

[54] Stahn, "*Jus ad bellum, jus in bello… jus post bellum*?" p. 939.

[55] Jeremy Waldron, "*Post Bellum* Aspects of the Laws of Armed Conflict," *Loyola of Los Angeles International and Comparative Law Review* 31 (2009), pp. 31–55, at pp. 55, 35.

[56] Michael Walzer, "Just and Unjust Occupations," *Dissent* (Winter 2004), pp. 61–66, at p. 61.

defense paradigm to the human rights paradigm provides for just war theory in general this link to political theory, to the principles of good governance. The human rights paradigm shows why the reestablishment of the vanquished state's self-determination is no longer all there is to the victor's *post bellum* obligations. For example, *jus post bellum* may require occupation, and an occupier must attend to principles of good governance in running the occupation. More importantly, when political reconstruction is required, the principles of good governance must be the basis for the reconstruction. This *post bellum* need to appeal to political theory does not take us beyond just war theory, for the human rights paradigm has already moved just war theory closer to the broader terrain of political theory. The exclusive focus on self-determination of the vanquished state is largely the product of looking at just war theory in terms of the national defense paradigm.

8.4 The general end of war

Is the general end of war possible? Can war be abolished, or is the hope for abolition a fantasy? Anti-war pacifists believe that war can be abolished, and realists generally believe that it cannot. *Should* war be abolished? Pacifists, of course, argue that it should. Realists would tend to view the question as pointless, given that abolition is impossible. Moreover, they would see serious risks in attempts to abolish war. An example of this that realists cite is the efforts in the 1920s to abolish war through treaty, such as the 1928 Kellogg–Briand Pact, a treaty abolishing the international use of force.[57] Realists claim that the treaty and other such efforts led to reluctance to confront Nazi Germany in the 1930s, making World War II more deadly than it might otherwise have been. Just war theorists, here as elsewhere, are in the middle. They are not sure whether war can be abolished, though they would like to see it abolished. Also, unlike the pacifists, they believe that war can serve justice. Thus, just war theorists side with pacifists in calling for efforts to end war, but their call for abolition is tempered by their belief that there are sometimes causes that justify war, injustices that can be corrected only through war. Just war theorists

[57] For the text of the treaty, see www.yale.edu/lawweb/avalon/imt/kbpact.htm, accessed January 16, 2011.

believe that the abolition of war may not be possible, and they appreciate that, even if possible, abolition would be a difficult and long-term project, and not without risks.

These contrasts among the three positions are related to their attitudes toward *jus in bello*. The guarded attitude of just war theorists on the prospects for abolition reinforces their commitment to *jus in bello*. If there really were a war able to end war, there would be little reason to adhere to *in bello* rules in that war, if adherence would at all interfere with victory.[58] Because there is no assurance that war can end, or that a war could end it, adherence to *jus in bello* remains a priority. In contrast, both pacifists and realists have problems with *jus in bello*. Pacifists tend to see *jus in bello* as in tension with the project of abolishing war. The task of *in bello* restraints is to *humanize* war, but however humanized war becomes, it would remain a grossly inhumane practice. Pacifists argue that focusing on humanizing war is a distraction from the moral urgency of ending it. These pacifist critics claim that just war theory is "a program for tolerating war, when what is needed is a program for its abolition."[59] It is not the inhumanity in war that is the enemy, but war itself. The prescription should be: don't mend it; end it.

From a moral point of view, attempts to humanize war are like attempts to humanize slavery by bettering the living conditions of slaves. Slavery should not be humanized, but ended. The slaves, however, may have a different view. Even if abolition is achievable, it would take time, and while that time passes, there is value in making the practice more humane. The worry is that the more the practice is humanized, the less will be the impetus to end it. A humanized condition of slavery would be more tolerable not only for the slaves, but also, in another sense, for the non-slaves, making them more likely to tolerate the continuation of the practice. Even if the humanization of war was at cross purposes with ending it, however, could we morally abide permitting those currently suffering from the practice, assuming this is necessary for the expected liberation decades hence, to be forced to suffer more? Similarly, if the abolition of war would take several generations, should we not do what we can for those who are currently caught up in wars? One should always be morally suspicious of

[58] Walzer, *Just and Unjust Wars*, p. 47.
[59] *Ibid.*, p. 45. Walzer does not endorse this view.

claims that we should allow greater suffering in the present to ensure that all suffering will end in the future. Those recommending this are seldom the ones doing the suffering.

Consider the realists' dislike of *jus in bello*. Realists often see adherence to *in bello* rules as interfering with efforts to win a war by imposing artificial constraints on the application of military force. They agree with the pacifists that focusing on humanizing war is a distraction from the moral urgency of ending it, but what they are concerned about ending are particular wars, not war in general. Realists (especially the moralized realists) sometimes make this argument by appealing to humane values. Attempts at *in bello* restraint only make war overall more destructive. Abiding by moral restraints within war makes it last longer and so makes it more destructive overall. Sherman seems to have held something like this view. Recall his claim that for the Union to win, it was necessary to make Confederate civilians feel "the hard hand of war." As military strategist Ralph Peters argues: "The paradox is that our humane approach to war results in unnecessary bloodshed." Speaking of the recent American wars in Afghanistan and Iraq, he asserts: "Had we been ruthless in the use of our overwhelming power in the early days of conflict … the ultimate human toll – on all sides – would have been far lower."[60]

An extension of this argument is that attention to *in bello* restraints makes wars not only more destructive, but also more frequent. When war is fought ruthlessly, its destructiveness is more apparent (as in "shock and awe"), and so states are more readily deterred from future wars. This may be so, even though ruthless wars may be overall less destructive. This seems paradoxical, but perhaps is not, because what determines the deterrent effect is the *perception* of destructiveness rather than the actual destructiveness. (Think of the proverbial frog who remains in the pot of water as it slowly boils, in contrast with the frog thrown into boiling water who promptly jumps out.) Perhaps a short intensely destructive war is a better deterrent of future wars than a long less intensely (but overall more) destructive war. A reason for this could be that belligerents usually go into war thinking that they will win a quick victory, thereby avoiding the

---

[60] Ralph Peters, "Wishful Thinking and Indecisive Wars," *Journal of International Security Affairs* 16 (Spring 2009), www.securityaffairs.org/issues/2009/16/peters.php, accessed September 20, 2010.

destructive effects of a long war. We saw this in the case of World War I, where both sides expected a quick victory. The idea that war becomes less frequent if its destructiveness is strongly imprinted in the minds of leaders is evident in the quotation from General Lee at the beginning of the chapter. But this argument is weak. Recall that one of the purposes of war is to achieve a just and lasting peace. If a war is made more destructive through ignoring *in bello* rules, it is less likely to achieve this purpose due to the resentments and grievances left in the war's wake, and this would tend to increase the likelihood of future wars of vengeance between those belligerents.

The argument that war will become less frequent (perhaps even disappear) if made more destructive is sometimes presented in terms of the expected impact of increasingly destructive military technology. This was the thinking of Alfred Nobel, the inventor of dynamite and the founder of the Nobel Peace Prize. Robert Holmes observes that Nobel "believed the key to peace lay with the development of war technology and that once the nations of the world acquired the capacity to annihilate one another – and he expressly included civilian populations here – war would disappear from the face of the earth." This is the "technologist's dream."[61] The quotation from Nobel at the head of the chapter, taken from a letter to an organizer of peace conferences, indicates his belief that weapons technology could be more effective at ending war than efforts to organize for peace.

This idea that war could be made less frequent or even abolished through technology reached its apogee in a way beyond Nobel's dreams with the invention of nuclear weapons in 1945. As discussed in Chapter 6, these weapons provide states with the capacity to destroy utterly an opponent's society, to bomb it "back to the stone-age," while also allowing the opponent, with a dead hand, to return the favor. This is the unprecedented two-way capacity referred to as *mutual assured destruction*. Some argue that such a capacity kept the United States and the Soviet Union from war during the long decades of the Cold War. But, while the terribleness of war, whether through weapons technology or through the disregard of *in bello* rules, may make war less frequent, it cannot abolish war, and for a simple reason. The psychological mechanism by which the terribleness of war is supposed to reduce the risk of its occurrence depends on the psychological

---

[61] Robert Holmes, *On War and Morality* (Princeton University Press, 1989), p. 4.

impact of the prospect of the terrible destruction on decision makers and the general public. But this impact necessarily fades with time. As mentioned earlier, the outbreak of World War I was facilitated by the fact that in 1914 general war had been absent from Europe for over forty years. The atomic bombings of Hiroshima and Nagasaki were a collective demonstration of the utter terribleness potential in nuclear war, but most people alive today have no memory of those 1945 events.

While just war theorists see the need for war as an instrument to rectify injustice, pacifists point out that it is not a very effective instrument for that purpose. The ineffectiveness of war as an instrument for justice at the *ad bellum* level is indicated in the quotation from Bertrand Russell at the chapter head. Half of wars are lost, and there is no guarantee that the just side in an armed conflict will prevail. Right does not make might. War causes tremendous suffering and does not ensure the result that alone can justify it. When the unjust side wins, war serves injustice rather than justice. War has been the main means by which powerful states perpetrate injustice against weaker states.

In addition, war may be morally unacceptable at the *in bello* level, even assuming general compliance with the rules. According to this argument, *in bello* rules are a much less effective restraint on the means of waging war than they may appear to be. Efforts to humanize war through the war convention have been largely a pretense and the rules a charade meant to make us more tolerant of war. Normative limits are inherent in war as a purposive activity, as noted in Chapter 1, but such *prudential limitations* (as we may call them) are below the level of restraint that justice requires and that *jus in bello* is meant to impose. But, in fact, the war conventions do not succeed in imposing a higher level of restraint. Chris Jochnick and Roger Normand claim that "despite noble rhetoric to the contrary, the laws of war have been formulated deliberately to privilege military necessity at the cost of humanitarian values." These laws "did not introduce restraint or humanity into war," which "has long been limited largely by factors independent of the law."[62] The laws of war that get adopted, and the way they are interpreted, are favorable to the military, and the

---

[62] Chris Jochnick and Roger Normand, "The Legitimation of Violence: A Critical History of the Laws of War," *Harvard International Law Journal* 35, no. 1 (Winter 1994), pp. 49–95, at pp. 50, 53. Their notion of military necessity is different from the one adopted in Chapter 6.

militarily powerful, allowing maximum use of the latest technology with little restraint beyond the prudential limitations. The result has been that "the development of a more elaborate legal regime has proceeded apace with the increasing savagery and destructiveness of modern war."[63] The legal regime *falsely legitimates* war, making it more vicious, more tolerated, and more likely. The regime "enables belligerents to suppress opposition to wartime conduct by cloaking such conduct in legal legitimacy," and succeeds in "undermining more realistic efforts to limit war."[64] In a similar vein, Robert Tucker claims that just war rules are "scarcely distinguishable from mere ideologies the purpose of which is to provide a spurious justification for almost any use of force."[65]

8.5 The morality of abolition

The goal of the abolition of war may be considered part of just war theory, and in this section we consider the criteria that this part of the theory should include. Our concern is the morality of abolition. Consistent with the tradition of using Latin phrases to label aspects of just war theory, let me refer to this part of the theory as *jus in abolitione belli*, justice in the abolition of war.[66] This aspect of just war theory is different from the others. *Jus ad bellum*, *just in bello*, and *jus extendere bellum* all govern the use of force. In contrast, *jus in abolitione belli* governs not the use of force, but rather the appropriate means to bring about the abolition of war. Abolition may or may not be possible, but the morality of abolition concerns moral limitations on efforts to achieve abolition and morally appropriate means that may help to get there. We have seen that the abolition of war is not a goal that war itself can achieve. The path to abolition, if we can get there from here, must lie along another route, and it is an appropriate moral capstone for just war theory to consider what that other route could and morally should be.

The criteria of *jus in abolitione belli* are related to the criteria of *jus ad bellum* specifically, they represent reminders that the *ad bellum* criteria must

---

[63] *Ibid.*, p. 55.   [64] *Ibid.*, pp. 65, 51.

[65] Robert W. Tucker, quoted in Jack Donnelly "Twentieth-Century Realism," in Terry Nardin and David Mapel (eds.), *Traditions of International Ethics* (Cambridge University Press, 1992), pp. 85–111, at p. 100.

[66] Thanks to my colleague Eugen Baer for help with this phrase.

continue to be respected and practical recommendations for how a course toward abolition could be charted consistent with that respect. The relevant *ad bellum* criteria are just cause, last resort, and legitimate authority. I propose these criteria of *jus in abolitione belli*.

(1) *Maximize feasible non-military alternatives to achieving justice*: multiply alternative means of rectifying injustices. Ensure that causes that might otherwise justify war may be resolved in alternative ways. Make the *ad bellum* last resort criterion more difficult to satisfy.

(2) *Bring greater legitimacy to international institutions*: allow more involvement by international institutions in inter-group conflict, including opportunities for the effective use of internationally sanctioned force.

(3) *Accept national sovereignty as a necessary moral fiction*: recognize the interim need, within the context of the human rights paradigm, to acknowledge respect for national sovereignty as a moral rule of thumb.

We now discuss these criteria.

(1) *Maximize feasible non-military alternatives to achieving justice.* For just war theory, war has a morally valuable use, namely, as a means to correct serious injustices in the absence of other effective means. From the perspective of pacifism, the abolition of war is a goal to be pursued without qualification. From the perspective of just war theory, abolition is a goal to be pursued, but only on the condition that alternatives will be available to rectify serious injustices that otherwise would justify the use of force. The goal of abolition is not to make these injustices disappear, which is a utopian prospect. As far as we can understand, there are and will always be real conflicts between groups of people that involve unjust treatment of some by others. These conflicts are not always simply the result of misunderstanding, and they cannot all be made to disappear through an increase in mutual understanding. Just war theory, by including the *ad bellum* just cause criterion, makes clear that war cannot, from a moral perspective, be abolished unless other means of rectification of those just causes continue to be available.

Given that war does not do well what it is supposed to do, rectify serious injustices, war is morally tolerated only because there are, in certain circumstances, no other means available to achieve this end. This is the import of the *ad bellum* last resort criterion. War is not justified if there are resorts other than military force available to rectify serious injustices that would otherwise be a just cause for war. Of course, these resorts must hold out a realistic prospect of success, especially given the costs in delaying the use of force, if they are attempted and fail, as discussed in Chapter 3. We may refer to resorts that satisfy this condition as *feasible resorts*. If feasible resorts are available, war may not be necessary, and if it is not necessary, the last resort criterion informs us, it is not justified. The purpose of this criterion is to set the limits on when resort to force is necessary. It makes justified war less likely by making the last resort criterion more difficult to satisfy. So the abolition of war is morally possible only if there are feasible resorts available in cases of serious injustice (and the resorts are in fact effective at rectifying the injustices). If war is to be abolished, it must be through the availability of other means of achieving justice in the sorts of cases where war has justifiably been relied on for this purpose. This is simply to state the point that the abolition of war morally requires alternative methods of conflict resolution.

Of course, making war more difficult to justify morally does not guarantee that it will become less frequent. For war to become less frequent, it must also become more difficult to justify politically or prudentially. Given the costs of war, however, increasing the number of feasible resorts should make it more difficult to justify prudentially as well as morally. Adherence to the second criterion should also make war more difficult both morally and prudentially.

(2) *Bring greater legitimacy to international institutions.* This criterion relates to the *ad bellum* criterion of legitimate authority. One way to reduce the opportunity for justified war is to invest international institutions with greater legitimacy. The reason is connected with the first criterion. When international institutions have greater legitimacy, they are able to provide a greater range of feasible resorts to the use of force by states (or sub-state organizations). This is how it works domestically: the greater legitimacy the legal authorities have, the more feasible resorts there are to the interpersonal use of force to rectify injustices. International institutions can be more effective at providing feasible resorts when their legitimacy extends to the use of force.

While many of the conflicts that bring war are real, distrust among groups is a contributing factor. Distrust can by itself lead to war, or it can exacerbate real conflicts making war more likely. The main source of distrust is that no group can be assured that its opponents will not take advantage of its trust. (This is the "cause of quarrel" that Hobbes refers to as diffidence.) The international distrust creates an *assurance problem*, and it sets up a dynamic which is referred to as the *security dilemma*.[67] In the absence of effective international institutions, each state must look after its own security. But due to general distrust, each state's efforts to make itself more secure can make its adversaries feel less secure. The resulting spiral of mutual distrust leads to war. Effective international institutions can break this cycle, turning individual security to collective security, and self-help to mutual help.

This dynamic is expressed well by Spanish diplomat Salvador de Madariaga, speaking of the effort to put an end to war through disarmament agreements.

> Nations don't distrust each other because they are armed; they are armed
> because they distrust each other. And therefore to want disarmament
> before a minimum of common agreement on fundamentals is as absurd
> as to want people to go undressed in winter. Let the weather be warm,
> and people will discard their clothes readily and without committees to
> tell them how they are to undress. Then, disarmament was tackled at the
> wrong end. A war is the *ultima ratio* in a conflict; a conflict is the outcome
> of a dispute that has got out of hand; a dispute is the consequence of
> a problem that has proved insoluble; a problem is born of a question
> that has not been tackled in time … It follows that disarmament is an
> irrelevant issue; the true issue being the organization of the government
> of the world on a cooperative basis.[68]

The liberal faith in institutions evidenced by de Madariaga was stated in the nineteenth century by the British philosopher John Stuart Mill. Speaking of the prospects for human happiness, he remarks: "The present wretched education and wretched social arrangements are the only real hindrance to its being attainable by almost all."[69] We simply need better

[67] On the security dilemma, see Robert Jervis, "Cooperation under the Security Dilemma," *World Politics* 30 (1978), pp. 167–214.

[68] Quoted in Michael Quinlan, *Thinking about Nuclear Weapons*, Whitehall Paper #41 (London: Royal United Services Institute for Defence Studies, 2005), www.rusi.org/downloads/assets/WHP41_QUINLAN.pdf, accessed September 30, 2010.

[69] John Stuart Mill, *Utilitarianism* (Indianapolis, IN: Hackett Publishing, 1979), p. 13.

social arrangements for the unhappiness of war to be avoided, and war is one of the chief causes of human unhappiness.

The international institutions whose legitimacy needs strengthening would be institutions of a "universalist politics."[70] As we saw, David Luban uses this phrase in the context of a discussion of the human rights paradigm, and the second criterion reflects the abandonment of the idea that state sovereignty has fundamental moral value and the switch from the national defense paradigm to the human rights paradigm. Given its abandonment of state sovereignty as its moral foundation, the human rights paradigm naturally fits an institutional structure at the global level. If these institutions were strong enough, they could abolish war by replacing it with policing. This institutional transition from traditional state sovereignty to effective international governance would track the transition in just war thinking from the national defense paradigm to the human rights paradigm.

(3) *Accept national sovereignty as a necessary moral fiction.* There is no guarantee, however, that international institutions can or will grow stronger and their legitimacy increase, and the applicability of the human rights paradigm does not depend on this happening. The feasibility of institutions of effective international governance involves questions not only of whether such institutions would work, but also of whether they could come into being. We seem to be riding a historical trend in their direction, but the future is open in this regard. The second criterion prescribes our promoting this trend, but other factors besides are at work in influencing our choices. Though we may be now in a long-term transition to effective international governance, we could as easily go backward as forward, and either way, while war may not be inevitable, it is likely to be with us for a long time. The third criterion is a recognition of this.

The case of humanitarian intervention shows vividly that we are now at a sort of *halfway house*, caught between a commitment to universal human rights as the moral foundation for military policy and a set of international institutions and habits of thought that, in practice, largely defers to traditional state sovereignty.[71] According to the human rights paradigm, the

---

[70] David Luban, "The Romance of the Nation-State," in Nardin and Mapel (eds.), *Traditions of International Ethics*, pp. 85–111, at p. 392.

[71] Kahn, Paul, "The Paradox of Riskless War," in Verna Gehring (ed.), *War after September 11* (Lanham, MD : Rowman and Littlefield, 2003), pp. 37–49.

alleged primacy of state sovereignty is a *moral fiction*, in two senses. In one sense, entailed by the human rights paradigm, the moral value of sovereignty is not primary, but derivative from the moral value of human rights and a state's effectiveness in respecting and protecting them. But this moral fiction is hardly yet a political fiction, and there continues to be some moral value in respecting it. This leads to the second sense in which the primacy of state sovereignty is a moral fiction. It is, to an extent, morally useful. This is the point of the third criterion. As we have discussed, there is considerable practical difficulty in applying the human rights paradigm directly. In the case of just cause, applying the paradigm requires the difficult task, conceptually and empirically, of determining whether the appropriate threshold of threatened human rights violations has been exceeded. Similar problems arise for applying *ad bellum* proportionality. These difficulties of application open the door for honest mistakes and situations of simultaneous ostensible justice, and also for international mischief making, for states making war founded on disingenuous claims about the justice of that war. In this sense, adopting the versions of the *ad bellum* criteria implied by the human rights paradigm carries significant moral hazard and may make war more likely.

As a matter of practice, these problems can be ameliorated if states generally act in matters of international force as if their chief moral concern is state sovereignty rather than human rights. Respect for sovereignty is often the best way, in the current state of things, to promote respect for human rights. The third criterion recommends that states generally, though not invariably, act as if state sovereignty has fundamental moral value. It recommends that considerations of just cause usually be governed by a *prima facie* moral rule of thumb that takes as fundamental the value of state sovereignty. But viewing state sovereignty as a moral fiction would mean that the rule would not be applied without exception, that states understand the source of the rule of thumb in the primacy of human rights and are willing to act in terms of human rights when it is clear that the situation requires it, as in the case of justified humanitarian intervention. Unless and until we achieve a level of international governance that turns warring into policing, the third criterion calls for us to recognize the power of state sovereignty in international politics.

The halfway house which we now occupy is between warring and policing. Policing is the ambition of effective international governance.

It is the ambition of the UN, which, in its Charter, outlawed aggressive war and assumed to itself (to the Security Council) the exclusive right to permit war in response to threats to international security. Indeed, the Korean War was authorized by the Security Council and was referred to as a "police action" (even though everyone called it a war). While national self-defense is left at the immediate discretion of the victim of aggression, given the need for a quick response, the defense is subject to retroactive endorsement by the Security Council. (This is like the domestic model, where, for example, a killing in self-defense is subject to after-the-fact legal assessment.) But in the other direction, pulling us back, is the power of states, the reality of state sovereignty. States control the force even while the force is supposed to be used for the universal goal of the protection of human rights. Paul Kahn notes: "A national army is not, and cannot be, an international police force. Effective international policing requires a credible separation of the application of force from national political interests."[72] An application of force that is not severed from the national political interests of individual states cannot have the public legitimacy that successful policing requires. Earlier I argued against understanding just war theory in terms of policing rather than warring, and this prescription remains so long as the preconditions for policing are absent. But the human rights paradigm points the way to the realization of those conditions.

The successful application of these criteria would help us to move from our current halfway house further toward the regime of international governance probably necessary for the abolition of war. Through *jus in abolitione belli*, just war theory may become the means to its own obsolescence.

---

[72] *Ibid.*, p. 38.

Bibliography

9/11 Commission Report, *Final Report of the National Commission on Terrorist Attacks upon the United States* (New York: Norton, 2004).

Albrecht-Carrié, René, *The Meaning of the First World War* (Englewood Cliffs, NJ: Prentice Hall, 1965).

Anscombe, Elizabeth, "War and Murder," in E. Anscombe (ed.), *Ethics, Religion, and Politics* (Oxford: Blackwell, 1981), pp. 51–61.

Aquinas, St. Thomas, *Summa Theologica*, trans. Fathers of the English Dominican Province, vol. 9 (London: Burns, Oates & Washbourne, 1916).

Aristotle, *Nicomachean Ethics* (Indianapolis, IN: Hackett Publishing, 1998).

Politics (Cambridge University Press, 1988).

Augustine, St., *City of God*, in Larry May *et al.* (eds.), *The Morality of War: Classical and Contemporary Readings* (Upper Saddle River, NJ: Prentice-Hall, 2006).

selections from *City of God*, *Against Faustus*, *Letter to Marcellinus*, *Letter to Boniface*, *On Free Choice of the Will*, *Questions on the Heptateuch*, excerpts in Reichberg *et al.*, *Ethics of War*, pp. 70–90.

Bass, Gary, "*Jus Post Bellum*," *Philosophy & Public Affairs* 32, no. 4 (2004), pp. 384–412.

Beitz, Charles, "Bounded Morality: Justice and the State in World Politics," *International Organization* 33, no. 3 (Summer 1979), pp. 405–424.

"Nonintervention and Communal Integrity," *Philosophy & Public Affairs* 9, no. 4 (1980), pp. 385–391.

Political Theory and International Relations, new edn. (Princeton University Press, 1999).

Bellamy, Alex, *Just Wars* (Cambridge: Polity Press, 2006).

Blumenfeld, Laura, "The Sole Survivor," *Washington Post*, June 11, 2007.

Boivin, Alexandra, "Complicity and Beyond: International Law and the Transfer of Small Arms and Light Weapons," *International Review of the Red Cross* 87, no. 859 (September 2005), pp. 467–496.

Bond, James E., *Rules of Riot: Internal Conflict and the Law of War* (Princeton University Press, 1974).

Boyle, Joseph, "Just War Doctrine and the Military Response to Terrorism," *Journal of Political Philosophy* 11, no. 2 (2003), pp. 153–170.

Buchanan, Allen, *Secession: The Legitimacy of Political Divorce from Fort Sumter to Lithuania and Quebec* (Boulder, CO: Westview Press, 1991).

"The Internal Legitimacy of Humanitarian Intervention," *Journal of Political Philosophy* 7 (1999), pp. 71–87.

Bull, Hedley, "The Importance of Grotius in the Study of International Relations," in Hedley Bull *et al.* (eds.), *Hugo Grotius and International Relations* (Oxford University Press, 1992), pp. 65–93.

"Recapturing the Just War for Political Theory," *World Politics* 31, no. 4 (July 1979), pp. 588–599.

Caney, Simon, *Justice beyond Borders: A Global Political Theory* (Oxford University Press, 2005).

Christopher, Paul, *The Ethics of War and Peace*, 2nd edn. (Upper Saddle River, NJ: Prentice-Hall, 1999).

Cicero, *On Duties* (Cambridge University Press, 1991).

Clark, John F., "Introduction: Causes and Consequences of the Congo War," in John F. Clark (ed.), *The African Stakes of the Congo War* (New York: Palgrave Macmillan, 2002), pp. 1–10.

Claude, Inis L., Jr., "Just War: Doctrines and Institutions," *Political Science Quarterly* 95, no. 1 (Spring 1980), pp. 83–96.

Clausewitz, Carl von, *On War*, ed. and trans. Michael Howard and Peter Paret (Princeton University Press, 1989).

Coady, C. A. J., "Escaping from the Bomb: Immoral Deterrence and the Problem of Extrication," in Henry Shue (ed.), *Nuclear Deterrence and Moral Restraint* (Cambridge University Press, 1989), pp. 163–226.

Morality and Political Violence (Cambridge University Press, 2008).

"Terrorism, Just War, and Supreme Emergency," in C. A. J. Coady and Michael O'Keefe (eds.), *Terrorism and Justice* (Melbourne University Press, 2002), pp. 8–21.

Coghlan, Benjamin, *et al.*, "Mortality in the Democratic Republic of Congo," International Rescue Committee, www.theirc.org/sites/default/files/resource-file/2006–7_congoMortalitySurvey.pdf, accessed July 12, 2010.

Cortright, David, "A Harder Look at Iraq Sanctions," *The Nation*, December 3, 2001.

Daponte, Beth, "A Case Study in Estimating Casualties from War and Its Aftermath: The 1991 Persian Gulf War," *Medicine and Global Survival* 3, no. 2 (1993), www.ippnw.org/MGS/PSRQV3N2Daponte.html, accessed January 13, 2010.

Dinstein, Yoram, "Comments on War," *Harvard Journal of Law & Public Policy* 27, no. 3 (Summer 2004), pp. 877–892.

The Conduct of Hostilities under the Law of International Armed Conflict (Cambridge University Press, 2004).

War – Aggression and Self-Defense, 4th edn. (Cambridge University Press, 2005).

Donnelly, Jack, "Twentieth-Century Realism," in Terry Nardin and David Mapel (eds.), *Traditions of International Ethics* (Cambridge University Press, 1992), pp. 85–111.

Dunlap, Charles, "Law and Military Interventions: Preserving Humanitarian Values in 21st Century Conflicts," Carr Center for Human Rights Policy Workshop Paper, Harvard Kennedy School (2001), www.hks.harvard.edu/cchrp/Web%20Working%20Papers/Use%20of%20Force/Dunlap2001.pdf, accessed August 22, 2010.

Eckhardt, William, "My Lai: An American Tragedy," www.law.umkc.edu/faculty/projects/ftrials/mylai/ecktragedy.html, accessed November 1, 2010.

Fearon, James, and David Laitin, "Ethnicity, Insurgency, and Civil War," *American Political Science Review* 97, no. 1 (February 2003), pp. 75–90.

Feil, Scott, "Preventing Genocide: How the Early Use of Force Might Have Succeeded in Rwanda," www.wilsoncenter.org/subsites/ccpdc/pubs/rwanda/frame.htm, accessed May 20, 2010.

Feinberg, Joel, "Voluntary Euthanasia and the Inalienable Right to Life," *Philosophy & Public Affairs* 7 (Winter 1978), pp. 93–123.

Feldman, Noah, "Choices of Law, Choice of War," 25 *Harvard Journal of Law & Public Policy* 457 (2002).

Fellmeth, Aaron Xavier, "Questioning Civilian Immunity," *Texas International Law Journal* 43, no. 3 (Summer 2008), pp. 453–501.

Fidler, David, "The Meaning of Moscow: 'Non-lethal' Weapons and International Law in the Early 21st Century," *International Review of the Red Cross* 87, no. 859 (September 2005), pp. 525–552.

Fleury, J. G., "*Jus in Bello* and Military Necessity," Advanced Military Studies Course 1 (Department of National Defense, Canada, 1998), www.cfc.forces.gc.ca/papers/amsc/amsc1/fleury2.htm, accessed June 29, 2010.

Forde, Steven, "Classical Realism," in Terry Nardin and David Mapel (eds.), *Traditions of International Ethics* (Cambridge University Press, 1992), pp. 62–84.

Fotion, Nicholas, "Reactions to War: Pacifism, Realism, and Just War Theory," in Andrew Valls (ed.), *Ethics in International Affairs: Theories and Cases* (Lanham, MD: Rowman and Littlefield, 2000), pp. 15–32.

Fullinwider, Robert, "Understanding Terrorism," in Larry May, Eric Rovie, and Steve Viner (eds.), *The Morality of War: Classical and Contemporary Readings* (Upper Saddle River, NJ: Prentice-Hall, 2006), pp. 306–315.

"War and Innocence," *Philosophy & Public Affairs* 5, no. 1 (Autumn 1975), pp. 90–97.

Gall, Carlotta, and Taimoor Shah, "Civilian Deaths Imperil Support for Afghan War," *New York Times*, May 7, 2009.

Gentili, Alberico, *On the Law of War*, excerpts in Gregory Reichberg *et al.* (eds.), *The Ethics of War: Classic and Contemporary Readings* (Oxford: Blackwell Publishing, 2006).

Gilbert, Paul, "Civilian Immunity in the 'New Wars'," in Igor Primoratz (ed.), *Civilian Immunity in War* (Oxford University Press, 2007), pp. 201–216.

Global Security, "The Iran–Iraq War," www.globalsecurity.org/military/world/war/iran-iraq.htm, accessed July 1, 2010.

Green, Michael, "War, Innocence and Theories of Sovereignty," *Social Theory and Practice* 18 (1992), pp. 39–62.

Grotius, Hugo, *The Rights of War and Peace*, trans. Jean Barbayrac (London: W. Innys, 1738).

The Rights of War and Peace, ed. Richard Tuck (Indianapolis, IN: Liberty Fund, 2005).

The Rights of War and Peace, trans. A. C. Campbell (Washington, DC: M. Walter Dunne, 1901).

Guthrie, Charles, and Michael Quinlan, *The Just War Tradition: Ethics in Modern Warfare* (London: Bloomsbury, 2007).

Gutman, Israel, *Resistance: The Warsaw Ghetto Uprising* (Washington, DC: United States Holocaust Museum, 1994).

Gutmann, Amy, "Freedom of Association: An Introductory Essay," in Amy Gutmann (ed.), *Freedom of Association* (Princeton University Press, 1998), pp. 3–32.

Hall Jamieson, Kathleen, *Eloquence in an Electronic Age: The Transformation of Political Speechmaking* (New York: Oxford University Press, 1990).

Hart, H. L. A., *Punishment and Responsibility* (Oxford University Press, 1968).

The Concept of Law (Oxford University Press, 1961).

Henckaerts, Jean-Marie, and Louise Doswald-Beck, *Customary International Humanitarian Law*, vol. I, *Rules*, International Committee of the Red Cross (Cambridge University Press, 2005).

Hobbes, Thomas, *Leviathan* (Indianapolis, IN: Hackett, 1994).

Holmes, Robert, *On War and Morality* (Princeton University Press, 1989).

Howard, Michael, "It Was a Terrible Error to Declare War," *Independent*, November 2, 2001.

Human Rights Watch, "Afghanistan: US should Act to End Bombing Tragedies," www.hrw.org, accessed September 13, 2009.

"Introduction and Summary," *Needless Deaths in the Gulf War*, www.hrw.org/legacy/reports/1991/gulfwar/, accessed June 18, 2009.

"Troops in Contact: Airstrikes and Civilian Deaths in Afghanistan," www.hrw.org, accessed September 4, 2009, pp. 35–36.

Hurka, Thomas, "Proportionality in the Morality of War," *Philosophy & Public Affairs* 33, no. 1 (2005), pp. 34–66.

International Commission on Intervention and State Sovereignty, "Responsibility to Protect," http://responsibilitytoprotect.org/ICISS%20Report.pdf, accessed January 4, 2011.

International Committee of the Red Cross, "International Humanitarian Law and the Challenges of Contemporary Armed Conflicts," *International Review of the Red Cross* 89, no. 867 (September 2007), pp. 719–757.

International Court of Justice, "Advisory Opinion on the Legality of the Threat or Use of Nuclear Weapons," *ICJ Report 1996*, pp. 226–267.

Jervis, Robert, "Cooperation under the Security Dilemma," *World Politics* 30 (1978), pp. 167–214.

Jochnick, Chris, and Roger Normand, "The Legitimation of Violence: A Critical History of the Laws of War," *Harvard International Law Journal* 35, no. 1 (Winter 1994), pp. 49–95.

Johnson, James Turner, *Ideology, Reason, and the Limitation of War* (Princeton University Press, 1975).

"Just Cause Revisited," in Elliot Abrams (ed.), *Close Calls* (Washington, DC: Ethics and Public Policy Center, 1998), pp. 3–38.

Just War Tradition and the Restraint of War (Princeton University Press, 1981).

"The Broken Tradition," *National Interest* (Fall 1996).

Kahn, Paul, "The Paradox of Riskless War," in Verna Gehring (ed.), *War after September 11* (Lanham, MD: Rowman and Littlefield, 2003), pp. 37–49.

Kaldor, Mary, *New and Old Wars*, 2nd edn. (Stanford University Press, 2006).

Kant, Immanuel, *Grounding for the Metaphysics of Morals* (Indianapolis: Hackett Publishing, 1993).

Kasher, Asa, "The Principle of Distinction," *Journal of Military Ethics* 6, no. 2 (2007), pp. 152–167.

Kilcullen, David, "Countering Global Insurgency," *Small Wars Journal* (2004), http://smallwarsjournal.com/documents/kilcullen.pdf, accessed June 9, 2010.

Kolb, Robert, "Origins of the Twin Terms *Jus ad Bellum/Jus in Bello*," *International Review of the Red Cross*, no. 320, pp. 553–562, www.icrc.org/web/eng/

siteeng0.nsf/htmlall/57JNUU?OpenDocument&View=defaultBody&style=custo_print, accessed September 2, 2010.

Koller, David S., "The Moral Imperative: Toward a Human Rights-Based Law of War," *Harvard International Law Review* 46, no. 1 (Winter 2005), pp. 231–264.

Koppel, Ted, "Nine Years after 9/11, Let's Stop Fulfilling bin Laden's Goals," *Washington Post* (September 12, 2010), p. B01.

Korab-Karpowicz, W. Julian, "Political Realism in International Relations," *Stanford Encyclopedia of Philosophy* (Fall 2010), http://plato.stanford.edu/entries/realism/, accessed December, 29, 2010.

Krause, Harry D., *Family Law in a Nutshell*, 2nd edn. (St. Paul, MN: West Publishing, 1986).

Kretzmer, David, "Civilian Immunity in War: Legal Aspects," in Igor Primoratz (ed.), *Civilian Immunity in War* (Oxford University Press, 2007), pp. 84–112.

Kutz, Christopher, "Fearful Symmetry," in David Rodin and Henry Shue (eds.), *Just and Unjust Warriors: The Moral and Legal Status of Soldiers* (Oxford University Press, 2008), pp. 69–86.

Lackey, Douglas, *The Ethics of War and Peace* (Englewood Cliffs, NJ: Prentice-Hall, 1989).

Lee, Steven P., *Morality, Prudence, and Nuclear Weapons* (Cambridge University Press, 1992).

Leitenberg, Milton, *Deaths in Wars and Conflicts in the 20th Century*, 3rd edn., Occasional Paper #29 (Ithaca, NY: Cornell University Peace Studies Program, 2006).

Lichtenberg, Judith, "War, Innocence, and the Doctrine of Double Effect," *Philosophical Studies* 74 (1994), pp. 347–368.

Luban, David, "Just War and Human Rights," *Philosophy & Public Affairs* 9, no. 2 (Winter 1980), pp. 160–181.

"The Romance of the Nation-State," *Philosophy & Public Affairs* 9, no. 4 (Summer 1980), pp. 392–397.

"The War on Terrorism and the End of Human Rights," in Verna Gehring (ed.), *War after September 11* (Lanham, MD: Rowman and Littlefield, 2003), pp. 51–62.

MacMillan, Margaret, "Ending the War to End All Wars," *New York Times* (December 25, 2010), www.nytimes.com/2010/12/26/opinion/26macmillan.html?scp=1&sq=margaret%20MacMillan&st=cse, accessed January 13, 2011.

Mattox, Henry E., "Like Father; Like Son," *American Diplomacy* (June 2004), www.unc.edu/depts/diplomat/archives_roll/2004_04-06/ed_father/ed_father.html, accessed May 26, 2010.

Mavrodes, George, "Conventions and the Morality of War," *Philosophy & Public Affairs* 4, no. 2 (Winter 1975), pp. 117–131.

May, Larry, *Aggression and Crimes against Peace* (Cambridge University Press, 2008).

"The Principle of Just Cause," in Larry May (ed.), *War: Essays in Political Philosophy* (New York: Cambridge University Press, 2008), pp. 49–66.

War Crimes and Just War (Cambridge University Press, 2007).

May, Larry, Eric Rovie, and Steve Viner (eds.), *The Morality of War: Classical and Contemporary Readings* (Upper Saddle River, NJ: Prentice-Hall, 2006).

Mayer, Jane, "The Predator War," *New Yorker* (October 26, 2009).

McCalpin, Jermaine O., "Historicity of a Crisis: The Origins of the Congo War," in John F. Clark (ed.), *The African Stakes of the Congo War* (New York: Palgrave Macmillan, 2002), pp. 33–50.

McDonnell, Michael, "The 'Conquest' of the Americas: The Aztecs," www.anzasa.arts.usyd.edu.au/ahas/conquest_overview.html, accessed August 3, 2008.

McDougal, Myres, and Florentino Feliciano, *The International Law of War: Transnational Coercion and World Public Order* (New Haven Press, 1994).

McKeogh, Colm, "Civilian Immunity in War: From Augustine to Vattel," in Igor Primoratz (ed.), *Civilian Immunity in War* (Oxford University Press, 2007), pp. 62–83.

McMahan, Jeff, "Innocence, Self-Defense, and Killing in War," *Journal of Political Philosophy* 2, no. 3 (1994), pp. 193–221.

"Killing in War: A Reply to Walzer," *Philosophia* 34 (2006), pp. 47–51.

"Liability and Collective Identity: A Response to Walzer," *Philosophia* 34 (2006), pp. 13–17.

"The Ethics of Killing in War," *Ethics* 114 (July 2004), pp. 693–753.

"War as Self-Defense," *Ethics & International Affairs* 18, no. 1 (2004), pp. 75–80.

McPherson, Lionel, "Innocence and Responsibility in War," *Canadian Journal of Philosophy* 34, no. 4 (December 2004), pp. 485–506.

Meron, Theodore, "Shakespeare's Henry the Fifth and the Laws of War," *American Journal of International Law* 86 (January 1992), pp. 1–45.

Metz, Steven, "The Next Twist of the RMA," *Parameters* (Autumn 2000), pp. 40–53.

Metz, Steven and Raymond Millen, "Insurgency and Counterinsurgency in the 21st Century: Reconceptualizing Threat and Response," Carlisle, PA: Strategic Studies Institute, 2004, www.strategicstudiesinstitute.army.mil/pdffiles/PUB586.pdf, accessed August 24, 2010.

Mill, John Stuart, *Utilitarianism* (Indianapolis, IN: Hackett Publishing, 1979).

Mollendorf, Darrel, *Cosmopolitan Justice* (Boulder, CO: Westview Press, 2002).

"Jus ex Bello," *Journal of Political Philosophy* 16, no. 2 (2008), pp. 123–136.

Montaldi, Daniel, "Toward a Human Rights Based Account of Just War," *Social Theory and Practice* 11, no. 2 (Summer 1985), pp. 123–161.

Montesquieu, Charles de, *The Spirit of the Laws*, excerpts in Reichberg *et al.* (eds.), *The Ethics of War: Classic and Contemporary Readings* (Oxford: Blackwell Publishing, 2006).

Morgenthau, Hans, and Kenneth Thompson, *Politics among Nations*, 6th edn. (New York: Knopf, 1985).

Motevalli, Golmar, "Analysis – Civilian Deaths Mount as the Afghan War Deepens," Reuters, www.reuters.com, accessed September 13, 2009.

Nagel, Thomas, "The Problem of Global Justice," *Philosophy & Public Affairs* 33, no. 2 (2005), pp. 113–147.

Nardin, Terry, "Ethical Traditions in International Affairs," in Terry Nardin and David Mapel (eds.), *Traditions of International Ethics* (Cambridge University Press, 1992).

Nardin, Terry, and Melissa Williams (eds.), *Humanitarian Intervention*, Nomos 47 (New York University Press, 2006).

National Conference of Catholic Bishops, *The Challenge of Peace: God's Promise and our Response* (United States Catholic Conference, 1983).

Neuwirth, Rachel, "The Hard Hand of War," *American Thinker*, www.americanthinker.com/2007/06/the_hard_hand_of_war.html, accessed July 30, 2010.

Nolan, Alan T., *Lee Considered: General Robert E. Lee and Civil War History* (Chapel Hill, NC: University of North Carolina Press, 1996).

Norman, Richard, *Ethics, Killing, and War* (Cambridge University Press, 1995).

O'Brien, William V., *The Conduct of Just and Limited War* (New York: Praeger, 1981).

Orend, Brian, "Jus Post Bellum," *Journal of Social Philosophy* 31, no. 1 (Spring 2000), pp. 117–137.

War and International Justice (Waterloo, Canada: Wilfred Laurier Press, 2000).

Pape, Robert, *Bombing to Win: Air Power and Coercion in War* (Ithaca, NY: Cornell University Press, 1996).

Peters, Ralph, "Wishful Thinking and Indecisive Wars," *Journal of International Security Affairs* 16 (Spring 2009), www.securityaffairs.org/issues/2009/16/peters.php, accessed September 20, 2010.

Pfanner, Toni, "Asymmetrical Warfare from the Perspective of Humanitarian Law and Humanitarian Action," *International Review of the Red Cross* 87, no. 857 (March 2005), pp. 149–174.

Pizan, Christine de, *The Book of Deeds of Arms and of Chivalry*, ed. Charity Cannon Willard (University Park, PA: Penn State University Press, 1999).

Plato, *Republic*, trans. C. D. C. Reeve (Indianapolis, IN: Hackett Publishing, 2004).

Pogge, Thomas, "Cosmopolitanism and Sovereignty," *Ethics* 103 (October 1992), pp. 48–75.

Power, Samantha, *A Problem from Hell: America and the Age of Genocide* (New York: Basic Books, 2002).

Primoratz, Igor, "Introduction," and "Civilian Immunity in War: Its Grounds, Scope, and Weight," in Primoratz (ed.), *Civilian Immunity in War* (Oxford University Press, 2007), pp. 1–41.

Pufendorf, Samuel, *On the Law of Nature and Nations*, excerpts in Larry May, Eric Rovie, and Steve Viner (eds.), *The Morality of War: Classical and Contemporary Readings* (Upper Saddle River, NJ: Prentice-Hall, 2006), pp. 89–95.

Quinlan, Michael, *Thinking about Nuclear Weapons*, Whitehall Paper #41 (London: Royal United Services Institute for Defence Studies, 2005), www.rusi.org/ downloads/assets/WHP41_QUINLAN.pdf, accessed September 30, 2010.

Rawls, John, *A Theory of Justice*, revised edn. (Cambridge, MA: Harvard University Press, 1999).

Justice as Fairness (Cambridge, MA: Harvard University Press, 2001).

The Law of Peoples (Cambridge, MA: Harvard University Press, 1999).

Reichberg, Gregory, "Is there a Presumption against War in Aquinas's Ethics?" in Henrik Syse and Gregory Reichberg (eds.), *Ethics, Nationalism, and Just War* (Washington, DC: Catholic University Press, 2007), pp. 72–98.

"Jus ad Bellum," in Larry May (ed.), *War: Essays in Political Philosophy* (New York: Cambridge University Press, 2008), pp. 11–29.

"Just War and Regular War: Competing Paradigms," in David Rodin and Henry Shue (eds.), *Just and Unjust Warriors: The Moral and Legal Status of Soldiers* (Oxford University Press, 2008), pp. 193–213.

Reichberg, Gregory, Henrik Syse, and Endre Begby (eds.), *The Ethics of War: Classic and Contemporary Readings* (Oxford: Blackwell Publishing, 2006).

Rengger, Nicholas, "The Jus in Bello in Historical and Philosophical Perspective," in Larry May (ed.), *War: Essays in Political Philosophy* (New York: Cambridge University Press, 2008), pp. 30–46.

Reuters Press, "List of 140 Afghan Killed in US Attack Includes 93 Children," www. informationclearinghouse.info/article22603.htm, accessed September 16, 2009.

Roberts, Adam, "NATO's 'Humanitarian War' over Kosovo," *Survival* 41, no. 3 (Autumn 1999), pp. 102–123.

"The Principle of Equal Application of the Laws of War," in David Rodin and Henry Shue (eds.), *Just and Unjust Warriors: The Moral and Legal Status of Soldiers* (Oxford University Press, 2008), pp. 226–254.

"The Road to Hell: A Critique of Humanitarian Intervention," *Harvard International Review* 16, no. 1 (Fall 1993), pp. 10–13.

Roberts, Adam, and Richard Guelff (eds.), *Documents on the Laws of War*, 3rd edn. (Oxford University Press, 2000).

Rodin, David, "The Ethics of Asymmetric War," in Richard Sorabji and David Rodin (eds.), *The Ethics of War: Shared Problems in Different Traditions* (Farnham, UK: Ashgate Publishing, 2006), pp. 153–168.

"The Moral Inequality of Soldiers: Why *jus in bello* Asymmetry Is Half Right," in David Rodin and Henry Shue (eds.), *Just and Unjust Warriors: The Moral and Legal Status of Soldiers* (Oxford University Press, 2008), pp. 44–68.

War and Self-Defense (Oxford University Press, 2002).

Rogers, A. P. V., "Unequal Combat and the Law of War," *Yearbook of International Humanitarian Law* 7 (2004), pp. 3–34.

Rousseau, Jean-Jacques, *The Social Contract*, in Rousseau, *The Social Contract and Discourses*, trans. G. D. H. Cole (London: Dent, 1923), p. 12.

Russell, Bertrand, *Portraits from Memory and Other Essays* (New York: Simon and Schuster, 1963).

Ryan, Cheyney, "Moral Equality, Victimhood, and the Sovereign Symmetry Problem," in David Rodin and Henry Shue (eds.), *Just and Unjust Warriors: The Moral and Legal Status of Soldiers* (Oxford University Press, 2008), pp. 131–152.

Sambanis, Nicholas, "What Is Civil War?" *Journal of Conflict Resolution* 48, no. 6 (2004), pp. 814–858.

Scanlon, Thomas, "A Theory of Freedom of Expression," *Philosophy & Public Affairs* 1, no. 2 (Winter, 1972), pp. 204–226.

What We Owe to Each Other (Cambridge, MA: Harvard University Press, 1998).

Schabas, William, *Genocide in International Law: The Crime of Crimes* (Cambridge University Press, 2000).

Schmitt, Michael, N., "21st Century Conflict: Can the Law Survive?" *Melbourne Journal of International Law* 8 (2007), pp. 443–478.

"Asymmetrical Warfare and International Humanitarian Law," *Air Force Law Review* 62 (2008), pp. 1–42, www.thefreelibrary.com/Asymmetrical+warfare +and+international+humanitarian+law.-a0188490581, accessed August 17, 2010.

"Humanitarian Law and Direct Participation in Hostilities by Private Contractors or Civilian Employees," *Chicago Journal of International Law* 5, no. 2 (Winter 2005), pp. 511–546.

"The Vanishing Law of War: Reflections on Law and War in the 21st Century," *Harvard International Review* 31, no. 1 (Spring 2009), pp. 64–68.

Scholz, Sally, "War Rape's Challenge to Just War Theory," in Steven P. Lee (ed.), *Intervention, Terrorism, and Torture* (Dordrecht, the Netherlands: Springer, 2007), pp. 273–288.

Seneca, Lucius, *Moral Epistles*, trans. Richard Gummere, Loeb Classical Library (Cambridge, MA: Harvard University Press, 1925), Epistle 88.

Shafritz, Jay M., *Words on War* (New York: Prentice Hall, 1990).

Shakespeare, William, *The Riverside Shakespeare* (Boston, Houghton Mifflin, 1974).

Sharp, Gene, *The Politics of Nonviolent Action*, 3 vols. (Boston: Porter Sargent Publishers, 1973).

Shaw, Martin, "Risk Transfer Militarism, Small Massacres and the Historical Legitimacy of War," *International Relations* 16, no. 3 (December 2002), pp. 343–360.

Sherman, William T., Letter to Mayor of Atlanta, 1864, http://freepages.genealogy.rootsweb.ancestry.com/~josephkennedy/Sherman_1864.htm, accessed July 1, 2010.

Shue, Henry, *Basic Rights: Subsistence, Affluence, and US Foreign Policy*, 2nd edn. (Princeton University Press, 1996).

"Do We Need a 'Morality of War'?" in David Rodin and Henry Shue (eds.), *Just and Unjust Warriors: The Moral and Legal Status of Soldiers* (Oxford University Press, 2008), pp. 87–111.

"Indiscriminate Disproportionality," www.allacademic.com//meta/p_mla_apa_research_citation/3/1/3/9/2/pages313921/p313921-1.php, accessed August 16, 2010.

"Laws of War," in Samantha Besson and John Tasioulas (eds.), *The Philosophy of International Law* (Oxford University Press, 2010), pp. 511–527.

"Limiting Sovereignty," in Jennifer Welsh (ed.), *Humanitarian Intervention and International Relations* (Oxford University Press, 2004), pp. 11–28.

"Targeting Civilian Infrastructure with Smart Bombs: The New Permissiveness," *Philosophy & Public Policy Quarterly* 30 (Summer/Fall 2010), pp. 2–8.

Shue, Henry, and David Wippman, "Limiting Attacks on Dual-Use Facilities Performing Indispensable Civilian Functions," *Cornell International Law Journal* 35 (2002), pp. 559–579.

Singer, Peter W., *Children at War* (Berkeley, CA: University of California Press, 2006).

"Outsourcing War," *Foreign Affairs* 84, no. 2 (March 2005), pp. 119–132.

Slaughter, Anne-Marie, "Beware the Trumpets of War," *Harvard Journal of Law and Public Policy* 25, no. 3 (Summer 2002), pp. 965–976.

"Tougher than Terror," *American Prospect* (January 2002).

Stahn, Carsten, "Jus ad bellum, jus in bello … jus post bellum? Rethinking the Conception of the Law of Armed Force," *European Journal of International Law* 17 (2006), pp. 921–943.

"*Jus ad Bellum – Jus in Bello – Jus post Bellum*: Toward a Tripartite Conception of Armed Conflict," European Society for International Law, available at www.esil-sedi.eu/fichiers/en/Stahn__838.pdf, accessed August 26, 2010.

"*Jus Post Bellum*: Mapping the Discipline(s)," *American University International Law Review* 23 (2008), pp. 311–347.

Stanton, Gregory, "Could the Rwandan Genocide Have Been Prevented?" *Journal of Genocide Research* 6, no. 2 (2004), pp. 211–228.

Steinhoff, Uwe, "In Defense of Guerrillas," *Diametros* 23 (March 2010), pp. 84–103.

Sterba, James, *Social and Political Philosophy: Contemporary Perspectives* (New York: Routledge, 2001).

Story, Joseph, U.S. Supreme Court Justice, *United States* v. *Le Jeune Eugenie*, 26 Federal Cases 832 (1822).

Tacitus, Cornelius, *The Complete Works of Tacitus*, trans. Alfred Church and William Brodribb (New York: Modern Library, 1942).

Tesón, Fernardo, "The Liberal Case for Humanitarian Intervention," in J. L. Holzgrefe, and Robert Keohane (eds.), *Humanitarian Intervention: Ethical, Legal, and Political Dilemmas* (Cambridge University Press, 2003), pp. 93–129.

Thomson, Judith Jarvis, *Rights, Restitution, and Risk: Essays in Moral Philosophy* (Cambridge, MA: Harvard University Press, 1986).

Thucydides, *The Peloponnesian War* (Oxford University Press, 2009).

United Confederation of Taino People, "Sacred Sites and the Environment from an Indigenous Perspective," www.yachaywasi-ngo.org/TainoSpeech.pdf, accessed August 6, 2008.

United Nations Commission on Human Rights, "Situation of Detainees at Guantánamo Bay" (February 15, 2006), http://news.bbc.co.uk/2/shared/bsp/hi/pdfs/16_02_06_un_guantanamo.pdf, accessed June 27, 2010.

United Nations International Commission on Intervention and State Sovereignty, *Responsibility to Protect* (Ottawa: International Development Research Center, 2001).

Vattel, Emer de, *Law of Nations*, ed. John Chitty (Philadelphia: T. & J. W. Johnson, 1883), www.constitution.org/vattel/vattel.htm, accessed June 15, 2011.

The Law of Nations, ed. Bella Kapossy and Richard Whatmore (Indianapolis, IN: Liberty Fund, 2008).

Vitoria, Francisco, "On the American Indians," in Anthony Pagden and Jeremy Lawrance (eds.), *Vitoria: Political Writings* (Cambridge University Press, 1991), pp. 231–292.

"On the Law of War," in Anthony Pagden and Jeremy Lawrance (eds.), *Vitoria: Political Writings* (Cambridge University Press, 1991), pp. 293–327.

Waldron, Jeremy, "*Post Bellum* Aspects of the Laws of Armed Conflict," *Loyola of Los Angeles International and Comparative Law Review* 31 (2009), pp. 31–55.

Walzer, Michael, *Arguing about War* (New Haven, CT: Yale University Press, 2004).

Just and Unjust Wars (New York: Basic Books, 1977; 2nd edn., 1992; 3rd edn., 2000; 4th edn., 2006; same text, different prefaces).

"Just and Unjust Occupations," *Dissent* (Winter 2004), pp. 61–66.

"On Involuntary Association," in Amy Gutmann (ed.), *Freedom of Association* (Princeton University Press, 1998), pp. 64–74.

"Regime Change and Just War," *Dissent* (Summer 2006), pp. 103–111.

"Responsibility and Proportionality in State and Non-State Wars," *Parameters* 39 (Spring 2009), pp. 40–52.

"Terrorism and Just War," *Philosophia* 34 (2006), pp. 3–12.

"The Moral Standing of States: A Response to Four Critics," *Philosophy & Public Affairs* 9, no. 3 (1980), pp. 209–229.

Thinking Politically: Essays in Political Theory (New Haven, CT: Yale University Press, 2009).

Wasserstrom, Richard, "Review of Walzer's Just and Unjust Wars," *Harvard Law Review* 92, no. 2 (December 1978), pp. 536–545.

Weber, Max, "Politics as a Vocation," reprinted in Michael Morgan (ed.), *Classics of Moral and Political Theory*, 4th edn. (Indianapolis, IN: Hackett Publishing, 2005), pp. 1213–1249.

Welsh, Jennifer, "Taking Consequences Seriously: Objections to Humanitarian Intervention," in Jennifer Welsh (ed.), *Humanitarian Intervention and International Relations* (Oxford University Press, 2004), pp. 52–68.

White, Hugh, "Civilian Immunity in the Precision-Guidance Age," in Igor Primoratz (ed.), *Civilian Immunity in War* (Oxford University Press, 2007), pp. 182–200.

Wolff, Christian von, *The Law of Nations Treated according to a Scientific Method*, excerpts in Reichberg *et al.* (eds.), *The Ethics of War: Classic and Contemporary Readings* (Oxford: Blackwell Publishing, 2006).

Zohar, Noam, "Collective War and Individualistic Ethics: Against the Conscription of 'Self-Defense'," *Political Theory* 21, no. 4 (November 1993), pp. 606–662.

Zupan, Daniel, "A Presumption of the Moral Equality of Combatants: A Citizen-Soldier's Perspective," in David Rodin and Henry Shue (eds.), *Just and Unjust Warriors: The Moral and Legal Status of Soldiers* (Oxford University Press, 2008), pp. 214–225.

Index